ROMANTIC PSYCHOANALYSIS

Romantic Psychoanalysis

The Burden of the Mystery

Joel Faflak

STATE UNIVERSITY OF NEW YORK PRESS

Cover art: "Saturn Devouring One of His Sons," by Francisco De Goya Y Lucientes, mural transferred to canvas, 146 x 83 cm. Used by permission, Museo del Prado, Madrid.

Published by
State University of New York Press, Albany

Printed in the United States of America

For information, contact State University of New York Press, Albany, NY
www.sunypress.edu

Production by Diane Ganeles
Marketing by Anne M. Valentine

Library of Congress Cataloging in Publication Data

Faflak, Joel.
Romantic psychoanalysis : the burden of the mystery / Joel Faflak.
p. cm.
Includes bibliographical references and index.
ISBN 978-0-7914-7269-9 (alk. paper)
ISBN 978-0-7914-7270-5 (pbk. : alk. paper)
1. English literature—19th century—History and criticism. 2. Romanticism—England. 3. Psychoanalysis and literature. 4. Coleridge, Samuel Taylor, 1772–1834—Criticism and interpretation. 5. Wordsworth, William, 1770–1850—Criticism and interpretation. 6. De Quincey, Thomas, 1785–1859—Criticism and interpretation. 7. Keats, John, 1795–1821—Criticism and interpretation. I. Title.
PR457.F29 2008
820.9'353--dc22

2007001779

10 9 8 7 6 5 4 3 2 1

For my sister Pat and brother Jim, who are greater influences than they know;
For my father Joe, who would have been proud;
For my mother Doreen, who is;
And for my partner Norm, who makes me smile and keeps my spirit light.

Contents

Acknowledgments

Apart from the writers, critics, philosophers, and theorists acknowledged in the bibliography, without whose voices both living and dead this book would be a rather diminished affair, its writing has been influenced, both directly and indirectly, by many people within and outside the academy, whose support it gives me great pleasure to acknowledge:

In the first instance, my understanding of Romanticism has been profoundly shaped by Tilottama Rajan and Ross Woodman. They hold me to the highest standard of engagement with literature, culture, the world, and myself. They allowed me to be fearless about speaking my critical voice, never assuming I should do anything else. They are colleagues, allies, and above all friends.

For her generosity, honesty, selflessness, loyalty, and humour; for the example of her scholarship and professionalism; and above all for countless acts of friendship, I thank Julia Wright, whose presence reminds me of what matters most in the academy.

Many people in the Department of English at the University of Western Ontario, past and present, have been helpful along the way: David Bentley, Joanne Buckley, Tom Carmichael, Patrick Deane, Stan Dragland, Kathleen Fraser, Paul Gaudet, Richard Green, J. Douglas Kneale, Marty Kreiswirth, Allison Lee, Cameron Macfarlane, Alan Pero, Geoffrey Rans, Jane Toswell, and Jennifer Venn. I thank the Department staff—Viv Lavers, Teresa McDonald, Beth McIntosh, Laura Nother, and Leanne Trask—who always hold back what they're really thinking, and that's not easy. I reserve a separate thanks for Pat Dibsdale and Anne McFarland, for being as beautiful as they are, and for saying what they *do* think; and for Angela Esterhammer and Allan Gedalof, for their honesty and loyalty. Among the faculty and staff at Wilfrid Laurier University, my first professional academic home, I thank Janet Bannister, Gary Boire, Joanne Buchan, Jane Campbell, Viviana Comensoli, Maria DiCenzo, Dianne Duffy, Sally Grey, Emmy Misser, Michael Moore, Helen Paret, Lynn Shakinovsky, Paul Tiessen, Eleanor Ty, and Jim Weldon, all of whom gave me a better sense of myself.

In so many incalculable ways, my motivation for research and writing comes from the classroom. My undergraduate and graduate students past and present have allowed me to inhabit a place where I can stand single, and hopefully they can as well, unconditionally and without the anxiety of approval. This rarely happens otherwise in my life, and it has been and continues to be a great gift indeed. I especially wish to thank Jeff Miles for his invaluable help with the index.

State University of New York Press has been wonderful in seeing this book through its various stages. I thank the two anonymous readers of my original manuscript for their generous and informed feedback. Among the Press's very helpful staff and administration, I thank Diane Ganeles and Christine Alexanian for a very humane editing process, and especially James Peltz for his faith, persistence, and humor. The staffs of the Weldon Library at the University of Western Ontario and the British Library have been, as always, superlative. Generous funding from the Social Sciences and Humanities Research Council of Canada has made the research and writing of this book possible. One of this funding's happy outcomes was a Governor General of Canada's Gold Medal for Research Excellence, awarded to an earlier version of this book.

Colleagues farther afield have been at all times generous and supportive in various capacities: James Allard, Alan Bewell, Christophe Bode, Fred Burwick, Steven Bruhm, Julie Carlson, Michael Eberle-Sinatra, Michelle Faubert, Jerry Hogle, Mary Jacobus, Theresa Kelley, Arnold Markley, Ghislaine McDayter, Mike O'Driscoll, Patrick O'Malley, Danny O'Quinn, Thomas Pfau, Jon Sachs, Karen Weisman, and John Whatley. I save a separate thanks for Joseph Wittreich for his continuing support and indulgence, and for a scholarly example I have never adequately acknowledged. I owe special debts to David Clark, Elizabeth Harvey, and Marion Woodman for their fearless singularity; and to Jodey Castricano, soul-mate in chaos, who helped me to grow up, and Jason Haslam, who understood if I didn't. For their friendship, superb minds, and (im)patience, I thank Jonathan Boulter and Jan Plug. I also thank David Shaffelburg for his capacity to transfer. This book would not have been possible without his being a witness to it. John Bloeman, Annabelle Fell, May Hilditch, Steven McLarty-Payson, Ed Panjer, Gillian Robertson,

Will Willemsen, Chris Winter, and Ryan Winter showed me how to believe in myself, in ways I can never adequately express.

My most profound thanks are in the dedication. My brother and sister have always been there for me, and that's a good feeling. My parents did everything they could to help me find a better way, and for their blindnesses as well as insights—which are now my own—I am eternally grateful, and for the fact that my Mother is still here to know this. To my niece Paula, who was pure spirit; to my brother-in-law Lyle and sister-in-law Nancy, who are never merely related; to my nieces and nephews, Darren, D'Arcy, Emily, and Sarah, who know how to love unconditionally; to Pat and Drew, who deserve the prizes they won; to my great-nieces and -nephews Alexis, Kaleigh, Luke, and Mason, princes and princesses extraordinaire—all of you make life beautiful.

So does the love of a good man, which, above all, forgives most things. This is for Norm.

ABBREVIATIONS

A Immanuel Kant. *Anthropology from a Pragmatic Point of View.* Translated by Victor Lyle Dowdell. Carbondale: Southern Illinois University Press, 1996. Cited by page number.

BL Samuel Taylor Coleridge. *Biographia Literaria; or Biographical Sketches of My Literary Life and Opinions.* Edited by James Engell and W. Jackson Bate. Princeton, NJ: Princeton University Press, 1983. Cited by volume and page numbers.

BT Friedrich Nietzsche. *The Birth of Tragedy and The Case of Wagner.* Translated by Walter Kaufmann. New York: Vintage Books, 1967. Cited by page number.

CJ Immanuel Kant. *The Critique of Judgement.* Translated by James Creed Meredith. Oxford: Clarendon Press, 1992. Cited by volume and page numbers.

CL Samuel Taylor Coleridge. *Collected Letters of Samuel Taylor Coleridge.* Edited by Earl Leslie Griggs. 6 Vols. Oxford: Clarendon Press, 1956–1971. Cited by volume and page numbers.

CN Samuel Taylor Coleridge. *The Collected Notebooks of Samuel Taylor Coleridge.* Edited by Kathleen Coburn. 4 vols. New York: Bollingen Series: Pantheon Books, 1957–1990. Cited by volume and page numbers.

CP Samuel Taylor Coleridge. *Coleridge's Poetry and Prose.* Edited by Nicholas Halmi, Paul Magnuson, and Raimonda Modiano. New York: Norton, 2004. Cited by line and/or page numbers.

CR Immanuel Kant. *Critique of Pure Reason.* Translated by Norman Kemp Smith. 1929. London: Macmillan, 1993. Cited by page number.

CWJ Carl Gustav Jung. *The Collected Works of C. G. Jung.* Edited by Sir Herbert Read, Michael Fordham, Gerhard Adler and translated by R. F. C. Hull. 21 vols. New York and Princeton, NJ: Princeton University Press, 1953–83. Cited by volume and page numbers.

KL John Keats. *Letters of John Keats.* Edited by Robert Gittings. 1970. Oxford: Oxford University Press, 1979. Cited by page number.

KP John Keats. *Complete Poems.* Edited by Jack Stillinger. Cambridge, Mass.: The Belknap Press of Harvard University Press, 1982. Cited by book, canto, page, and/or line numbers.

P William Wordsworth. *The Prelude: 1799, 1805, 1850.* Edited by Jonathan Wordsworth, M. H. Abrams, and Stephen Gill. New York: Norton, 1979. I use the 1805 version, cited by book and line numbers, unless otherwise noted as *1799* or *1850*, or *1805* to avoid confusion.

SE Sigmund Freud. *The Standard Edition of the Complete Psychological Works of Sigmund Freud.* Translated by James Strachey. 23 vols. London: Hogarth Press, 1953–1974; London: Vintage, 2001. Cited by volume and page numbers.

SPP Percy Bysshe Shelley. *Shelley's Poetry and Prose.* 2nd edition. Edited by Donald Reiman and Neil Fraistat. New York: Norton, 2002. Cited by page number for the prose works and act, scene, and/or line numbers for the poetry.

WDQ Thomas De Quincey. *Works of Thomas De Quincey.* Edited by Grevel Lindop et al. 20 vols. London: Pickering and Chatto, 2000–2003. Cited by volume and page number.

WL William Wordsworth. *The Letters of William and Dorothy Wordsworth.* Edited by Ernest de Selincourt. 2nd edition. Vol 1. *The Early Years, 1787–1805.* Revised by Chester L. Shaver. Oxford: Clarendon Press, 1967. Vol 2. *The Middle Years, Part 1, 1806–1811.* Revised by Mary Moorman. Oxford: Clarendon Press, 1969. Cited by volume and page numbers.

WP William Wordsworth. *Poetical Works.* Edited by Thomas Hutchinson. Revised edition by Ernest de Selincourt. 1936. Oxford: Oxford University Press, 1988. Cited by book and/or line numbers for the poetry and by page number for the prose.

WWR Arthur Schopenhauer. *The World as Will and Representation.* 2 vols. Translated by E. F. J. Payne. New York: Dover, 1958. Cited by volume and page numbers.

Introduction

> I tried to arrive at a sense for each text I encountered (it was my private touchstone for when an interpretation had gone far enough to leave for the moment) that psychoanalysis had become called for, as if called for in the history of knowledge.
>
> —Stanley Cavell, "Freud and Philosophy"

An Unnatural Thought

Let me begin with a case study of what I call one of the ur-scenes of Romantic psychoanalysis. The text, to which I will return at greater length in Chapter Two, is "The Ruined Cottage," composed by Wordsworth in 1797–98 as one of his earliest writings for *The Recluse*. The text opens by describing a noonday summer idyll "Pleasant to him who on the soft cool moss / Extends his careless limbs beside the root / Of some huge oak whose aged branches make / A twilight of their own," where "the wren warbles." This "dreaming man," who might or might not be the Narrator, is only "Half-conscious of that soothing melody." "With sidelong eye [he] looks out upon the scene," which seems natural only insofar as the Narrator construes its natural*ness* (10–15).[1] Indeed, both the dreamer's "sidelong" suspicion and his "half-conscious" state become symptomatic of a *preter*natural ideality, repeated through the darker scene within the *mise-en-scène*: the separate "twilight" shadowed by the tree's "aged branches." From the poem's opening, there is a counter-signing that leaves its mark yet remains, as we come to find, traumatically untold. This counter-signing propels the Narrator, nonetheless, toward a different telling. As a representation of nature and naturalness, his perception of things becomes the symptom of his displacement from the scene:

> Other lot was mine.
> Across a bare wide common I had toiled
> With languid feet which by the slippery ground
> Were baffled still; and when I stretched myself
> On the brown earth my limbs from very heat
> Could find no rest . . . (18–23)

The passage necessitates overcoming the perceptual and psychological struggle occasioned by the Narrator's separation from his world by *seeking out* and *constructing* this struggle ("Other lot was mine") as the subject's native position. To be empirically displaced from nature and the natural is to live in the world of "dreaming man." The Narrator removes himself from this imaginary realm, but not without first marking its visionary hold on his consciousness.

The Narrator is thus caught between two solitudes of his human nature: a nature that is anything but natural; a humanity that is his natural bourn but that he experiences preternaturally. As the "twilight" within the scene emerges in a clearer—and more clearly traumatic—form, we begin to understand what is at stake in his dilemma. He encounters another displaced wanderer, a Pedlar "Alone and stretched upon the cottage bench," "beneath a shade / Of clustering elms that sprang from the same root" in front of "a ruined house, [with] four naked walls / That stared upon each other" (29–34). The single "root" suggests an organic origin behind the cottage's bleak humanity: however traumatic, this uniformity makes sense of and naturalizes the scene. But the cottage is also spectrally anthropomorphized as a kind of inaccessible primal scene blankly gazing on its own lack of meaning. The scene mirrors the individual psychologies of the Narrator and the Pedlar, but also the subject of their ensuing dialogue: the madness of Margaret and her unremittingly bleak and traumatic life. Simultaneously within and apart from nature, the scene acquires a phantasmal life of its own that compels conversation between the Narrator and the Pedlar in their attempt to make sense of this life, as if to tell the record of humanity itself.

But the attempt to displace the threat of madness in the conversation between men fails, for they become mutually mesmerized by their attempt to make sense of Margaret's life. Their transference prolongs as much as it attenuates madness, and they become desperate to restore a 'naturally' sane state of affairs, which the text from its very beginning is clear to displace. The trees' uniformly "clustering" shape begins to suggest the psychic fragmentation of multiple personalities. This oppressive psychology prevents either man from connecting the past and present in a meaningful way. Their final reduction of Margaret's life to "spear-grass" marks, ironically, the return in their own psyches of a nature they would rather set aside. This threat of madness—of a sense of profound loss coupled with a traumatic inability to know the truth of one's identity—remains immanent within the text as a part of a nature that will not go away, an incipient madness that is also the title of one of Wordsworth's earliest writings for "The Ruined Cottage."

But whose madness is it: a) Margaret's; b) the Narrator's or the Pedlar's; c) Wordsworth's? According to *The Prelude*, the answer is 'c.' Certainly the trauma of loss had greatly affected Wordsworth by the time he began writing *The Prelude* in 1798. By 1783, at thirteen, both his parents were dead. His political hopes for the French Revolution had dissipated, and he had left behind in France Annette Vallon and their illegitimate child, Anne Caroline, precipitating his 1796 crisis of moral, spiritual, and psychological confidence. This crisis was a primary reason for his expansion of *The Prelude* first to five books between January and March 1804. Coleridge's departure for Malta (he did not return until 1806) left Wordsworth unable to continue with *The Recluse* and provoked a further expansion to thirteen books completed by May 1805, three months after the death of Wordsworth's brother John at sea. Further exacerbating the situation was the strain of his growing estrangement from Coleridge, whose poetic and philosophical support in the mid- to late-1790s had been so crucial to Wordsworth's own creative development. We should not be surprised, then, that at the opening of *The Prelude*, like that of "The Ruined Cottage," the poet stretches himself "in the sheltered grove" (*P* 1.78) beneath an oak tree. Here he is "Cheared by the genial pillow of the earth," but only after recognizing in the "gentle breeze" of nature, "half conscious of the joy it gives," the "redundant energy" of his own "corresponding mild creative breeze" (1.88, 1, 4, 46, 43). The struggle between these forces occasions the text's dialogue between Wordsworth and Coleridge as a phantom-like silent screen to ease the "burthen of [Wordsworth's] own unnatural self" (1.23).

Whatever historical or political contingencies have impacted upon this dialogue, however, become inseparable from the text's crises of psychological representation played out between Wordsworth and Coleridge as the text's coauthors. This transference uncannily replicates the situation of the poet who is both at home and not at home in his 'natural' environment. The struggle to hold these two states in consciousness simultaneously produces dialogue about the state of the self in nature as a site of traumatic displacement. This crisis of his natural state, at once unnatural and preternatural, necessitates in the poet the struggle to manage his "Unmanageable thoughts" (1.149) in order to gain "clearer insight" (1.238). The text's problematic empiricism—its struggle to locate the subject in the world—is also an epistemological problem, the trauma of not knowing or being able to comprehend this position. This lack of knowledge is one way of understanding Wordsworth's description of his "brain / Work[ing] with a dim and undetermined sense / Of unknown modes of being" (1.419–21), the way in which the empiricism of perception itself, as Laura Quinney notes, mobilizes the unconscious as a force with which the mind must then reckon.[2]

To accommodate this process Wordsworth figures himself as "couched" on the "ground" in "[a] perfect stillness," "Passing through many thoughts, yet mainly such / As to [him]self pertained" (78–81). In the process he writes one of the first case histories of psychoanalysis, an epochal moment Wordsworth marks by saying that "it is a thing unprecedented in Literary history that a man should talk so much about himself" (*WL* 1:586–87). Both *The Prelude* and "The Ruined Cottage" 'couch' the analytical subject within a scene of psychoanalysis built around a past trauma necessitating a cure. All of the elements of the Freudian setting are here: the couch; the scene of 'stillness' clinically separated from nature and the social sphere; an analysand and an analyst; the process Freud describes as remembering, repeating, and working-through the past, with its attendant phenomena of repression and repetition; a reliance on the importance of dreams and phantasy as a key to unlocking the secrets of the unconscious; the primal scene as a site of trauma necessitating the analytical process in the first place; the affective and psychic bonding between analyst and analysand in the transference/countertransference. These clinical features, remarkable enough in Wordsworth's texts, repeat themselves throughout a body of writing that we have come to call Romantic, although this rubric in no way fits the period's heterogeneity.

For reasons that I will outline in the next section, this book will read differently from Romantic criticism's recent historical, ideological, and cultural turns, and therefore will not explore a cultural so much as a psychological history of psychoanalysis as it emerges in Romanticism. This is also to say that I employ criticism here, amidst its other valences, as an essentially psychological venture. When criticism returns to the past, it does so by confronting that past's validity, which is also to say the validity of the return and thus of criticism itself. We wrestle to make sense of the past within the theater of our critical imaginations, where *imagoes* of the past—of the various artifacts, textual or otherwise, that mark the past's revenance—as well as the *imagoes* of our attempt to come to grips with this past form parts of the same associative critical matrix within which past and present, while often distinguishable, are nonetheless intermixed. Put another way, in its attempt to make sense of a past that is always traumatically absent to it, criticism is inevitably itself traumatic and thus implicitly psychoanalytical, always engaged in the (im)possible task of remembering, repeating, and working through to some understanding of a past that perpetually shifts with our attempts to comprehend it.

I belabor this explanation of criticism's psychoanalytical nature precisely because my object of inquiry is the emergence *of* psychoanalysis in Romanticism. One of this book's assumptions is that Romanticism's concern with the trauma of self-identity is one of the ways it coheres as an historical entity, but that this historical identity is always subject to the psychoanalysis that is so much a part of its emergence, a psychoanalysis that both consolidates Romantic identity and places it under erasure. I do not doubt that there are clear historical precedents for this emergence somewhere between 1789 and 1832, to name two arbitrary markers of the British Romantic period with which this book primarily concerns itself. The birth of Romantic psychiatry during this period would form one set of both material and discursive conditions for this emergence; mesmerism, which *is* central to this book's concerns for reasons that will later become apparent, forms another.[3] Again, rehearsing a material, discursive, or cultural history of these phenomena is not my primary concern here, and those concerned with Romanticism's history will find such a decision problematic, even negligent. A definitive critical history of Romantic psychiatry and its relationship to literature remains to be written, and I applaud whatever can or might be done to write one.[4] But my present argument is that it is not at the level of history and its materialities, at least not strictly or in the first instance, if one can name such an instance, that Romantic psychoanalysis itself takes shape. And I hope that this book, by addressing itself to *this* phenomenon, will offer some productive commentary on the *im*possibility of writing such a history, despite whatever critical resistances one might otherwise have to this book's methodology. For it is precisely in the nature of psychoanalysis at its emergence in Romanticism to disclaim such a purchase on 'reality,' although it may claim a rather more radical purchase on what we might call 'the real.'

This study takes shape, then, around the issue of how Romanticism constitutes itself as a scene of psychoanalysis to deal with the trauma of Romanticism's search for itself. More remarkable is the emergence of what I will call the scene of Romantic psychoanalysis in the metaphorical and seemingly *un*clinical terrain of poetry, and at a time when in the Preface to *Lyrical Ballads* Wordsworth warns against "frantic novels, sickly and stupid German Tragedies, and deluges of idle and extravagant stories in verse" (*WP* 735) or Shelley, somewhat later in *A Defence of Poetry*, refers to poets as the "*un*acknowledged legislators of the world" (*SPP* 535; my italics). One of the purposes of this book will be to examine Romantic poetry's anxiety about articulating a language of the psyche that resists articulation, an anxiety that in turn demands psychoanalysis. From early on Romanticism submits the idealism of its visionary and imaginative apparatus to psychoanalysis. Indeed, it is one of my central assumptions that the emergence of this apparatus is concerned with its own psychoanalysis, an idealism that generates its own demystification. Romantic psychoanalysis takes place as part of a monumental philosophical effort to explain human existence. In his early 1799 manuscript version of the Prospectus to *The Recluse*, which was to have contained both "The Ruined Cottage" and *The Prelude* as part of its larger structure, Wordsworth writes:

> On man, on nature, and on human life,
> Thinking in solitude, from time to time
> I find sweet passions traversing my soul
> Like music; unto these, where'er I may,
> I would give utterance in numerous verse. (*WP* 1–5)

Philosophy, or in Wordsworth's case eighteenth-century British empiricism and early nineteenth-century philosophical idealism, meets poetry and the visionary imagination to produce the hybrid of what Coleridge calls "the first & finest philosophical Poem" (*CL* 2:1034). Yet the moment the poet puts himself on his own couch, he is compelled to confront other facets of his psyche, which makes him irrevocably complicit in his own analysis.

In the texts that stand in for what I will call the absent body of *The Recluse*, the poetry of "dreaming man" gives way to the contemplation of philosophy ("Other lot was mine"), the stance of man "thinking in solitude" in order to figure out what's wrong. But this stance produces "no rest." Instead there is the third "lot" signified by the Narrator's seeking dialogue with an other. This stance is constructed from the sense of the first two being themselves *un*natural or *preter*natural constructions of the human condition. Psychoanalysis emerges as this third thing, ostensibly as a solution to a dilemma left unresolved by poetry or philosophy, but rather more problematically as the mobilization of uncanny forces in both. Psychoanalysis remains vulnerable to this haunting, which affects the reader in turn as an interloper upon its uncanny terrain. Poetry and philosophy may not have all the answers, but psychoanalysis is equally set aside as a self-alienating gesture within both. Put another way, once psychology enters philosophy to produce psychoanalysis, psychoanalysis immediately becomes alien to itself. Philosophy turns to poetry, or vice versa, to produce psychoanalysis at the site where thinking man discovers that human nature is neither *human* nor *natural*, his own perception having constellated how this separation manifests itself precisely at the moment he perceives himself to be *other*wise part of the world.

Hence this book's argument, in short: Romantic poetry, by confronting the unconscious of philosophy, *invents* psychoanalysis. When Freud admits that his case histories "lack the serious stamp of science" (*SE* 2:160) and read more like "short stories" than confirmed diagnoses, he marks psychoanalysis as a seismic confrontation between the reason of philosophy and the phantasy of literature and the literary. This concession responds to the fact, as Freud states in *The Ego and the Id*, that the "psychology of consciousness" understood by philosophy "is incapable of solving the problems of dreams and hypnosis" (*SE* 19:13). Focusing specifically upon the latter, Mikkel Borch-Jacobsen argues that "by invoking hypnosis against the philosophy of consciousness, Freud calls up a phenomenon that escapes his own theory of the unconscious." Whereas early on in his writings Freud saw dreams as a rationalizable bridge between conscious and unconscious life, hypnosis, which suspended the consciousness of reason and of philosophy, was beyond explanation. It confronted psychoanalysis with an inalienable part of itself that was at the same time utterly alien and beyond its grasp. Borch-Jacobsen continues by asking, "Could Freud have been trying to tell us that psychoanalysis is not really 'itself' or 'at home' except when estranged from itself?"[5] The question, especially because of the strange confluence of post-Enlightenment thought, Romantic poetry, and mesmerism that is one of this book's central concerns, leads us to wonder how philosophy and poetry before Freud complicate their own idealisms in an attempt to deal with this blind spot in Freudian insight. Put another way, how is philosophical idealism complicated by Romantic poetry's response to it to produce a psychoanalysis before Freud? We know that the encounter between reason and phantasy is hardly novel to psychoanalysis after Freud, nor is it the exclusive province of Romantic literature. Yet it might be that such an encounter, as it produces psychoanalysis, might be very particular to Romanticism.

One salient fact should galvanize our attention here: Coleridge coined the term "psycho-analytical" in a September 1805 notebook entry, coincidentally the same year that Wordsworth completed his thirteen-book *Prelude* in Coleridge's absence and in place of the missing *Recluse*. Kathleen Coburn first pointed out the neologism in the 1970s.[6] But

Romantic studies have yet fully to internalize the term's astonishing resonance within a psychoanalytic imaginary that includes, besides Freud, British Romantic poetry, and its relationship to eighteenth-century empiricism and philosophical idealism, especially as all of these are haunted by the specter of mesmerism. What is troubling about mesmerism, as I will suggest in the next chapter, partly explains why the "psycho-analytical" took so long to make it from Coleridge's notebooks into common parlance. Informing this psychoanalytic imaginary is a scene of understanding both articulated and clouded by its own experience, that experience residing, paradoxically, in a traumatic and traumatizing lack of comprehension. Against a "disciplinarian closure of identity," Sonu Shamdasani and Michael Münchow argue, "psychoanalysis reveals an unmasterable exteriority encrypted within itself."[7] Romantic poetry stages this encryption at one of the inaugural moments of psychoanalysis as it is engaged in its own impossible disciplining. Romantic poetry, that is, confronts psychoanalysis as its own impossibility. The "greatest speculative power" of psychoanalysis, Derrida writes, is its "greatest resistance *to* psychoanalysis," a deconstructive gesture within enlightenment Reason that "remain[s] forever heterogeneous to the principle of principle."[8] Keats will refer to this as being able to live with the "Burden of the Mystery" (*KL* 92), a burden which, as we shall see in the poetry itself, Romantic psychoanalysis 'understands' only too well.

Romanticism and Psychoanalysis

For the sake of argument, then, this book defines Romanticism as a body of writing struggling to find its own identity, what Tilottama Rajan calls a "literature involved in the restless process of self-examination."[9] A telling symptom of this process is the fact that subjects in key Romantic texts spend a lot of time talking to themselves and to others about the trauma of who they are: the Ancient Mariner and the Wedding Guest, the Narrator and the Pedlar in "The Ruined Cottage," the Narrator and Moneta in "The Fall of Hyperion," Wordsworth in *The Prelude*, De Quincey in *Confessions of an English Opium Eater*, among others. Like Freud, the Romantics undertake analyzing "an unmasterable exteriority encrypted within themselves," a taking in of the world through subjective experience that finds its origins in Enlightenment thought and that leaves the subject bewildered by an attempt to make sense of this subjectivity and thus of the world itself. In this way we can say that Romanticism parallels psychoanalysis, which emerges at the end of the nineteenth century when Freud advocates a talking cure through which his patients can make sense of their symptoms, hysterical ones in the first instance, such as these symptoms betray a fundamental glitch in the subject's experience of the world. Criticism has rarely observed this parallel, however. Genealogies constructed to link Romanticism and psychoanalysis have tended to diminish Romanticism as an earlier blindness cured by the theoretical insight of a later psychoanalysis. This is to follow Matthew Arnold's observation that, in general, Romantic writers "did not know enough"[10] and so were unable to bring their own insights to proper fulfillment by turning all that mental effort of self-scrutiny outward to public action—to master an "unmasterable exteriority" in order to demonstrate the subject's ability to bring the world under his control. For Arnold, Romanticism evoked something heterogeneous in need of Victorian prescription; and so, compensating (ironically) for his own Romantic past, he treats literature as a body of knowledge that other disciplines need to regulate, a Victorianizing privileging of psychoanalysis over literature that lasted well into the twentieth century.

Freud's own historicization of psychoanalysis betrays a similar Victorianizing impulse. In his 1923 "A Short Account of Psycho-Analysis" he writes that psychoanalysis

> did not drop from the skies ready-made. It had its starting-point in older ideas, which it developed further; it sprang from earlier suggestions, which it elaborated. Any history of it must therefore begin with an account of the influences which determined its origin and should not overlook the times and circumstances that preceded its creation. (*SE* 19:191)

The sensitivity about precedents betrays a deeper concern about how this history could or should be written. "For," Borsch-Jacobsen writes, "it remains that Freud *does* oppose psychoanalysis to philosophy, and he found no better way to do so than by calling on a phenomenon that remains estranged not only from philosophy but from psychoanalysis itself."[11] That phenomenon, hypnosis, as Freud writes in "Group Psychology and the Analysis of the Ego," thwarted "rational explanation" and contained "a great deal in it which we must recognize as unexplained and mysterious" (*SE* 18:115). Explaining hypnotism becomes the Holy Grail of psychoanalysis, the secret mechanism of the psyche that psychoanalysis could claim to make sense of, where other disciplines had failed. Yet hypnotism is precisely what sets psychoanalysis beside itself, marking its fundamental failure to distinguish itself from philosophy and thus to claim the authority Freud seemed desperate to achieve for the 'science' he invented. We can thus read hypnotism back to its earlier precedent in mesmerism, which will emerge in the present examination as the specter haunting Romantic psychoanalysis in the same way that Freud's theoretical rationalism remains haunted by hypnotism in the early twentieth century. What "sprang from earlier suggestions" to produce psychoanalysis in both its Romantic and Freudian incarnations is an unexplainable suggestibility transacting between subjects, played out in the transference relationship between them.[12] And this transference bears the traces of a subjective interiorization of the world that, by virtue of its dependence on others' similar (or often not so similar) experiences, constitutes a slippery slope of human comprehension.

That literature becomes an equally occult strain of Freud's exploration betrays the powerful cathexis between literature and mesmerism in the cultural imaginary of psychoanalysis that this study explores. The power of the literary, that is, its ability both to conjecture and to replicate the imaginary space of human comprehension, *hypnotizes* or *mesmerizes* both philosophy *and* psychoanalysis in their attempt to rationalize the subject. We need only remind ourselves of the fact that, even as the child of earlier precedents, Freud both uses his theories to parent literature and uses literature as a scapegoat for his theories. Setting aside for the moment the question of how psychoanalysis itself construes experience at the intersection of literature and philosophy, I would note how this trend influenced the locating of psychoanalysis within literary studies and thus of psychoanalysis *against* literature. In his 1947 "Freud and Literature," Lionel Trilling marks what Harold Bloom calls a "classical" antithesis between the disciplines by recalling Freud's admission that the "'poets and philosophers before [him]'" discovered the unconscious and that "[w]hat [he] discovered was the scientific method by which the unconscious can be studied."[13] Again, whatever precedence Freud gives to philosophy or poetry he then takes away by announcing psychoanalysis's scientific precedence over both. Trilling followed Freud's suggestion by arguing that literary analysis needed to become more scientific, which Bloom famously disputed by calling Shakespeare "the inventor of psychoanalysis" and Freud "its codifier."[14] Overturning the precedence, however, doesn't quite get at literature's more disruptive psychic legacy. Whereas Bloom would examine how literature overcomes its own psychic paternity, we also need to examine how literature displaces a theoretical paternity in which the child (theory) has become father of the man (literature). We need to remember, as Ned Lukacher writes, that "Literature is always what philosophy/psychoanalysis forgets in its progress toward the Spirit of Absolute Knowledge."[15] It is this radical sense of literature and the literary that will concern us here.

If "psychoanalysis did not drop from the skies ready-made" but "sprang from earlier suggestions," one is led to wonder what omissions psychoanalysis has made in suggesting its own history to itself. Shoshana Felman's 1977 "To Open the Question" has been one of the most effective statements against the master/slave relationship between literature and psychoanalysis. As noted earlier, however, discussions of Romanticism *and* psychoanalysis have nonetheless tended to oppose Romantic literary blindness to the theoretical insights of psychoanalysis.[16] To borrow Felman's terms, the issue appears to be one of disciplinary hygiene: one studies *either* literature *or* psychoanalysis, but must avoid having one contaminate the "interiority of the other" because "a theoretical body of thought always is traversed by its own unconscious, its own 'unthought,' of which it is not aware, but which it contains in itself as the very condition of its disruption, as the possibility of its own self-subversion."[17] Felman's account is a telling gloss on the relationship between Romanticism and psychoanalysis in Romantic studies, which has traditionally contained psychic interiority as the privileged site of Romantic consciousness. Northrop Frye and M. H. Abrams, for instance, associated Romantic idealism with the mythopoeic imagination and its ability to overcome political and social disillusionment and to transcend the narrowness of Enlightenment materialism and rationalism. Bloom and Geoffrey Hartman foregrounded how the Romantic transcendental *mythos*, redeeming the mind from natural determinism, in fact produces in the subject a desire to return to a "self-less self" from the alienating *excess* of consciousness, an oddly proto-Victorian answer to Arnold's later concern about the Romantics.[18]

More recent posttranscendentalist versions of Romanticism have thoroughly de-privileged the metaphysics of Romantic interiority. Reading consciousness as a textual effect, deconstruction questions this effect as what Paul de Man called one more "metaphor[ ] of primacy, of genetic history, and, most notably, of the autonomous power to will of the self."[19] New historicism internalizes deconstruction's hermeneutics of suspicion so as to replace what Joseph Litvak calls the "deconstructive abyss" with a "cultural reality" that is "shocking and even painful."[20] Jerome McGann, for instance, has critiqued a Romantic ideology that sublates the material conditions of the human, and hence the materiality of the subject, by repressing history in both Romantic literature and the criticism it valorizes, whether logocentric or deconstructive.[21] The point, as Clifford Siskin argues, is to historicize Romanticism's own stake in constructing "a self-made mind, full of newly constructed depths."[22] Such a process maps the shifting cultural contexts within which Romanticism's various models of the mind emerged. Recent historical and cultural criticisms, reading the subject as the unstable effect of sociohistorical discourses, are thus committed to demystifying the category of "the subject" in order to avoid reifying any singular account of the psyche or, more accurately, to document what forces have profited from the reification where it has occurred.

This book turns its attention to a psychoanalysis of this spectralizing emergence of the subject precisely as this process marks the emergence of psychoanalysis itself as a radically phantasmal and destabilizing process of nonetheless considerable imaginal and critical power. This is necessarily also to return to the question of agency and interiority, usually figures of false consciousness in deconstructive, new historical, or cultural practice. Mary Jacobus asks the "question of how things get . . . from the outside to the inside—simultaneously establishing the boundary between them and seeming to abolish it": "What does it mean to call this 'interiority'? Where is this place that has neither outside nor inside, and by what process does it come into being?"[23] Jacobus draws on both post-Lacanian and post-Kleinian object relations psychoanalysis to argue that interiority, rather than protecting the category of the subject, in fact radicalizes, and is radicalized in turn, by the transference/countertransference between subjects within this space. For our later purposes the work of Julia Kristeva, herself influenced by both Lacanian and Kleinian models, will become central to thinking through this interiority. Via Kristeva's revision of Freud's legacy, I wish to return to the ramifications of an earlier criticism's concern with imagination and mythopoeia as figures of psychic interiority and psychoanalysis and hence to read these figures post-transcendentally.

In *The Psychic Life of Power* Judith Butler argues that the subject is formed from his subject*ion* to "regulatory power" by "producing and exploiting the demand for continuity, visibility, and place." The subject's psychic life is determined by power's "iterability" as the inbred effects of social regulation. This iterability, paradoxically, constitutes the subject's agency, the way in which power acclimatizes him to its arbitrary nature by repeating itself so as to appear natural or given. However, Butler continues, agency also "consist[s] in opposing and transforming the social terms by which it was spawned."[24] The repetition of power's effects offers the *possibility* of transformation, not as transcendence, but as the subject's opportunity productively to alter, recreate, or transgress these effects—as it were, to *de*naturalize their cultural authority. As Andrea Henderson argues in a recent study of how varieties of subjectivity constructed in the Romantic period take on a life of their own, Romantic interiority evokes the "notion of a heart or core in either society or the individual [that] is threatening because such a core becomes, in both cases, the center of movement or circulation, a place of dangerous fluidity."[25] As I will show in the opening sections of my first chapter, eighteenth-century empiricist models of the mind generate this fluidity as the threat of psychology to the philosophy by which it is generated. This generation of the self at the phantasmal matrix of its own mobilization gives the concepts of the self and subject their own particular power and dark legitimacy.

If Romanticism generates an overdetermined depth model of subjectivity, an interiority inconsistent within itself, then the Gothic is surely the place to investigate its haunting and haunted locus. As Andrew Smith argues, "The Gothic does not merely anticipate the arrival of Freud, it also . . . identifies the inconsistencies and incoherences which govern Freud's accounts of the unconscious and the uncanny."[26] Indeed, Gothic studies at the present moment, as in the recent work of Jerrold Hogle, David Punter, or Anne Williams, can claim to be one of the most fertile sites for investigating the prehistory of psychoanalysis or psychoanalytic imperatives in nineteenth-century literature and culture.[27] Terry Castle considers the Gothic as part of the invention of the uncanny in the late eighteenth century, so that "psychoanalysis seems both the most poignant critique of romantic consciousness to date, and its richest and most perverse elaboration."[28] Castle's work, like Hogle's, Punter's, Smith's, or Williams's, helps to rewrite the narrative of progressive enlightenment that has traditionally informed the critical movement from Romantic literature to psychoanalytic theory. Somewhat differently, my approach subsumes the Gothic as a force of destabilizing articulation within a broader investigation of Romantic poetry and eighteenth- and nineteenth-century philosophy. In the manner of Williams's poetics of Gothic, that is, I would trace a *poetics of Romantic psychoanalysis*.

As much as recent ideological interrogations have questioned the reductivism of an earlier transcendentalist view of Romantic interiority, then, it is also possible to read within Romantic texts an immanent self-critique that is already a critique of the ideology that Romantic interiority had been thought to protect.[29] Specifically, one can explore this autocritique in the form of a psychoanalytical apparatus that allows us in turn to reflect on the ideologies generated by the text without reinscribing another ideology. How, that is, can one account for the generation of psychoanalysis in Romanticism before a theoretical or metapsychological framework existed through which to read Romanticism's psychoanalytical insights? This is to address in Romanticism the radical power of phantasy within the literary imagination that always disrupts the very authority of science and truth it makes possible—the kind of phantasy of truth, for instance, that makes possible the theoretical distinctions of the Freudian metapsychology. For the current study, to answer the previous question is to frame a set of philosophical and theoretical concerns more than cultural or sociohistorical ones. That is to say, I wish to trace in the emergence of Romantic psychoanalysis the tension between a scientific *consciousness* associated with philosophical enlightenment and a literary *unconscious* associated with both mystification and self-making. Rather than reading either consciousness or the unconscious as the exclusive domain of a particular discipline, however, I read across the disciplines for a particular phenomenology of the philosophical *cogito*, whose consciousness is unsettled by the *literature* or *poetry* of its own unreason, especially as this phenomenology can be traced within literature or poetry itself.[30]

Ultimately, I am concerned to explore in certain Romantic texts a confrontation with the work of reason, more particularly with reason's tenacious resistance to unreason in the work of the imagination. Romanticism evolves an aesthetic or literary approach to the subject partly because philosophy's systematization of reason is threatened by the psychic determinism of an unconscious that philosophy generates in the first place. This meeting between philosophy and poetry *in literature*, I am suggesting, is the breeding ground of a particular psychoanalytic hybridization of the subject at the encounter of his psychic determinism with his self-making potentiality. By reading Romantic psychoanalysis before psychoanalytic theory, then, one can intercept the discourse of psychoanalysis that emerges within Romantic texts themselves, but intercept this emergence within the broader *philosophical* currents of Romanticism's emergence, the topic of my first chapter. I am not therefore concerned with the 'discovery' of the unconscious *per se*, which already has a rich and complex scholarly history.[31] Instead, I address how certain Romantic texts attempt to read the effects of the unconscious by evolving a psychoanalytic apparatus for its exploration before Freud. In particular, I want to address how the positivism of Romantic self-discovery unmasks within itself an undecidable encounter with the trauma of not knowing, a trauma that continually turns Romanticism back upon the radically self-making and phantastic terms of its own epistemology. It is Romanticism's gradual acceptance of the radically mythopoeic nature of its psychoanalysis that we can read in advance of modern psychoanalysis' own struggle to return itself to the poetry-making ground of the *cogito*. Although conceding the influence of literature on his metapsychology and admitting the role of phantasy in the psyche's self-constructions, Freud essentially repressed the poetics of psychoanalysis within his confirmed scientism. Romanticism, I would argue, repeats Freud's repression, but by remaining skeptical about and even psychoanalyzing its terms as antithetical to the very project of inventing psychoanalysis that Romanticism undertakes.

Let me briefly suggest the terms of this invention. Romanticism offers many forms of psychic interrogation that look uncannily like psychoanalysis: Keats's "Large Mansion of many Apartments" or "vale of Soul-making" as metaphors of psychic development (*KL* 95, 249); De Quincey's interpretation of dreams; the repetition of texts in displaced and problematic forms, as in Keats's two *Hyperion*s, De Quincey's *Confessions*, or Wordsworth's writings toward *The Recluse*, which repetition constitutes a larger traumatic hermeneutics of self-understanding. One could allegorize these phenomena within a later theoretical framework such as psychoanalysis to produce a psychoanalytical or psychological reading of Romantic texts. Yet this is to assert both a theoretical and historical precedence over literature. Rather than being the nascent form of psychoanalysis, Romanticism has become its unconscious, a receding literary scene within the theoretical mind of psychoanalysis.[32] Yet a psychoanalysis *avant la lettre* is equally the primal scene of Romanticism, for in the search for psychic origins the Romantic subject comes to the self-receding scene of his own identity which it is the particular endeavor of psychoanalysis to find.

In *The Order of Things* Foucault argues that the "mere emergence" of "man" as an epistemic category "impl[ies] an imperative that haunts thought from within," an "imperative lodged within thought and its movement towards the apprehension of the unthought."[33] This study will read psychoanalysis archaeologically back through Romanticism in order to find disruptions that manifest the unconscious or "unthought" between them and within the conscious shape of the *anthropos* that they both share. The knowledge Romanticism comes to have of itself suggests what is unthought about its subjectivity. Moreover, within the process of what I shall examine as a Romantic psychoanalysis both *terminable* and *interminable*, Romanticism is frequently blind to its own insights. Yet it also articulates itself within an analytic apparatus that allows it to apprehend these blindnesses without necessarily giving them cognitive shape and thus making them conform to reason. Applying literature to a psychoanalysis that literature generates and always exceeds, this study returns to the future of psychoanalysis in Romanticism, but not as the disciplined child of a later theoretical parent. Instead, I shall argue that Romanticism *invents* psychoanalysis as the struggle for an identity radically divided between its scientific—by which I also mean theoretical and philosophical—and literary or aesthetic impulses.

The Authority of Psychoanalysis

The object lesson of (post-)Freudian psychoanalysis offers a particularly instructive way of reading Romanticism's struggle to avoid the prescriptive terms of its own unfolding. Freud's attempt to make sense of the unconscious suggests a kind of theoretical rationality that in turn evokes his desire for acceptance by the scientific community from which he emerged.[34] *The Interpretation of Dreams*, for instance, systematizes the dreamwork in the way that Kant's first critique maps the conscious mind's architectonic:

> In the pages that follow I shall bring forward proof that there is a psychological technique which makes it possible to interpret dreams, and that, if that procedure is employed, every dream reveals itself as a psychical structure which has a meaning and which can be inserted at an assignable point in the mental activities of waking life. I shall further endeavor to elucidate the processes to which the strangeness and obscurity of dreams are due and to deduce from those processes the nature of the psychical forces by whose concurrent or mutually opposing actions dreams are generated. (*SE* 4:1)

Yet Freud's scientism seems to overshadow the fact that his metapsychology derives much of its explanatory power from literature and phantasy. Moreover, this scientism is subverted by Freud's case histories, in the same way that Coleridge's case history of a woman's nervous "fever" (*BL* 1:112), as we shall see, disrupts the theoretical authority of his *Biographia Literaria* (1817). In the case history narrative invades science to expose both Coleridge and Freud to later revision. In these narratives both analyst and analysand, as well as subsequent readers, remain vulnerable to an unconscious that escapes narrative's signification itself.

That Freud's psychoanalysis is overdetermined by its own evolving theoretical framework is the point of Lacan's return to Freud, the fact that, according to Jeffrey Mehlman, "Freud's discovery of repression was itself necessarily and constantly threatened with being repressed"[35] and that Freud's theories are unsettled by the negativity of the psychological mechanisms they seek to rationalize. Lacan's Freud, Althusser argues, comes before the "fall of psycho-analysis into biologism, psychologism and sociologism," before Freud's radical insights "fall into [the] ideology"[36] of Freudianism itself, particularly that of American ego psychology. Yet Lacanianism's demystification of Freud carries its own scientific authority. Frederic Jameson argues that Lacan's work is not "the transformation of Freud into linguistics" but "the disengagement of a linguistic theory which was implicit in Freud's practice, but for which he did not yet have the appropriate conceptual instruments."[37] Figuring Lacan as a Victorian who clarifies Freudian blindnesses, Jameson inscribes a Lacanian paternity in place of Freud's. The Lacanian theoretical child becomes the father of the Freudian man in order to enforce the hegemony of the de-idealizing signifier.[38] Lacan himself writes that "[Freud] is not only the subject who was supposed to know. He did know, and he gave us this knowledge in terms that are indestructible."[39]

For Todd Dufresne the whole debate is "rotten to the core of psychoanalysis." By *Beyond the Pleasure Principle* (1920), Dufresne argues, Jung and Adler had defected from Freud's camp and psychoanalysis had gained little scientific respectability. Enter the death drive and the repetition compulsion, ideas "immune to [future] criticism." The death drive is a theoretical ruse designed to insure for psychoanalysis a potent if spectral half-life. Freud's *thanatos* is the crux of a "metapsychology [that] became the delicate inner space of psychoanalysis, a theater or cave from which everything began and will return again and against which nothing truly critical can be said." Lacan plays an important role in this half-life for, "having found the place of Truth empty in light of the deaths of God and Man, [he] nonetheless continued to play the role of resurrected father; like Freud, Lacan occupied a privileged reference point in the transmission of psychoanalytic knowledge."[40] My purpose generally in this study is to extract from the theoretical endgame Dufresne describes "the delicate inner space of psychoanalysis" in order to explore this space otherwise in Romanticism. At present I would note that a telling feature of "the transmission of psychoanalytic knowledge" Dufresne critiques is the fact that Lacan does not employ case histories in support of his own theory. On one hand, this absence fits with his essential denial of any constitutive subject position. On the other, it occludes the literary dimension of psychoanalysis as self-writing or self-dramatization, protecting it from external critique, or else internalizing a self-critique hermetically sealed within the discipline's private theoretical domain.

This Lacanian hermeticism is symptomatic of another repetition compulsion in psychoanalysis. Following a pattern set by Freud, one way that psychoanalysis has sought to consolidate its authority is by abjecting as occult strains threats to its disciplinary and institutional purity.[41] By criticizing Freud's scientific reductivism, for instance, Jung marked Freud's 'fall into ideology' precisely by rejecting Freud's materialism, just as Lacan displaces Freudian positivism, but to different ends.

Among other disagreements, Jung rejected Freud's medical prejudice against art as a neurosis, because it suggests that the psyche is determined wholly by infantile sexuality or repression. As Jung writes in "Psychology and Literature,"

> The reduction of the vision [of the artist] to a personal experience makes it something unreal and unauthentic—a mere substitute ... The vision thus loses its primordial quality and becomes nothing but a symptom; the teeming chaos shrinks to the proportions of a psychic disturbance. We feel reassured by this explanation, and turn back to our picture of a well-ordered cosmos. (*CWJ* 15:93).[42]

In Jung's more 'literary' conception of the psyche, the subject finds his identity as it calls to him from the collective unconscious, like the "magus Zoroaster ... / [Meeting] his own image in the garden" (*SPP* 1.192–93) in Shelley's *Prometheus Unbound*. But this process of imaginary individuation also offers a self-making response to the psychic determinism of this unconscious, a process of transformation rather than transcendence. By occupying a transitional space between a 'literary Jung' and a 'literary Freud,' Julia Kristeva's writings encrypt a return *of* Jung through a rereading of Lacan's Freud. The network of theoretical possibilities generated by reading *between* Freud, Jung, and Lacan is remembered, repeated, and worked-through in a Kristevan encounter between psychoanalysis and literature. This encounter reads both dialectically and dialogically rather than hierarchically or antithetically between scientific and literary conceptualizations of the subject. Kristeva (dis)locates the subject between Freud's tempering of the pleasure principle of phantasy by the reality principle of the death drive and the determinism of Lacan's desiring subject, and thus also between Freudian psychic determinism and Jungian self-making, resisting the former and remaining, not unlike Jung, ambivalent about the latter.[43]

Kristeva revises the psychoaesthetics of Lacan's distinction between the imaginary and the Symbolic, which itself revises Freud's Oedipal schema. The imaginary's narcissistic dynamics dramatize the child's relationship to the Mother as preparation for the subject's inscription *as subject* by the Symbolic intervention of the Father. In Lacan's words this mirror stage "situates the agency of the ego, before its social determination, in a fictional direction" and mobilizes subjectivity before it is objectified within the language of the Symbolic, which "projects the formation of the individual into history." The mirror stage is a "drama ... which ... machinates the succession of fantasies which go from an image of the body in bits and pieces to a form which we will call orthopaedic of its totality." But this *imago* is also, paradoxically, the signifier of Symbolic identity as fragmentary and dependent (the child's separation from the Mother and castration by the Father). The Symbolic is a type of deterministic repetition of the mirror stage ("which will mark with its rigid structure the subject's entire mental development"), "the assumption of the armor of an alienating identity."[44] The paradox is this: the subject inhabits the imaginary only symbolically, but in turn inhabits the Symbolic in only an imaginary manner. Yet Lacan also reads the imaginary as prior to and thus separate from the Symbolic and thus privileges the Symbolic for its significative complexity. Correspondingly, he reads the "fictional direction" of the mirror stage as seducing the subject with the illusion of an autonomy she cannot possess except in a purely hypothetical manner. The fiction and "drama"[45] of the mirror stage mark self-making potentiality as an illusory dimension that masks Symbolic determinism. The Lacanian subject is both identity-less and trapped by the Symbolic's arbitrary effects, her own performative and fiction-making power greatly reduced.

Kristeva recuperates this power in the same way that Keats reclaims from the Wordsworthian "egotistical sublime" (*KL* 157) its self-making potentiality. Kristeva recasts the Symbolic as a monological and univocal mode in order to address how the semiotic (her renaming of the imaginary) functions ambivalently *within* the Symbolic. This Kristevan imaginary is a primordial and necessary positing of the subject as a site of generative self-fashioning and *productive* illusion. The Kristevan subject emerges from a semiotic *chora*, an "essentially mobile and extremely provisional articulation constituted by movements and their ephemeral stases." The *chora* functions like the primary processes and registers the drives as "'energy' charges as well as 'psychical' marks." As the psychic 'binding' of the subject's instinctual and libidinal "motility," the semiotic is associated with the infant's biological attachment to the mother, but also with the intersubjective and imaginary relationship between them. This (m)other is both material and psychic, its identity constituted through "inseparable" semiotic and symbolic modalities "within the *signifying process* that constitutes language."[46] Kristeva calls this process *poetic* and associates it with what she calls "the dramaturgy of the drives,"[47] which both overdetermine and are overdetermined by an unconscious negativity that Kristeva does not read exclusively through Lacanian speech and language. The *chora* re-visions the genetic gradualism of Freudian materialism, yoking the 'scientific' subject of Freud's psychoanalysis to an immanent aesthetic potentiality through which her identity, like the physiological processes of the body, is continually (de)constituted.

Whereas the Lacanian unconscious produces self-alienation, Kristeva reads it as a site of *jouissance*: "The analysand knows the unconscious, orders it, calculates with it, yet he also loses himself in it, plays with it, takes pleasure from it, lives it."[48] Kristeva thus speaks of an "adolescent imaginary," which she associates with the novel as an "open psychic structure." This mode (rather than genre) suggests a "semiotic practice that facilitates the ultimate reorganization of psychic space, in the time before an ideally postulated maturity." The ambivalent economy of imaginary writing "construct[s] a discourse that is not 'empty,' but that [the subject] lives as authentic," that is to say, as *intentionally* provisional and illusionary.[49] This writing suggests how the Symbolic of literature encrypts self-contesting forces of signification that continually shift the predicative and monologic boundaries of Symbolic identity toward the heterogeneous site of its own self-making.[50] Moreover, the adolescent imaginary signifies the subject's psychic production in both art/literature and psychoanalysis/theory without privileging either. Displacing a philosophical and psychoanalytical progress toward Absolute Knowledge, Kristeva's analytical schema, it can be said, reclaims psychoanalysis as the heterogeneous literature of the self.

I do not mean to suggest that this account subsumes Freud, Jung, or Lacan by locating Kristeva as a later subject presumed to know in the history of modern psychoanalysis. Rather I mean to indicate how the theoretical hegemony of any metapsychology needs to be placed "in process/on trial"[51] at the revisionary site of its own constitution. Kristeva psychoanalyzes the scientism of Freudian and post-Freudian theory by unmasking at the scene of this theory's authority the psychodynamics of a dramatic dis-location of the subject that theory would presume to know. By suggesting how psychoanalysis eventually developed a resistance to its own theory, Kristeva offers the possibility of reading psychoanalysis before its incarnation as theory. This psychoanalysis can be traced to Romanticism's exploration and dramatization of the subject, a 'romanticism' within psychoanalysis that resists Freudian, Jungian, Lacanian, or Kristevan prescriptions, although these models can be used intermittently to gloss Romantic versions of psychoanalysis. Romantic psychoanalysis is more a question of how a literary approach to the self is discontinuous with a scientific one. The literariness of the self is evident in Freud's emphasis on narrative (case studies) or on drama or cinema (the analytic scene, projection, acting out) and in Jung's view of individuation as a process of self-imagining, hence in the priority both give to self-writing. The literary is later evident in Lacan's emphasis on the imaginary as a place where the subject encounters the fictionality of her identity and in Kristeva's emphasis on the 'adolescent imaginary' as a site of creative psychic production. That the scientific is often incompatible with the literary in psychoanalysis, however, is part of a larger allegory of the scientific vs. the aesthetic that stretches back in the philosophical and literary history of psychoanalysis to the Enlightenment, as we shall see in the next chapter.

The Scene of Romantic Psychoanalysis

Romanticism's heterogeneous literature of the self emerges through what I shall term the scene of this literature's psychoanalysis, in that Romanticism both constructs and is analyzed by its own figures and mechanisms of self-exploration. As I have suggested, Romanticism offers numerous metaphors of this scene: the silent analytic presence of Coleridge in *The Prelude*; *Endymion*'s Cave of Quietude as the analytic office of Greek mythology; the case history of De Quincey's *Confessions*; Wordsworth's spots of time as inscriptions of the primal scene; numerous Romantic couches. These examples in turn both suggest and generate contemporary models, the Symbolic language of which we can adopt. From time to time we *shall* adopt this language (as set out in the previous section, for instance) as a way of gauging the body of knowledge that Romantic psychoanalysis produced. When reading *between* these models and the Romantic metaphors before them, however, we might remind ourselves that in the struggle to codify the psyche, to make it speak its language, science and literature themselves speak in radically different ways.

The dialogue between Romantic studies and the cognitive sciences suggests a viable alternative to the frequently antihumanistic hermeneutics of suspicion offered by poststructuralist psychoanalytic theory. Alan Richardson argues that the return to Romantic brain science, read "through the lens of contemporary neuroscience, which has returned (in its own way) to one after another concern of Romantic psychology," demonstrates "how innovative, exciting, and threatening the theoretical and experimental work of leading Romantic-era brain scientists might once have appeared."[52] Richardson's approach suggests that methodologies such as psychoanalysis have taken us so far, but that now neuroscience or cognitive science will get us that much farther in understanding the complexities of how Romantic discourse and culture come to understand the subject and her cognitions. This New Psychology provides a corrective to our perception of Romantic cognitive theories as primitive and naive, although one remains ambivalent about this project's promise of enlightenment. Following in the footsteps of the cognitive revolution, the New Psychology offers a more sophisticated mental model whereby we can gain insight into the mind's complex workings, a claim it makes on behalf of Romanticism itself. This reading of psychic reality in the nervous adventures of the human mind avoids simple materialism as surely as Coleridge suspected David Hartley's mechanistic work of associationism; moreover, its contribution to knowledge about the period's history is invaluable. But the New Psychology also evokes a type of neural rationalism, which claims that the psyche, despite its darknesses, *can* be mapped and thus made visible: a Human Neurone Project. The philosophical and scientific confidence behind all versions of the brain, Romantic or otherwise, needs to be treated with some skepticism given the psyche's fundamental resistance to enlightenment that characterizes Romantic psychoanalysis and that it makes part of its own imaginative mapping of the psyche.

Furthermore, then, this study tries to avoid letting scientific or theoretical discourse subsume entirely the imaginary self-writing of the literary. Romantic figures and mechanisms of psychoanalysis are now part of our Symbolic language, but since they do not receive a similar formulation in the Romantic period, they exist because of the Romantics' refusal to encode them, at an imaginary or semiotic level. They are part of what displaces the Symbolic order of the texts that contain them. At the same time, however, naming these figures and mechanisms, even if they had not entered a Romantic Symbolic, still allows us in turn to name those displacements that, in Wordsworth's or Keats's time, had not yet been given a name or had been named less prescriptively as part of the shifting rhetoric of Romanticism's self-making discourse. To name them within the rhetoric of psychoanalysis also simplifies them, so that we must subsequently use the texts as sites to interrogate our psychoanalytic tropes. Perhaps most importantly, however, Romanticism's own psychoanalytic figures and mechanisms disclose a process of *imagining* psychoanalysis before its codification by a theoretical language. That is to say, psychoanalysis had to be imagined in order to become the subject of theoretical debate, a debate always undone by the psychic process that made it possible. This ability to imagine psychoanalysis, as it is staged by the subject's imagining himself in the face of a psychic determinism he cannot comprehend, is at the core of the Romantic psychoanalytic scene.

What is this traumatic unknowing that takes place in Romantic psychoanalysis? In the Freudian analytical session, the analysand attempts to read his psychic otherness in the presence of the analyst in the form of archaic attachments to the objects repressed in his unconscious, a forgetting usually occasioned by some traumatic event or loss. The analysand at first acts out or *repeats* the effects of the past by projecting their negativity onto the analyst through the largely unconscious process of transference operating between them. Helping the analysand to *work-through* or interpret these projections at a more conscious level of self-understanding, and thereby to withdraw them, the analyst helps him to *remember* the past. However, the patient often refuses to remember, a resistance complicated by the transference/countertransference between analyst and analysand which continually produces for analysis a potentially endless proliferation of psychic material that endlessly stalls the cure.[53] Put another way, not only the patient but the process itself becomes trapped in a search for the diagnosis that can become "something evermore about to be" (*P* 6.542). This endless deferral characterizes Christabel's inability to tell her trauma or Saturn's inability to remember his past in *Hyperion*. The analytic scene, built around this resistance, offers a radical ontological and epistemological reconstruction of identity. In "From the History of an Infantile Neurosis" (1918), Freud hypothesizes behind the Wolf-Man's dream a primal scene of sexual trauma. Conceding that this scene's empirical reality could only be validated as a psychical event after the fact, however, Freud reached an epochal conclusion: he could "venture upon no decision" (*SE* 17:97) whether the primal scene was a real event repressed or a phantasy reconstructed from the unconscious. Moreover, the distinction was irrelevant. It was more important to recognize how phantasy reconstructs the past, for the primal scene could only be remembered through one's imaginary reconstruction of it anyway.[54] The primal scene is in this way inseparable from the analytic scene of its reconstitution as a remembering of the past forever receding from the subject's view. (Wordsworth seems implicitly *un*able to learn this fact in his ongoing revisions to *The Prelude*.) History conceals the subject from himself to suggest, not a specific episode or trauma, but the more profound trauma of a subject lost between remembering and forgetting, as we shall see, for instance, in De Quincey's two versions of *Confessions of an English Opium-Eater*.

But despite its negativity, the phantasy of the analytic scene also suggests the performativity of how the subject reimagines, reenacts, or reconstitutes himself. As a dialogic (rather than monologic) communication between two destabilized (rather than full-fledged) subjects "in-process/on trial," the indeterminacy of the analytic scene is part of a process by which subjects dramatize, and are dramatized by, the unconscious psychic life circulating between them.[55] Jung argues that the "primeval chaos" encountered in the transference creates an alchemical combination that leaves both subjects "altered," so that the unconscious hybridization of identity is "continually producing new formations." The unconscious "yields an endless and self-replenishing abundance of living creatures, a wealth beyond our fathoming" (*CWJ* 16:182, 177–178). The Romantic texts we will go on to examine struggle to comprehend this pathology of imagination "beyond our fathoming," not as a psychic dis(-)ease, but as a site where the subject reimagines his psychic determinism within the interminable psychic process of finding his identity. The unconscious marks the Romantic subject's alienation from himself; but it is also the site of a sublime imaginative *jouissance*.

Through transference, then, the analytic scene constellates both an affective and psychic attachment between subjects and the constitutional effect of this attachment as an intersubjective or transpositional exchange/decentering of identities between them. This hybridization of the subject by the mutating forces of his unconscious is one of the central concerns of Romanticism's struggle to understand the shifting nature of its psychoanalytical identity. The aesthetic economy of Romantic psychoanalysis, responding to its own interminability, is thus itself a hybrid form. The interiority of the Romantic subject has been traditionally associated with the Romantic ode or the conversation poem, which express a monologic constitution of the *cogito*.[56] But lyric is psychologically complex in ways that upset this monologism. Keats's "Ode on a Grecian Urn," for instance, is addressed by the self to the self across the screen of an object, real or ideal, that functions as a type of analyst of the poet's desire. Wordsworth's "Tintern Abbey" and Coleridge's "Dejection: An Ode" function as lyric case histories which, by retracing the evolution of psychic creativity or its anxiety, displace through narrative the genetic history of the self's autonomy. The conversation poem, such as Coleridge's "This Lime-Tree Bower My Prison," addresses itself to the silent screen of an auditor, whose absent presence in the poem establishes a dialogic pretext for an analysis of the poet's thoughts. However, although concerned with psychic interiority, these lyric forms do not fully inscribe the presence of the other-as-analyst and are thus ultimately more meditative than psychoanalytical.[57] Where meditation suggests the 'cure' of psychic self-alienation, psychoanalysis inscribes a dialogue with otherness, rather than consolidating otherness within the lyric totality of a bounded *cogito*. Lyric in the psychoanalytic scene suggests a particular attention to the form of speaking, as it embodies the subject's encounter with his own psychic interiority.

In this sense, lyric signifies a type of close self-reading whose hermeneutic is entrenched within the form of what I shall explore as the psychosomatic body of lyric utterance.[58] To articulate this body, Romantic psychoanalysis emerges through an aesthetic economy that mixes lyric with narrative and dramatic elements. Where lyric expresses a single consciousness, narrative temporalizes or dramatizes the *cogito* as a dialogue with its/an analytic other/s.[59] Considered as textual modalities rather than separate genres, narrative and drama hybridize lyric totality by inscribing within it the affect of other identities and voices that expose it to both temporal/narrative and performative/dramatic influences. Keats's *Hyperion* or *Endymion*, for instance, attempting to tell the monologic narrative of a single character, mutate into the narrative forms of other characters, whereas *Suspiria de Profundus*, radicalizing the already prose terrain of *Confessions*, tells the dramatis personae of De Quincey's unconscious by staging the monodrama of his psychic evolution as the heterogeneous site of multiple personalities. In the way that transference calls forth self-differentiating aspects of the analysand upon the stage of the analytic session, the lyric form of single authorship mutates into various selves, some recuperative, some dissenting and contradictory, within the 'personal' or 'interior' limits of its discourse. Moreover, that the struggle to articulate the scene of Romantic psychoanalysis produces frequently open-ended and problematic textual forms implicitly, and not so implicitly, inscribes the reader within the text's transferential field of reading. Our inability to master the text's meaning, that is, mirrors uncannily the text's call for knowledge and interpretation that is built into its very structure. What Dufresne critiques as the "delicate inner space of psychoanalysis" is, as Jacobus suggests, the impossible space of reading that marks the impossibility of psychoanalysis, the impossible space of an interiority that both defines and loses our identities at the threshold of meaning.

We can read this heterogeneous aesthetic modality through the apparatus of analytic figures (the unconscious, the dream, conversation/dialogue, the case history, the primal scene) and mechanisms (transference, repetition, remembering, projection, resistance) that comprise the Romantic psychoanalytic scene. These elements converge largely in the relationship between an analyst and analysand. Yet we often encounter the disparate appearance and functioning of these elements at different times within the text rather than always as part of an analytic scene itself. Therefore, this study will read the emergence of the analytic scene locally, in order to trace its figurative and psychical appearance within specific texts, as well as abstractly, as a metadiscursive frame within which to witness the phenomenology of the Romantic psychoanalytic subject's attempt to deal with the psyche's interminability. One *topos* of this scene is what Maud Ellman calls the Freudian psychic theater: "If dreams resemble drama, drama also owes its form to dreams; rather than mirroring the outer world, the theater gives external form to the internal dramaturgy of the mind, where anything may be invoked and brought to life."[60] But dreamwork alone does not explain this scene's functioning or shape. The scene of Romantic psychoanalysis evokes a hybrid form signified by no single genre or text, but providing its metaphors to—and thus *inventing*—a psychoanalysis within Romanticism, whose shifting scene is constituted between various analytic encounters in various texts, and through our encounters with these texts.

What this study examines, then, is the unseen/scene of reason in Romantic literature. Chapter One thus begins by examining reason's undoing within philosophy, from the Enlightenment subject to an emerging critique and revisioning of this subject in Romanticism and beyond. This trajectory reads a struggle between scientific materialism and literature in the Romantic subject. Coleridge's term "psycho-analytical" is symptomatic of how Romantic psychology rethinks associationist psychology, and how Romantic epistemology evolves a psychoanalytic concern for the self out of eighteenth-century empiricism. I thus use mesmerism, the eighteenth century's version of psychoanalysis, to frame the literature of subsequent chapters. Signifying idealism and scepticism at the same time, mesmerism anatomizes the specter of the Enlightenment's absent psychosomatic body, the evidence of an invisible phenomenon that defies empiricism, a body that eighteenth- and nineteenth-century philosophy attempts to (de)rationalize. Where Locke and Hume describe the associationist subject as a presence threatened by its own psychology, Kant and Coleridge use the dynamism of the transcendental imagination to rethink this subject, Kant in largely descriptive terms, not unlike Locke and Hume, Coleridge in an attempt to psychoanalyze imagination. More specifically, one can read after Hume the absent psychosomatic body of Kant's *Anthropology*, which Coleridge's *Biographia Literaria*, by hybridizing psychology and philosophy, both accepts and resists. The presence of Coleridge's interest in the unconscious concurrent with his philosophy of imagination suggests in the latter a desire to repress within an organic paradigm of identity what it is unwilling to confront about itself in the former. That is, Coleridgean imagination ostensibly subsumes yet is symptomatically radicalized by associationist psychology. The secularization and radicalization of the unconscious, and resulting destabilization of the subject, from Locke to Coleridge emerges as open critique in Schopenhauer and Nietzsche, whose metaphysics is displaced by its own psychology. Nietzsche re-stages Schopenhauer's will and representation as the aesthetic economy of Apollo and Dionysus in order to examine the unconscious as a depth within an internal drama of the mind. Between Locke's rationalism and Nietzsche's Dionysus one can apprehend darkly a Romantic subject who both totals and exceeds the sum of her Enlightenment parts.

Subsequent chapters trace the emergence of this subject through a genealogy of texts that reads the development of the scene of Romantic psychoanalysis. Chapters Two and Three examine Wordsworth and Coleridge respectively as subjects presumed to know.[61] Because of their investment in philosophy, both writers were presumptuous about the limits of their knowledge; in their hands Romantic psychoanalysis becomes the case of what its inventors *presumed* to know about themselves and about the self-investigation they undertook. Marking the mind's terminability, they then appear anxious about its interminability. Wordsworth speaks the anthropological voice of Kantian reason against the de-humanizing threat of the Coleridgean psyche in *The Rime of the Ancient Mariner* and *Christabel*. The aphasic anxiety of these texts, however, recalls the pretext of *The Recluse* in "Incipient Madness" and "The Baker's Cart" as an inability both to tell and to understand the story of Margaret's psyche. "The Ruined Cottage," like the Prospectus and *The Prelude* after it, subsequently represses this gap through a hermeneutics of sociophilosophical reparation. All are what I describe as missed encounters with psychoanalysis. Coleridge's poems, however, demonstrate how unreason suspends reason, the collapse of philosophy's terminability into the interminability of the psyche. Contemporary with *The Recluse*, these texts critique its unrealizable Kantian idea in terms of Coleridge's own desire for a philosophical system. Just as the interminable life-writing of *The Prelude* stalls Wordsworth's magnum opus, Coleridge's writings record a similar inability to proceed with his *Logosophia*. Written early in his career, *Mariner* and *Christabel* signify the unconscious of the philosophical *anthropos*, to which Coleridge responds variously through metaphysics in *Biographia Literaria* and mesmerism in the *Notebooks*. Psychology mesmerizes metaphysics, however, to suggest Coleridge's struggle to work-through a psychoanalytical apparatus commensurate with his self-observation, so that he remains compelled to return to his early poems as the primal scene of his inability to write the *Logosophia*.

This book's penultimate chapter addresses De Quincey's *Confessions of an English Opium-Eater* and *Suspiria de Profundis* as the psychic anatomy of Wordsworth's and Coleridge's missed encounters with psychoanalysis. These texts confess the "*burden of the Incommunicable*" (*WDQ* 2:170) as the unreason of Kantian reason neither Wordsworth nor Coleridge could confront, and in De Quincey's shifting attitude toward the mode of autobiography, one can read the unfolding of his philosophical identity as the disclosure of philosophy's interminably confessing other, a mode of confession which marks De Quincey's exploration of psychoanalysis as a distinctly *post*-Kantian undertaking. Yet he encounters his own conflicts with psychoanalysis, first in his 1821 *Confessions* and then in its 1856 revision for *Selections Grave and Gay*, the first British collected edition of his writings. A collected De Quincey subsumes the confessor's psychic dis-ease, associated with Romantic psychoanalysis and the absent psychosomatic body, within the more acceptable rubric of his formal Autobiography, which orders the chaos of psychic life as the developmental Victorian history of the social subject. Yet this schism between (early) confessions and (later) Autobiography remains symptomatic of an internally divided psychoanalytical content in both *Confessions.* De Quincey is caught between autobiography, which tells the chronology of the addict's life in "Preliminary Confessions," and confession, which explores this life's repetitive interiority in the "Pleasures" and "Pains" of opium. The 1856 revisions repeat the 1821 text in ways that both conserve and further exacerbate the earlier text's disruptive psychoanalytic content. But the 1821 text itself attempts to conserve this content in ways that make the earlier text oddly parallel with its own later revision. Moreover, this revision is tempered by the 1845 *Suspiria de Profundis.* Whereas *Confessions* evolves what I call a *chronic* or symptomatic psychoanalysis challenged by its own resistances, *Suspiria* reconstitutes this resistance as psychoanalysis's determinate moment. This *acute* encounter with the unconscious accounts for the astonishing mythopoeia of Romantic psychoanalysis as a self-making dialogue with psychic determinism. *Suspiria* constructs the visionary dimensions of the psychoanalytic subject as the decentred organicism of his disparate parts.

The division between the empirical and mythopoeic subjects of psychoanalysis, however, persists in De Quincey's corpus. The suffering subject of *Confessions*, as if always tied to his couch, is exiled from his self-making other in *Suspiria*, a subject who imagines his liberation from the couch, but who then seems oddly dissociated from any sense of its *lived* experience. Despite the fact that the 1821 *Confessions* was published only a year before Keats died, Chapter Five reads Keats *after* De Quincey within this study's genealogy of Romantic psychoanalysis. Keats deploys the De Quinceyan idea of philosophy as interminable speculation by exposing poetry to its own psychology. I first trace this interrogation in *Endymion. Endymion* explores the romance of Greek mythology as the mutating or wandering unconscious of the Greek pantheon, which splits into a multiplicity of tellings. Endymion's attempt to read these forms evolves into a peripatetic scene of psychoanalysis, which seems mesmerized within a text unable to break free of the hegemony of romance. Moreover, this psychoanalysis plays out the subtextual drama of gender in Wordsworth, Coleridge, and De Quincey. The fancy that Coleridge sets aside in his theory of imagination becomes for Keats the fancy that "cannot cheat so well / As she is famed to do" [*KL* 73–74]). Associated increasingly with romance and sensibility in the early nineteenth century, this fancy comes to signify a wandering or interiorized discourse of the imagination feminized as a threat to the masculine Romantic visionary tradition. Keats finds this tradition in Miltonic epic, which he uses to discipline Titanic melancholy in *Hyperion*. Revising *Endymion*'s scene of psychoanalysis, *Hyperion* offers a mobile tableau of analytical figures both male and female who constellate the text's dialogic mode but remain unable to accept its cognitive darkness. Leaving behind epic and romance, and psychoanalyzing the gendered psychology of their Symbolic production, *The Fall* revises *Hyperion* by staging Romantic psychoanalysis as the primal scene of poetry itself, revisited as if in a dream. *The Fall* interrogates the subject's ability to tell his dreams, as his struggle to surmount poetry's own psychic determinism without succumbing to the metapsychology poetry inevitably produces from this process. If *Suspiria de Profundis* marks the first determinate invention of the scene of Romantic psychoanalysis, *The Fall* marks this psychoanalysis as determinately *interminable*, the *lived* experience of a Dionysus who, seeing himself reflected in the Apollonian representations of his female analyst, Moneta, cannot forget how the art of the subject always emerges from a core of eternal suffering. Together, *Endymion*, *Hyperion*, and *The Fall of Hyperion* constellate an unfolding scene of gender in Romantic psychoanalysis, which reads its masculine science of the mind as a feminine phantasy of reason, but in order to confront the 'masculine' and 'feminine' as both constitutive *and* destabilizing categories within this process.

The Romantics, insofar as they remained true to the acausality rather than causality of psychic evidence, both sacrificed and deconstructed a metaphysical framework of the psyche that is the counterpart of Freud's materialistic/scientific one. It is within the pioneering and heroic nature of Romanticism that it does not *name* the unconscious, does not make its dark empiricism answerable to a metapsychology, and therefore does not theorize the manner in which it might be named except as the literary and aesthetic form of its own psychic processes. The *burden* of this psychic struggle in Wordsworth and Coleridge becomes in De Quincey the "*burden of the Incommunicable*" or in Keats the "burden of the Mystery." This burden manifests itself through the psychosomatic effects of the unconscious as it resists the thrust of interpretation toward its own termination, the sovereignty of the mind's pursuit of the unknown as what Wordsworth calls the "exalted mood" of reason. The struggle to terminate psychoanalysis as an exploration of the unreason within reason is always unsettled by the unconscious, which cannot be known and which emerges in Romanticism through the often disruptive functioning of imagination. The struggle to overcome the burden of the unconscious as it produces Romantic psychoanalysis subsequently produces a conflict between a psychoanalysis terminable—the desire to provide a theoretical and therapeutic closure to the work of the psyche—and interminable—the acknowledgment that the psyche tenaciously resists closure. In its effort to accept the latter over the former, Romanticism produces its most radical form of psychoanalysis.

One of the cultural effects of this 'acting out' is the analytic session, during which the subject, as Mikkel Borch-Jacobsen suggests, is staged by the dramatis personae of his psyche.[62] Phillip Rieff argues that the short-lived and transitional Enlightenment "ideal of economic man" produced instead the post-Enlightenment emergence of "psychological man," a subject who "lives by the ideal of insight" and who "has constituted his own careful economy of the inner life." Both Romanticism and psychoanalysis, Rieff argues, use cathartic "[self-]expression" to gain "[aesthetic or therapeutic] self-mastery" and thus to illuminate, as if by the desire of the Enlightenment itself, the subject's psyche. In therapy, however, the patient's "obligation to the therapist . . . to tell all he knows in order to be told all he does not know" must avoid the efficiency and rationality of normative discourse in favor of a "deliberate anti-efficiency" of an analytical discourse that explores what is unsettlingly inexpressible for the patient. Suspended between catharsis and analysis, between self-expression and knowledge, the psychoanalytic subject produced by psychological man is at war with the self as "the last enemy."[63] The ideal of an enlightened subject is thus unsettled by an ambivalence between self-mastery and self-defeat by unconscious forces beyond her rational control. This ambivalence is symptomatic of a broader Kantian concern to construct a metaphysics of psychological man out of the Enlightenment legacy of Locke, who casts a long shadow over eighteenth-century thought. Romanticism's post-Kantian discourse, however, places within the arena of aesthetic contemplation the Enlightenment analysis of a human psychology that is both pliant *and* intractable. Romanticism looks, as Wordsworth attempts to look in the "Prospectus" to *The Recluse*, "Into our Minds, into the Mind of Man" (*WP* 40), only to find there what Shelley calls in *Prometheus Unbound* "the world unknown" (*SPP* 2.2.190). The contours of this psychic *terra incognita* emerge in mesmerism, a world where reason and unreason encounter one another and where a repressed Enlightenment anxiety about the subject returns in Romanticism.

ONE

The Psychology of the Romantic Subject

> The mind is a kind of theatre, where several perceptions successively make their appearance; pass, repass, glide away, and mingle in an infinite variety of postures and situations.
>
> —David Hume, *A Treatise of Human Nature*

> The point of excess for the imagination . . . is like an abyss in which it fears to lose itself.
>
> —Immanuel Kant, *Critique of Judgement*

Coleridge and the "Psycho-analytical"

"The first step to knowledge," Coleridge writes, ". . . is to dare commune with our very and permanent self."[1] This daring turn to discover the quintessential self is a quintessentially Romantic gesture. The self that Romanticism came to know, however, turned out to be anything but "permanent," or was permanent in ways it had not at first anticipated. Let us start with this book's conceptual origin, an excerpt from an 1805 entry in Coleridge's notebooks:

> Among the numerous examples of confusion of Heathen & Christian Mythology in the Poets of the 15th Century (pleasing inasmuch as they prove how intimately the works of Homer & Virgil &c were *worked* in & *scripturalized* in their *minds*—I. was taught this hour, the other the next—or both together &

> by the same man with the same countenance, with the same seriousness and zeal, at the same early age—& in a time when Authority was all in all—and what was publickly *taught* of Aristotle, was individually & perhaps more generally, *felt* of *Homer* in the various broken reflections of him throughout the Latin Poets & all men of Education & in the original & the echoing series of the other Greek Poets to the Politians, & c &c,—indeed, it requires a strong imagination as well as an accurate psycho-analytical understanding in order to be able to conceive the *possibility*, & to picture out the reality, of the *passion* of those Times for Jupiter, Apollo &c & the nature of the *Faith* (for a Faith it was—it vanished indeed at the Cock-crowing of a deliberate Question, in *most* men; but in the ordinary unchecked stream of Thought it moved on, as naturally as Contraband & Legal Goods in the same Vessel, when no Revenue Officers are on the Track.) (*CN* 2:2670)

It seems apt that the first appearance of the term "psycho-analytical" in the English language should come in a passage concerned with two issues: faith and the present's ability to read the past. Coleridge alludes to how Renaissance poets (he goes on to cite Ariosto), 'con-fusing' the "Heathen & Christian" as part of the same "mythology," "*worked* in & *scripturalized*" Homer or Virgil. That is to say, they treated ancient poetry as a form of belief, not as religious doctrine, but because it expressed the nature of faith itself. Poetry was a fundamental expression of how "Jupiter, Apollo & c" were daily merely present in the minds and imaginations of the ancients. Faith was not a question of the gods' existence, but of a passion *for* the gods. Or rather, there was no question of faith itself; it simply *was*. Only with the dawn ("cock-Crowing") of Enlightenment in the Renaissance was the question ("a deliberate Question") posed. At this point, Coleridge claims, faith "vanished," and, the passage suggests, poetry was called upon to speak for the reality of the gods that the ancients took for granted as surely as Christianity spoke for the existence of God.

But a schism emerged. The Renaissance made Aristotle the paradigm of its scientific mind and took Homer and Virgil as its literary paradigms. Philosophy and science found themselves in the singular intellect of Aristotle, whereas literature had to find itself through the rather more intuitive paths of feeling, as the "broken reflections" or "echoes" of multiple personalities. This division of labor between "what was publickly *taught* of Aristotle" and what "was individually . . . *felt* of *Homer*" generated binaries around which the public sphere took shape: outside and inside, public and private, social and individual, mind and heart, cognition and feeling, sense and sensibility.

Yet faith never really vanished. It moved on "in the ordinary unchecked stream of Thought," "as naturally as Contraband & Legal Goods in the same Vessel [of thought that contains philosophy and science], when no Revenue Officers are on the Track." In *Biographia Literaria* (1817) Coleridge, aligning poetry with myth and belief, speaks of the "poetic faith" that comes from a "willing suspension of disbelief" (*BL* 2:6). This formulation treats the psychology of faith as desire and illusion as well as hope and certainty. Coleridge is not talking about the delusions of ideology's social *mythos*, although the 1805 passage suggests that the "deliberate Question" of rationality stakes its own belief claims on reality. Rather, Coleridge addresses the human capacity *to* believe, especially what we do not necessarily know to exist or to be true, what in *Biographia* he examines as the "supernatural," like the preternatural reality that must be accounted for in "The Ruined Cottage." This psychology of faith constitutes an *other* register of cognition that goes underground. This is not the Freudian unconscious *per se*, the depth or interior of a repressed or buried psychic half-life. Rather, it is a "Contraband" reality buried within the everyday, in the "ordinary unchecked stream of Thought," a shadow economy within reason, the unseen part of its operations. It is thus also "naturally" or semiotically part of the "same Vessel" as reason, consciousness, the visible. Poetry speaks of and from this Hades (in "Ode to a Nightingale" Keats will say that the work of poetry is always borne "Lethe-wards" [*KP* 4]), where the dead, never really dead, continue to wander in a forgetting that, as Freud will remind us, is its own form of remembering.

The resilience of this other form of memory, Coleridge seems to say, comes from its being "*felt*" rather than seen, from its resistance to enlightenment's demand for visibility. Its transmission from past to present is thus different from reason's 'public' education, and its knowledge and historical form elude official expression. For one thing, faith is felt "individually," invoking in Coleridge's time the post-Revolutionary specter of a knowledge that might counter the status quo. Faith is truly radical, that is, because of its psychological dimension. It cannot be located in the origins or ends of identity but rather makes itself felt throughout history, an other trajectory of feeling that transmits itself as "broken reflection" and "echoes." This body of feeling registers thought's cognition as it is, to paraphrase Wordsworth in "Tintern Abbey," felt along the pulses before it passes into the purer mind. Yet, as Coleridge suggests, thought can never overcome or set feeling aside. Rather, feeling is the psychosomatic body of cognition integral to thought. And to apprehend this body, the passage calls upon an *other* way to "conceive the *possibility*"—as opposed to 'explain the meaning'—of "the *passion* of those Times." Again, the point is not to understand reality itself but to comprehend one's passion *for* this reality, knowledge's human dimension. This "requires a strong imagination as well as an accurate psycho-analytical understanding." One invokes the Enlightenment precision of reason, while the other invokes a Romantic faith in imagination. But the "psychoanalytical" con-fuses the psyche with reason, introducing the psychological as a third component between imagination and reason. This third thing is like the "tertium aliquid" of the Coleridgean dialectic in *Biographia Literaria*, "an inter-penetration of . . . counteracting powers, partaking of both" (*BL* 1:300). Psychology is the reciprocity of understanding between imagination and the analytical, but as mimesis—"to picture out the reality" of things—and phantasy—"to conceive the possibility" of that reality. That is, psychology *conceives* or *imagines* how the mind *makes* reality.

Coleridge's Romantic response to Renaissance poetry's response to faith, then, questions how one believes in what one thinks and writes as essential marks of the human. Speaking of German idealism's rethinking of the Cartesian *cogito*, Slavoj Žižek addresses the human "symbolic (re)constitution" of the world's "natural environs," the ongoing "construction of a symbolic universe that the subject projects onto reality as a kind of substitute-formation, destined to recompense us for the loss of the immediate, pre-symbolic real." Žižek calls this (re)constitution of the real through the "symbolic virtual environs" of subjectivity the "founding gesture of 'humanization.'"[2] He links this gesture to psychoanalysis, which comprehends that subjectivity is always a "substitute-formation." Attempting to correct such formations when they turn pathological—that is, when they get out of synch with the reality to which they correspond—psychoanalysis strikes at the very heart of subjectivity itself. Always a projection of its own symbolic nature onto the real, subjectivity is always at some level implicitly pathological. The work of writing and the Symbolic, where the human meets the real and reason meets its phantasy, is thus the pathology of being that requires, interminably, the cure of writing's pathology, the pathology of writing's cure—Derrida's *pharmakon*. The work of thought and writing in Coleridge's notebook entry betrays this mark of humanization as the "substitute-formation" of subjectivity itself, a psychology that can never step outside itself because it has become its own 'work,' the pathology of thought that makes thought possible. The moment the psychoanalytical emerges, that is, it becomes immediately symptomatic.

It seems equally fitting, then, that it should emerge in Romanticism as if unawares, like the Ancient Mariner's act of faith in blessing the water snakes "unawares," as if through the missed encounter of its own cognition and signification. For to suspend one's disbelief in a reality that literature and its mythological nature makes felt is also to *be suspended by* this disbelief in feeling, caught in a struggle of faith that by its nature can never be resolved. "Poetic faith" *is* the struggle that makes itself felt as the possibility *of* faith. In this *suspension* we find what I shall call the *absent* psychosomatic body of our subjectivity that psychoanalysis emerges to account for. Let us turn finally to what is perhaps the passage's most maddening transition: "I. was taught this hour, the other the next—or both together & by the same man with the same countenance, with the same seriousness and zeal, at the same early age—& in a time when Authority was all in all." The "same man with the same countenance" seems to be Coleridge himself, but could be any number of figures named or unnamed (perhaps one of Coleridge's earlier teachers) con-fused into the singular persona of Coleridge as speaker. The passive "was taught," however, dispels the "infinite I AM" (*BL* 1:304) of Coleridge's primary imagination into the multiple personalities of the subject and his cognates. The passage seems to anthropomorphize history itself as the allegory of how literature transmits knowledge as a matter of faith to its subjects, through which process the subject is meant to find himself. Without beginnings or ends, however, this history is instead the process of its own making, which explains the passage's anxiety about origins. Between the simultaneous movement forward from the "original" through its "echoing series" and backward from later "broken reflections" to this original, origins vanish, except insofar as the past makes itself *felt* in the present. The stable "I" goes missing, displaced by a subject "in-process/on trial," constituted by the psychology waged between his "accurate psycho-analytical understanding" and "strong imagination" of things.

This process also accounts for the passage's strange temporality. "This hour, the other the next" is the uncanny meeting of the past and present in the present's understanding of a past it *feels* but cannot *know* definitively, or rather can only feel *that* it knows with some certainty. This "both together" produces the synchronic "same countenance" of past and present in the strange time of psychoanalysis. Dominick La Capra argues that psychoanalysis makes sense as neither an Aristotelian diachronic temporality nor synchronic atemporality, but "is understood both in stabilizing terms . . . and in more disconcerting ways."[3] Whereas the scientific mind moves consciously, progressively, deliberately, the literary mind moves intuitively, repetitively, and is more difficult to locate within the public sphere. This is the temporality of transference, which con-fuses the identities of who analyzes and is analyzed. One both reads the past and is read by the past, both reads the past and reflects upon one's ability *to* read the past. Within this transference, the present can only "conceive" the "times" of the past as part of an indefinite and interminable future. The passage's circuit of representation returns to a past that catches us in its future, where we are required to suspend our disbelief in what Coleridge is saying. Coleridge's notebook entry evokes the "psychoanalytical understanding" it incidentally expounds, generating meaning as a pathology beyond understanding, where thought requires an equally "strong imagination."[4] Between the writing that finds thought and the one that loses it we find the strange subjectivity of cognition itself, registered as the psychosomatic effects of thought's struggle to find itself. Yet this struggle pursues its goal through its *feeling* dissemination through an interminable future in which the form of thought, of which writing is both an essential and incidental expression, is determined by the ongoing nature of thought's process.

Psychoanalysis emerges, then, as if against its will, as a resistance to itself. For the remainder of this chapter I want to explore this resistant emergence in a specific history of philosophy, which in turn calls for Romantic poetry's invention of psychoanalysis. For it is in philosophy's meditation on the work of reason within philosophy itself as it reflects upon the rationality of the scientific mind that philosophy then turns upon an *analysis* of reason to which Romantic poetry will respond. This intervention of philosophy into science comes at a time when the sciences, as David Knight notes, still "lacked sharp and natural frontiers," and disciplinary boundaries were as yet indistinct. Instead, "the realm of science, governed by reason," was distinguished from "practice, or rule of thumb; and apostles of science hoped to replace habit by reason in the affairs of life."[5] Science sought to regulate the habit or practice of eighteenth-century experience. How the mind rationalized experience, however, could exceed this systematization. In *Essay Concerning Human Understanding* (1690), Locke says that the white page of the mind gathers all its "materials of Reason and Knowledge" from "*Experience*."[6] Hume, however, finds himself "*pretending* . . . to explain the principles of human nature." In the Abstract to *A Treatise of Human Nature* (1740), he "promises to draw no conclusions but where he is *authorized* by experience," although experience will have to do because "we can never arrive at the ultimate principles."[7] His later *Enquiry Concerning Human Understanding* (1748) continues with the "most determined scepticism" (xiv) to argue more locally for an "ordering and distinguishing . . . of the operations of the mind": "And if we can go no farther than this mental geography, . . . it is at least a satisfaction to go so far."[8] If Locke is somewhat uneasy, Hume is openly ambivalent about reason's ability to organize the mind's empiricism. Between *rationalism*, which guarantees the *cogito*'s order, and *empiricism*, which by attempting to explain how reason functions must confront what exceeds reason, there is a great divide that Kant will attempt to bridge in his critical philosophy, so influential upon Coleridge's and Romanticism's own thought.

In many ways the apotheosis of Western philosophy's struggle to come to terms with this divide is Nietzsche's critique of metaphysics. For Nietzsche, Socrates represents the kind of authority that philosophy would claim for reason, "the unshakeable faith that thought, using the thread of causality, can penetrate the deepest abysses of being, and that thought is capable not only of knowing being but even of *correcting* it" (*BT* 95). Nietzsche is reacting against the spirit of scientific positivism in the later nineteenth century, by which time science had become rather more institutionalized and a clinical concern with the mind's functioning had produced an ethos of mental hygiene, of minds properly understood and thus properly located within the public sphere. Knowing the ruse of this proper management all too well, Nietzsche rejects rationalism as a "sublime metaphysical illusion" and argues instead that "it is only as an *aesthetic phenomenon* that existence and the world are eternally *justified*" (95, 52). What emerges in the trajectory from Hume's "determined scepticism" to Nietzsche's "sublime metaphysical illusion," is a Coleridgean "willing suspension of disbelief" in the mind's empiricism, a "poetic faith" in the phantasy of reason as the guarantor of the mind's ontological and thus of its epistemological moorings. In *Biographia Literaria* Coleridge turns from eighteenth-century British empiricism in Locke, Hume, and Hartley, among others, toward German philosophy, through which he attempts to recover a metaphysics of subjectivity that rationalism had yielded to empiricist/associationist models of the mind.

Between associationism and metaphysics, however, intercedes the psychoanalytical practice of Coleridge's inquiry, which remains troubled by what in these models still exceeds reason's perception. There are, as I suggested in the Introduction, numerous historiocultural reasons for the emergence of the "psycho-analytical": the rise of an interest in the neuroscientific, the psychological, and the psychiatric, all of which in one way or another reflect a fallout from various philosophical, political, and social revolutions in post-Enlightenment thought and culture. This chapter's present concern is to trace within this matrix of forces a certain phenomenology of the philosophical *cogito* as it confronts the imagination of its own reason. This phenomenology, focused in Romanticism's own struggles with philosophy's truth-value, its ability to reconstitute the world in human terms, reproduces an Enlightenment crisis of reason in a

Romantic body of philosophical thought that leaves this body, in a word whose importance will emerge more clearly as this study unfolds, *mesmerized* as much as it is *ordered* by reason. That is to say, one particular form of this excess is the body of knowledge and of knowing that was mesmerism. As we shall see in Chapter Three's more in-depth exploration of his notebook writings, Coleridge was fascinated by the psychosomatic, and thus with mesmerism as it evoked the psychosomatics of subjectivity. Thus in many ways mesmerism haunts the unconscious of the 1805 passage cited above as the specter of an unthought body of cognition that challenges metaphysical explanation. Between the real and the unreal, the seen and the unseen, psychoanalysis emerges to question, not reality itself, but *how* we believe in it, especially when that reality makes itself known via other means than common sense. At the core of this crisis of empiricism is a scene of mesmeric crisis, the mesmerizing of reason by its own phantasy.

One can thus trace from around the time of Mesmer to the end of the nineteenth century a parallel genealogy that both supplements and unsettles the scientific evolution toward Freudian psychoanalysis. This trajectory reads the psychic dynamism of mesmerism, particularly its resistance to rational explanation, recircuited through a philosophical concern for the subject in Romanticism. Mesmeric transference signifies a post-Enlightenment, post-Kantian consciousness unsettled by the unconscious as a radically disruptive rather than transcendental force, both a transpsychical phenomenon and a symptom of Romantic consciousness. Eventually we shall read this disruption in Schopenhauer and Nietzsche, the most immediate precursors in philosophy of Freudian psychoanalysis. Beyond this in subsequent chapters, however, we shall read what philosophy eventually confronts in Schopenhauer and Nietzsche in Romanticism's radical reimagining of this body of thought. Romantic poetry stages a confrontation with the psychosomatics of reason that produces psychoanalysis. That is, it uses an aesthetic economy to re-stage the subject that science could not broach intellectually, because it lacked the conceptual means to do so, and would not broach systematically, because this subject's unconscious threatened science's inherent rationalism.

John Barrell argues that the period's political imagination fed off the law's protean nature, a pathology that equally informs Romanticism's obsession with imagination and its cognates. As Barrell notes,

> aesthetics was anxious to pass the concept [of imagination] over to psychiatry; for when the imagination slipped the lead of the will or judgment, often when "heated" by the overwhelming

> power of the passions, it became "disordered," and produced elaborate structures of ideas associated on accidental rather than on substantial grounds. The relation between insanity and the imagination had been a subject of a famous dispute in the late 1750s . . .[9]

I would like to elaborate on these insights within the context of a certain array of philosophical texts from Locke to Nietzsche that trace the genealogy of a struggle with reason. We can then read this struggle within the specific terrain of Romantic poetry, which poetry, rather than 'passing off the concept of imagination to psychiatry,' was all too familiar with the imagination's radically unsettling impact on the subject and her mind, mesmerism being the most challenging precedent for this impact. Like concepts of the imagination themselves in the late eighteenth and early nineteenth centuries, the psychoanalytical becomes a signifier of what lies arbitrarily *between* the science or philosophy and the literary. The "permanent self" that speaks back to Coleridge and to the broader unfolding of Romanticism within which he is situated, and that speaks to us in turn, is a subject we cannot presume to know, but with whom we "dare to commune."

The Enlightened Imagination

In general terms, Enlightenment rationalism sees the mind as a type of inductive associative mechanism through which the external world both expresses and buttresses the integrity of the subject. Perception was the representation in the mind of sense impressions as ideas. These ideas were then rationalized in increasingly complex ways so as to produce the revelations of a subject presumed to know—that is, to inculcate principles of belief, opinion, and conduct through which the social order could cohere. Or at least Enlightenment positivism thought so. What the mind might do with its representations was a matter of some speculation, for Enlightenment thinking was unable to accommodate entirely within its rationalist empiricism the work of the imagination, which comes to signify, like empiricism itself, the radical contingency of the mind's functioning.[10] In his chapter "Of the Association of Ideas," added to the fourth edition of the *Essay Concerning Human Understanding* (1700), Locke argues that associationism creates "a natural Correspondence and Connexion one with another." Yet this process also generates autonomous mental processes threatening the subject's conscious personality:

> This wrong Connextion [sic] in our Minds of *Ideas* in themselves, loose and independent one of another, has such an influence, and is of so great a force to set us awry in our Actions, as well Moral as natural, Passions, Reasonings, and Notions themselves, that, perhaps, there is not any one thing that deserves more to be looked after.

Like Johnson, Locke associates the aberrancy of empiricism with madness and the imagination's "violence."[11] He expresses a general eighteenth-century desire to pathologize the imagination for raising disturbing moral and ethical questions about the social subject. Imagination evokes an internal functioning that unsettles this subject's external constructedness, which requires that much more "all the Light we can let in upon our own Minds" to illuminate what is "Dark to our selves."[12] As Henri Ellenberger writes, this eighteenth-century "mental hygiene [is] based on the training of the will and the subordination of passions to reason."[13]

For Locke dreams were a particularly disturbing threat to this hygiene because they threatened the soul's permanence. A subject is "sensible" of her soul only through waking reflection, Locke argues. There is "no Reason . . . to believe, that the *Soul thinks before the Senses have furnish'd it with Ideas*": "For if we take away all Consciousness of our Actions and Sensations . . . it will be hard to know wherein to place personal Identity." The soul had to be protected at all costs because ultimately for Locke it reveals to us the rationality of God's plan: "'Tis true, we have sometimes instances of Perception, whilst we are *asleep*, and retain the memory of those *Thoughts*: but how *extravagant* and incoherent for the most part they are; how little conformable to the Perfection and Order of a rational Being, those who are acquainted with Dreams, need not be told." Locke is careful to limit reason and understanding: "We shall not have much Reason to complain of the narrowness of our Minds, if we will but employ them about what may be of use to us; for of that they are very capable."[14]

Such mental hygiene thus also became essential to protecting social order. Locke was greatly influenced by Anthony Ashley Cooper, third earl of Shaftesbury (1671–1713), who writes against Hobbes's vision of a purely materialistic society. Cooper was anxious to let "certain humors in mankind . . . have vent": "as there are strange ferments in the blood, which in many bodies occasion an extraordinary discharge; so in reason, too, there are heterogeneous particles which must be thrown off by fermentation." Cooper fears the "contagion of enthusiasm" that might result from an uncontrolled *sympathy*, and so prescribes that the "only way to save men's sense, or preserve wit at all in the world, is to give liberty to wit" in the interchange between subjects.[15] *This* sympathy would function, as James Engell writes, as "an instrument of virtue and as an act of the imagination permitting the self to identify with others," a moral sympathy that anticipates Adam Smith's *Theory of Moral Sentiments* (1759) and *Wealth of Nations* (1776), in which Smith, in a curious inversion of Hobbesian self-interest through the transference between subjects, "will be more likely to prevail if he can interest [his brethren's] self-love in his favour."[16] As Julia Wright argues, sympathy can also be read within later medical concepts of the nervous body, as in the writings of William Cullen (1710–1790), John Brown's *The Elements of Medicine* (1780), or Thomas Trotter's *A View of the Nervous Temperament* (1807), "particularly as they relate to philosophical constructions of sensibility and emerging organicist notions of the place of the individual within the nation."[17] These notions play off the idea of a nervous economy that achieves equilibrium through its ability to self-regulate disease and pathology, and are in concert with the empirical balancing act of Locke's associationism. Read forward to Romantic theories of the imagination, as we shall see, this sympathetic dynamism suggests a metatransference beyond perception, integrating mind with the external world in a kind of mutual relevance.

But although Locke articulates an intellectual utilitarianism that continues well into the Victorian period, his writings are also symptomatic of what this utility masks. Cathy Caruth argues that Locke's scrupulous rationality, which reads in the association of ideas the soul's formation, disguises a traumatic lack of self, the "textual 'trauma' [in Locke's writings] that is displaced in the neurosis of empiricism": the fact that "associative substitutions are displaced versions of the attempt to establish a unified self-consciousness."[18] Writing after Locke, Hume see this neurosis as empiricism's norm. If, paradoxically, sympathy also posits a subject displaced by metaphysical agency, then Hume rejects any metaphysics of identity by paring down the subject to a reductive associationist logic tied to experience:

> . . . [T]here is no impression constant and invariable. Pain and pleasure, grief and joy, passions and sensations succeed each other, and never all exist at the same time. It cannot, therefore, be from any of these impressions, or from any other, that the idea of self is deriv'd; and consequently there is no such idea. . . . [M]ankind . . . are nothing but a bundle or collection of different perceptions, which succeed each other with an inconceivable rapidity, and are in perpetual flux and movement.

Identity exists by the "action of the imagination" tied to memory, which "does not so much *produce* as *discover* personal identity, by showing us the relation of cause and effect among our different perceptions" and so remains faithful to the "correspondent impressions" that produced it.[19] Imagination, on the other hand, "is not restrained to the same order and form with the original impressions." Contrary to Hobbes's notion of imagination as "decaying sense," Hume's imagination is "the vivacity of our ideas," a type of *jouissance* of associationism from which "memory, senses, and understanding are . . . all . . . founded." It internalizes the bodily changes of sensory perception to create an "easy transition of the imagination from one situation of the body to another" and toward some "*common end* or purpose," and it restores psychic equilibrium when the will threatens to overtake the *cogito*.[20]

But the tenuous empirical syntax of this imaginary ontology also evokes anxiety in Hume's writing. Through the imagination we

> feign the continued existence of the perception of our senses, to remove the interruption; and run into the notion of a *soul*, and *self*, and *substance*, to disguise the variation. . . . [W]e may further observe, that where we do not give rise to such a fiction, our propension to confound identity with relation is so great, that we are apt to imagine something unknown and mysterious, connecting the parts, beside their relation.[21]

Because identity and the soul are fictional rather than essential, imagination also produces a psychic inertia protecting identity from sensory decomposition, a kind of death drive of associationism. The imagination's autonomy, associated with the will, unsettles Humean empiricism to suggest the mind's less rational functioning, its capacity to mis-recognize itself:

> Nothing is more free than the imagination of man; and though it cannot exceed that original stock of ideas, furnished by the internal and external senses, it has unlimited power of mixing, compounding, separating, and dividing these ideas, in all the varieties of fiction and vision. It can feign a train of events, with all the appearance of reality, ascribe to them a particular time and place, conceive them as existent, and paint them out to itself with every circumstance, that belongs to any historical fact, which it believes with the greatest certainty. . . . We can, in our conception, join the head of a man to the body of a horse; but it is not in our power to believe, that such an animal has ever really existed.

Because the psychology of imagination can effect a type of physiological deconstruction that distorts reality and loses site of the *cogito*'s anthropological form, Hume must distinguish between the discipline of belief, the habitual and customary work performed on associationism, and the volatility of fiction, which constitutes associationism's irregularity and caprice. That both involve imagination means that ultimately it must be superseded by belief, "the vivid, lively, forcible, firm, steady conception of an object, . . . what the imagination alone is never able to attain."[22]

Hume's psychological dynamism, threatening to displace the univocal subject, is a paradigmatic expression of eighteenth-century anxiety about the enlightened subject, a key feature of the Romantic aesthetics of identity:

> The mind is a kind of theatre, where several perceptions successively make their appearance; pass, repass, glide away, and mingle in an infinite variety of postures and situations. There is properly no *simplicity* in it at one time, nor *identity* in different; whatever natural propension we may have to imagine that simplicity and identity. The comparison of the theatre must not mislead us. They are the successive perceptions only, that constitute the mind; nor have we the most distant notion of the place, where these scenes are represented, or of the materials, of which it is compos'd.[23]

Here, the mind's associationist logic is reinscribed at the site where empiricism falters and where the psyche is staged beyond consciousness. The dramatic reality of these scenes holds no cognitive value for Hume, but he nonetheless places us in a proto-Freudian theater of the mind to offer, like Freud's dreamwork, an "example of the processes occurring in the deeper, unconscious layers of the mind, which differ considerably from the familiar normal processes of thought." Once the "preconscious material of thought" has been condensed and its "psychical emphasis" displaced, it is "translated into visual images or *dramatized*, and completed by a deceptive *secondary revision*" (*SE* 20:45). This psychic dramaturgy parallels yet exceeds consciousness. Like Hume, Freud is skeptical of this psychic performativity by framing it within a "deceptive" secondary process. We apprehend the mind's original performance, then, through a structure overdetermined by the heterogeneity of inaccessible unconscious material. In order to make the structure at all comprehensible, this material must be repressed. Repression, then, negatively recuperates empiricism's fear of association by placing limits on the mind's potentially uncontrollable functioning. Repression and repetition in the psychic apparatus reproduce in the free associationism of psychoanalysis Hume's fear that "we are apt to imagine something unknown and mysterious, connecting the parts, beside their relation."

Hume marks a key moment in the shift from the Enlightenment to Romanticism, for in the above passages his skepticism produces logical conclusions that seem to exceed their own utterance, a sort of hysterical rationalism whose symptoms betray the psychoanalysis stirring within philosophy's unconscious. That is, the writing is not itself hysterical; rather it so obviously (and paradoxically) persists in the certainty of its skepticism, that it inevitably calls upon a psycho-analytical understanding of which it remains as yet unenlightened, an other writing that is the uncanny double of enlightenment thought. Yet within this suspended psychoanalysis the idea of imagination begins to emerge as a mobile figure for the unconscious, which signifies both the negativity and potentiality of the *cogito*. On one hand, an expanded imagination merely extends Enlightenment positivism into Romanticism by further assimilating the mind's disjointed faculties. Like sympathy, imagination "brings the whole man together—heart, soul, body, brain, and feelings—and it establishes the individual's place in society" with other men.[24] Imagination's unifying power leaves no aspect of mind unaccounted for; what had been pathologized was now transcendentalized as 'secret' or 'obscure' (Wordsworth's "hiding places of man's power" in *The Prelude*). On the other hand, this idealism betrays a curiosity about the unconscious and thus about its own unconscious. As Andrea Henderson argues, imagination marks the subject's "core" as "the center of movement or circulation, a place of dangerous fluidity." Curiosity about this center, I would argue, is symptomatic of how Romantic organicisim represses what it is unwilling to confront about itself, what David Farrell Krell calls the *contagion* of idealism.[25] If, as Engell argues, Romanticism "overturn[ed] an abstract and mechanistic formalism found in the first half of the [eighteenth] century," and if self-understanding became central to this project, the "dominant prescription [of which] is poetic and aesthetic," it was only inevitable that imagination, upon which so much came to depend as an agency of Romantic self-understanding, would become a site of some overdetermination.[26]

Kant's Imagination

A key figure in this overdetermination is Kant. The ability "to imagine something unknown" beyond empiricism's contingency is the focus of Kant's metaphysics of Reason. For Kant, Hume "was one of those geographers of human reason who have imagined that they have sufficiently disposed of such questions [about what lies beyond the horizon of all the possible objects of our knowledge] by setting them outside the horizon of human reason" (*CR* 606). For Kant, however, all that we can know with certainty is what constitutes this horizon beyond. As Gilles Deleuze argues of Kant's transcendental method, if "a final end is a being which possesses the reason for existence in itself," then "[t]he only one who can be is the one who can develop a concept of ends; only man as rational being can find the end of his existence in himself." What we can know, that is, is a reason that "posits nothing other than itself," a reason enclosed by its own 'pure' unfolding.[27] But to describe this unfolding, Kant evokes a reason that struggles to define its own boundaries, the empiricism of a reason challenged to know itself in space and time.

Enlightenment reason struggles to order the determinism of sense data in order to guarantee reciprocity between the world within and the world without, an externally constructed subject commensurate with his own sense perceptions. Romanticism refashions external constructedness by social forces, as in Locke and Hume, as internal constructedness by past and present trauma and thus by an unconscious whose psychic determinism both discloses and conceals identity. Romanticism, that is, confronts empiricism's traumatic lack of self as an internal phenomenon. Yet it does so through Kant, to whom Coleridge turns, as we shall see in the next section, in order to critique empiricism's passivity. That Coleridge appropriates Reason's transcendental nature by conflating it with imagination's more radically creative nature places Kant at the cusp between the Enlightenment and Romanticism. Kantian reason addresses the systematization or architectonic of an internal constructedness lacking in the external constructedness that troubles empiricism. The psychology of empiricism presents challenges to Kant, to be sure, but by shifting crucially from the phenomenal to the noumenal, to the ground or conditions of existence that form the matrix of the phenomenal, Kant is able to move past empiricism's ground in experience to Reason as the ground *of* experience, if not to know the in-itself, at least to intuit the categories by which the mind structures experience. As Schopenhauer will argue, Kant's idealism attempts "to pass beyond the phenomenal appearance to that which appears" (*WWR* 2:177).

Kant's interest in the psychology of reason's creativity seems at first negligent. At the end of the *Critique of Pure Reason* (1781), Kant allows that empirical psychology must have "some sort of place (although as an episode only) in metaphysics" (*CR* 664). He places this psychology beside applied philosophy, "the *a priori* principles of which are contained in pure philosophy." But the applied is "not to be confounded with" the pure, so that psychology does not infect the contemplative. Nonetheless, Kant studies how the mind creates rather than just passively receives the phenomenal world through the categories, and so cannot avoid being as much a psychologist of the imagination as its metaphysician. In the "Transcendental Analytic" of his first Critique, Kant distinguishes two modes of imagination. The reproductive or empirical imagination unifies manifold impressions derived from perception into singular images or ideas. What realizes this "synthesis of apprehension" as "the affinity of all appearances" is the productive imagination, which is for Kant "the transcendental function of imagination" (133, 146). This function is "grounded *a priori* on rules" that obey the logic of the categories to then impose upon ideas the "formal and pure condition of sensibility" through the understanding's concepts or "schema" (145, 182). That the productive subsumes the reproductive imagination, reason subsuming the understanding, or what one might call the 'pure' subsuming the 'empirical,' insures that empiricism remains under the control of the "abiding and unchanging 'I'" (146), which Kant calls "pure apperception" and Coleridge will call the "infinite I AM." "Thus the order and regularity in the appearances, which we entitle *nature*, we ourselves introduce" (147) through the understanding, which profits from the synthesizing work of imagination, a profit that ultimately accrues to reason.

That a synthesis of imagination must take place between the pure and the empirical, the ideal and the real, however, means that Kant ends up producing conscious and unconscious versions of imagination. Kant famously states that "pure reason leaves everything to the understanding—the understanding [alone] applying immediately to the objects of intuition, or rather to their synthesis in the imagination" (318). The "*schema* of sensible concepts [is] . . . a monogram . . . of pure *a priori* imagination, through which . . . images themselves become possible" (183). But moving past imagination, the "schematism of our understanding . . . is an art concealed in the depths of the human soul, whose real modes of activity nature is hardly likely ever to allow us to discover, and to have open to our gaze" (183). By abandoning "everything to the understanding," Kant still dissociates the pure "I" of reason from its self-understanding, its head from its body, as it were. And this rift begins at the most fundamental stage of reason in the sensibility of perception, where an imagination "subjected to the laws of association" is dissociated from one that is "productive and exerting an activity of its own" (*CJ* 1:86).

Not until his exploration of the sublime in the *Critique of Judgement* (1790) does Kant seem to broach the psychology of this interiority, one that "constantly divides us from ourselves, splits us in two."[28] The sublime is "to be found in an object even devoid of form, so far as it immediately involves, or else by its presence provokes, a representation of *limitlessness*," as distinct from the beautiful, which "consists in limitation" (1:90). Where in aesthetic judgements about the beautiful the mind is in "*restful* contemplation" (1:107), in apprehending the sublime, the mind is in constant flux. The sublime evokes the psychosomatic body of reason as "a feeling of displeasure, arising from the inadequacy of imagination in the aesthetical estimation of magnitude to attain to its estimation by reason" (1:106). Whereas the perception of natural beauty "conveys a finality in its form making the object appear, as it were, preadapted to our power of judgement," the sublime is an "outrage on the imagination" (1:91). It wreaks havoc on the work of synthesis by which imagination renders up the objects of perception for understanding's comprehension under the transcendental authority of reason. Yet by invading the realm of the noumenal, where reason addresses itself to itself, the imagination, by contemplating the nonobject of sublime apprehension, makes reason confront its own unconscious. Or as Kant writes, "[t]he point of excess for the imagination (toward which it is driven in the apprehension of the intuition) is like an abyss in which it fears to lose itself" (1:107). As the imagination reaches beyond conscious empiricism toward the purely psychical or unconscious—understood as the 'purely' rational—its ability to represent itself and thus to fulfill the Kantian categorical imperative of rational understanding falters.

Deleuze, of course, reads the third Critique as the "foundation of Romanticism"[29] because it uncovers the negativity of a dynamism suppressed in the orderly functioning between imagination, understanding, and reason in the first two Critiques: Kant figuring himself as a post-Kantian for Romanticism's sake. This is certainly a tempting view. Whereas for "the beautiful in nature we must seek a ground external to ourselves," for the sublime we must seek for "one merely in ourselves and the attitude of mind that introduces sublimity into the representation of nature." The sublime infects the psychic domain of Kant's internal constructedness, opening the subject to the abyss of the interior. Yet does he just as quickly repress this option in the next sentence, which "entirely separates the ideas of the sublime from that of a finality of *nature*, and makes the theory of the sublime a mere appendage to the aesthetic estimate of the finality of nature" (*CJ* 1:93)? By making the sublime merely supplementary ("a mere appendage"), Kant reinvokes the transcendental guarantee of reason in the first two Critiques as if to stave off Deleuze's incipient Romanticism.

Making the sublime supplementary, however, also implicitly marks an excessiveness that returns in Kant's own *corpus*. Written late in his career, Kant's *Anthropology from a Pragmatic Point of View* (1798) both fears and is fascinated by unconscious facets of the imagination that skew the work of reason and thus exceed Kant's ability to systematize them.[30] Marshall Brown argues that in eighteenth-century Germany science often engaged imaginatively with phenomena such as mesmerism that existed between empiricism and metaphysics, even though philosophy largely expelled this enthusiasm from within itself as the pathology of its own rationalism. The repression of discourses such as mesmerism, then, took a subtler philosophical form than in France, where the aristocracy and then the Revolution both forced a political disengagement from all things threatening to the social body. Brown outlines a number of psychological sources that both transmitted and transformed Kant's ideas, so that the trajectory from "the *Critique of Pure Reason* to a growing interest in abnormal or paranormal behaviour and psychic states" is not as discontinuous as one might think. Kant knew, or knew of, many of these psychologists and read them, although he condemned "the enthusiastic excesses of mesmerism."[31]

To rationalize this excess, Kant distinguishes between physiological anthropology, or "what Nature makes of man" (the determinism of memory, neurophysiology, etc.), and pragmatic anthropology, or "what man makes, can, or should make of himself as a freely acting being" (*A* 3). Part of his way of setting aside the former in favor of the latter, "understood as *knowledge of the world*" (4), is to categorize and thus pathologize the mind's aberrant cognition—dreams, madness, hypochondria, mania, fantasy, the visionary, etc.—as if to contain its threat to man's rational health. Distinguishing between the productive or "poetical" and reproductive or "merely recollective" faculties, for example, Kant argues that imagination is never wholly creative "because it does not have the power to produce a sense impression which has never before occurred to our senses" (56–57). Here the performance anxiety of Hume's psychic theater returns as Kant reins in associationism's volatile autonomy. The anxiety is especially acute when Kant revisits the issue of genius, which the third Critique defines as "the exemplary originality of the natural endowments of an individual in *free* employment of his cognitive faculties" (*CJ* 1:181). In the *Anthropology* genius is the "[o]riginality (nonimitative production) of the imagination . . . when it harmonizes with notions" of "a rational being," that is, with the "form of man" (*A* 62).[32] In the later work Kant immediately contains the psychology of the free movement of cognition described in the third Critique, however, by separating genius from fanaticism, or when imagination is not in harmony with man's anthropology. Fanaticism "may border on genius," as when it can "spring up unexpectedly like poetic inspiration (*furor poeticus*)"; as a "facile but uncontrolled flood of ideas," however, it "affects reason" (98). Naming what genius *is* according to what it threatens *to become* locates the subject within an organic structure of rational being that pathologizes aspects of the imagination but also implicitly includes this pathology as part of the structure's integrity.

Kant's fear of fanaticism, echoing Cooper's earlier panic about enthusiasm and Coleridge's later warning about *Schwärmerei* in *Biographia Literaria* (indeed, in Coleridge's own description of genius), is of an effusion or free association of ideas that 'swarms' the mind, as in dreams.[33] Fanaticism is thus linked to dreams as a way of invoking the hygiene of pure reason from the first Critique. The physiological anthropology of dreams in Kant's late text, however, recuperates the threat of physiological deconstruction that Kant confronts in empiricism. For Kant the dream is a type of vitalistic or physiological mechanism important to the survival of the subject: "[d]reaming seems to belong so necessarily to sleeping that sleeping and dying would be just the same thing, if the dream were not added as a natural, though involuntary, agitation of the inner vital organs by means of the imagination." Kant recounts the personal case history of playing, falling asleep, and then immediately awakening, having dreamed that he was on the point of drowning: "[t]his was probably caused by the reduction of the breathing activity of the chest muscles, . . . and consequently, with the reduction of breathing, the action of the heart is impeded so that the imagination of the dream tries to restore the rate of breathing again" (*A* 82).

I would note two important shifts here. First, whereas the productive imagination of the first Critique synthesizes perception and apprehension in the service of understanding and reason, here the dream evokes Kant's psychosomatic body as the embodied, empirical form of reason returning in Kant's critical method. To be sure, Kant links imagination to the subject's vitality and thus to the survival of the *anthropos*. This survival is not without its discontinuities, however, as when dreams dramatize "difficulties and perilous situations, because such ideas excite the powers of the soul more than when everything goes along as we wish and will" (*A* 82).[34] Moreover, Kant introduces personal narrative and the psychology of self-writing into the discourse of philosophy, so that the psychoanalytical momentarily emerges to displace philosophy—or rather more potently, to submit philosophy to self-examination.

Both at the level of the text's psychology and of its letter, the work of the literary imagination, as evoked through dreams and psychosomatic symptoms, emerges in post-Enlightenment thought as a Romanticism that will emerge more forcefully as part of a larger effort to account for an incipient psychoanalysis in philosophy that it becomes the business of

Romanticism to explore. Moving beyond Locke's behaviorism and Hume's skepticism, Kant foregrounds, although ultimately resists, radicalizing Romanticism's turn inward as a psychoanalytical issue concerned with what the mind cannot know about itself. The psychosomatic and the dream suggest a transference between mind and body, between consciousness and the unconscious, that accounts for identity's radical discontinuity, as in the sublime. The psychosomatic itself is both an imaginative response to and effect of this discontinuity because it signals the imagination's unconscious. Hume fears the imagination's ability to return ideas to their original state as immediate impressions, so as to convince the mind that these impressions are sensorily real: the mind ends up with a body of its own, and this body has a mind of its own. For a later psychoanalysis, the hysterical symptom was the physiological manifestation of a repressed psychological state, a site where the body quite literally had a mind of its own that Freudian psychoanalysis emerged in the first instance to cure. Before Freud, however, this body, while the object of some fear and loathing, was equally the site of desire and fascination.

Mesmerism, Psychoanalysis, and the Absent Psychosomatic Body

The tension between a rational Kant and one interested in the "mysterious vitality" of the world, especially via phenomena such as mesmerism, exposes within the post-Enlightenment imagination a fatal suture between reason and the psychosomatics of its cognates—what I will call the absent psychosomatic body of reason. Mesmerism becomes a crucial focus of our study at this point, both because of its simultaneously legitimate and occult influence on eighteenth-century thought and culture and beyond, and because in the imaginary of psychoanalysis that this book explores, mesmerism marks the cultural genesis of a psychoanalytical practice from which Romantic psychoanalysis will take its cue. The immediate characteristics of mesmerism would not, however, make this kinship apparent. Franz Anton Mesmer (1734–1815) posited a "universally distributed and continuous fluid . . . of an incomparably rarefied nature." This fluid "fills and connects all bodies, celestial, earthly, and animate," like the "mutual influence" between magnets (hence the alternate name 'animal magnetism' for Mesmer's practice). When unevenly distributed, it was thought to produce bodily disease, cured by the magnetizer's channeling the fluid in individuals or in groups in order to restore its equilibrium and thus to eliminate "nervous disorders directly and other disorders indirectly." Arguing that in animal magnetism

"NATURE AFFORDS A UNIVERSAL MEANS OF HEALING AND PRESERVING MEN," Mesmer believed his practice "would thus reach its final stage of perfection" through its "art of healing."[35]

Prerevolutionary France treated mesmerism as both rational high science and occult pseudoscience. Mesmerism forms part of a larger cultural text that attempts to explain gravity, galvanism, or electricity as universal forces compelling the motion of bodies in the universe, or the synthetic force of imagination, what Coleridge, after Kant, calls the mind's "*esemplastic power*" (*BL* 1:295).[36] Yet as much as mesmerism exemplified an Enlightenment faith in progress and in conquering the unknown, it also challenged this faith. For one thing, the existence of a mesmeric fluid was purely conjectural, a hypothesis that resisted empirical validation. Regardless, its effects were all *too* real. Controlled by the agent's look and touch, mesmerism produced a type of physical catharsis or *crisis* in its patients.[37] As Mesmer's materialism became quickly superceded by the psychological explanations of later practitioners, beginning with his disciple Puységur (1751–1825), focus shifted toward explaining mesmerism in terms of the client's suggestibility. Yet while this explained and thus legitimated mesmerism on one hand, on the other it only deepened the problem. That mesmerism generated psychic reactions beyond the body created a different crisis of empiricism: a transference between minds and bodies beyond as much as within the jurisdiction of the individual will. Mesmerism, that is, threatened the body politic. A 1784 report commissioned by Louis XVI (and chaired by Benjamin Franklin) concluded that mesmerism, preying on the suggestibility of its clients, might, as Maria Tatar writes, "taint further generations of Frenchmen."[38] Mesmerism, then, might exploit the imaginations of individuals by swaying them toward revolution. Although Mesmer's clients were predominantly wealthy and educated, among whom Revolution was already a contentious issue, there was a further fear that mesmerism might spread among the working class. Mesmerism was thus further discredited on the other side of the Revolution and of the English Channel, where it posed a threat to the progress of individual freedom but also conservation of social order. In Elizabeth Inchbald's 1788 play, *Animal Magnetism*, mesmerism, the target of farce and satire, registers an imminently 'French' threat on the eve of the 1790s and the subsequent aftermaths of a tension between revolution and reaction. As Nigel Leask notes, however, mesmerism's revival in France and Germany in the 1810s, which was a significant influence on both Coleridge's and Percy Shelley's writings, was equally felt in England, where mesmerism continued to haunt Britain's political unconscious well into the next century through its philosophy, aesthetics, and science.[39] Tim Fulford locates the influence even earlier in the radical politics of the 1790s and its reactionary aftermaths. Fulford notes that "Mesmerism . . . was a menacing political force. . . . Revolution . . . was a creature of the imagination—spread not by rational argument but through the mesmerist's hypnotic touch. It was a matter of excessive and fanatical mass belief—belief of which millennial religion and magical medicine were both the symptoms and carriers."[40]

It was mesmerism's psychological effects that most were disturbing, however. As we have suggested, the "rapport" established between the agent and his subject to produce the crisis had less to do with physiology than with an interpsychic relationship between subjects. Puységur hypothesized that "the real agent in the cure was the magnetizer's will," and used magnetic sleep, what was also called automatic somnabulism and what the English physician James Braid in 1843 later named hypnotism, to access latent material in the patient's psyche. Puységur "learned that magnetism should be used only for therapeutic purposes and not for experimentation and demonstration."[41] He thus moved mesmerism toward the therapeutic and the practical, away from both science and the sensational, meaning that mesmerism did not "[leave] only the memory of a transient psychic epidemic."[42] Between Mesmer's fluidism and Puységur's psychological animism, however, emerged a Cartesian split between treatments that persisted into the late nineteenth century. Two key influences on Freud's 1895 *Studies on Hysteria* were the work of Pierre Charcot (1825–93), associated with the Saltpêtrière School, and Hippolyte Bernheim (1837–1919), associated with the Nancy School, both of whom employed hypnotism in their treatments. Whereas Charcot's neurophysiology explained hypnotism as somatic alterations effected by the nervous system, Bernheim read hypnotic phenomena as psychic effects. Just as the mesmeric crisis evoked a loss of identity, hypnotic sleep, while often returning the subject to his proper self, was also thought to alter his identity by exposing other personalities within the psyche. Worse, through the power of the agent's suggestion, it might even manufacture these other selves. In the preface to his 1888 translation of Bernheim's *Suggestion* (1886), Freud speaks of hostile reaction to hypnotism as an "'experimentally induced psychosis'" (*SE* 1:76), a trauma *created* rather than *cured* by the analyst, as part of some experiment that indulges itself in the carnivalesque of the artificially provoked psyche.

Anxious about scientific legitimacy, and about ethical boundaries, Freud thus early on abandoned hypnotism because dream interpretation and the talking cure offered up the same unconscious material for analysis, yet at a more objective distance.[43] Thereafter, Freud adopted the classical stance of sitting behind the analysand, who reclines upon a couch unable to see the analyst. He chooses the rationality of speech (albeit in the rather less orderly arena of free association) in order to avoid the occult taint of mesmerism's nonverbal mysticism. Yet was psychoanalysis any less disturbing if a patient's alien identities were part of her *waking* as opposed to *hypnotized* life? Interpretation might disclose in what the dream or symptom was *not* saying what it *meant* to say; yet the fact remained that the subject *was hidden* from himself, *had* hidden selves. Moreover, as Freud knew only too well by the time of his case of the Wolf-Man (1918), and certainly by the time of his late "Analysis Terminable and Interminable" (1937), the analytical transference, through which unconscious phenomena manifested themselves in the analyst's office, proved difficult to manage, producing as much new material for future analysis, including the patient's own resistance to analysis, as it worked through. The psychosomatic effects of the patient's unconscious life, that is, could never be put to rest definitively.

So, if psychoanalysis emerges from the postmesmeric history of dynamic psychiatry, it remained haunted by the kind of irreducible postempiricist dilemma first posed by mesmerism.[44] Mesmerism marks the at-once ambiguous and tenacious suture between psyche and soma, wherein the transference of mesmerism produces a body of evidence that resists empirical validation. Just as the hysteria of Freud's first patients registered psychic trauma in the somatic symptom, the trans-psychical force of mesmerism exceeded the physiological except to register its psychical effects in the body, a force of seemingly primal energy both constituting and exceeding the constitution of subjects. The rise of mesmerism is symptomatic of several philosophical and psychological conflicts: spirit/mind vs. body; science and philosophy vs. psychology and the imagination; rationalism and empiricism vs. the irrational and unknown; consciousness vs. the unconscious. It is the first of these dualisms, however, that, in philosophical terms, registers most potently for our present concerns. In short: mesmerism, like psychoanalysis after it, encounters the subject's absent body. Drew Leder uses this idea of the absent body to critique a Cartesianism that privileges the cognition of the subject as presence. Citing Merleau-Ponty's radicalization of Husserl, and reading between medicine and philosophy, Leder describes the body as "never just an object in the world but that very medium whereby our world comes into being." Expanding on Merleau-Ponty's phenomenology of embodiment, Leder evolves a phenomenology of bodily absence that signifies how the subject's body is projected into the world: "the embryonic body prior to birth, the autonomous rhythms of breathing and circulation, the stilled body of sleep, the mystery of the corpse."[45] This bodily negativity or (dis)embodiment, Leder suggests, both conceals and discloses the subject's identity.

Seventeenth-century Cartesianism treats the body as a physical entity that submits itself to materialist scientific description. As Descartes writes in the *Meditations* (1641), "body, figure, extension, motion, and place are merely fictions of my mind." The imagination "turns towards the body, and contemplates in it some object conformed to the idea which it either of itself conceived or apprehended by sense"; but imagination "is in no way necessary to my [nature or] essence,"[46] so that this imagined body is a phantasy easily set aside, and imagination itself poses no threat at the border between mind and body. Science anesthetizes the body, the purpose of which is to house the mind or spirit. Coleridge points to this tranquilization when he notes that medicine in his time was "too much confined to [the] *passive* works—as if fevers & c."—of the body. A "Gymnastic Medicine," he continues, might address itself to "forcing the Will and *motive faculties* into action" in the examination of illnesses such as madness that involved both the mind and body.[47]

Leder adopts Husserl's and Merleau-Ponty's distinction between *Korper* as the physical body and *Leib* as the living or 'lived' body in order to subvert a Cartesian division between *res extensa* and *res cogitans*, the physical body divided from the decorporealized mind. *Leib* situates "corporeality as generative principle, . . . the body as lived structure [and as] a locus of experience," which articulates the self "as an integrated being." *Leib* extends beyond "one's immediate sensorimotor grasp upon the world" to the subject's "faculties of abstract cognition." This 'lived' body, however, is ontologically and empirically also an absent body because it can never be perceived at one go. We cannot, that is, witness the interior or exterior of our bodies in their entirety, except by artificial means or through the gaze of the other, and even then only in parts. Exceeding science's ability to apprehend it, the body inhabits a phenomenological interspace where it is "witnessed from the third-person and first-person perspective alike, articulated by science as well as the life-world gaze." This body is a temporal and heterogeneous psychosomatic complex fundamentally resistant to analysis.[48]

I would revise Leder's formula to suggest that an *absent psychosomatic body*—the body of mesmerism—haunts both Enlightenment and Romantic attempts to theorize imagination. (It needs also to be stated that Coleridge coined the term "psycho-somatic."[49]) The specter of the psychosomatic was of some concern during the eighteenth century. That the mind could somatize itself in terms of organic diseases, either by producing a physical lesion to which the subject's response was greatly exaggerated or, even more disturbingly, by operating purely psychogenically, in which case no physical lesion existed, did not fit with prevailing epistemologies. Edward Shorter traces a concern for the psychosomatic in the eighteenth-century "revolution in the neurosciences." This begins early in the century, Shorter notes, with Friederich Hoffman's 1718 hypothesis of a "'nervous ether' radiating out from the brain and setting the rest of the body mechanically in motion" and culminates in William Cullen's 1777 identification of 'neuroses' as part of his nosology or classification of diseases.[50] This breakthrough produced, in very general terms, two theories: one of the irritability of the nervous system, centered in John Brown's 1780 hypothesis of the excitability of bodily tissues; the other, more influential and wide-ranging in its implications for post-Enlightenment thought, the reflex arc centered in the spinal cord. First hypothesized by Robert Whytt in the 1750s, the reflex arc anatomized the body's interiority as a circuitry of nervous forces, rooted in the central nervous system, but also mobilizing the body as a kind of heterogeneously dynamic organism. All of these theories attempted to trace the evidence of the psyche in the body. Unconscious or immaterial phenomena were thus divided between legitimate and illegitimate symptoms, the former traceable to an organic source and the latter pathologized as the work of fancy and mental illness.[51]

Eighteenth-century psychosomatics, including mesmerism, presented a "range of nervous phenomena that could be understood with reference to apparently scientific concepts of physics"[52] rooted in the determinism of physiology. These gave way to later nineteenth-century ideas of a patient-doctor relationship that attempted to interpret or read the body's symptomalogy. What interests me presently is the automatism of mesmerism, its power to alter the subject as if physiologically, yet through the autonomy of some nonphysiological power, especially as this power resulted in the pathologizing of certain aspects of the imagination. In short, and to revise my own earlier statement: mesmerism confronted the eighteenth century with the specter of its absent psychosomatic body. This body resisted definition by contemporary epistemologies, precisely because it became the locus of a psychic dis-ease characterized by a host of pathologies such as madness, delusion, hysteria, and hypochondria. However, the fact that the phenomenology of this dis-ease infiltrates the subtext of post-Enlightenment philosophy and its emergent concern with imagination and the unconscious suggests a compelling, alternative response within philosophy to science's psychic materialism.

Coleridge's Imagination

Irreducible to Enlightenment norms and challenging post-Enlightenment idealisms, mesmerism haunts the Enlightenment *cogito* as the other of reason. If eighteenth-century empiricism had stumbled upon the unconscious in theory, mesmerism embodied it in practice as a psychosomatic register that evaded science's apprehension. Crossing reason with unreason, it turned science toward the radical contingency of its observation of experience and thus existed on the cusp between the Enlightenment and Romanticism, particularly via their mutual concern with imagination. In terms of this chapter's genealogy of mesmerism's impact on the philosophic mind, we now return to Coleridge's theory of imagination and its crucial interception in Romantic philosophy of the British empiricist and German idealist traditions. The errant imagination Kant would set aside returns in the writing of Coleridge, who turns to German idealism out of a dissatisfaction, not unlike Kant's, with empiricist/associationist models of the mind. We can, of course, read Coleridge's reading of Kant as the Romantics' way of buttressing the idealism of their own theories of imagination. Yet as he follows Kant inward to establish a metaphysics of imagination, as in *Biographia Literaria*, Coleridge encounters empiricism's central trauma of lost identity. Romanticism does not eliminate the constructedness of the subject with which the empiricists struggled; it merely displaces this constructedness inward, so that Coleridge's attempt to recover what rationalism yields to empiricism becomes symptomatic of a return to the empirical subject as *already lost* to himself. In doing so, Coleridge explores the interiority of philosophy that Kant only describes.

Coleridge begins *Biographia* hoping that its "narration" will unify its "miscellaneous reflections" on "Politics, Religion, and Philosophy, and the application of the rules, deduced from philosophical principles, to poetry and criticism" (*BL* 1:5). He uses metaphysics to "reconcile personality with infinity" (1:201), thus articulating the mastery of his personal views on philosophy and literature within a larger critical system. But this narrative abreacts elements of psychology and thus of the unconscious through the text's self-writing. The psychology that was supposed to make philosophy cohere ends up exceeding the text's program. Coleridge admits early on in the text that "metaphysics and psychology have long been my hobby-horse" (1:85). From an early age Coleridge has "bewildered himself in metaphysicks," and in later life has "sought a refuge from bodily pain and mismanaged sensibility in abstruse researches" (1:15, 17). As both cure and illness, "metaphysicks" (the archaic spelling is itself symptomatic) lodges itself uneasily in Coleridge's philosophy: "To lie in ease yet dull anxiety for hours, afraid to think a thought, lest some thought of Anguish should shoot a pain athwart my body, afraid even to turn my body, lest the very bodily motion should introduce a train of painful Thoughts—" (*CN* 3:3149). Reason's reflection leads to "thoughts of Anguish," which produce physical distress, which in turn produce a psychosomatic or symptomatic rationality, "a train of painful Thoughts." This disturbance of identity at the threshold between mind and body is typical of a Coleridgean anxiety about philosophy that makes writing—and particularly the writing of the *Biographia*, as we shall see in Chapter Three—as painful for Coleridge as reading the text is often agonizingly frustrating for its readers.

His compulsion to explore the psychology of philosophy stems from his concern about the lack of agency in the associationism of eighteenth-century empiricism, particularly in the work of David Hartley (1705–57). For Coleridge, Hartley reduces mental events to a physiology of sense perception and the identity of mind, and thus soul, to habit. This materialism leaves the subject "divided between the despotism of outward impressions, and that of senseless and passive memory," and reduces "the will, the reason, the judgment, and the understanding" to the "mechanical *effects*" of the mind's association of ideas (*BL* 1:110–11). "[A]ll acts of thought and attention," rather than "being distinct powers, whose function it is to controul, determine, and modify the phantasmal chaos of association" under the guidance of the will, are instead "parts and products of this blind mechanism" (1:116). In short, associationism, the most reductive form of Locke's empiricism, conducts to "absolute *delirium*" in which the subject vanishes altogether: "the whole universe co-operates to produce the minutest stroke of every letter, save only that I myself and I alone, have nothing to do with it, but are merely the causeless and *effectless* beholding of it when it is done" (1:111, 119).

Here we reach a key moment in the narrative of Romantic psychology this chapter is tracing. What appears most to threaten Coleridge is that, without the imagination's synthesizing influence, associationism becomes *free-associationism*, in which the mind fires away at will, just as it appears to do in the passage with which we started this chapter. The threat of empirical deconstruction that Locke, Hume, and Kant merely describe, Coleridge thus analyzes within an organicist paradigm of imagination that is meant to contain the threat: "[t]he fairest part of the most beautiful body will appear deformed and monstrous, if dissevered from its place in the organic Whole" (1:234). But Kant's repressed psychology returns in Coleridge, who seems compelled to repeat how the psychic errancy of associationism has become the trauma empiricism had been unable to speak. The phantasmal madness and pathology of the mind's unconscious life disfigures the "physiognomy of the Being within," which expresses organicism's "true Image": "The organic form . . . is innate; it . . . shapes as it developes itself from within, and the fullness of its development is one & the same with the perfection of its outward form."[53] But organicism's natural growth is also autonomous and suggests parasitical mutations within its own evolution. Organicism has a mind of its own, and thus an unconscious beyond the mind's conscious "controul."

The organic continuity of thought promised early in the *Biographia* is most traumatically de-formed by an imagination he seems incapable of theorizing in the text. He begins this theory in Chapter Four, then stalls the discussion until Chapters Twelve and Thirteen, at which point the text is crucially interrupted. Addressing Kant's idea of the synthetic imagination and, implicitly, Schelling's and Fichte's, Coleridge begins describing the "tertium aliquid" that is "an inter-penetration of . . . counteracting powers, partaking of both." At this point, he breaks off and inserts a letter from a friend of "practical judgment" (*BL* 1:300), who is most likely Coleridge himself. The letter, Coleridge's *fait accompli* for excluding his still unwritten chapter on imagination, takes us back to the future of Chapter Thirteen in Chapter Four, not to pick up where its theory left off, but to explain the effect of the absent chapter upon his understanding as the writing of a "'bull'" (1:301). Coleridge's note to Chapter Four defines a bull as a written statement that "consists in the bringing together two incompatible thoughts, with the *sensation*, but without the *sense*, of their connection," as in "'*I was a fine child, but they changed me*'" (1:72n). If "I" expresses personal identity and "me" the object represented to the self as "it imagined itself previously to have existed," there should be a continuity between self-consciousness and the image "in and by which the mind represents that act to itself, the result and symbol of its individuality" (1:73n). By an act of textual legerdemain, that is, Coleridge means to demonstrate how his theory of imagination functions in its own absence, to describe the *sensation*, rather than the *sense*, of its "esemplastic power."

The word "changed," however, changes everything:

> The man *feels*, as if he were standing on his head, though he cannot but *see*, that he is truly standing on his feet. This, as a painful sensation, will of course have a tendency to associate itself with the person who occasions it; even as persons, who have been by painful means restored from derangement, are known to feel an involuntary dislike toward their physician. (1:73n)

The subject's absent psychosomatic body (the "sensation" of "connection") turns intellect (or "sense") on its head to offer an alternative cognition difficult to overlook. This "painful sensation" creates a "tendency," a painful transference or association between self and other ("an interpenetration of counteracting powers, partaking of both") like that between the 'deranged' subject and the physician who cures him, although the cure is equally "by painful means." Like the repetition of trauma in the analytical transference or the crisis of a mesmeric session, the transference between "sense" and "sensation" both repeats and contains the trauma-as-cure, prolongs the suffering it intends to mitigate, and passes this suffering of reason along to the reader. The synthesizing effects of imagination produce instead a feeling of profound dissociation in all.

This transference returns with the "bull" in Chapter Thirteen to evoke a "palpable darkness not without a chilly sensation of terror," as the friend reads the "*stone-work images of great men*" in a Gothic cathedral. Although he is "familiar" with the imagery, "[they] looked upon me with countenances and an expression, the most dissimilar to all I had been in the habit of connecting with those names. Those whom I had been taught to venerate as almost super-human in magnitude of intellect, I found . . . as grotesque dwarfs; . . . In short, what I had supposed substances were thinned away into shadows, while every where shadows were deepened into substances." What was to have been in Coleridge's text a kind of summation of his "CONSTRUCTIVE PHILOSOPHY" becomes instead a Gothic cathedral that unsettles the "habit of connecting" things in a way that makes sense (*BL* 1:301–2). Kant, Fichte, Schelling, and Wordsworth, cornerstones of Coleridge's theory of imagination, are disembodied from their 'substance' to haunt Coleridge's own imagination as revenants within a psychic tableau that terrorizes the philosophical identity they were supposed to guarantee.

As if to dramatize the primal scene of Coleridge's thought, these phantasms—philosophy's gothic poetics—disorder the chapter's return to philosophy as it theorizes two levels of imagination. The primary level is the "living Power and prime Agent of all human Perception, . . . a repetition in the finite mind of the eternal act of creation in the infinite I AM." The secondary imagination then "dissolves, diffuses, dissipates," but only "in order to re-create; or where this process is rendered impossible, . . . still . . . to idealize and to unify" (*BL* 1:304). Two imaginations necessitate a synthesis that the theory can be shown to facilitate, a Kantian sublimation rather than a Humean repression of the imagination's ability to conquer what it divides. Yet the division also suggests that the imagination's primary autonomy haunts, and is thus *in need of* control by, the secondary's "conscious will," even if they are "identical" in the "*kind* of [their] agency." The symptom of this potentially hazardous fission, like the potentially uncontrollable effects of mesmerism, is Coleridge's marginalization of Fancy. Fancy is "no other than a mode of Memory emancipated from the order of time and space" that "receive[s] all its materials ready made from the law of association" (1:305). This return of association in Coleridge's theory functions as if to set aside the threat of free-associationism implicit in the imagination's primary autonomous functioning. But by having to name a function it cannot set aside, the theory repeats rather than overcomes the earlier letter's practice: to manifest the imagination's obscure and indeterminate operation within a divided economy of imagination that exceeds theory's systematization, an excess or creative autonomy of the Romantic mind that Shelley in his 1821 *A Defence of Poetry* associates with "inspiration" rather than "composition" (*SPP* 531).

Coleridge's post-Enlightenment ambivalence about the imagination's autonomy anticipates Freud's dreamwork, which reads condensation, displacement, and representation through a secondary revision that conceals how these primary processes dramatize the unconscious to itself, a deception of consciousness that betrays Freud's own anxiety about the *poesis* of the unconscious. Conflated with genius, creativity disrupts Coleridge's metaphysics of imagination. The secondary imagination attempts to frame or finish the primary's activity, against Fancy, which produces only a valueless reprint of associations. But Fancy's work can be neither discounted nor avoided, for the psyche can also create personae which to the conscious mind appear aberrant but which are more troubling because they are produced by the same imagination the Romantics were attempting to transcendentalize. Consciousness becomes infected by its own dissemination, staged according to the imagination's unconscious revisionism.

The letter *should* rationalize the absence of Coleridge's theory of imagination.[54] Instead, it suggests between metaphysics and psychology a psychosomatic suture of shadow and substance that, by this suture's earlier association with nervous fever and delirium, disrupts the Coleridgean *cogito* and the synthetic power of imagination that gives it its integrity. Partly to refute Hartley's philosophy, Coleridge in Chapter Six presents the case history of a young woman "who could neither read, nor write" and was "seized with a nervous fever." She had been found "incessantly talking Latin, Greek, and Hebrew" as if she were "*possessed* . . . by a very learned devil":

> The case had attracted the particular attention of a young physician, and by his statement many eminent physiologists and psychologists visited the town, and cross-examined the case on the spot. Sheets full of her ravings were taken down from her own mouth, and were found to consist of sentences, coherent and intelligible each for itself, but with little or no connection with each other.

Eventually, the voice of her "ravings" is identified as that of her pastor/guardian, who read aloud from "his favourite books," among them "rabbinical writings, together with several of the Greek and Latin fathers." For Coleridge, the case proved "that reliques of sensation may exist for an indefinite time in a latent state," that "all thoughts are in themselves imperishable" (*BL* 1:112–14), and above all that Hartley's "principle of contemporaneity" as the "sole *law*" (1:110) of association was wrong: it is not only impressions existing contemporaneously with one another that produce ideas, for there is clearly a deeper connection of ideas that gives evidence of the will or soul.

Moreover, the reactivation of psychic vestiges suggests that "if the intelligent faculty should be rendered more comprehensive, it would require only a different and apportioned organization, *the body celestial* instead of *the body terrestrial*, to bring before every human soul the collective experience of its whole past existence." Coleridge thinks beyond the Cartesian *res extensa* to the collective unconscious, a kind of metaphysical body of thought like von Hartmann's unconscious:[55] "this, perchance, is the dread book of judgement, in whose mysterious hieroglyphics every idle word is recorded," although "it is a profanation to speak of these mysteries." There exists a "living chain of causes, to all whose links, conscious or unconscious, the free-will, our only absolute *self*, is co-extensive and co-present" (1:112–14). However, this Jungian subject is still tied to her Freudian precedence as if psychosomatically sutured between two halves of a divided self. The fever is also a "delirium" not unlike the "phantasmal chaos of association" Coleridge would refute. Moreover, while this identity is unique, it is also alien; it has its own integrity, but as an other personality. And this character, again in an uncanny reflection of associationism, is composed of—or rather decomposed by—the fragments of archaic texts.

Perhaps most telling, the fever reproduces itself fever*ishly* in the labor of science (the psychologists and physiologists) and philosophy (Coleridge's own text) to document and analyze the woman's case. This veritable mesmeric 'crisis' of analysis leaves the *Körper* or physical body of science and philosophy arrested by the *Leib* or lived body of the female patient because its "will, and reason are perhaps never wholly suspended" at any point to submit to empirical analysis. The associative fragments of the woman's mind are "coherent and intelligible"; but there is "little or no connection with each other" to form an essential subject. And yet the metaphysical unconscious to which Coleridge later appeals is no more egocentric than the alien "nervous system" of the woman's psyche. The subject has gone missing, and reason must work like mad to think and write itself out of the dilemma by "identifying so many passages with those taken down at the young woman's bedside, that no doubt could remain in any rational mind concerning the true origin of the impressions made on her nervous system" (1:112).

Coleridge's nervous woman is also philosophy's way of gendering its confrontation with the potential madness of its own imagination, a move typical of many of the figures we shall study in the following chapters. *Biographia* is symptomatic of how philosophy and theory manage to do the talking for women, as in the metapsychological capital Freud will make from his female hysterics.[56] The tableau of so many men at "the young woman's bedside," like the doctors around the corpse in Thomas Eakins's painting *The Agnew Clinic* (1889), offers a prototypical *mise en scène* of the psychoanalytical session: the embodiment of masculine scientific rationality eager to receive and document the viscera of its own psyche, yet equally eager to turn this psyche's 'raving' psychosomatic presence into a disembodied, codified, and theorized absence, to set aside its embodied effects as merely women's fancy.[57] Yet it is also important to note that the Romantic writers treated herein put *themselves* on the couch, and that the evasions and repressions of the psychoanalytical scene they orchestrate are as important as material of which they seem more conscious. Coleridge's case history marks a key expression of this ambivalent psychoanalysis. As the biographical recounting of the facts of the case itself, the case history introduces narrative into the exposition of science and philosophy. This episode attempts to medicalize the woman's psychoanalytic history by submitting narrative to the empirical demands of science, but it also records the cognitive faltering of science around the trauma of associationism and fancy, in that the psychoanalytical content of the story becomes a pathological presence within the organic form of Coleridge's philosophy. Narrative uses the literary to explain a symptom that metaphysics and reason cannot. As located within the *Biographia*, the case in turn frames Coleridge's encounter with philosophy as philosophy's *lack* of identity, its inability to read itself *as truth*.

Schopenhauer's Unknowing Subject

If Locke, Hume, and Kant describe the imagination's psychosomatic determinism, in Coleridge this description becomes symptomatic, although in the end Coleridge resists giving these symptoms cognitive value. In the end, in his "official" philosophy, especially in his final published work *On the Constitution of Church and State* (1829), Coleridge expounds a positivist organicism. Yet there still remains the problem of the philosophical consciousness or phenomenology of organicism—that is, the problem of the absent psychosomatic body of Romanticism's experience of imagination. As it emerges in Locke's and especially Hume's empiricism, this body's psychoanalytical content is as much repeated as it is worked-through in Kant. Coleridge uses Kant's critical philosophy, compounded by the influence of Schelling's idealism, to transcend the traumatically absent subject of empiricism. But the primal scene of Coleridge's theory of imagination points to what cannot be remembered in Kant, a kind of transgenerational haunting of philosophy by the very problem of reason itself. Coleridge's imagination is a hybrid, an aesthetically *deconstructed* organicism prone to psychoanalysis. This hybridity signifies both a generic duality and an immanent errancy in organic form. It synthesizes disparate elements into a third strand, but retains traces of the dialectic. The hybrid functions as a coherent unity, but is also the mark of its difference(s) and is thus divided against itself as mind vs. body, waking vs. dreaming, consciousness vs. the unconscious.

For an analysis of *this* phenomenology of organicism in philosophy we must turn to Schopenhauer's *The World as Will and Representation* (1819), published two years after *Biographia*. That Coleridge read Schopenhauer is unlikely, for the text went almost entirely unnoticed for the first half of the nineteenth century. But *The World as Will* is important for our present purposes to investigate how Schopenhauer's psychology of metaphysics, as if responding to a Coleridgean positivism, eventually produces in Nietzsche's *The Birth of Tragedy* (1871) an aesthetic staging of the symptomatic, proto-Romantic subject of imagination.[58] Both texts come at the end of a philosophical trajectory that moves from the protobehaviorist de-centering of identity in the subject of empiricism, through the fragile reassembling of identity in both rationalism and the organicist paradigm, to an organic or aesthetic de-centering of subjectivity that the writers we shall explore in subsequent chapters will stage as the subject of Romantic psychoanalysis. *The World as Will* anthropomorphizes the empirical subject as the subject of imagination fatally sutured between will and representation. This hybridity marks organicism's psychoanalytical content, the psychic determinism of which empiricism was unable to work through and Kantian idealism was unable to sublimate. In Schopenhauer's text, imagination becomes the embodiment of reason as an absent psychosomatic body that perpetually recreates itself in its desire to know itself, an interminable process ultimately doomed to failure.

Kant internalizes the mind's empiricism in advance of the world as if to determine its form *a priori*, bracketing off the categories from empiricism, as if to abstract Being from being. For Schopenhauer Kant's idealism too easily sublates the mind's relationship to being, the *in-itself* or touchstone of perception. For Kant, "nothing whatsoever can be asserted of the thing in itself," although it can *be thought*, for "otherwise we should be landed in the absurd conclusion that there can be appearance without anything that appears" (*CR* 87, 27). Schopenhauer begins with this paradox in the Kantian subject, who reverts to perception only "to convince [himself] that [his] abstract thinking has not strayed far from the safe ground of perception, . . . [as] when walking in the dark, we stretch out our hand every now and then to the wall that guides us" (*WWR* 1:449). For Schopenhauer, the Kantian categories that guarantee existence are merely representations. Moreover, Schopenhauer argues, by setting aside the objective world as the inscrutable touchstone of empiricism, Kant suppresses how this contingency resists being subsumed *a priori*. This resistance forms the kernel of Schopenhauer's idealism, which starts with the principle of sufficient reason, wherein "the pure *a priori* concepts . . . serve solely as *a priori* conditions of a possible experience" without constituting this experience except as representation. Sufficient reason governs how consciousness functions *within* rather than *apart from* the world, lest idealism veer off into complete abstraction.[59]

What Kant sets aside as the unknowable in-itself, Schopenhauer examines as the "will," which we know only through its representation, a negative knowledge that subverts reason. In will, reason's sufficiency, more pragmatically than transcendentally idealistic, marks a baffling limit: the subject reenters from Kant's abstract world as the *principium individuationis*, but as a mere appearance interminably contending with the will's mastery. The will is untiring and metaphysical, the "first and original thing" to which the intellect or representation, treated as physical and thus exhaustible, is a "secondary thing," a "mere slave and bondsman to the will" (*WWR* 2:202, 212). The will is a "blind irresistible urge," not "subject to the principle of sufficient reason" in the world of representation, although the will mobilizes representation as its "*appearance*" or "*phenomenon*" (1:275, 106). Representation, that is, is the will's imagination, the secondary expression of the will's primary functioning that does not between them, however, materialize the "infinite I AM." Evoking a psychology at odds with Reason's abstraction, Reason's *dis*traction by the body of the will creates the subject as a "stable and unwavering phantom" (1:278n) at the fault line where will and representation mutually supplement and deconstruct one another, an impossible imagination that leaves the subject ultimately bereft.[60]

Book Two examines the will as an *urgrund* anchoring the first Book's representation of it. But the will finds a more ambivalent manifestation in the subject, who emerges as a troubled hybrid between two strains of the same ontology. The subject impossibly suspended between will and representation, as if by a willing suspension of disbelief, is the absent psychosomatic body *par excellence*. Schopenhauer describes this body as the *cogito* of Romantic organicism divided against itself:

> As we know, [the plant] has two poles, root and corona; the former reaching down into darkness, moisture and cold, and the latter up into brightness, dryness and warmth; then as the point of indifference of the two poles where they part from each other close to the ground, the collum or root-stock (*rhizoma, le colet*). The root is what is essential, original, perennial, whose death entails the death of the corona; it is therefore primary. The corona, on the other hand, is the ostensible, that which has sprouted forth, that which passes away without the root dying; it is therefore the secondary. The root represents the will, the corona the intellect, and the point of indifference of the two, namely the collum, would be the *I*, which, as their common extreme point, belongs to both. (*WWR* 2:202–3)

The "I" emerges at the "point of indifference" between intellect and the will, consciousness and the unconscious. But the "I" and its intellect are fundamentally rooted in the organism's body, which is "will itself; embodied will, in other words, *will* objectively perceived in the brain." The will's physiological functions are "enhanced and accelerated by the . . . emotions," which are registered more acutely by the intellect, but the intellect is in turn the "mere function of the *brain*, which is nourished and sustained by the organism only parasitically. Therefore every perturbation of the *will*, and with it of the *organism*, must disturb or paralyze the function of the brain, a function existing by itself, and knowing no other needs than simply those of rest and nourishment" (2:216). In short, Schopenhauer's deconstructive organicism encrypts the subject or "I" as the repetitive compulsion of the will's paradoxically vital drive toward death.

As symptom of the will's dis-ease, then, the subject is constituted by the very thing that subverts this constitution. This symptomatic subject bears the burden of proof for a body of evidence that is his own, yet also utterly alien to him. As "will become visible" (1:107), the body is both representation or "knowledge *a posteriori* of the will"—*embodied* will—*and* will or "knowledge *a priori* of the body"—*dis*embodied representation. The will thus interiorizes the contingency between the subject and the world as an internal otherness or foreign body within the subject of philosophy itself. As Terry Eagleton writes, while Schopenhauer "privileges the inward in Romantic style, he nevertheless refuses to valorize it."[61] The will grounds the subject in the body of her experience through a type of Romantic immediacy between the self and its interiority. But the subject is then denied access to any definitive knowledge of this embodiment, so that interiority is radically displaced within itself, as if to reexteriorize or alienate itself. Inevitably, representation succumbs to its ceaseless effort to know the will, which appears as "a continual rushing of the present into the dead past, a constant dying" or "constant suffering" (*WWR* 1:311, 267). Representation is the fated repetition of the subject through the forms of his knowledge, the mere repetition of the will's endless striving as a drive toward the exhaustion of the knowing subject.[62] Rather than the enlightened, practical correction of a Kantian abstraction, then, sufficient reason becomes the symptom of Reason's traumatic inability to know the will. Although representation exists to know the will, "there is no permanent fulfilment which completely and for ever satisfies its craving" (1:262). The will is the "strong blind man" who carries the "sighted lame man" (2:209) of the intellect on his shoulders, so that insight illuminates a blindness essential to its own constitution. The will is both Reason as if yet without consciousness *and* Reason's unconscious, both the *prima mobile* of the subject's desire for enlightenment and a force utterly oblivious to this desire.

Once the *a posteriori* effects of representation are subsumed by their *a priori* ground in the will, a different story begins to emerge. The "game" of "Eternal becoming" and "endless flux," although it reveals the will's "essential nature" through a "constant transition from desire to satisfaction," cannot prevent existence from "showing itself as a fearful, life-destroying boredom, a lifeless longing without a definite object, a deadening langour" (1:164). The "subject of willing is constantly lying on the revolving wheel of Ixion, is always drawing water in the sieve of the Danaides, and is the eternal thirsting Tantalus" (1:196). The first of these metaphors suggests a radicalization of the Freudian couch, whereon the subject's experience of his unconscious would otherwise end in the cure of his suffering. In Schopenhauer, however, the desire for knowledge produces a kind of epistemological futility in which idealism's desire for psychoanalysis is never satisfied by the cure of enlightenment. Books Three and Four appear to respond to this futility by ending the will's suffering through a suspension of the willing body in representation's *end* rather than *ends*. In Book Three representation momentarily transcends itself through the aesthetic contemplation of the Ideas, which stage representation's finiteness as a type of absolute limit. Here the imagination appears to return to its metaphysical home in the "I AM." Deriving from Plato's Ideas and from Kant's transcendental ideality of phenomena, the Ideas, which "lie quite outside the sphere of [the subject's] knowledge" (1:169), manifest the will for knowledge in a form least adulterated by the will's exhaustible iteration of itself via representation. Grasped intuitively as the gestalt of representation, the Ideas are a type of self-consciousness that transcends the desire for enlightenment. The highest forms of this sublimation of idealism's contingency with its own interiority are philosophy and, finally, music. In both, "knowledge tears itself free from the service of the will precisely by the subject's ceasing to be merely individual, and being now a pure will-less subject of knowledge" (1:178), an Idea expressing itself as if without the help of phenomena. The aesthetic liberates the subject from empiricism via a cognizant body that, paradoxically, suspends its own body of knowledge by "abolishing individuality in the knowing subject" (1:169).

As much as the aesthetic subsumes the body's contingency within the Idea, however, by wishing away the will's subjectivity as "vanished illusions" (1:164), the Ideas stage the subject's (dis)appearance as the symptom of Kant's original problem with empiricism. Like Heideggerian *Schein*, wherein being is at once revelatory and illusory, or like the Lacanian gaze, wherein the *cogito* and its consciousness do not add up to the same subject, the apparition of the Idea marks a type of paralyzed mirror stage. Ceasing to be individual, the subject merely *appears* in a momentary retreat back into an imagined yet unsustainable unity of Being.[63] If, as Eagleton argues, the "aesthetic is what ruptures for a blessed moment the terrible sway of teleology, . . . plucking an object for an instant out of the clammy grip of the will and savoring it purely as spectacle," Book Four surrenders to this fate.[64] Schopenhauer reads Freudian *thanatos* not as an absolute resistance to enlightenment but as the "*denial of the will-to-live*" (*WWR* 1:283), that is to say, an elimination of desire itself. Book Four turns to asceticism, which *starves* or *suppresses* the will's appetite in the body, not to eliminate the body, as in suicide, but in order to *be* the will as a suspension of any desire for phenomenalization and thus for enlightenment. The ascetic uses the Idea, where "the will can reach full self-consciousness," to "abolish[ ] the essential nature at the root of the phenomenon"—the striving of the will as the knowledge or *knowing* of representation—"whilst the phenomenon itself still continues to exist in time." The ascetic thus "brings about a contradiction of the phenomenon with itself" (1:288). Left is a type of bodiless knowledge, a will that no longer desires to know itself. This gnosis releases the subject into the "real present," where he is no longer subject to the phenomenality of "abstract thoughts" or of the past or future, which are the "cause of our pain as of our pleasure" (1:279, 293). Such thoughts are "often unbearable to us," as "in the case of intense mental suffering," because they "lie[ ] for the most part not in the real present." That is, the temporal form of the will's suffering in the body becomes the symptom of the mind's suffering, so that "we cause ourselves physical suffering in order . . . to divert our attention from the former to the latter" (1:299).

However, once again one cannot eliminate the body as the hysterical symptom of the mind's struggle to know the will without eliminating the subject altogether. To escape the blindness of representation's 'illumination,' then, is to accept insight itself as a kind of blind determinism: "We are like entrapped elephants, which rage and struggle fearfully for many days, until they see that it is fruitless, and then suddenly offer their necks calmly to the yoke, tamed for ever" (1:306). Rather than transcend the will through enlightenment, we radically accept the will in order no longer to remain susceptible to it. We desire, that is, not the cure of enlightenment but an end to the desire *for* enlightenment. The ascetic's acute acceptance of the will unravels into a chronic denial of desire that "must always be achieved afresh by constant struggle" (1:391). The desire for psychoanalysis, never satisfied, becomes the crucible of human existence, a chronic psychoanalysis whose own chronic nature must be set aside, but cannot. In the end, Schopenhauer's philosophy confronts the trauma of Reason, in which philosophy, denied the absolute state of its existence, becomes an impossible telling: it must speak what it cannot know and, in telling, expose more than it knows without then having, or by no more desiring, access to this knowledge. The aesthetic and the ascetic suspend the will all the more pointedly to invoke its presence as a pathology resisting their cure. In either case, consciousness fails the subject and is symptomatic of philosophy's ambivalent relationship with the interiority of its own idealism. Schopenhauer puts philosophy on the couch to confront this interiority, but suspends it beatifically in the midst of its own suffering for knowledge, in a moment of impossible enlightenment. *The World as Will* evokes a representational crisis about philosophy's ability to express this impossibility. Philosophy emerges from this crisis as a telling body that is the symptom of the dis-ease of enlightenment with which the will infects the knowing subject, a symptom from which there is no relief.

It goes without saying that Schopenhauerian analysis works against the Hegelian Spirit of Absolute Knowledge. By displacing the subject's identity into the circuit of representation, the will is "[t]hat which knows all things and is known by none" (1:5). The subject is a complete stranger to herself: "the intellect remains so much excluded from the real resolutions and secret decisions of its own will that sometimes it can only get to know them . . . by spying out and taking unawares; and it must surprise the will in the act of expressing itself, in order merely to discover its real intentions" (2:209). The subject is, like the Humean subject, merely the repetition of his own forms of knowledge who must, then, suffer the pain of never knowing himself: "the in-itself of life, the will, existence itself, is a constant suffering, and is partly woeful, partly fearful" (1:267). Schopenhauer refashions the Enlightenment *cogito* as the sum/SUM of its deconstructive parts. This subject is invaded by an other subjectivity at once alien and essential. The will's asymmetrical relationship to representation suggests the Freudian dreamwork, a deceptive veneer of consciousness masking the internal dramaturgy of the unconscious. Yet although "sighted" within consciousness, representation is blind to and blinded by the will's unconscious, unable to read its "real resolutions and secret decisions." Subject to this dramaturgy, however, the subject who would know is compelled to read its effects. Representation is thus an endless psychoanalysis of the will's life, itself a traumatic absence that compels the intellect to confess the will's secrets, which are forever unspeakable.

Nietzsche's Theater of Psychoanalysis

Ultimately, *The World as Will* cannot mourn the subject lost to the will's determinism. Kristeva speaks of the "melancholy cannibalistic imagination" as a "repudiation of the loss's reality and of death as well." The psyche digests rather than abjects the lost object: "Better fragmented, torn, cut up, swallowed, digested . . . than lost."[65] The mourning that comes with representation's attempt to speak and master the body of a will that resists articulation encrypts the object's absent body, an impossible mourning suggested by the shape of Schopenhauer's text itself.[66] Schopenhauer's knowing subject instantiates her own unknowable otherness. This is Deleuze's Kantian interiority that "constantly divides us from ourselves, splits us in two" as much as exteriority tells us how we have been made against our wills: an interiorized or embodied exteriority that maps our impossible subjectivity. For its desire to understand this psychological terrain *The World as Will* is immanently psychoanalytical in nature, and its symptomatic staging of imagination is, as we shall see in Chapter Four, crucial to De Quincey. Nietzsche's *The Birth of Tragedy* radicalizes this tacit moment in Schopenhauer as the explicit staging of the psychoanalytic *content* of the subject within an aesthetic *form*. In this way, Nietzsche offers psychoanalysis as an art of the absent psychosomatic body performed within an analytic scene that dramatizes the primal scene of its own deconstruction. This birth of the tragic subject is a type of antithetical *Interpretation of Dreams*, one that critiques the rise of a scientific/metaphysical illusion used to hypothesize the subject's unconscious origin. For Nietzsche, the subject ambivalently poised between the Dionysian and the Apollonian, his terms for will and representation, evokes an *aesthetic* determinism that reimagines the body's psychosomatic determinism. Where Schopenhauer sees the will as a negativity suffered by the subject, and representation as a defense against this negativity, Nietzsche's Dionysus endures the will by embracing its dark fate.

As separate heuristic categories, the Apollonian and the Dionysian are inseparable modalities at the level of experience, just as the semiotic and Symbolic coexist within the same signifying process.[67] The Dionysian's return to primal unity evokes an idealism that is demystified as a repression of Dionysian heterogeneity. *The Birth of Tragedy* reads between illusion and reality a suture between dreaming and waking which, insofar as it is associated with the genesis of the subject, troubles those writers we have examined before Nietzsche. Nietzsche associates Apollo with dreams, whereas Dionysus is associated with intoxication. Both are "physiological phenomena," so that the economy of the subject emerges as if from the unconscious or absent psychosomatic body as "energies which burst forth from nature herself" (*BT* 33, 38). Where in Coleridge or Kant the analysis of dream phenomena is ultimately more heuristic than substantive, Nietzsche distinguishes experiential modes of the dream's psychic functioning. Hence, where the dream is Dionysian, a disruptive addiction to something that cannot be explained, as in Kant or Coleridge and especially in Schopenhauer, it is also Apollonian, an aesthetic cure for Dionysian intoxication. But the Dionysian is itself an orchestration of what is invisibly dissolved and dissipated in the primal mobilization of the subject, so that the primary processes of Dionysus and Apollo's secondary revision coexist as part of the same signification. Behind this process lies an even more primal force of the Dionysian. Rajan calls this the "*presence* of difference,"[68] the site of the subject's body as the Lacanian Real, which can only be known through its representational effects. This chaos of presence, even prior to the Kristevan *chora*, is a kind of 'pure' psychic energy not yet differentiated by the drives, much like Freud's death instinct: "*an urge inherent in organic life to restore an earlier state of things*" (*SE* 18:36).[69] As dream, then, Apollo is Dionysus' metaphysical other rather than its repression, but a metaphysics *as* otherness, or more specifically, the "symbolical dream image" (*BT* 38, 49) of this otherness. Both transcendental and deconstructive, Apollo's dream is where the "world of the day becomes veiled, and a new world, *clearer, more understandable*, more moving than the everyday world *and yet more shadowy*, presents itself to our eyes in continual rebirths" (*BT* 66; my italics). Apollo demystifies Dionysian intoxication within a "clearer," "symbolical" language; but it is likewise a "shadowy," "deceptive" manifestation of the Dionysian's more primal force, a representational ambivalence we shall see repeated in the unfolding of Romantic psychoanalysis.

The terror-filled affect of the Dionysian is expressed collectively through the throng of revelers who surrender themselves to the god's power. This process entails a radical loss of identity that submerges the subject within a more archaic web of experience, "as if the veil of *māyā* had been torn aside and were now merely fluttering in tatters before the mysterious primordial unity" (*BT* 37). The experience of the Dionysian dithyramb means that "the entire symbolism of the body is called into play, not the mere symbolism of the lips, face, and speech but the whole pantomime of dancing, forcing every member into rhythmic movement" that is the "collective release of all symbolic powers" in a state of complete "self abnegation" (40–41). Apollo is the calm reflection of this primordial unity through which the astonished subject sees his Dionysian self abjected, although this abjection is "mingled with the shuddering suspicion that all this was actually not so very alien to him after all, in fact, that it was only his Apollonian consciousness which, like a veil, hid this Dionysian world from his vision" (41). Apollo sees himself as Dionysus, but darkly, as in a "transfiguring mirror" (43), as if to dramatize the aesthetic logic of the Lacanian subject. The only means by which he knows himself is through a reflection that is always an alteration of who he is as who he is not. The Apollonian and the Dionysian, then, mutually supplement and deconstruct one another, "in new births ever following and mutually augmenting one another" (47).

This reconstructive/deconstructive process means that, in the end, Apollo and Dionysus are dissociations of one another within the same identity. Whereas waking reality orders the Real, the dream, both Dionysian "rapturous vision" and Apollo's "pleasurable illusion"—the "*mere appearance of* [the] *mere appearance*" of empirical reality—mirrors the "eternal contradiction" of reality in order to redeem it. Whereas Dionysus is "eternally suffering and contradictory," Apollo is the "inchoate, intangible reflection of the primordial pain" of Dionysus and therefore *is*, 'essentially,' Dionysus: "The image that now shows [Dionysus] his identity with the heart of the world is a dream scene that embodies the primordial contradiction and primordial pain, together with the primordial pleasure, of mere appearance" (45, 49). This Apollonian subject is, by virtue of his simultaneity with Dionysus, also not yet a subject. Nietzsche envisions this subject of the dream through the tragic chorus of Dionysian satyrs as the "*dramatic* proto-phenomenon" of Dionysian subjectivity. The chorus is not Schiller's 'ideal spectator,' a "living wall that tragedy constructs around itself in order to close itself off from the world of reality" (58). Instead, it is a "community of unconscious actors" who behold the "visionary world of the scene" of Dionysus, except that the scene, as it were, is an absent scene in that only the power of the god is present. The chorus is a "proto-tragedy, the mirror image in which the Dionysian man contemplates himself" (63) at the scene of his absence.

Nietzsche thus radicalizes as the aesthetic constructedness of the entire subject within Greek tragedy Hume's theater of the mind. The concentric and terraced arcs of the Greek theater "made it possible for everybody to actually *overlook* the whole world of culture around him and to imagine, in absorbed contemplation, that he himself was a chorist" (63). Here, I would argue, we have an invention of the scene of psychoanalysis as an aesthetic phenomenon. But Nietzsche goes further by destabilizing the boundary between the analyst or spectator as a subject presumed to know and the analysand who suffers in the midst of the scene. Rather than obeying the boundary between the observer and the observed, all subjects participate in the "primal ground of tragedy" (65). This ground is most powerfully expressed through the "Dionysian chorus which ever anew discharges itself in an Apollonian world of images, . . . the womb that gave birth to the whole of the so-called dialogue, that is, the entire world of the stage, the real drama." This Apollonian staging of the Dionysian, then, stages the idea of 'theater' before there was 'Drama.' Yet this staging continually reminds its dramatic subjects—the analyst and analysand—of the primal scene of theater always taking place behind their dialogue, a dialogue that is, nonetheless, a necessary form through which to intuit this primal scene. The form of the psychic theater, that is, is fundamentally traumatic, wherein subjects know the parameters of their identities only through the transfiguring mirror of the transference.

Anthony Kubiak suggests that the condition of 'theater' is the primal condition of the subject before he enters the Symbolic, like Lacan's mirror stage, where the subject's identity is found in a moment of recognition and integration that is also its moment of self-alienation.[70] The mirror stage's specular relation between the self and other, which precedes the fissured and imaginary assumption of Symbolic identity, stages the subject's absent identity. The subject's identity, that is, *is* the stage, theatrical and self-alienating, "painful and contradictory," always ready to assume his part within a Symbolic Drama, but constantly haunted by identity's primordial condition as theater. Dionysus is not yet a character at the center of his own tragic performance. Between a primal semiotic theater and the Drama of an imaginary Symbolic subjectivity, identity both emerges and collapses in a transpositional space of difference between the prototheater of the primal scene and the Drama of the analytic scene as inseparable signifying functions.

Dionysus is thus imagined before the chorus became part of a Drama and thus before the consciousness of science overtakes the unconscious of art. Unlike Socrates, he is not a subject presumed to know, and his emergence through the motility of the Greek chorus also enacts a type of transference as a process of both creativity and disruption:

> Here we have something different from the rhapsodist who does not become fused with his images but, like a painter, sees them outside himself as objects of contemplation. Here we have a surrender of individuality and a way of entering into another character. And this phenomenon is encountered epidemically: a whole throng experiences the magic of this transformation. (*BT* 64)

Nietzschean psychoanalysis is the experience of the subject as the experience of a "whole throng." Through this affective staging of 'affected' subjects, the subject's identity is both refigured and disfigured. In this way, the tragedy of Nietzsche's psychoanalysis parallels the group therapy of mesmerism as a type of psychic 'epidemic' that the mesmerist seeks to bring under his individual psychic control. Whereas the scene of mesmerism is still inflected by the enlightenment culture of science within which it emerges, however, Nietzsche's scene of psychoanalysis, resisting science's metaphysical illusion, places the psychoanalysis of the subject within the aesthetic or dramatic space of the Apollonian staging of his Dionysian absence. Moreover, this staging "epidemically" threatens the scientific or philosophical *cogito* with the "excess of life" (41), a heterogeneity figured in the multiple personality of the Greek chorus. As the staging of Dionysian subjectivity, the chorus is the *dramatis personae* of a psyche unbounded by the illusion of his self-knowledge. This process functions through a transformation or transfiguration (like Jungian transference) of its own (Freudian/Lacanian) negativity. Nietzsche warns against overstepping the "delicate boundary" of the Apollonian dream into the "pathological effect" (35) of the Dionysian's ceaseless flow. Yet what science would consider sanity is, for Nietzsche, the madness of sanity's illusion. Instead, Nietzsche refashions the broken thread of memory, the continuity between self and other, past and present, which guarantees the rational stability of the *cogito*, as subjectivity's essential condition.

As an extended exploration of the psychic dimensions of the destabilized enlightenment subject within the context of aesthetics, *The Birth of Tragedy* mounts a psychoanalysis of the post-Kantian *cogito* in order to produce what we can think of as the Romantic, de-centered subject of a contingent rather than transcendent existence. Nietzsche, like Freud after him, digs archaeologically back through the archives or cultural effects constituting the subject in order to designate the primal ground of the subject's being. That this origin does not exist is manifested by a Freudian transference or Nietzschean eternal recurrence, a perpetual restaging of the subject through his representational or aesthetic effects.[71] As Daniel Chappelle argues, the fate of the subject in transference, considered as eternal recurrence, becomes, because of its psychic determinism, paradoxically liberating:

> The analytic situation, by means of the transference phenomena taking place in it, forms a self-contained eternity in which linear history is abolished and in which life repeats itself endlessly in timelessness. The paradox of eternal return in transference consists herein, that the analysand must inescapably undergo it by surrendering to the repetition compulsion and that he simultaneously evades the fate of a life lived in the mode of eternal return by remaining unconscious of the compulsive, ritualistic, and symbolic repetitiousness of his actions in transference. In brief, transference presents before the analyst a Sisyphus who is unaware of his Sisyphean identity and fate.[72]

Nietzsche's tragedy enacts this analytical subject. She participates in the performance of her psychoanalysis by encountering the dramatic effects of a past that analysis (re)constructs for her. By thus reexamining her psychic origins, however, she is also already in a theater as part of the audience/chorus of psychic characters, both performing and witnessing the spectacle of her psychic life—frequently, necessarily, blissfully *un*aware that she has seen the play before.

This self-making potentiality in the face of psychic determinism, the eternally recurring representation to the Romantic analysand of her own unknowability, is the subject of this study's remaining chapters. The Sisyphean nature or *interminability* of this eternal recurrence, which the poet of Keats's *The Fall of Hyperion* accepts as he begins his agonizing ascent up the marble stairs of Saturn's temple, is, I shall argue, not a fact of psychic exploration that the Romantics seem at first to entertain. The invention of Romantic psychoanalysis in Wordsworth, Coleridge, De Quincey and Keats is, like the trajectory of philosophy's attempt to deal with the agitating subtext of its own psychoanalytical content we have just traced, arduous. As we shall now see, the resistance to the psychoanalytical content of Romanticism's own struggle to make poetry and literature function as philosophy begins with Wordsworth's *The Recluse*, the specter of which haunts Romantic psychoanalysis.

TWO

Analysis Terminable in Wordsworth

> What must orient here is [Wordsworth's] discovery of a mode of conversation, now most easily recognized outside of poetry in the domains of the authentic psychoanalyst and a certain kind of expert teacher too tentative to know or say for sure what he "really" thinks.
>
> —Thomas Weiskel, *The Romantic Sublime*

Romantic Psychoanalysis and the Wordsworthian Primal Scene

In the Prospectus to *The Recluse* Wordsworth claims to inaugurate a poetry of the psyche. And yet, conceived early in Wordsworth's career and thus early in the genealogy of High Romanticism, *The Recluse* also forms the primal scene of Romantic psychoanalysis, a troubled origin Romanticism can neither name nor understand. Riffing off Freud's sense of its phantasmal nature, Ned Lukacher argues that the primal scene is always already a scene of analysis, an "ontologically undecidable intertextual event that is situated in the differential space between historical memory and imaginative construction, between archival verification and interpretive free play."[1] This undecidability makes identity, dependent upon a stable and continuous association with the past, an equally undecidable proposition. Yet we can make two assumptions about the primal scene's indeterminate effects: as either a real or phantasized event, it precedes the subject's reconstruction of it, and this reconstruction both obscures and amplifies the effects of the event.

The Recluse thus 'originates' in the poems comprising the "undecidable intertextual event" of its conception in 1797 as a work that would present Wordsworth's "*views of Nature, Man, and Society*" (*WL* 1:214). Examining these texts takes us back to the future of *The Recluse. The Recluse* is a metonymy for Wordsworth's desire to invoke a system or structure of thought comprehensive enough to recuperate all differences within his *corpus*.[2] This desire is intensified by Coleridge's conviction that Wordsworth would write the "FIRST GENUINE PHILOSOPHIC POEM" (*BL* 2:156) in British literature. The poem's anatomy, as we shall see, suggests the conscious shaping of a shapeless imaginative content. Its '*corpus*,' however, suggests an aesthetic interiority or organism functioning systemically within and beyond consciousness. Wordsworth generates this ambiguity by refusing "formally to announce a system" (*WP* 589) for the poem. By "conveying to the [reader's] mind clear thoughts, lively images, and strong feelings," he enjoins the reader to "[extract] a system for himself," thus treating the text as a transparent mediation between subjects. But even the systematic psychology of a reader response requires more of the text than Wordsworth ever provides. Indeed, the text invites us to read against the grain of its aesthetic promise to gloss the absent body of a desire that remains unfulfilled. Like Kant's aesthetic ideas, *The Recluse* is a "representation of the imagination which induces much thought, yet without the possibility of any definite thought whatever . . . being adequate to it" (*CJ* 175–76). Kant recuperates this dissociation between form and content by privileging the transcendental function of genius and the imagination. This is the "something evermore about to be" that Wordsworth himself calls "clearest insight, amplitude of mind / And reason in her most exalted mood" (*P* 13.169–70) and that signifies the potentiality of the imagination's unconscious within the otherwise "steadiest mood of reason" (5.1). Again, however, Wordsworth's plan offers no 'definite thought adequate to it' because it reproduces in the reader the poet's ambivalence toward his own ability to realize his conception. The "mood" of reason, that is, manifests the unsteadiness of its "idea."

Like Coleridge, who uses the metaphor of organic life to figure the imagination's invisible workmanship, in the Preface to *The Excursion* Wordsworth uses architecture as a metaphor for coherence, and thus foregrounds how the transcendental imagination regulates its own organic growth: a cathedral built to the glory of intellectual divinity. He explains the relation between the disparate parts of his writings, both completed and projected, as that of "little cells, oratories, and sepulchral recesses" within the "body of a gothic church" (*WP* 589). The church itself was *The Recluse*, of which *The Excursion* formed an "intermediate part" and *The Prelude* formed the "ante-chapel"; the Prospectus appended to the Preface was then intended to outline the "design and scope of the whole Poem," a blueprint for its finished structure. But the church is more absent than completed, and we are left with its interiority—organs without a body. And as we shall see in the next chapter that Coleridge cannot entirely suppress how the imagination's unconscious mutates the imagination's organic form, Wordsworth finds that the solitude in which the imagination finds its higher form as the SUM also produces a psychic otherness troubling this transcendental schema. *The Prelude* describes this irritation as the "tempest" or "redundant energy" within the "corresponding mild creative breeze" that is the mind's meeting with Nature (*P* 1.46, 43). This "energy" comes from the "sepulchral recesses" of the mind's sanctuary inaccessible to its intellect. The symptomology of *this* body of thought demands psychoanalysis. The 1814 Prospectus to *The Recluse* seems to satisfy this demand by announcing a poetry that wonders what happens "when we look / Into our Minds, into the Mind of Man," although in the end it cannot deliver on the "fear and awe" of psychoanalysis it promises (*WP* 38–40). However, the 1800 manuscript draft of the Prospectus points us toward the psychic genesis of *The Recluse* in "The Ruined Cottage" and the earliest fragments of its conception, "Incipient Madness" and "The Baker's Cart." Even if the later Prospectus looks forward to a systematic philosophy of "*Nature, Man, and Society*," the receding textual origin comprised by these fragments lies in madness. They are the unconscious of *The Recluse*. The Prospectus marks itself as the 'natural' origin of Wordsworth's epic, but these earlier texts materialize an ambivalent psychoanalytical content within its already gothic body.

The Prelude attempts to work-through this ambivalence, and so this chapter, beginning with an examination of various writings for *The Recluse*, will end with Wordsworth's "Poem on [his] own life" (*WL* 1:586), which eventually subsumes *The Recluse*. Wordsworth undertakes his self-analysis as "a theme / Single and of determined bounds," a way of avoiding *The Recluse*'s "ampler or more varied argument," in which he "might be discomfited and lost" (*P* 1.668–72). Yet as a "preparatory poem" (*WP* 589) *The Prelude* was intended as an analysis terminable, a type of extended curriculum vitae outlining his self-apprenticeship for a greater "work that should endure" (*P* 13.278): "[it] is biographical, and conducts the history of the Author's mind to the point when he was emboldened to hope that his faculties were sufficiently matured for entering upon the arduous labour which he had proposed to himself" (*WP* 589). Well into the poem, however, Wordsworth confesses that the "motions retrograde" (*P* 9.8) of his analysis, compounded by his struggle to work through the experience of the French Revolution, have produced an internal "revolution" (10.237). This "stride at once / Into another region" (10.240–41) leaves his "brain confounded" (10.378). He thus turns to the imagination as a philosophical and aesthetic compensation for and sublimation of psychological turmoil.

But Wordsworth's continual revisions to the poem, which forever stalled its publication, suggests an *in*terminability registered symptomatically in the structure of the Wordsworthian imagination. He said of *The Prelude* that it was "a thing unprecedented in Literary history that a man should talk so much about himself": "I had nothing to do but describe what I had felt and thought" and "therefore could not easily be bewildered" (*WL* 1:586–87).[3] Freud repeats this self-initiated self-exploration a century later in *The Interpretation of Dreams*. Favoring analytical self-observation over philosophical contemplation, he argues that the "success of psychoanalysis depends upon [the analysand] noticing and reporting whatever comes into his head and not being misled, for instance, into suppressing an idea because it strikes him as unimportant or irrelevant or because it seems to him meaningless" (*SE* 4:101). While contemplation "leads [the analysand] to reject some of the ideas that occur to him after perceiving them, to cut short others without following the trains of thought which they would open up to him," self-observation, like "poetic creation," overcomes the "violent resistance" to confronting "involuntary thoughts" that present themselves during analysis and does not limit the work of the unconscious (*SE* 4:101–2).[4] Yet Freud grants this tolerance cognitive value only insofar as it helps to demystify the psyche. Like Kant, he implicitly closes off within the contemplativeness of the beautiful ego the unconscious threat of the self's sublime confrontation with itself as a subject unknown to himself—an *interminable* subject. Ultimately for Freud only contemplation can produce the interpretive coherence demanded by analysis. He turns free association back into a controlled associationism that evokes an earlier philosophical empiricism's disciplining of the psyche, the imposition of a type of scientism upon a process that is otherwise inscrutable.

The transference between analyst and patient during self-observation brought Freud to this impasse by suggesting that a therapeutic cure was unattainable and that the process of interpretation was interminable. Freud is wholly Wordsworthian in this respect. Wordsworth's reading of his psyche is, I would argue, ultimately contemplative, a stance he associates with the "steadiest mood of reason." Contemplation is Wordsworth's way of responding to the psyche's self-observational poetry, which ultimately confronts him with the textual trauma of an identity that lacks clearly definable empirical contours. He experiences this trauma in his analysis of solitude, wherein he confronts a psychic otherness that then gets repeated in his transferential encounters with other subjects. *The*

Prelude is, in short, the analytic scene of his inability to proceed with "the promised work" (*1850* 7.15) of *The Recluse*. Wordsworth remains "Halted without a struggle to break through" (*1805* 6.530) the psychic material of *The Prelude* to a realization that he has already looked into the "Mind of Man" by looking into the interminable darkness of his own. This psychological complexity repeats his conflict in *The Recluse*, a complexity that, again, was psychological rather than philosophical in origin. Implicitly psychoanalyzing the Wordsworthian imagination of *The Recluse*, but remaining blind to its own analytical insights, *The Prelude* marks the idea of *The Recluse* as an analysis interminable that Wordsworth must interminably resist.

Incipient Madness in *The Recluse*

The genesis of *The Recluse* comes from the most creative period of Wordsworth's and Coleridge's relationship, which began in the summer of 1797 and ended with Coleridge's departure for Malta in 1804. During that time they were "joint labourers," "Prophets of Nature" speaking "A lasting inspiration, sanctified / By reason and by truth" (*P* 13.439–44). Coleridge called Wordsworth "the first & greatest philosophical Poet" (*CL* 2:1034). But he did so, as the story goes, because Wordsworth was "to realize what Coleridge thought," so that without Coleridge Wordsworth could not write *The Recluse*.[5] The poem emerges separately in Wordsworth's mind. In early 1797 Coleridge contemplated a "gigantic poem on a Miltonic scale" that would contain "all modern scientific and historical knowledge" (1:320).[6] Whereas Coleridge's epic would assimilate all knowledge, however, Wordsworth in *The Recluse* "contrive[s] to convey *most* of the knowledge of which *I* am possessed" (*WL* 1:212; my italics). The shift is crucial. For one thing, it suggests his resistance to the philosophical identity Coleridge assigned to him. Moreover, it foregrounds a hermeneutic that, while limited to personal knowledge, also circumscribes the psychology of the subject within its boundaries, even though Wordsworth ultimately resists this knowledge.[7] The next chapter will examine a similar resistance in Coleridge, but for now our focus is Wordsworth, to whom the burden of writing the epic of the mind quickly reverted.

The history of *The Recluse* from 1797 onward is written over the palimpsest of its heterogeneous and conflicting textual presences.[8] The process of tracing this history asks the reader to take up a relationship with a lost textual object that places one in a countertransference with Wordsworth's epic textual desire. The first sustained version of *The Recluse* was "The Ruined Cottage," and the genesis of its first full draft

(MS. B, March 1798) can be traced to the incomplete draft of MS. A and to miscellaneous pieces from this manuscript and from the Racedown Notebook, all of which date between 1795 and early 1797.[9] This MS. A version of "The Ruined Cottage," as Helen Darbishire famously surmised, "must [have been] a short bare narrative of unrelieved distress"[10] resembling nothing like the ambitious schema Wordsworth conceived under Coleridge's influence. The surest signs of the text's painful origin are "Incipient Madness" and "The Baker's Cart," likely the earliest writings for "The Ruined Cottage." These fragments comprise a type of primal scene or psychic pre-text for a fixation on aberrant and traumatic empirical phenomena. That is to say, they fetishize rather than either repress or redress psychopathology (also a recurrent feature of *Lyrical Ballads*) and so evoke a displacement of reason that signals a fundamental inability on Wordsworth's part. Witnessing in the Reign of Terror a suspension of reason that resulted in social chaos, Wordsworth experienced this deterioration as a traumatic psychological collapse. "I lost / All feeling of conviction" (*P* 10.897–98), he writes, to which he adds in 1850, "This was the crisis of that strong disease" (11.306).

The primal scene of *The Recluse* suggests both a fascination with and fear of the other within which this "disease" manifested. A creative schizophrenia splits *The Recluse* between an allegory of the "Mind of Man" and a psychoanalysis of its disturbing growth, a double consciousness of imagination likewise described at the start of *The Prelude.* This rupture can be traced to "The Ruined Cottage," which employs a mode of conversation that Wordsworth will exploit differently in *The Prelude* to cure himself. The first full drafts of "The Ruined Cottage," MSS. B and D, eventually swerve away from a conversation that confronts ruptures within and between psyches. Instead they evolve a hermeneutics of psychosocial containment—a *psychotherapy* that treats trauma philosophically—in order to deal with the specter of psychopathology that is their traumatic core in "The Baker's Cart" and "Incipient Madness." As later texts struggle especially to find a narrative apparatus to mediate the abject content of Margaret's life, they leave behind the possibility of psychoanalysis. The Narrator and the Pedlar emerge as coanalysts who speak about and for Margaret, whom one can say is the ur-Romantic analysand. To do this they construct her life *as* traumatic in order to demonstrate their sure ability to overcome trauma. The next section will explore how they botch this therapy, like Freud and Fleiss deciding Emma Eckstein's fate or like Freud himself reeling from Dora's sudden departure, at which point psychoanalysis has to confront a variation on its most radical impossibility. But before "The Ruined Cottage" activates the trauma it would interpret, "Incipient Madness" and "The Baker's Cart" describe the pathology of the psyche as an indeterminate textual identity that resists analysis. Within the transference of this process, Margaret (as yet unnamed) and a speaker (as yet unidentified) seem mesmerized by a trauma neither can speak, an inability to make sense of things that becomes inseparable from trauma itself. The speaker conflates the Narrator and Pedlar before they become distinct identities through which Wordsworth later constitutes his own ego. He thereby splits himself into supplementary *cogitos*, as if to avoid identifying with Margaret's madness; but this self-division, the uncanny reflection of the split itself, also reexposes him to madness.

"Incipient Madness" and "The Baker's Cart" present the story of madness (maybe Margaret's) through the speaker's visits to the cottage and its progressive decay.[11] In "The Baker's Cart" the speaker approaches a "wretched hut" with five children who appear "not born to live" (9, 5). A "loaded wain" (3) has just passed by, suggesting a social abundance at odds with their abject poverty. He watches "with involuntary look" as the cart disappears and is addressed by a woman, who says, "'That waggon does not care for us'" (9, 16). It is the *only* thing she says, and the text's remaining lines are his attempt to make sense of the scene's bare phenomenology reflected in her 'simple words.' This incipient psychoanalysis becomes, in "Incipient Madness," a repetition compulsion. Three times the speaker visits a "hut" (2), which we presume to be the previous text's scene of absence, yet this time to enter the cottage as a scene of trauma beneath the first text's social veneer. Both fragments function as metonymies of either the narrator's or his subject's frame of mind, which is symptomatic of an *in*ability to make sense of experience. Both constellate the threat of an *internal* psychic other and an *external* social other, which "The Ruined Cottage" will attempt to suppress.[12] Suspended between the public and the private, however, the fragments cannot leave madness behind, which returns through a conversation with the social other that repeats internal disturbances. In "Incipient Madness," the narrator attempts to work through a "grief" that has "Become an instinct" because it is more repeated than remembered (8–9). In "The Baker's Cart," his description of the woman establishes a transference that destabilizes both identities while also securing his speaking authority through her discourse of the other. In either text conversation is managed ambivalently to secure the narrator's fragile identity.

I suggested earlier that "The Baker's Cart" and "Incipient Madness" are the unconscious of *The Recluse* and thus a site for its potential later signification. Yet they are also an unconscious that cannot be read except as trauma, or rather, an unconscious traumatically resistant to interpretation: a primal scene within Wordsworth's *corpus* that makes psychoanalysis necessary. Nicholas Abraham and Maria Torok describe *endocryptic identification* as the

> exchanging of one's own identity for a fantasmatic identifiction with the 'life'—beyond the grave—of an object of love, lost as a result of some metapsychological traumatism. . . . In all cases, the goal of this type of construction is to disguise the wound because it is unspeakable, because to state it openly would prove fatal to the entire topography.[13]

The existence of "The Baker's Cart" and "Incipient Madness" suggests that the entire structure of *The Recluse* fantasizes this endocryptic topography by way of dealing with what it cannot say about itself. This explains why in *The Prelude* Wordsworth can deal with reason's displacement or suspension, but not its death, for such an admission would threaten the entire topography, however traumatically realized, upon which his selfhood depends. But Romantic psychoanalysis will eventually admit this insight: psychoanalysis *is* an attempt to deal with the subject himself *as* lost object; it exists precisely to admit this absence—*and nothing more.* This is the trauma of "The Baker's Cart" and "Incipient Madness" that *The Recluse* cannot leave behind. As "spots of time" (*1799* 1.288) or "fragments of a drama, moments in a single action which has retired beyond the reach of direct expression,"[14] they erupt, like the drowned man of Esthwaite, "bolt upright" (*1805* 5.471) into a textual landscape without any aesthetic framing. Their effect upon the reader, as upon the narrator of their painful utterances, is to emerge with a force of trauma that leaves us mesmerized. We are unable to discern clearly the texts' embryonic psychoanalytic scene, and thus are equally baffled to understand the larger picture of Romantic psychoanalysis as it comes into focus. Caruth writes that "one's own trauma is tied up with the trauma of another, the way in which trauma may lead . . . to the encounter with another, through the very possibility and surprise of listening to another's wound."[15] This encounter, in the first instance at least, is reparative. As it is encrypted within "The Baker's Cart" and "Incipient Madness," it creates a psychodynamic that finds speaker/author and listener/reader both mesmerized by trauma and compelled to speak—that is, to interpret and understand—its secret.

This psychodynamic is manifested through a tension between the diachronic space of narrative, which comprises a type of social science within the scene it expresses, and the synchronic mode of a stark lyric compression, which expresses the narrator's singular frame of mind.[16] Named only by her association with her children ("we"), the woman in "The Baker's Cart" emerges surreptitiously. She seems to be for the narrator what Christopher Bollas calls the "transformational object," the mother as a "region or process of transformation" that defines the self's "nascent subjectivity." This process establishes the experiential matrix that "promises to transform the self"[17] in later life by remembering the transformational potential offered in the first instance of the infant's experience of the mother's life-altering influence. Here the chance for transformation is rather more limited, however, as the narrator recognizes her as having been "neglected and denied / The common food of hope" (19–20). He thus distinguishes her mental distraction from his sound reflectiveness within the social order. Yet this mastery silences social and psychic difference: his subsequent diagnosis empathizes with her distress but ultimately contains it according to Symbolic law by subsuming it within the text's imaginary identity. Within his discourse, her brief speech is only a diacritical marker rather than a site of potential dialogue offering any cognitive value. Working-through her grief becomes a moot point, because his narcissism disallows exposure to the other. Yet as much as he elides her narrative (self-)difference, by noting her affect, he also implicitly identifies *with* it. His ability to make sense of things, that is, depends on *her* "low and fearful voice" (15). The "words" of her language are "simple," but "their meaning" is "[m]ade up" by the semiotic affect and demeanor of "her look and voice." Her "Sick and extravagant" mental disposition, through which "the rebellious heart to its own will / Fashions the laws of nature" (21, 24–25), transgresses what appears to be the text's social and Symbolic law. The Narrator would objectify himself as the scene's analytical authority, but he is mesmerized "with involuntary look" (9) within it. Her affect compels from him a countertransferential relationship that destabilizes his textual identity.

"Incipient Madness" seems to interiorize this disturbing affect as the narrator's own, as if told from the point of view of the countertransference that turns him into the patient. In his first visit to the ruined cottage, he obsesses within its "fractur'd walls" about a "broken pane," which becomes a metonymy for his "settled temper of the heart" (28, 5, 8). He describes this "grief" as a melancholy associated with his inability to introject the lost object, fetishized in the text as a "speck of glass" (9, 13). Abraham and Torok describe introjection, after Sandor Ferenczi, as "[l]earning to fill the emptiness of the mouth with words" to compensate for the mother as lost object.[18] Hence, the narrator's second visit reads the glass as "more precious to [his] soul / Than was the moon in heaven," an introjection of the object that his third and final visit accepts *as lost*: the "glow worm" is now "seen no more," the "blackbird" has "disappear'd," and the "linnet" has "vanish'd" (23–24, 38–43). But the text also describes incorporation (the essential mechanism of endocryptic identification) as the obstacle to introjection, when "[f]ailing to feed itself on words to be exchanged with others, the mouth absorbs in fantasy all or part of a person—the genuine depository of what is now nameless." Words "fail to fill the subject's void," who takes up the denial of the void by filling it with "an imaginary thing" that supplies the fantasy that the void has indeed *been* filled. The narrator's grief having "[b]ecome an instinct, fastening on all things / That promise food," and "doth like a sucking babe / Create it where it is not," expresses this imaginary sustenance in particularly disturbing terms (9–11). And, that the "speck of glass" remains both "undisturbed" and "more precious than heaven" at his second visit suggests repetition avoidance rather than acceptance, as if no mourning can take place here (22).[19]

The speaker's third visit thus precipitates a series of ontological collapses in the empirical world that are merely the text's pathetic fallacy for the narrator's melancholy. He says his "heart claimed fellowship" with the "I [that] alone / Remained," the "winds of heaven [that] remained," and the "beams / Of dawn and of the setting sun," an affective reconstitution of his relationship with the world in spite of loss (45–49). But this could also figure his obsession with absence projected onto the world as being one with his mind: an identification with the empirical world that is so intense that it begins to suggest his complete obliteration of all objects including the disconcerting presence of the woman in "The Baker's Cart." This perceptual cannibalization of the world marks his psychotic break from it. The light that illuminates the scene, just as the "broken pane" that "glitter'd in the moon . . . seemed akin to life," turns parasitical and "seemed / To live and linger on the mouldering walls" (6–7, 48–49). The narrator's initial fixation, reproduced in solitude, returns in the text as if to exceed its control, there being no hope of conversation with the other to save the day.

Ultimately, "The Baker's Cart" and "Incipient Madness" are what Rajan calls textual abjects, paraphrasing Kristeva's notion of that which "does not fit, and which therefore produces a sense of dis-ease in the body of the Kantian or Cartesian subject."[20] They evoke psychic aberrancies that Wordsworth will attempt to absorb into the SUM of *The Recluse.* Yet they unsettle the metaphysics of this transcendental subject in advance of its articulation. Put another way, the texts evoke a preSymbolic experience of primal loss or trauma that exceeds later attempts to give this experience a discernible explanatory shape.[21] A scene of psychoanalysis is possible: in "The Baker's Cart" the speaker appears to be responsive to the woman's distraction, and in "Incipient Madness" he appears to negotiate her loss as his own. Yet both texts would remain equally invulnerable to the unconscious, going so far as to imagine the loss of the other in order to avoid dealing with its heterogeneous and unrepresentable presence *as* other.

Speaking of Margaret: "The Ruined Cottage"

By uniting and then fleshing out the bare scenarios of "Incipient Madness" and "The Baker's Cart," "The Ruined Cottage" promises a fuller exploration of the potential for psychoanalysis left untapped in the shorter texts. MS. A "begins abruptly with the Pedlar's contrast between the ruined cottage he now sees and the way he remembers it from the time when Margaret was alive."[22] Wordsworth still seems compelled to give a fuller account of the "unrelieved distress" of Margaret's psychology, using the cottage to indicate Margaret's physical and psychic deterioration.[23] Yet in revisions between the first full drafts of the poem, MS. B (early 1798) and MS. D (February–November 1799), a resistance to Margaret's life and thus an incipient gendering of psychoanalysis begins to emerge. This resistance takes the form of a narrative apparatus that attempts to impose coherency in place of a previous psychic rupture created by a confrontation with what remains unspeakable. This structure displaces Margaret's story within the Narrator's encounter with a Pedlar, who recounts his visits to the cottage to the Narrator as a third party. This framing relocates the dialogue between the narrator and Margaret as a triangulated exchange that recuperates Margaret's alterity dialectically in the conversation between men. Together they evolve a model of *correct* interpretation by transforming the narrative of sensibility, set aside as the troubling psychosomatic embodiment of the feminine psyche as wayward feeling, into metadiscourse, which asserts its masculine prerogative over this body by rationalizing it away.

The result is telling on several fronts. For one thing we can see the contours of nation and Empire emerge through a reaction against revolution: Wordsworth refigures Margaret's life as cautionary tale to warn against how psychopathology can lead to social disintegration. The backdrop for this decay is the life made useless because, to paraphrase Arnold's later indictment of Romanticism, there was everything to be endured yet nothing to be done. To accomplish this end, the Narrator's conversation with the Pedlar pits the Pedlar's philosophical case history against Margaret's psychological profile.[24] In place of an earlier potential for psychoanalysis in the narrator's exposure to external disruption we now find a hermeneutic that secures his analytical voice through the Pedlar's, which becomes the text's epistemological center. The Pedlar's telling acquires cognitive and thus therapeutic authority through its ability to absorb the cottage's disturbing phenomenology within the text's main exposition: to educate the narrator, through the example of the Pedlar's meditative life, about the dangers of solitude. In turn, Margaret's story becomes a philosophical lesson upon, rather than a psychoanalysis of, her psychic etiology. But this early attempt to preempt within *The Recluse* the threat of psychoanalysis is not entirely successful. Conversation in the text is supposed to attenuate the "passing shows of being" (522) associated with Margaret's affect. Instead, it mobilizes the return of a psychic content that the manuscript cannot entirely repress.

Both MSS. B and D open with the analytic scene I described in the Introduction. The spectral mirroring of repose and solitude between the Narrator and Pedlar in B, however, does not mark a relation between analyst and analysand, whereas in D the Narrator recognizes the Pedlar "With instantaneous joy" (36). Moreover, their communication as "fellow-travellers" precludes working-through psychic complexities and transfers philosophical authority immediately to the Pedlar, who makes clear what the Narrator "cannot see" within the primal scene: the transience of life (40–41, 68).[25] To compensate for this loss, the Pedlar notes how lyric "Poets," "in their elegies and songs," "call upon the hills and streams to mourn" (73–74). However, lyric turns mourning into melancholy by tranquilizing the "foolishness of grief" (119). In lyric the poet is more "Obedient" than responsive to "human passion" as a "strong creative power" rather than an unsettling affective force (75–76). Lyric closes off the poet to a dialogue with himself and with others by expressing the philosophical mediation of "Sympathies . . . / More tranquil, yet perhaps of kindred birth, / That steal upon the meditative mind / And grow with thought" (79–82). The passage invokes Smith's moral sympathy, so that grief is not so much worked-through as contained within a communal 'one life' that sublimates and aestheticizes grief as pathetic fallacy: "Beside yon spring I stood / And eyed its waters till we seemed to feel / One sadness, they and I" (82–84).

MS. D's appeal to lyric preempts the affective pull of Margaret's life by contextualizing the Pedlar's transference with Margaret in philosophic terms that produce a terminable analysis of things. The Pedlar presents Margaret's case as an illustration for rather than an analytical challenge to the Narrator. Lyric suspends transference by maintaining the Pedlar's analytical authority within the Narrator's own telling. In this context, dialogue is a controlled and conscious exchange between two fully constituted subjects, but is really ultimately monologic: the telling of no more than one subject and version (and gender) at a time that excludes the threat of the other, who in turn implicitly agrees to the other's speaking authority. In MS. B, however, the Narrator's identification with the Pedlar through his case history of the Pedlar's moral and spiritual education figures the Narrator's attempt to work-through the other's example of solitude. In both drafts, the Pedlar is a type of autochthonic poet who emerges as if fully developed at the breast of (mother) Nature and in the absence of the (social) father. MS. B's genealogy of the Pedlar as a wanderer "born of lowly race," who, "untaught, / In the dead lore of schools undisciplined," "[flashes] poetic fire," supports this identity at the same time that it represses the oedipal scene of his history (47, 72–75).[26] Yet the *telling* of his story by the Narrator in MS. B assigns the Pedlar's solitude a psychic content and exposes his philosophical authority to the Narrator's psychoanalytical interrogation.

The Pedlar's life purports to teach the reader by example what the Pedlar's account of Margaret has taught the Narrator. He was educated in a "school that stood alone, / Sole building on a mountain's dreary edge," an isolation that prepares him in his "far" wanderings into the world "of men" to adopt the "passions" and "feelings . . . / Essential and eternal in the heart" (54–63). He is the prototype of Wordsworth's poet in the Preface to *Lyrical Ballads* and of Wordsworth himself in *The Prelude*: he speaks a "language really used by men" and he is "possessed of more than usual organic sensibility," having "thought long and deeply" (*WP* 734–35). A budding Victorian who has learned to temper his excessive Romantic sensibility in the service of the public good, he is thus a "chosen son" who has "deeply felt / The voice of Nature in the obscure wind," and "To every natural form" given a "moral life; he saw them feel / Or linked them to some feeling" (MS. B 76–83). In passages from the Alfoxden Notebook, however, Wordsworth also describes the Pedlar's ability to hear the "ghostly language of the antient earth," which contains a "visionary power" that does not speak to "our purer mind / And intellectual life" but to a remembering of "how [the soul] felt but what she felt / Remembering not retains an obscure sense / Of possible sublimity."[27] The Pedlar feels a primal, affective "spontaneous overflow of feeling" (*WP* 734) beyond the intellect, a realm of "strange meaning," where lyric is disrupted by the otherness of its own solitude (MS. B 85). Untouched by social engagement, the Pedlar's isolation reflects his psychic and social marginality:

> He had a world about him 'twas his own,
> He made it for it only lived to him
> And to the God who looked into his mind.

> Such sympathies would often bear him far
> In outward gesture, and in visible look,
> Beyond the common seeming of mankind.
> Some called it madness. (87–93)

In this blueprint for moral sympathy the man looks within so that he can feel properly without also producing divine madness. The Pedlar's commune with Nature unleashes, not a divinatory communication, but a type of Natural metatransference that threatens to subsume identity. Indeed, the passage conflates the transcendental imagination and the later dissociative affect of Margaret's life, as if itself hysterical about the subject's semiotic ground in (Mother) Nature. In turn, the Narrator's case history of potential madness *in the Pedlar* becomes symptomatic of a desire to suppress its psychic difference: Wordsworth removed the passage from the later draft, and the Narrator and Pedlar together address Margaret's story as impartial interpreters, as if clear of the feminine threat of her disruptive sensibility.

But their homoanalytical meditation cannot maintain its reflective composure. As the Pedlar begins Margaret's story in MS. B, affect overcomes exposition, as he is overwhelmed by his description of the cottage's desolation: "You will forgive me, Sir, / I feel I play the truant with my tale" (170–71). MS. D turns distraction into self-admonishment and the cottage's visceral reality into picturesqueness: "You will forgive me, Sir, / But often on this cottage do I muse / As on a picture, till my wiser mind / Sinks, yielding to the foolishness of grief" (116–19). Refiguring feeling as contemplation ("I muse") suppresses psychoanalysis in favor of aesthetics and philosophy. Nonetheless, conversation creates a transference through which the Narrator and Pedlar, as if unable to confront themselves through Margaret, project psychic responsibility for the tale onto one another. In both drafts, the end of Part 1 breaks the "unrelieved" distress of Margaret's story, pausing after her first speech, in which, seeing her husband's madness reflected in her children's fear, her "heart bleed[s]" (185). Defending against her despair, the Pedlar asks the narrator if, "feeding on disquiet," they should "disturb / The calm of Nature with [their] restless thoughts?" (197–98). As an evasion of grief's self-reproduction, the question is both an admonition and appeal to the Narrator, who confirms the Pedlar's ambivalence at the beginning of Part Two: "He spake with *somewhat* of a solemn tone" (199; my italics). The Narrator, as if also anxious to suspend grief, reads this ambivalence as "a look so mild / That for a little time it stole away / All recollection" (201–3). In both versions he 'begs' the Pedlar to continue, and in MS. B he is "impelled / By a mild force of curious pensiveness" (276–77), suggesting the mesmerizing effects of the Pedlar's telling in the Narrator, so that he is both *pensively* drawn to his own thoughts and *curiously* drawn to the Pedlar. Responding to this influence projected in the narrator, the Pedlar warns that to indulge in the narrative "were a wantonness" that "would demand / Severe reproof," "A momentary pleasure never marked / By reason" (221–26; MS. B). Distinguishing philosophy's moralization from the mesmerized stance of the "idle dreamer," which the Pedlar cautions the narrator against, the Pedlar defends his narrative's analytical authority against the shapeless content of Margaret's life, a "[common] tale of silent suffering, hardly clothed / In bodily form." He resecures his identity against the Narrator's curiosity about Margaret's life in order to resume his narrative: "at your bidding / I will proceed" (231–37).

If not by speech, however, Margaret insists on being heard in other ways. The affect of her voice continues to mesmerize the Pedlar.[28] Although his conversation with her "[builds] up a pile of better thoughts," subsequent visits confirm her mental deterioration (279, 512). She repeats to strangers the "same sad question" about her husband's fate, insisting upon her listener's attention in also reading the affect of her grief, and the Pedlar, like Coleridge's Wedding-Guest, remains drawn into her grief, which both "seemed to cling upon [him]" parasitically and to infect his heart like a virus from within (512, 256). MS. B closes with the death of Margaret, "[l]ast human tenant of these ruined walls" (528), implying an end to melancholy and a purging of the narrative's affective taint. But the specter of the cottage itself takes us back to the text's future as the Pedlar laid outside its "four naked walls / That stared upon each other," compelling us to read in his visits a repetition compulsion echoing Margaret's own. He seems continually drawn back to a primal scene he appears unable to work-through (he remains *outside* the cottage). Is this refusal in the nature of the text's resistance to its own psychoanalysis, or because it recognizes in psychoanalysis its own selfresistance? Despite the fact that the text draws us into a repetitive epistemological ambivalence, it does not finally stage itself as an artifact demanding transference with its readers. In fact it seems anxious to curtail this relation as a way of interpellating our response. In MS. D the Pedlar's last visit is a "final parting" (444), and Margaret's death terminates her life's telling to prepare for the text's coda—in all respects he is clear that he will not return to Margaret's story. Here the Pedlar, as if to cure the "impotence of grief" transferred to the Narrator, dismisses it as "an idle dream that could not live / Where meditation was" (500, 523–24). "Admonished thus," the Narrator and Pedlar reenter the social order of a "rustic inn," presumably to resume their meditative—and meditatively uncomplicated—lives (538).

The return to the social is in keeping with MS. D's opening sequence, which foregoes the Pedlar's case history and joins the Pedlar and Narrator as "fellow-travellers." But this happens only at Margaret's expense, and by overlooking their transference with her. If Margaret is sacrificed for the sake of social stability, this stability is preempted by an earlier passage. Here the Pedlar's meta-commentary, used to contain narrative affect, ends up reproducing its effects. Feeling the "story linger in [his] heart," and noting that his "spirit clings / To that poor woman," he feels in his "walks / A momentary trance [come] over [him]" (363–69). He defends against this mesmerizing suspension of reason by 'musing' on Margaret as "one / By sorrow laid asleep" (371–72). But Margaret's grief registers beyond his attempt to distinguish intellect from the chaos of her unconscious. He repeats "It would have grieved / Your very heart to see her" fourteen lines later as "it would have griev'd / Your very soul to see her" (361–62, 375–76). Grief bores deeply to infect the subject's very being against his will: instead of griev*ing*, he *is grieved*. Moreover, the repetition turns exposition into entreatment, the symptom of the Pedlar's attempt to project melancholy onto the Narrator and thus to implicate the Narrator in a transference that upsets both men. Lyric utterance, which was supposed to teach the Narrator how to grieve properly, produces its own dialogue that keeps reanimating Margaret's ghost. And the text itself, by so carefully parceling out the rare times it allows Margaret *to* speak, insures, by virtue of her viscerally spectral presence, her continued half-life in the minds and hearts of readers.

Therein lies the text's central problem: Margaret—the woman's question/the question of woman that will not go away. Certainly her dispossessed and deracinated body returns by the very conspicuousness of its absence through the text's attempt to abstract through rational interpretation this body's otherwise chaotic presence. But it is this body's psychosomatic, symptomatic aftereffects as feeling that compels its repetition. This return draws us back to her phantasmal yet almost overpowering manifestation through speech in "The Baker's Cart": "'That waggon does not care for us.'" Her *unheimliche* and unnamed presence becomes in later texts an all too *heimlich* recurrence. "Who cares for us?" Margaret asks of the Pedlar and the Narrator, as she asks of her later readers. This call to countertransference arrests our attention and demands our interpretation at the same time. The Pedlar cannot, in fact, get rid of lyric's internalized grief, associated in the text with the madness of solitude. Lyric mourning becomes lyric melancholy. His attempt with the Narrator to return Margaret, through the violence of interpretation, to her 'natural' state as "spear-grass" (*essentially* to return her to Mother Nature) outside the ruined cottage, always catches them unawares, so that the philosophical authority of lyric contemplativeness cannot compose itself. It is as if Margaret would turn that violence back upon them and upon us to remind us of a body—our own feelings—that reason cannot possess. Yet ultimately "The Ruined Cottage" decidedly, albeit conflictedly, turns the possibility of psychoanalysis in its earliest texts toward psychotherapy, as if making Wordsworth's vision of the philosophical *anthropos* in *The Recluse* fit to tell.

Pathologizing the Prospectus

In the Prospectus the multiple half-lives of Margaret's body become the monolithic voice of the Bard projecting his own disembodied voice onto Nature and into the future, like one of the "mirrors of the gigantic shadows which futurity casts upon the present" in Shelley's "A Defence of Poetry" (*SPP* 535). The Prospectus fulfils several interconnected functions: it indicates how *The Excursion*, which absorbs "The Ruined Cottage" into its first Book, fits within the larger pattern of *The Recluse*; it indicates that *The Recluse* is still a viable project in Wordsworth's mind; it renders the archetypal stance of Wordsworthian meditation; and it thus displaces the threat of Margaret definitively. Yet by wresting philosophical stability from the psychology of solitude explored in "The Ruined Cottage," the Prospectus is also conflicted. *As* archetype, it tries to terminate once and for all the inherently psychoanalytical and interminable nature of Wordsworth's project. At the end of *The Prelude* his mission is clear: with Coleridge he will "Instruct [mankind] how the mind of man becomes / A thousand times more beautiful than the earth / On which he dwells, above this frame of things / . . . / In beauty exalted, as it is itself / Of substance and of fabric more divine" (13.446–52). Wordsworth can now undertake "building up a work that should endure" (13.278), and the Prospectus formally announces and dedicates itself to this effort. Epic projects the poet's identity onto a broader sociophilosophical screen, where the mind's internal divisions are recuperated through its marriage to Nature. This much is Wordsworth's "high argument." His focus on the mind, then, reveals, paradoxically, a move away from psychic interiority, foregrounding the mind's "quality" (*1850* 14.452) in lieu of its "substance" (*1805* 13.452). The shift turns the possibility of psychoanalytical life-writing into meditative epitaph, exchanging psychological exploration for epic ritual, psychic motility for aesthetic form. The changeable psychic shape of "biographic verse" (13.341) becomes instead a "monument of glory" (*1850* 14.434) to a changeless Imagination.

Insofar as the Prospectus marks this shift, it formally redirects the psychoanalytical impulses of his earlier writings into the larger philosophical frame of *The Recluse*. Although not published until 1814, the Prospectus was first written after MSS. B and D of "The Ruined Cottage" but before the bulk of *The Prelude*.[29] Publishing the Prospectus seems part of Wordsworth's effort to monumentalize himself—the first collected edition of his poems appeared the following year. But the manuscript seems more fragment than manifesto, an intention that does not work, a prelude to *The Prelude* more than to *The Recluse*. Indeed, its forward-looking ethos takes us *back* to the future of *The Prelude* as much as it defines *The Recluse*'s prospective shape.[30] In "The Ruined Cottage" Wordsworth moves beyond the opening reverie of the reclining subject because it poses the dangers of solitude. The Prospectus revisits these dangers as part of the challenge of epic poetry. His exchange with Milton appears to be suppressed within a univocal, monologic channeling of the "prophetic Spirit" that inspires all "mighty Poets" (83, 87). The Pedlar's solitude, we can now see, prepared for Wordsworth's incarnation as solitary Bard.

Both the manuscript and the 1814 text adopt the cadence of Miltonic verse: "On Man, on Nature, and on human Life" (1). Where the later version begins as epic contemplation by "Musing in solitude" (2), however, the manuscript begins in analytical self-observation by "Thinking in solitude" (2). The difference is this: 'thinking' suggests that in the rest of the text Wordsworth talks to himself *through* Milton in order to psychoanalyze him, whereas 'musing' suggests his attempt to outdo Milton's achievement and thus controvert his transference with Milton's ghost: "For I must tread on shadowy ground, must sink / Deep, and ascend aloft, and breathe in worlds / To which the Heaven of heavens is but a veil" (16–18 [MS]; 28–30 [1814]).[31] One situates the *The Recluse* within epic tradition, the other places both Milton's and Wordsworth's symbolic identities in process/on trial. If Milton does not (read: "cannot") venture *far enough* into his own psyche, then epic must be faulty, which is why Wordsworth asks for a "greater muse." Therefore, the text entertains the interminable psychological process of the poet wandering through the "shadowy ground" of his own thoughts: "from time to time / I find sweet passions traversing my soul / Like music" (2–4). The tension in the subtext between the "inviolate retirement" of "th'individual mind" and its indeterminate activity ("from time to time"), which "consists / With being limitless" (8–10), is only partly attenuated by an appeal to the "one great Life" and to its universal character "Of Truth, of Grandeur, Beauty, Love, and Hope" (6).

Changing "Thinking" to "Musing" (a more formal appeal to classicism?) uses "moral strength" and "intellectual power" to sustain the "the law supreme / Of that Intelligence which governs all" (17, 21–22). It objectifies internal processes by collapsing psychic difference into the monolithic external identity of the "great consummation" (58) between mind and Nature, the prototype of Wordsworth's vision of a community of like minds joined by imagination. As Mary Jacobus writes of this process in the Snowdon episode in Book Thirteen of *The Prelude*, "Positing a mirroring or specular relation between nature and imagination externalizes (and hence manages) the split [between them] as an exterior, consolidating reflection rather than as internal division." The maneuver also serves an anthropomorphic function: "to naturalize (and so to preserve) the human against figuration."[32] I would argue further that anthropomorphism denies psychic interiority by suppressing its autonomous and transferential functioning, setting aside the imagination as a free-associative mechanism. In the manuscript Wordsworth aligns this potentiality with the "soul of man," which is really the work of Fancy, the delirium of associationism that Coleridge sets aside in his theory as a feminine and feminizing threat to imagination.[33] But in Wordsworth's writing the madness of solitude, so integral to the genesis of *The Recluse*, returns as the madness of imagination. And in the Prospectus—its 1814 publication carefully orchestrated to gauge readers' interaction with the radically unfinished gothic body of Wordsworth's *corpus*—the specter of psychoanalysis that haunts the text as a mode of possible interpretation alters in rather fundamental ways how psychoanalysis comes to be invented in Romanticism.

Kant sets aside physiological anthropology as a threat to pragmatic anthropology. The soul's activity is equally problematic for Wordsworth because it de-centers the anthropological identity that secures Wordsworth's aesthetic against its psychological excesses. Soul, or psyche, is neither internal nor external and evokes a complex of opposing forces—intellectual/affective, physiological/psychological, personal/social, conscious/unconscious—rather than a single identity. For Wordsworth the soul is profoundly de-humanizing, the negativity of what Keats calls the "wordsworthian [sic] or egotistical sublime" (*KL* 157).[34] Keats defines this "negative capability" as essential to "poetical Character," which exists as part of an interminable deconstruction of identity within the world as a "'vale of Soul-making,'" which "will not admit of [perfectibility]." "Soul" is the intersection between the intelligence or mind, the heart, and "the *World* or *Elemental space* suited for the proper action of *Mind and Heart* on each other for the purpose of forming the *Soul* or *Intelligence destined to possess the sense of Identity*." Specifically, soul-making is a "Place where the heart[, which is the Mind's experience,] must feel and suffer in a thousand diverse ways," reproducing the subject's provisional identity as the absent psychosomatic body of emotional and psychological struggle (249–50).

The archetypal psychology of James Hillman, indebted to a Romantic rethinking of soul as a psychoimaginative rather than theological concept, offers a useful gloss on the psyche's de-humanizing potential. The subject is situated "in the midst of psyche" as an experiential locus rather than as an ego that masters his psychological being, and so the psyche continually displaces anthropological exclusivity. Hillman argues for a "*poetic basis of mind* and a psychology that starts neither in the physiology of the brain, the structure of language, the organization of society, nor the analysis of behavior, but in the processes of imagination." Both heterogeneous and destabilizing, this imaginal process is mobilized by pathology and personification. Substantially different from anthropomorphism, personification, which "[*saves*] *the diversity and autonomy of the psyche from domination by any single power*," respects the imagination as a mutating or pathologizing function, its "autonomous ability to create illness, morbidity, disorder, abnormality, and suffering in any aspect of its behavior and to experience and imagine life through this deformed and afflicted perspective." Locke and Hume would have been horrified. Through this process, "body and soul lose their borders, neither more literal or metaphorical than the other," so that the subject exists as a "fantasy system of complexes, symptoms, tastes, influences and relations, zones of delight, pathologized images, trapped insights."[35] This "fantasy system" suggests a parallel between fantasy, fancy, and the madness of imagination that Wordsworth and Coleridge would redress.

Whereas the manuscript of the Prospectus explores the imagination's dehumanizing potential, the 1814 text struggles against it, anthropomorphizing imagination as a "dread Power! / Whose gracious favour is the primal source / Of all illumination" (100–2). For instance, in the later text Wordsworth contemplates the mind's workings as part of an objective psychic tableau: "I oft perceive / Fair trains of imagery before me rise, / Accompanied by feelings of delight" (2–4). He remains "conscious of affecting thoughts / And dear remembrances, whose presence soothes / Or elevates the Mind, intent to weigh / The good and evil of our mortal state" (6–9). In the manuscript, however, inherent psychic morality becomes instead threatening psychic autonomy:

> The darkest Pit
> Of the profoundest hell, night, chaos, death,
> Nor aught of blinder vacancy, scoop'd out
> By help of dreams, can breed such fear and awe
> As fall upon me often when I look

> Into my soul, into the soul of man —
> My haunt, and the main region of my song. (23–29)

The "soul of man," more terrifying than the "blinder vacancy" of the unconscious, breeds the psychosomatics of fear and awe within the "haunt" of the text's millennial vision. As a poet who "must tread on shadowy ground," Wordsworth is "in part a fellow-citizen, in part / An outlaw, and a borderer of his age" (16, 69–70). He is poised to emerge "unalarmed" (23) into the dark psychology of his vision, the frontier where psychoanalysis and philosophy converge.

The 1814 text changes "soul" to "Mind," anthropomorphizing the 'shadowy soul' as the "genuine [philosophic] insight" of "the individual Mind that keeps her own / Inviolate retirement, subject there / To Conscience only, and the law supreme / Of that Intelligence which governs all" (88, 19–22). Instead of wedding heterogeneous "minds" to "this outward frame of things," Wordsworth proposes marrying the "discerning intellect" to "this goodly universe / In love and holy passion" (38–39, 52–54). And upon the shapeless "region" of his "song," he imposes the doctrinal shape of "high argument":

> How exquisitely the individual Mind
> (And the progressive powers perhaps no less
> Of the whole species) to the external World
> Is fitted; and how exquisitely, too—
> Theme this but little heard of among men—
> The external world is fitted to the mind;
> And the creation (by no lower name
> Can it be called) which they with blended might
> Accomplish. (63–71)

The "creation" of solitary poetic vision is the *fitting* or *blending* of a "great consummation" (58) that elides imagination's transferential power as dialectic. This resolves the "madding passions mutually inflamed" within the "tribes / And fellowships of men" into the "holy passion" of universal man and synthesizes "Man" and "Nature" to produce "Human Life" (73–75). Hence, the heterogeneous "human soul of the wide earth" (55) in the MS. is replaced by the transcendental ego of the "human Soul of universal earth, / Dreaming on things to come" (84–85). Moreover, "the human Soul" suppresses transference as anthropomorphism. *This* Soul places the individual dreaming subject under a "dread Power, the primal source of all illumination," producing one "Vision" (98) that erases Wordsworth's transference with Milton.

By objectifying the psychology of "Thinking in solitude," Wordsworth represses the psychosomatic identity of the *anthropos* he constructs. This affective subject's "fear and awe," like the empiricism of Margaret's body, lacks definite contours. Whereas in the manuscript Wordsworth promises to probe the soul, in 1814 he asks for "A gift of genuine insight" so that his "Song" might secure "its place" "from all malevolent effect / Of those mutations that extend their sway / Throughout the nether sphere!" (88–93). Like Locke and Hume, Wordsworth sets aside the mind's "mutations" within a "nether sphere." This shift refigures poetic vision's "growth of common day" as "A simple produce," exchanging psychic proliferation for aesthetic containment (40, 55). Therefore, the 1814 text addresses the "personal form" rather than the manuscript's "forms of the imagination's activity" (32, 20). The limitless psychology of "profoundest hell, night, chaos, death" becomes in 1814 the Miltonic cosmography of "Chaos" and "the darkest pit of lowest Erebus" (35–36), the unconscious classicized and aestheticized by an epic metapsychology.[36]

The later Prospectus defines the mind rather than imagines it as soul. Soul finds identity through self-discovery; its organicism *breeds* within a limitless potential rather than *bredes* the mind as a static object of aesthetic contemplation. Mind works by a process of self-enlightenment to produce a stable *cogito* separated from the "nether sphere" of what it refuses to confront within itself. Whatever range of feeling is provoked by the imagination is closed off to leave what is "Pure, and with no unpleasing sadness mixed." And the imagination's psychosomatic body is intellectualized within a type of theoscientific empiricism idealized for its "moral strength" and "intellectual Power." In his note to "The Thorn," Wordsworth writes that "poetry is passion," but passion as the "history or science of feelings" (*WP* 701), and in his 1802 addition to the 1800 Preface to *Lyrical Ballads* he anthropomorphizes poetry's "spontaneous overflow of powerful feelings" as "the impassioned expression which is in the countenance of all Science" (701). Science's "solitude" is then yoked to the Poet's "song," "in which all human beings join with him, [rejoicing] in the presence of truth as our visible friend and hourly companion."[37] The "infinite complexity of pain and pleasure" produced by poetry becomes instead "the breath and finer spirit of all knowledge," the finding of "similitude in dissimilitude," that closes off the abstract philosophy of the poetic mind to the psychosomatic body of its poetry (738–40).

The 1814 text replaces psychology with anthropology to produce a static subject. The psyche's dynamism is stabilized by intellect, and self-exploration becomes collective contemplation ("*we* look / Into our Minds"). This social science of the mind, like Kant's pragmatic anthropology, closes off the mind's deconstruction by diverting the threat of the other *within* the subject. But Wordsworth's attempt to systematize interiority within an epic vision of the mind gets sidetracked. Emphasizing the radical nature of the second, antithetical movement of how Nature is fitted to the Mind ("Theme this but little heard of"), Wordsworth disrupts their dialectical synthesis. The texts we have examined so far call for another analysis, their primal scene remaining the madness of solitude, the fear of being alone with one's own mind. The Prospectus searches for an image of the mind that will suffice, a prototype for Wordsworth's psychological entry to *The Recluse* in *The Prelude*. But this work of "single and determined bounds" threatens to proliferate, "like the overflowing Nile" (*P* 6.548), into an interminable psychoanalysis.

The Prelude Interminable: 1799

There are, we know, at least four different *Preludes*: two parts (1799), five Books (1804), thirteen Books (1805), and fourteen Books (1850). Always under revision, *The Prelude* seems compelled to speak its own psychology as a kind of ongoing closet psychodrama. The poet uses the text's clinical space to work-through trauma, leaving it to reenter the public domain through other, less personal texts. The earliest drafts and fragments for the two-part *Prelude*, contained in MS. JJ, were written in 1798, the year after Wordsworth's first version of "The Ruined Cottage" and before the 1800 Prospectus. Reading the Pedlar's "moral life" as speaking "perpetual logic to his soul" rather than indicating madness, Wordsworth recasts his biography as his own in order to introduce the reader to *The Recluse*'s future author.[38] Beginning *The Recluse* as personal history, however, *The Prelude* is likewise haunted by that poem's psychic past, except that now the primal scene of *The Prelude* lies in aberrations within Wordsworth's *own* mental development signified by various traumas: the deaths of his parents; the death of the social Father in the Reign of Terror and Wordsworth's subsequent breakdown; and most specifically for the present discussion, Coleridge's psychic disappearance. "To fix the wavering balance of [his] mind" (*P* 1.650) after the French Revolution, Wordsworth calls upon Coleridge. But by figuring Coleridge as an absent screen, Wordsworth ultimately abjects the Romantic psychoanalysis of his own imagination. Bollas writes that the analyst develops in himself not only the capacity for self-exploration but the capacity of the "self-analytic element," the "ability to receive news from within the self only on its own terms" rather than by those imposed externally—philosophical, psychological, even metapsychological.[39] What Wordsworth hears from within himself, which he would describe and explain in the first instance, he would ultimately make answerable to an external reality. The one exception to this rule, as we shall see, is the case of the Dream of the Arab in Book Five, where Wordsworth evolves the capacity to let the inner life stage itself on its own terms.

The Prelude is a personal case history preceding *The Recluse*'s social history, the psychological foundation for a philosophical edifice. It sets the stage for a larger systematization by evolving its own metapsychology for the growth of the poet's mind. This apparatus formalizes various mechanisms—dreaming, conversation, transference, the free association of poetic vision and reverie—and tropes—the dream itself, the couch, the spots of time as primal scenes—that we have encountered in one form or another so far in Wordsworth.[40] At times, and especially in Wordsworth's later revisions to the poem, this formalization is more aesthetic, at the most psychotherapeutic, than psychoanalytical. It defines Wordsworth's history within the framework of his dialogue with Coleridge, but this exchange seems more like philosophical contemplation. Wordsworth orchestrates his life *for* Coleridge more than he solicits his auditor's interpretation, retreating into the aesthetic rationality of his own solitary moral instruction by Nature. The scene of this instruction works not by transference but by "imagination" (13.166), which produces "clearest insight" and "amplitude of mind." Wordsworth personifies this as "reason in her most exalted mood," which produces a vision of "life endless, the one thought / By which we live, infinity and God" (13.183–84). By locating psychic self-observation within the Prospectus' contemplative framework, Wordsworth reconstructs psychology as metaphysics, the psyche as "majestic intellect" (*1850* 14.67) and "sovereign voice" (10.183). More doctrinal than heuristic, the text's psychic economy is subsumed by an aesthetics that closes off the cognition of the psyche as a developing and developmental, rather than fixed, identity. Moreover, while he idealizes reason's feminine form, at the same time he is careful to offload her excess as women's work 'up there,' just in case something goes wrong, a tactic of Romantic psychoanalysis we shall explore in greater detail in Chapter Five.

But in other respects the poem's philosophy *is* unsettled by its psychology. *The Prelude* is insistently self-fashioning, in terms of its self-writing content and its generation from earlier drafts and fragments, both biographical and autobiographical, and its circulation among friends and family, in manuscript and through letters and recitations. This economy suggests the mobility of Wordsworth's textual personae and the evolution of a certain self-idiom for working-through relations with psychic objects. Dialogue constellates this changeable narrative scene as a shifting scene of analysis. Wordsworth's developmental paradigm, anchored metadiscursively and metaphysically through the "spots of time" passage in Part 1 of the 1799 text (1.288–327) and the "infant babe" passage in Part 2 (2.267–310) is contested by the interminability of telling "who he was." Wordsworth's increasingly conservative revisions to the text from 1805 onward thus signal his reaction *against* the radical implications of psychoanalysis in his early writings. But the trauma of his inability to remember himself signifies an unsettling psychic ontology, his inability to master "who he is." His ongoing revisions are thus symptomatic of a subjectivity on trial/in process inscribed within the origins of the poem as a two-part structure. In the 1799 text, Wordsworth experiences the "vacancy" between the past and present as a "tranquillizing spirit" that presses on his "corporeal frame" and that is associated with imagination (2.25–28). In "Tintern Abbey" he will turn to this spirit for "Abundant recompense" to lighten "the burden of the mystery" (*WP* 88, 38). Yet the psychic exertion of this unconscious force agitates the heterogeneous and psychosomatic complex of his identity at the same time that it tranquillizes this body through philosophy. The past "days," otherwise absent to his conscious intellect, "yet have such self-presence in [his] heart" that he *seems* to exist as "Two consciousnesses—conscious of [himself], / And of some other being" (*1799* 2.27–30). Wordsworth's anthropology is here unsettled by a protopsychoanalytic dialogue between self and (self-as-)other, his personification of his psychic interior as a mutated and alien presence "disowned by memory," a "stranger" amid "No body of associated forms" (1.405, 445, 406). As the narrative of a split subject, the poet confronted by the darkness of what he cannot intuit, *The Prelude* is Wordsworth's most explicit confrontation with psychoanalysis.

The 1799 text begins as if to analyze the moment of reverie bypassed at the beginning of "The Ruined Cottage" as the gap between a psychic past and his present ambivalence:

> Was it for this
> That one, the fairest of all rivers, loved
> To blend his murmurs with my nurse's song,
> And from his alder shades and rocky falls,
> And from his fords and shallows, sent a voice
> That flowed along my dreams? (1.1–6).

The question catches the poet free-associating *in medias res.* The antecedent for "this," repeated twice more (6, 17), is never stated. The text reverts to an origin that can only exist in the future of its self-exploration, a stream of consciousness or "ceaseless music" (9) that is genealogical rather than teleological.[41] This "steady cadence" composes the poet's "thoughts," but his insight is only in "dim earnest" (1.10, 11, 14).

The question also appeals to Coleridge, who is "More deeply read in [his] own thoughts" (2.249–50) than Wordsworth. But his authority is the illusion of the Lacanian *sujet supposé savoir*, a screen to whom Wordsworth addresses his self-questioning. Coleridge is thus praised as the analyst who "has sought / The truth in solitude" (2.505–6), but Wordsworth also teaches him to "know / With better knowledge how the heart was framed / Of him [he] lovest" (1.456–58). Wordsworth needs Coleridge's knowledge to learn more about himself in order to teach Coleridge more about Wordsworth. This is Wordsworth's projective identification with Coleridge, but certainly also a countertransference badly in need of self-analysis. Wordsworth distinguishes Coleridge's traumatic development in the "great city, 'mid far other scenes" (2.497) from his own normative evolution in nature. Wishing Coleridge "the quiet of a healthful mind" (2.510), he projects his own fears in solitude onto the other's mental anxiety, amplified in *1805* when he describes Coleridge as "too weak to tread the ways of truth" (13.431).[42] But Wordsworth also reads as "impotent" his own "desire" that self-knowledge will lead "[t]o honourable toil" (*1799* 1.451–54). This further casts doubt on the past he would make a "visible scene" (1.463) in order to secure this self-knowledge.

The dialogue with Coleridge, then, becomes an indeterminate *exchange* of analytical knowledge and identities that, as the poem evolves, Wordsworth tries to control. He wants to maintain lyric autonomy, but he *needs* Coleridge to hear (as much as to *over*hear) his self-questionings, "to fix the wavering balance of my mind," he adds in 1805 (1.690).[43] Conversation or dialogue, like narrative, calls for the other within this self-image. Differentiating Romantic narrative from lyric, Rajan argues that the former evokes a "kind of mirror stage in which the [latter's] search for a unified self-representation is enacted and called into question," "the displacement of the self into an objective world that will disclose it as other than itself."[44] Karen Weisman associates this de-idealized lyric utterance with transference, which is "never 'what' is heard . . . [but] is *how* hearing is experienced" ("the soul— / Remembering how she felt, but what she felt / Remembering not retains an obscure sense / Of possible sublimity"). Romantic lyric consciousness suggests "the curative possibilities of transferential exchange," which in Freud create "a process that happens between *essentially* rational creatures, one of whom is seeking to reconstitute . . . a [Kantian] moral law within, and one of whom (the doctor) seeks to hear the fragments of its dispersed body." Weisman calls this the "sound of rational thought."[45] I would argue that Wordsworth hears the sound of "internal thought / Protracted among endless solitudes" (*P*

5.145–46), a reason that lies "couched" in the "blind and awful lair / Of . . . madness" (5.151–52). Coleridge is the text's silent presence because Wordsworth does not want to hear his own thinking projected in Coleridge. What he does not want to hear, that is, is the sound of the Mariner or of Christabel, a spontaneous overflow of feeling that exceeds, as we shall see in the next chapter, the "language really used by men."

Resisting his internal voice, Wordsworth retells his past as a commentary or metadiscourse that erases difference and rewrites lyric as what Rajan calls "the absence of narrative, constituted on the trace of what it does not tell." But this metadiscourse is often more self-observational than contemplative, more conversational and narrative than lyric. This search for an image of the self also requires an "expansion of lyric, a mode that embodies desire in the world."[46] The text reads as sessions recounting "moments [that] chiefly seem to have their date / In our first childhood" (*1799* 1.295–96) and that record the progress of psychic life. These episodes evolve a series of interpretations meant to gather the force of doctrine that will shape the re-telling of "days / Disowned by memory." These "spots of time / Which with distinct preeminence retain / A fructifying virtue" (1.288–90), anchor free association in self-interpretation and metapsychology and figure the imagination's work as metaphysics rather than psychology.[47] Yet as self-contained lyrics they are conflicted by an unconscious that keeps "breaking in upon the unity" of Wordsworth's "argument," disrupting the text's forward trajectory (1.253–54). The descriptions of woodcock snaring (1.27–49) and hanging above the raven's nest (1.50–66), for instance, mark "Low breathings coming after [him], and sounds / Of indistinguishable motion," and winds that blow "strange utterance" (47–48, 64). If "the mind of man is fashioned and built up / Even as a strain of music," there is also trouble in the poet's "favored being," figured within Wordsworth's commentary as an ambivalence between "gentle visitation" and "severer interventions" (1.67–79).[48]

In the boat-stealing episode (1.81–129) Wordsworth seems to examine the mind's "troubled pleasure" (1.91). Memory becomes "a living thing" that works "with a dim and undetermined sense / Of unknown modes of being" (1.113, 121–22). Wordsworth confronts this otherness as "solitude, / Or blank desertion," which is "the trouble of [his] dreams" (1.123–24, 129). By not anthropomorphizing this force ("huge and mighty forms that do not live / Like living men" [1.127–28]), the 1799 text exerts the symptomal force of Wordsworth's unconscious life, the "alien sound / Of melancholy" (1.166–67). On one hand it (re-)produces "characters / Of danger and desire" that "Work like a sea" (1.194–95, 198). On the other, however, it signifies his "unconscious intercourse / With eternal beauty," creating the "first-born affinities that fit / Our new existence to existing things / And, in our dawn of being, constitute / The bond of union betwixt life and joy," the heterogeneous sea now directed toward a specific psychic source (1.394–95, 387–90).

By the end of Part 1, Wordsworth refigures associationism as an aesthetic determinism through which the ego appropriates the external world:

> The scenes which were a witness of that joy
> Remained, in their substantial lineaments
> Depicted on the brain, and to the eye
> Were visible, a daily sight. And thus
> By the impressive agency of fear,
> By pleasure and repeated happiness—
> So frequently repeated—and by force
> Of obscure feelings representative
> Of joys that were forgotten, these same scenes,
> So beauteous and majestic in themselves,
> Though yet the day was distant, did at length
> Become habitually dear, and all
> Their hues and forms were by invisible links
> Allied to the affections. (1.429–42)

Association's delirium (in *1805* the "work supposed / Of evil-minded fairies" [618–19]) is ordered by an imagination that is dissociated from the unconscious and given a "beauteous and majestic" purpose, repeating the dialectical movement of the Wordsworthian imagination described by Hartman.[49] But memory's "obscure feelings" also evoke its less habitual work, which has "invisible" links to the affections and thus to a psychosomatic real of cognition within the rationality of Wordsworth's postassociationist system.[50]

An autonomous association of ideas divorced from perception produces alien selves that threaten the *cogito* with the force of trauma.[51] Memory produces "archetypes" that "know no decay," "spectacles and sounds to which / [He] often would repair, and thence would drink / As at a fountain" (1.287, 368–70). He is "nourished and invisibly repaired" by this "imaginative power" (1.293–94). Yet memory, like "Follow[ing] his [father's] body to the grave," can also advance in "indisputable shapes" (1.352, 367), an archetype that repeats itself compulsively. These evoke the mind's "independent life" (286), which is perhaps why the text figures the past as "Rememberable," yet "lifeless . . . and doomed to sleep" until it is awakened procreatively by the imagination's conscious will: "Until maturer seasons [call it] forth / To impregnate and to elevate the mind"

(1.420, 424–26). In the 1805 passage on the drowned man of Esthwaite, Wordsworth will neither *pathologize* nor *personify* (in Hillman's usage) the imagination's "peculiar" (1.407) functioning. Instead, he aestheticizes what is de-humanizing: "Thence came a spirit hallowing what I saw / With decoration and ideal grace, / A dignity, a smoothness, like the words / Of Grecian art and purest poesy" (5.478–81).

If Part 1 of the 1799 *Prelude* would connect its spots of time in order to legislate memory, Part 2 thematizes this process as a commentary upon psychic origins. But between the terminability of narrative and the interminability of the psyche still lies the problem of connecting "who he was" with "who he is." Wordsworth remembers the "first beginning in [his] thoughts to mark / That sense of dim similitude which links / Our moral feelings with external forms" and argues that his "soul would send a longing look" to the "Fair scenes" that guide his moral education (2.163–65, 168–69). But he is mesmerized by the soul's work in greeting the past, which "held [him] like a dream": "these words / Were uttered in casual access / Of sentiment, a momentary trance / That far outran the habit of my mind" (2.214, 175–78). Wordsworth now questions the genetic images or "habit" of his mind's associationism: "Who knows the individual hour in which / His habits were first sown even as a seed? / Who that shall point as with a wand, and say / 'This portion of the river of my mind / Came from yon fountain'?" (2.245–49). To whom is Wordsworth addressing this question? Coleridge? Himself? Us? The gestalt of the question, the powerful affect of its appeal, produces an experience in the other that uncannily mirrors Wordsworth's own: a missed encounter with the mind's unconscious which throws us back on all that is left: the process of interpretation itself in the midst of a profound unknowing. When in the 1805 text Wordsworth calls upon "Imagination" as the "overflowing Nile" that "hides" the mind's identity within a semiotic "access of joy," he speaks of "infinitude," of "something evermore about to be" (6:547–48, 539, 542). The imagination's "unfathered vapour" possesses a sublime "strength / Of usurpation" that means the ego is clearly not the psyche's master (6.527, 532–33). Such are the implications of this missed insight that in *1850* Wordsworth, *contemplating* the overwhelming autonomy of what he cannot apprehend within himself, speaks of "beatitude"that "Poured from his fount of Abyssinian clouds / To fertilise the whole Egyptian plain," *tranquilizing* as transcendental imagination the autonomous self-mutation of the psyche (6.613, 615–17).

The 1799 *Prelude* applauds Coleridge's ability to avoid that "false secondary power by which / In weakness we create distinctions" (2.251–52) and mistake them for reality. Coleridge's imagination has intuited the "unity of all" (2.256). But for Wordsworth it is a "plastic power" "at times / Rebellious, acting in a devious mood" (2.411–13). This "first creative sensibility" means that "by the regular action of the world / [His] soul was unsubdued" (2.409–11). But he finds it "Hard task to analyse a soul," for it "hath no beginning" (2.262, 267). He can only give one of his "best conjectures" to "trace / The progress of our being" from the "first / Poetic spirit of our human life"—the archetype of the "[infant] babe who sleeps / Upon his mother's breast" and "Doth gather passion from his mother's eye . . ." (2.268ff). Yet that "Such feelings pass into his torpid life / Like an awakening breeze," leaving "his organs and recipient faculties / . . . quickened," evokes an absent psychosomatic body that is both determined and capable of self-creation (2.274–75, 282–83):

> From Nature largely he receives, nor so
> Is satisfied, but largely gives again;
> For feeling has to him imparted strength,
> And—powerful in all sentiments of grief,
> Of exultation, fear and joy—his mind,
> Even as an agent of the one great mind,
> Creates, creator and receiver both,
> Working in alliance with the works
> Which it beholds. (2.297–305)

This narrative of the developmental self does not fit the "uniform control" (2.307) of lyric totality. The passage constructs identity in embryo as part of a transcendental ego or "one beloved presence," but also makes this ego answerable to the reality principle: "Emphatically such a being lives, / An inmate of this *active* universe" (2.285, 295–96).

By returning to life-telling, the "broken windings" of a "path more difficult," Wordsworth marks this origin as heuristic and provisional (2.318–19). Narrative breaks lyric's illusion of autonomy, the "gravitation and the filial bond / Of Nature," to record an "intercourse of touch," "mute dialogues with [his] mother's heart" (2.293–94, 312–13). In the mirror stage between self and mother as transformational object, the "Great birthright of our being" (2.316) becomes a transferential exchange through which the subject enters his absent psychosomatic identity.[52] From this self-alienation "a trouble came into [his] mind / From obscure causes," "yet the building [of his psyche] stood, as if sustained / By its own spirit" (2.321–26). Whereas the Pedlar's solitude threatens madness, the subject here threatens interminability as Wordsworth questions how to "trace the history, where see / The origin of what [he] . . . felt" (2.395–96). The skepticism turns him inward, wherein he "forgot / The agency of sight, and what [he] saw / Appeared like something in [himself], a dream, / A prospect in [his] mind" (2.398–401). Processed through the associative mind, the external world grows "darker in the presence" of the "auxiliar light" of the mind (2.423, 417). The 1805 *Prelude* will refer to this as the "strength / Of usurpation . . . / . . . when the light of sense / Goes out in flashes that have shewn to us / The invisible world" (6.532–35). This "Creative agency" is an "interminable building reared / By observation of affinities" (6.431–33). The terminability of contemplating the "one life" (6.460), the 'building' of his psyche as a fixed structure, remains conflicted by the interminability of its unconscious functioning and thus of narrative telling, a building that remains unfinished.

The Prelude Terminable: 1805 to 1850

The 'glad preamble' to Book One of the larger *Prelude* (1–54) glosses over the conflict between terminability and interminability by offering a blueprint of the mind's visionary awakening. This pattern moves dialectically between Wordsworth's temporal predicament and the infinity of imagination. But the passage is also framed as a potential, yet reluctant, scene of psychoanalysis between Wordsworth and Coleridge: "Thus far, O friend . . ." (55 ff.). Like the "blessed Babe" passage, the preamble supplies a missing origin. But it also reproduces the 1799 split between consciousness and the unconscious, philosophy and psychoanalysis, metadiscourse and narrative. The later text appears to begin in psychic health. Wordsworth sheds the "burden" of his "own unnatural self" (1.23). He is now "free, enfranchised and at large" (1.9). But his "clearer insight" is disturbed by "Trances of thought and mountings of the mind" (1.20). The "gentle breeze" that personifies Wordsworth's renascence is met by the "correspondent mild creative breeze" or "vital" potentiality of his psyche. But this internal force becomes "A tempest, a redundant energy / Vexing its own creation," the spectral unconscious of the external breeze's half-consciousness. Inspiration is also tied to irritability, a psychosomatic conflict of the "breeze" against and within the "body" that registers the imagination's symptomal power. Wordsworth greets it as "a power / That does not come unrecognized" because it suggests "vernal promises" of "some work / Of glory, . . . forthwith to be begun" (1.46–48, 50, 84–85). Has the analysis ended or is it just beginning? He lies down on "the genial pillow of the earth" (1.88) or "soft couch" (*1850* 1.86) and is back at the start of "The Ruined Cottage." He is "couched" (*1805* 1.78) between self-revelation and self-mystification. Pulled from other poetic themes toward "Some tale from [his] own heart, more near akin / To [his] own passions and habitual thoughts," he finds that the "fabric" of this endeavor "seems to lack / Foundation, and withal appears throughout / Shadowy and insubstantial" (1.221–28). He cannot absorb into the rationalism of a larger aesthetic economy the inscrutability of the mind that the imagination places before him (even the later 1850 version describes how "the unsubstantial structure melts / Before the very sun that brightens it" [1.225–26]). Finally, he begins, again, the work of retrospection, bringing his past identity forward to meet a future self by returning to the two-part text as the primal scene of his inability adequately to contain the earlier text's threat of free association.

But as Wordsworth expands the earlier text, the projected work of memory works against the teleology of the "Wisdom and spirit of the universe" (1.429). The prolonged encounter with memory only exacerbates a repetitiveness that returns him to the unconscious of his imagination, the "solitude, / Or blank desertion" that is the "trouble of [his] dreams" (1.422–23, 426) preventing the mind's "revival." The longer text thus also magnifies the tension between self-observation and contemplation by contrasting Wordsworth as a *reclining* psychological "sojourner" and a walking philosopher.[53] Upright Wordsworth moves diachronically forward into (his) history. Lying on a "couch," he moves synchronically through the variegations of his psyche by blanking out the external world. The projection of his inner psychodrama onto a cultural stage, however, finds him less able to separate phantasy from reality. Trying to conduct an analysis while walking through the phenomenal world interferes with one's psychic reconstruction of it, so that the trauma of empiricism conflates with the trauma of analysis. Two episodes play out this split in the text: the dream of the Arab in Book Five and Wordsworth's account of the Reign of Terror and his subsequent psychological breakdown in Book Ten. The dream analyzes the poet's unconscious life but is left suspended as an abject interpretation of dreams within the text's egotistical sublime. The later episode turns outward to the culture that precipitated Wordsworth's breakdown. It attempts to analyze civilization and its discontents by projecting the psyche on the epic scale of political revolution. Politics gets (con)fused with analysis, the march of history with the psyche's evolution. The split is between psychoanalysis and the social anthropology that (according to the Prospectus) Wordsworth would have his work become. Finally, by projecting madness onto the Reign of Terror, Wordsworth subsequently distances his psychic origins into the primal *cultural* scene of a Druidic past in his experience on Salisbury Plain.

At the beginning of Book Five Wordsworth argues that "Even in the steadiest mood of reason" he "grieves" for the "state" of "man" (5.1, 3). This grief becomes symptomatic of reason's excess, a negativity both within and beyond reason, associated with 'moods' rather than the intellect, with passion as opposed to "highest reason in a soul sublime" (5.40).[54] The 1850 text will subdue this excess through "Contemplation," which "sends deep / Into the soul its tranquilizing power" and is only "sometimes" disrupted by the poet's mourning for what disturbs him psychically (5.1–4). The difference between these stances suggests at large Wordsworth's desire to contain the unconscious of the dream, although the dream also marks a culmination of sorts of the larger text's psychoanalysis. "Hitherto / In progress through this verse" Wordsworth has addressed the humanized and humanizing "intercourse" of man with Nature, the "speaking face of earth and heaven" and his "prime teacher" (*1805* 5.10–13). Governing this relationship is the "Sovereign Intellect" (5.14), image of the *anthropos* as transcendental ego. The reflection of this participation in the "soul divine" in man's "commerce of [his] nature with [itself]," however, produces self-alienation, imaged in the fact that man's self-created "Things worthy of unconquerable life" "must perish" (5.16–21). Thus asking why "hath not the mind / Some element to stamp her image on / In nature somewhat nearer to her own?" (5.44–46), Wordsworth looks inward to the unconscious through the dream of the Arab. Implicitly expecting to find there an immortality that would secure the *cogito*'s psychic moorings, he also places the "Sovereign Intellect" on trial/in process as a *de*humanized as well as humanizing force.

The prologue to the dream is structured as dialogue, during which Wordsworth "give[s] utterance" to his self-doubts "in hearing of a friend" who has "Yielded to kindred hauntings." Their transference yields a mesmerizing of reason: "Sleep seized him and he passed into a dream" (5.49–70). Moreover, in a rare gesture in *The Prelude* the friend speaks as analyst of Wordsworth's self-questionings, though by offering the dream *as* interpretation rather than actually interpreting it. Like the Discharged Soldier of Book Four, the Bedouin appears surreptitiously at the dreamer's side and is engaged in conversation. Whereas the poet both solicits and recounts the soldier's "history" (4.441), however, the dreamer relinquishes analysis to the Arab, who emerges as if to answer the friend's "Distress of mind" (5.74) within the dream. Their conversation places Wordsworth's walking or contemplative identity on the couch by spectrally mirroring Wordsworth's resistance to the psychology of his reclining stance and thus to Coleridge's analytical presence. This return of the text's repressed psychoanalysis refigures his free-associative identity in *1799* ("characters / Of danger and desire" that "Work like a sea") as the "unknown tongue" of the shell that "foretold / Destruction to the children of the earth / By deluge now at hand" (5.94–99). In the Reign of Terror this deluge will become a "devouring sea" (9.4) that the Arab identifies in the "glittering light" as "'the waters of the deep / Gathering now upon us'" (5.129–31).[55] That this "deluge" is also a "prophetic blast of harmony," and thus associated with transcendence, is challenged by the dream's free-association of identities, wherein the Arab and Don Quixote become "neither" and "both at once," just as, waking in "terror," the dream of the sea merges with the actual "sea before [him]" (5.96, 126, 137–38).

Wordsworth's reaction to the dream is ambivalent. Professing his "reverence" for the Arab's psychic experience, he also humanizes him as a "living man" (5.150, 143). In this conscious manner he has imagined the "semi-Quixote" "Protracted among endless solitudes," so that in this "blind and awful lair / Of such a madness" he finds reason "couched" (5.142, 146, 151–52). Even in his "sober contemplation of the approach / Of such great overthrow" he can sympathize with "that maniac's anxiousness" (5.157–60). In Wordsworth's ensuing commentary on the dream (5.166 ff.), however, he distances himself from this self-observation of his psyche by consigning its potential madness to the "nether sphere" of the text's untold spots of time:

> That portion of my story I shall leave
> There registered. Whatever else there be
> Of power or pleasure, sown or fostered thus—
> Peculiar to myself—let that remain
> Where it lies hidden in its endless home
> Among the depths of time. (5.193–98)

Instead, he dedicates himself again to the anthropology of "Nature's self / And things that teach as Nature teaches" (5.230–31). Finally, his 1839 revisions to the poem appropriate the dream as his own, its psychic threat safely immured from his later "maturer" selfhood. But he also thus claims the dream's unconscious, exposing his psychic interior to an analysis that he cannot seem to avoid.

In Book Nine of *The Prelude*, written, like most of the latter half of the 1805 text, in Coleridge's absence, Wordsworth enters upon a sustained analysis of his own psychological turmoil during the French Revolution. Here, he projects the madness of his dream across a cultural screen and onto Coleridge. Then, seeing the reflection of his own most disturbing psychic otherness, he abjects its psychological implications by rewriting the primal scene of the self as a return to a more distant past that evokes the nation's cultural prehistory, Wordsworth himself remaining "as far as angels are from guilt" by "Looking as from a distance on the world / That moved about [him]" (10.127, 9.23–24). Wordsworth's Revolutionary idealism takes "The attraction of a country in romance"

(10.696), a reverie writ large on the social stage. As a sign of his later conservatism, he avoids Britain's response to Revolution as a "Reality too close and too intense" (10.641) and tends to aestheticize the experience as "chivalrous delight" (9.503) or the "obscurity [of] a tragic tale" (10.550). But he tells his "own history" (10.658) as if suspended in a mesmeric trance in which Enlightenment insight is the cause of trauma: "Reason seemed the most to assert her rights / When most intent on making of herself / A *prime enchanter* to assist the work / Which then was going forward in her name" (10.697–700; my italics). A "universal ferment" (10.165) threatens the mind of "Reason" in the Reign of Terror. Even characters in the romance, like Vaudracour, "breaking down in heart and mind," end up in the madness of solitude, "Cut off from all intelligence with man," "wasted, an imbecile mind" (10.751, 929, 935). Wordsworth removed the story of Vaudracour and Julia after 1805, of course, as an account too close to his relationship with Annette Vallon. But this purging only serves to highlight within the text's life-telling a psychoanalytic romance that, with its separate publication in 1820, becomes formal romance.

The irony is that, in its absence, we proceed more quickly to Wordsworth's own breakdown, so that the teller/analyst is turned back into the suffering analysand. Book Ten recounts the "ravage of this most unnatural strife / In [Wordsworth's] own heart" (10.250–1). He is an "uninvited guest / Whom no one owned" as Britain's declaration of war against France breaks the spell of his idealism and leaves him with a "conflict of sensations without name" (10.272–73, 265). This absent psychosomatic body of feeling at war with itself compels him to "speak bare truth, / As if to [Coleridge] alone in private talk" (10.371–72). The scene of analysis that emerges brings him closest to disclosing his encounter with the irrationality of his unconscious, unmasking himself to Coleridge as a "soul / to thee unknown" (10.200–1). He has "ghastly visions . . . of despair, / And tyranny" to leave his "brain confounded" and create a "sense / Of treachery and desertion" in his "own soul" (10.374–80). But his history is too closely associated with that of the "goaded land waxed mad" in which "the crimes of the few / Spread into the madness of the many" (10.312–13). Confusing the reason of "eternal justice, thus / Made manifest" in Robespierre's death with his own "vengeance," he offers us a "madness . . . declared and visible" rather than an encounter with his own madness (10.540–41, 274, 550). Now "swept away" in "Rivers of blood," the return of sanity allows Wordsworth to contemplate "schemes . . . framed more calmly, when and how / The madding factions might be tranquillized, / And . . . / The mighty renovation would proceed" (10.547–56). Where he is "interrupted by *uneasy* bursts / Of exultation," he returns in memory to the "wantonness . . . / Of schoolboys" (10.555–64; my italics). What he remembers, in effect, is Book Two and the "pinnacle of self-deification at the age of seventeen, which is the controlling metaphor of the 1799 *Prelude*. . . ." The madness was only the fancy of adolescence, a prelude to a later maturity. By sublimating psychopathology as social justice, Wordsworth protects the "Sovereign Intellect" from the madness of "a soul in the process of making itself."[56]

Here especially we can read how the later 1850 text, by reinforcing how Reason sublates the earlier text's ambivalent passion for psychology, points to this passion's implicit threat. Before recounting his breakdown, Wordsworth anticipates within "Society's unreasoning herd / A domineering instinct," a "sovereign voice . . . within the soul, / Arbiter undisturbed of right and wrong" (10.168–69, 183–84). This later addition consolidates the earlier text's appeal to "reason's naked self," which validates "self-knowledge and self-rule" (10.817, 819). It also dissociates the intellectual from the "transport of the outward sense," so that history has been "chiefly told / Of intellectual power" (10.187, 42–43). This "resolute mastery" evokes the Kantian "freedom of the individual mind, / Which, to the blind restraint of general laws / Superior, magisterially adopts / One guide—the light of circumstances, flashed upon an independent intellect" (10.821–829). Reborn as a "creative soul" (11.256), he now inserts the "spots of time" passage as a doctrine of the psyche. This allows him to ascribe a monolithic power to the mind as "lord and master" (11.271).[57] He rewrites his inability to reconstruct his "former years" (1.649) as the "mystery of man" (11.328). In 1805 he seems in the midst of the imagination's inscrutability: "The days gone by / Come back upon me from the dawn almost / Of life; the hiding-places of my power / Seem open, I approach, and then they close" (11.333–36). In the final text he contemplates imagination as if from a distance: "the hiding-places of man's power / Open; I *would* approach them, but they close" (12.279–80; my italics). Earlier he "*would* enshrine the spirit of the past" (11.341; my italics); he later actively "enshrin[es] / . . . the Past" (12.284–85) as a dead figure of allegory. The challenge of the earlier "spots of time" passage, to remember "who he was," is now the melancholic object of "who he is." Wordsworth has become the Pedlar: an analyst as elegist whose precise function is to *prevent* the subject from mourning. The "independent intellect" now secure from trauma, Wordsworth can recount his father's death (*1805* 11.344–88; *1850* 12.287–335), perhaps the poem's most traumatic event, without being affected. He climbs Snowdon to feel "chastisement" from "God, who thus corrected [his] desires" (*1805* 11.369, 374). He names death, but does not mourn.

In Book Twelve Wordsworth attempts to shore up the unsettled boundaries of psychological trauma within a kind of metaphysics of Britain's ancient heritage—to merge the subject's history with his culture's archetypal history. Recalling walking at night on "the plain of Sarum" (12.314), he writes: "While through those vestiges of ancient times / I ranged, and by the solitude o'ercome / I had a reverie and saw the past" (12.318–20). Here time is the medium of an unexpected and autonomous return in which the poet "might be discomfited and lost." As he called upon the night, "a midnight darkness seemed to come and take— / All objects from [his] sight" (12.328–29). He 'fancies' that he hears ("how deep the groans!" [12:332]) the "obscurities of time" (12:355) return, or sees in the "mystery of shapes" carved in the ground "With intricate profusion" how the "Druid covertly expressed / Their knowledge of the heavens" (12.340–346). Such evidence embodies psychosomatically the poet's confrontation with the past as a primordial scene at once impossibly distant and uncannily present. Like his time in France as a "country in romance," Wordsworth seems compelled to defuse this confrontation as an "antiquarian's dream" by which the poet is "gently charmed" (12.347–48). The text figures the individual's de-centering return back to his future as a merely beguiling scene of mesmerism from which the subject remains immune. In the next passage, Wordsworth explains how, under the "persuasion" of Coleridge, his mind "exercised / Upon the vulgar forms of present things / . . . / A higher power." This process gave him "sight / Of a new world . . . fit / To be transmitted and made visible / To other eyes, as having for its base / That whence our dignity originates," the ground of an "ennobling interchange / Of action from within and from without" (360–77).

But even this nod to the Prospectus and the Romantic ideology of the mind's binding union with the external world cannot set aside the occult residue of the earlier passage, wherein the subject is left suspended rather than transported/transformed by reverie. The mention of a "new world" suggests that Wordsworth's poetry does not so much return to the past as return the past to an archetypal form it does not otherwise have. This return obliterates the past's potentially defamiliarizing influence as a force beyond the mind's ken. Changes to the 1850 text make the further containment of this still-lingering threat apparent. Here the overdetermined eruption of the past as reverie repeats itself instead as the dream's more coherent interpretation: "Time with its retinue of ages fled / Backwards, nor checked his flight until I saw / Our dim ancestral Past in vision clear" (*1850* 13.318–20). The passage anthropomorphizes time as a body distinctly present rather than troubling to the senses. This body figures the past as "a work . . . / Shaped by the Druids, so to represent / Their knowledge of the heavens" (13.339–41) rather than as hieroglyphics scattered in "intricate profusion," which "covertly expressed" the past. *Representation* rather than *expression* consolidates an alien Druidical past by making it empirically visible rather than psychosomatically felt or heard. No wonder, then, that Wordsworth is now "charmed / Into a waking dream, a reverie" that he can see with "believing eyes" (13.342–44).[58] He can now willingly turn himself over to the past because he has carefully refigured its influence, as if gazed upon by the "open eye of Reason" (12.67). The 1850 text not only "[makes] visible" this "new world"; it reifies it through "fixed laws / Whence spiritual dignity originates" (13.372–73).

Such a shift seems to preempt the dark and inscrutable workmanship of the "brooding soul" (*1805* 13.165) that still threatens the stability of reason in the poem's climactic scene on Mount Snowdon. Again, the 1850 text reins in the immanent dangers of imagination by locating intellectual power, even after all this proliferating growth of the poet's mind, on "the Almighty's Throne" (*1850* 14.187) whereon Reason sits "in her most exalted mood." Once and for all the psychoanalytical stream of consciousness seems to be teleological and unbroken: "we have traced the stream / From darkness, and the very place of birth / In its blind cavern" (*1805* 13.172–74) to "The *feeling* of life endless, the one thought / By which we live, infinity and God" (13.172–74, 183–84; my italics). But even the psychosomatic motility of this "moving soul" (13.171) has to become a "feeding source" (*1850* 14.193); and even then the potentially dehumanizing and semiotic "sound of waters" (*1805* 13.175) that evokes the undercurrent of the mind's self-cannibalization at its supposed origin must in 1850 be further anthropomorphized as a "natal murmur," the telos of which is "Faith in life endless [rather than the 'feeling' of life endless], the sustaining thought / Of human Being, Eternity, and God" (14.196, 204–5). And *beyond even this*, "absolute strength" (*1805* 13.168), still symptomatic of the mind's autonomous will to its own unassimilable power, has to become Reason as a monotheistic "absolute power" (*1850* 14.190). Whereas the Father's absence ("an unfathered vapour") urges an object relations that can never recover the self, Wordsworth now submits for "chastisement" to a transcendental *cogito*. The final solution, that is, is for God to do Wordsworth's thinking for him.

One clearly gets the feeling as well that Wordsworth means to do the reader's thinking *for him*. But the effect of his revisions are startlingly sterile in this respect. Theologized, the unconscious signified by Wordsworth's metapsychology comes to have little cognitive value, except that its erasure comes to signify that much more viscerally in the reader's mind. The developmental pathology generated by the madness of the poet's free-associationism is a missed encounter with psychoanalysis. Or is it? As the narrative of a transference both with himself and with Coleridge, the poem also leaves Wordsworth unsure of who he is. "The true subject of *The Prelude* behind its veil of representation," writes Robert Young, "is the indeterminacy of its subject."[59] In places the poem's psychoanalysis takes us out of its own enlightenment into this indeterminacy, always returning us to the Wordsworthian primal scene of *The Recluse* in "Incipient Madness" and "The Baker's Cart." Such a return makes the 1850 revision less a cure or transformation of past inscrutability than a compulsive repetition of this past's psychosomatic effects in the future of our own present. In Book Four the unconscious rises like "Some fair enchanting image in [the poet's] mind" (*1805* 4.104) and exerts a mesmerizing potential so troubling that *1850* changes "enchanting" to "lovely" and exchanges semiotic motility for epic simile: "like Venus rising from the sea" (4.114). Looking into the pool of his psyche, Wordsworth cannot tell depth from surface, for there is "Something . . . that perplexed / Th' authentic sight of reason" (*1805* 4.295–96). He brackets off this "under-presence" (13.71) by turning poetic vision into a type of gnosticism: "I made no vows, but vows / Were then made for me" (*1805* 4.341–42; *1850* 4.334–35).[60] In *1850* he argues that "Solitude" is "benign" and "Most potent when impressed upon the mind / With an appropriate human centre" (4.356–59). Solitude's "self-sufficing power" (*1799* 2.77) rises again in Book Four, however, in a passage removed from *1850*. Here the psyche's "harmonious imagery" (4.393) rises "As from some distant region of [the poet's] soul":

> And came along like dreams—yet such as left
> Obscurely mingled with their passing forms
> A consciousness of animal delight,
> A self-possession felt in every pause
> And every gentle movement of [his] frame. (4.395–99)

Here the internal reconstitution of the external world repeats itself symptomatically in the poet's and the text's body. Attempting to bring to insight the psyche's associative functioning, Wordsworth encounters its free-associative, transferential logic. The royal road to the unconscious—and thus to Romantic psychoanalysis—is a broken stream of consciousness that leaves us broken subjects in its wake.

In his case of the Wolf-Man Freud submits metapsychology to narrative, which refashions the subject of the primal scene as a phantasy. In the transference *between* subjects, as in the mesmeric trance, the phantasy of the absent psychosomatic body—an idiom where the subject *feels* the experience of the other but cannot *know* it—holds sway. *The Prelude*, like "The Ruined Cottage" before it, is confronted with this transference as the constitutive position of being human. But Wordsworthian analysis is split between Enlightenment and Romantic impulses. The Enlightenment subject reverts to the transcendental imagination because naming the unconscious confronts him with the limits of empiricism. And as imagination moves toward its own idealization as "Reason in her most exalted mood," it subtends a Romantic impulse to liberate the subject from the psychic determinism of the unconscious. However, Romanticism engages with this determinism through a refashioning of its psychic effects as they disrupt the imagination's 'one life.' Romanticism possesses the Enlightenment desire to suture the rift, to sublimate its disruptiveness. But this desire fails to *cure* the soul's body by putting it to rest within an ego located at the center of its world. In Wordsworth the poet is caught between the closure of an enlightened or analyzed subject and what we have been calling the Romantic subject of an analysis interminable. The ambivalence threatens Wordsworth's metapsychology by reproducing the "Sovereign intellect" as the "unsubstantial structure" of a free-associating psyche. Analysis interminable is an idealism without absolutes, a Romantic subject caught between two poles: his metaphysical extension beyond the psyche and the darkness of a collapse of identity that this extension entails. Like Wordsworth's lack of awareness that he had crossed the Alps in Book Six, by writing *The Prelude* he may have written *The Recluse* without knowing it. *The Prelude* analyzes *The Recluse* as the unconscious of the not being said in what Wordsworth was trying to say in *The Recluse*. After conceptualizing *The Recluse*, there was nothing else to think, but everything more to say.

THREE

Analysis Terminable in Coleridge

It is an instinct of my Nature to pass out of myself, and to exist in the form of others.

—Coleridge, notebook entry

It moaned as near, as near can be
But what it is she cannot tell.

—*Christabel*

Coleridge and *The Recluse*

By anthropomorphizing imagination, Wordsworthian philosophy is all the more unsettled by psychoanalytical self-writing. By self-writing I also mean self-making, the writing both of and by the self as part of the creative act, but also, and more crucially, the fact that the subject, by writing the self, *is written* in turn by the imagination's free-association. Self-writing is both active and passive, both possessed by and possessing the subject. For if Wordsworth's examination of the psyche suggests Kant's pragmatic anthropology, Coleridge's interest in the psychosomatic body suggests the return of a physiological anthropology—the autonomous functioning of the subject's 'nature'—within the contemplative domain of the Wordsworthian *cogito*. Both *Biographia Literaria*, Coleridge's uneasy conflation of autobiography and philosophy, and the *Logosophia*, his philosophical magnum opus,[1] are chapters within the ontologically undecidable intertext of *The Recluse*. Insofar as *Biographia Literaria* returns to the scene of his relationship with Wordsworth, that is, it also returns to the *Logosophia*, which in 1814 Coleridge described as his "most important work" (*CL* 3:533).[2] Yet it remained virtually unwritten, an absence more profound than that of *The Recluse*. The *Logosophia* thus evokes within *Biographia* itself a loss of philosophical authority that Coleridge explores in his manuscript writings. The self-observations of Coleridge's *Notebooks* collapse the boundary between poetry and philosophy, experience and theory. Coleridge's specific interest in mesmerism, a recurrent theme of the *Notebooks*, signifies between metaphysics and psychology an overdetermined psychoanalytical inquiry that he both entertains and resists. Yet mesmerism's absent psychosomatic body—the bodies of Christabel or the Mariner—resists interpretation by expressing the imagination as a free-associative rather than transcendental force. Ultimately, then, the self-writing of *The Rime of the Ancient Mariner* and *Christabel* takes us back in Coleridge to the future of psychoanalysis, but a future whose potential for self-exploration is aborted.

The mesmerizing force of psychoanalysis in Coleridge's writings registers symptomatically in Wordsworth's sense of its threat to his philosophical identity. Specifically, he reads in Coleridgean solitude a disruptive unconscious within reason. Describing Coleridge as having "sought / The truth in solitude," Wordsworth also wishes him the "quiet of a healthful mind" that would cure solitude's dis-ease. During Coleridge's absence Wordsworth is left alone with his own mind, which confronts him with his fear of Coleridgean unreason that requires the therapy of his own "meditative history" (*P* 13.418). Wordsworth speaks as one redeemed from madness in the French Revolution by a "strong and sanative" (10.977) philosophical knowledge. He organizes his wandering thoughts into a "ladder for [Coleridge's] spirit to reascend" (10.978). To do so, however, he has to turn Coleridge into a "lonely wanderer . . . , by pain / Compelled and sickness" (10.983–94), a feminized figure of excessive sensibility not unlike Margaret. Wordsworth himself turns to Dorothy who, "speaking in a voice / Of sudden admonition," "Maintained for [him] a saving intercourse / With [his] true self" and "preserved [him] still / A poet" (10.909–19).[3] Wordsworth implicates Dorothy in a psychoanalytical dialogue that, like the Narrator and the Pedlar rationalizing Margaret's madness, finds them undertaking Coleridge's therapy in his absence and thus avoiding contamination by the other. Moreover, Wordsworth doubly sets aside the threat of the feminine by speaking on Dorothy's behalf. He preempts the potential of a psychoanalytic dialogue with Coleridge, or of his consultation with Dorothy, by using the poetry of "pure Imagination" (*1850* 8.423) to do Coleridge's, as well as

Dorothy's, feeling for him. "I feel for thee, must utter what I feel" (10.986), he writes.[4] Yet Wordsworth's feeling *for* the Coleridge he has thus implicitly feminized signals the return of a homosocial transference that his text is unable to repress. Coleridge's madness seems to be Wordsworth's projected fear of his own isolation *from* Coleridge, and thus of psychic aberrancy. In *The Prelude* Coleridge is silent, then, because Wordsworth does not want to hear the sound of his own "internal thought" projected in Coleridge as other.[5]

Wordsworth speaks the anthropological voice of Kantian Reason against the de-humanizing threat of Coleridge's psyche, particularly as expressed in Coleridge's poetry. In the language of *Christabel*, the story of the psyche 'cannot be told,' an aphasic anxiety that recalls the pretext of *The Recluse* in "Incipient Madness" and "The Baker's Cart," both fragments unable to *tell*—that is, both to *speak* and to *understand*—the story of Margaret's psyche. As attempts to construct a hermeneutics of sociophilosophical reparation, "The Ruined Cottage," the Prospectus, and *The Prelude* all subsequently evolve as missed encounters with psychoanalysis. In *The Ancient Mariner* and *Christabel*, however, the unreason of the unconscious suspends reason, collapsing philosophy's terminability into the psyche's interminability. Contemporary with the conception and initial writings for *The Recluse*, they implicitly critique its unrealizable Kantian idea in terms of Coleridge's own desire for a philosophical system in the *Logosophia*. As the interminable life-writing of *The Prelude* signifies Wordsworth's inability to finish *The Recluse*, Coleridge's writings similarly record the stalling of his magnum opus. Written early in his career, *The Ancient Mariner* and *Christabel* signify the unconscious of the philosophical *anthropos*, to which Coleridge responds both through metaphysics in *Biographia Literaria* and the psychology of mesmerism in the *Notebooks*. Coleridge's psychology mesmerizes his metaphysics, however, making it difficult to work-through a *psychophilosophical* or *psychoanalytical* apparatus commensurate with his self-observation. The result is that he seems compelled to return to *Mariner* and *Christabel* as the trauma of his inability to write the *Logosophia*. This chapter will trace the narrative of this return as Coleridge's missed encounter with psychoanalysis.

Biographia Literaria, the *Logosophia* and the Poetry of Philosophy

In "To William Wordsworth" Coleridge writes: "thou hast dared to tell / What may be told, to th' understanding mind / Revealable; and what within the mind / May rise enkindled" (*CP* 6–8). Yet the compulsion in both writers "to tell" confronts what *cannot* be told, the conflict between what the active mind can *reveal* and what is *enkindled* by the mind as the excess of reason.[6] This is the anxiety of Coleridge's "Dejection : An Ode," which suspects that what we "receive" from "Nature" is a "redundant energy" undoing what we create (47–48). For Coleridge, the "shaping spirit of Imagination" (86) is disrupted by its own unconscious as the "part [that] infects the whole" of his being and "now is almost grown the habit of [his] soul" (92–93).[7] Dejection foregrounds as affect the antithetical movement of the Wordsworthian dialectic of imagination—how Nature is 'fitted' to the Mind—by pointing to the 'unfitness' of a Nature internalized by the mind: Nature become *human* nature. Dejection thus implicitly critiques how the Wordsworthian *cogito* avoids psychosomatic interiority as an excess that does not fit within a philosophy of imagination.

Coleridge's plan in the 1790s to write a "gigantic poem on a Miltonic scale" was quickly eclipsed by his joint labor with Wordsworth, which produced *Lyrical Ballads*. According to Coleridge, his portion of the labor was an "interpolation of heterogeneous matter" (*BL* 2:8). Of the composition of *The Ancient Mariner* Wordsworth later refers to himself as impeding the growth of Coleridge's thought: "our respective manners proved so widely different that it would have been quite presumptuous in me to do anything but separate from an undertaking upon which I could only have been a clog."[8] How the poets' individual conceptions of poetry do or do not overlap is not my present concern so much as what remains incommensurable *within* their writing, what it *could not* tell. Wordsworth and Coleridge seem not so much to abandon the unrealizable idea of *The Recluse* as they appear unable to think through the "shadowy ground" of the contemplative "Mind of Man." Whereas in the Prospectus Wordsworth muses upon the "Mind" as a stable object of study, Coleridge addresses it as a dynamic *process*, but remains haunted by the prospect that psychology does not conduct to a higher unity.

As we have seen, *The Recluse* is a metonymy for Wordsworth's desire to invoke a system of thought that imposes its reflective identity on the empiricism of poetic observation, more to clarify the role of philosophy *in* poetry. This is especially true of *The Excursion* (1814), which, instead of offering a philosophy *of* poetry, narrativizes the philosophical life. Coleridge, however, sees philosophy separately, and his admiration of *The Recluse* marks his own desire to write a *philosophical* rather than *poetic* masterwork.[9] His 1815 criticism of *The Excursion* describes a *Recluse* that is as theoretically rigorous as Wordsworth's is poetically ambitious.[10] In this criticism Coleridge's relentless advance toward "Idealism" imposes an intractable Kantian architectonic of reason over the sepulchral recesses of his vision's potential execution. This vision sublimely suspends the reader's, and thus Wordsworth's, ability to contemplate its execution, although one suspects that was Coleridge's intention.

My suggestion here is that Coleridge seems able to articulate the rational *structure* of philosophy, so long as he does not have to contemplate its heterogeneous embodiment. Put another way, in *Biographia Literaria* Coleridge's philosophy of poetry is unsettled by the *poetry of philosophy*.[11] I use this phrase to evoke the conflict between philosophy and psychology that persists in Wordsworth's and especially Coleridge's writing. Philosophy, argues Robert Smith, is essentially autobiographical in that it must tell its own story in order to work-through and eliminate what threatens its "conceptual organization": the chance or contingency that "cannot be accounted for in advance" in the work of reason.

> It is *always possible* that contingency will startle philosophic anticipation; it takes the form of the future and opens historical change. And, being *always* possible, it amounts in its invariant categoriality to a necessary condition or a priori, therefore *also* taking the form of the (absolute) past. As such, any philosophy worth its salt will be obliged to take it, the always possible chanciness of contingency, on board. But paradoxically, doing so brings on the destitution of philosophy: chance, which is necessarily a-philosophical, the limit of reason, is where philosophy runs out; a non-philosophical a priori.[12]

This work of unreason within reason, paradoxically, makes reason possible. To eliminate contingency from its rational operation, philosophy must account for its identity "at the cost of total rational purity." Moreover, to prove itself, philosophy, against its own will, must wait for contingency to erupt in order to eliminate it. The philosophical method thus contains within itself a "certain philosophic unconscious," and philosophy's anthropomorphization, its autobiography or self-identity, is only realized by suppressing the psychic darkness of its embodiment, what Smith calls the *poetics of reason*.[13] This poetics recalls Coleridge's struggle with associationism, which signifies "between the despotism of outward impressions" and "senseless and passive memory" the "mere lawlessness" of a subject without agency, "the absence of all interference of the will, reason, and judgement." Bracketed off as fancy, this "*delirium*" returns to unsettle the primary imagination's transcendence, which exists beyond the "conscious will" and suggests a transpositional subject-in-process (*BL* 1:111).

This contingency returns in Coleridge's struggle with the *poetics of metaphysics*: "*All* metaphysics . . . is in its origin poetic: & in Poe~~try~~sy, that highest in which Phil. & Poetry interpenetrate, & mutually co-inhere it must end" (*CN* 4:4692). The correction of "Poetry" to "Poesy" is telling. In the theory of Poesy, as opposed to poetry's practice, perception, aesthetics, and philosophy are synthesized through imagination, where associative ideas are transformed into the ideal, the SUM that transcends the psyche.[14] The psyche's primary work or primary imagination of the SUM generates thought but does not control it. It installs at the core of imagination reason's darkness, the poetry of philosophy as self-difference rather than self-identity. Coleridge's philosophy of poetry, his metaphysics of imagination, thus finds in what it sets out to theorize a "redundant energy": the free-associative poetry of the psyche. In an 1803 notebook entry Coleridge associates this poetry with an analysis of the interior life: "Seem to have made up my mind to write my metaphysical works, as *my Life*, & *in* my Life—intermixed with all the other events/or history of the mind & fortunes of S. T. Coleridge" (*CN* 1:1515). But his attempt to "define with the utmost impartiality the real *poetic* character of the poet" (*BL* 1:5), then, breeds an uneasy mix of autobiography and philosophy, especially in *Biographia Literaria*.

Coleridge describes the *Biographia* as an "immethodical . . . miscellany" (1:88) that seems to delay its own fulfilment as if to avoid the project he intends to write, the *Logosophia*. The same interminable "motions retrograde" delay *The Prelude*, but despite Wordsworth's endless talking, self-observation never appears to overtake contemplation.[15] Coleridge's *Biographia*, like *The Prelude*, was to effect philosophy's 'cure' as an analysis terminable; but its miscellaneous form suggests an unremedied process of cognition. The text's scene of composition exposes in the ineffectual therapy of reason a conflict between critical contemplation and what Freud, as we have seen, calls the poetic tolerance of free-association. While trying to overcome his opium addiction, Coleridge dictated much of the *Biographia* to his amanuensis, John Morgan. This silent screen liberates Coleridge's psyche from its own empiricism: he can free-associate without having to 'compose' his thoughts through the materiality of writing.[16] But freedom has its price: it alienates Coleridge from himself at the same time that it allows him to work toward intellectual self-definition. The *Biographia* reads like the case history of his attempt to remedy his creative inactivity through writing; but this narrative's lack of organic wholeness produces instead a history of thought's trauma. At the primal scene of this trauma is Coleridge's absent psychosomatic body in a state of opium-induced torpor, a body that infects the intellect in the form of a free-associationism that the text is unable entirely to contain as much as Coleridge seems unable to proceed with writing.

Coleridge partly manages this conflict by projecting onto Wordsworth the inability to impose philosophy's "matter and arrangement" on poetry's body. In an 1815 letter he writes,

> the Poem on the growth of your own mind was as the ground-plat [sic] and the Roots, out of which the Recluse was to have sprung up as the Tree—as far as the same Sap in both, I expected them doubtless to have formed one compleat [sic] Whole, but in matter, form, and product to be different, each not only a distinct but a different Work. (*CL* 4:573)

Coleridge contains *The Prelude* within an organicism that implicitly quarantines that text's psychology, which pictures him as a failed poet, from the philosophy of *The Recluse*, which was partly his brainchild. He tells Wordsworth that "It is hard . . . to confess the whole Truth even of one's Self—Human Nature scarce endures it even *to* one's Self," and that "It is for the Biographer, not the Poet, to give the *accidents* of *individual* Life." He adds: "Whatever is not representative, generic, may be indeed most poetically exprest, but is not Poetry" (*CL* 4:571–72). Poetry must have a *determinate* form; indeed, without philosophy it would not be poetry, at least not of a terminable kind. This seems to be why *The Excursion*'s peripatetic narrative signifies to Coleridge Wordsworth's inability to transcend self-observation and why in the *Biographia* he is dissatisfied with Wordsworth's poetics: "My friend has drawn a masterly sketch of the branches with their *poetic* fruitage. I wish to add the trunk, and even the roots as far as they lift themselves above ground [and] are visible to the naked eye of consciousness" (*BL* 1:88). Philosophy shapes poetry's shapelessness and reveals poetry's internal unity as an unconscious that poetry cannot read. Thus, when Coleridge pits imagination against fancy in Chapter Four and again in Chapter Thirteen of *Biographia Literaria*, he seems to repress the psychological within philosophy.

But the repressed returns. After expounding his work's organic authority in Chapter Four and refuting associationism in Chapters Five to Seven, Coleridge digresses in Chapters Eight and Nine into a case history of philosophy. This narrative moves from Descartes to German Idealism's 'cure' of associationism as if to complete Coleridge's rationalization of Wordsworth's incomplete philosophy of poetry.[17] But the use of narrative becomes problematic, as it was in the case of the woman's nervous fever in Chapter Six and in the "letter from a friend" in Chapter

Thirteen. Interpolating the psychology of self-writing into philosophy foregrounds Coleridge's affective relationship to the writing of the *Biographia*. As his response to Wordsworth's *Excursion* and 1815 *Poems* and Preface, and more distantly to *Lyrical Ballads*, the *Biographia*'s incomplete philosophy is symptomatic of an inability to move beyond Wordsworth's poetry. This sense of melancholy colors the text's more immediate relationship to philosophy, which Coleridge defines as an "affectionate seeking after the truth" (*BL* 1:142). Just before he recounts his debt to German Idealism, and to Kant's "Critical Philosophy, more than any other work," Coleridge writes: "After I had successively studied in the schools of Locke, Berkeley, Leibniz, and Hartley, and could find in neither of them an abiding place for my reason, I began to ask myself; is a system of philosophy, as different from mere history and historic classifications, possible?" (1:153, 140–41).[18] The question raises the specter of the absent *Logosophia*, which promises to answer definitively Coleridge's debate with associationism. But making plans for the future also diverts the reader's attention away from his current text's fragmentary nature. Breaking off Chapter Eight's refutation of materialism, Coleridge says: "I shall not dilate further on this subject; because it will . . . be treated of at large and systematically in a work, which I have many years been preparing, on the PRODUCTIVE LOGOS human and divine" (1:136). He promises a prospectus to the work in Chapter Eight, and again in Chapters Twelve and Thirteen.

Chapter Nine had apparently finished the philosophical case history, after which Coleridge digresses with two autobiographical chapters. Chapter Twelve then marks a return to 'formal' philosophy, except that its overlong ontology digresses yet again from the very transcendental system it promises, further deforming an organic shape the text clearly cannot assume. Chapter Twelve begins with this appeal: "In lieu of the various requests which the anxiety of authorship addresses to the unknown reader, I advance but this one; that he will either pass over the following chapter altogether, or read the whole connectedly. The fairest part of the most beautiful body will appear deformed and monstrous, if dissevered from its place in the organic whole." The chapter's argument states that it will concern itself with "requests and premonitions concerning the perusal or omission of the chapter that follows" (1:232–34). The *following* chapter could be Chapter Thirteen, which largely 'omits' the text's long-delayed theory of imagination, or it could be the ensuing *current* chapter. Either way, Coleridge asks for readers to indulge his philosophy's self-writing, and thus his identity as 'auto-philosopher,' especially given our (by this point) considerable frustration. The text's digressiveness, that is, comes to express philosophy's *desire* more than its reason: the poetry of philosophy reflecting the absence of a coherent identity that Coleridge, by appealing to the reader, models as transference—the desire for the desire of the other—that will somehow complete the text's search for truth. The text's final reference to the *Logosophia* finds the author speaking from the other side of this transference through the fictional letter writer: "Be assured . . . that I look forward anxiously to your great book on the CONSTRUCTIVE PHILOSOPHY, which you have promised and announced: and that I will do my best to understand it" (1:302). The statement constructs a *mise en scène* of textual psychoanalysis that, like the opening of Chapter Twelve, models our countertransference as a struggle to understand the text-as-patient's inability to speak its complete history. Tellingly, the "friend" alludes to "To William Wordsworth" and thus introduces the absent body of *The Prelude* in the form of Coleridge's affective response to its "tale *obscure* of high and passionate thoughts" (1:302)—and beyond this to the absent *Recluse* as the primal scene that Coleridge's current text is compelled to repeat as the idea of the *Logosophia*.[19]

But Coleridge is also asking his universal "PUBLIC" to read the text's part as the promise of its organic whole, to gloss over its deformity, and thus to avoid any psychoanalysis of its ruin. This idealization is the symptom of that other nagging subtext of Coleridge's relationship to his sources, particularly to German philosophy. Although for Coleridge Kant is master, and Schelling (and to a lesser extent Fichte) completes Kant's "revolution in philosophy" (1:163), Coleridge places himself outside the family romance of German idealism by silencing Kant's heirs, as if he alone can manifest its latent truths. "I regard truth as a divine ventriloquist," he writes; "I care not from whose mouth the sounds are supposed to proceed, if only the words are audible and intelligible" (1:164). Now we see why Coleridge belittled his precursors as "*grotesque dwarfs*" (1:301) in Chapter Thirteen. He reads philosophy's unconscious as a determinism he cannot control, speaking a truth for which he then bears little responsibility. This idea of philosophy that speaks its own mind without Coleridge's control produces a rather telling account of his authority as a subject presumed to know—and philosophy's ability to know—the truth of things at the end of *Biographia Literaria*. Coleridge begins the chapter by explaining how criticism that bears little or no relation to the author's work it attacks produces in the author a "dull underpain that survives the smart which it had aggravated" because the "consolatory feeling that accompanies the sense of a proportion between antecedents and consequents" does not exist. The cause is constitutional: "we are so framed in mind, and even so organized in brain and nerve, that all confusion is painful" (2:234). More specifically, however, the psychosomatic effects of the wound are not from the attack itself but from the dissociating effect of an untruth, the way in which it produces symptoms in the otherwise sound body of philosophy.

To explain the symptom, Coleridge turns to medical science:

> It is within the experience of many medical practitioners, that a patient, with strange and unusual symptoms of disease, has been more distressed in mind, more wretched, from the fact of being unintelligible to himself and others, than from the pain or danger of the disease: nay, that the patient has received the most solid comfort . . . from some new symptom or produce that had once determined the name and nature of his complaint, and rendered it an intelligible effect of an intelligible cause: even though the discovery did at the same moment preclude all hope of restoration. (1:234–35)

A form of talking cure alleviates the symptom, the compulsion of the "[a]fflicted to communicate their sorrows" (1:240) that renders symptoms "intelligible" and thus points to philosophy's ability to make sense of the truth in spite of the body's suffering. This is to make sense of the nervous body by what Foucault calls a "transformation into discourse, a technology of power, and a will to knowledge."[20] But Coleridge seems to avoid the increasingly utilitarian imperatives of nineteenth-century medical psychology by looking elsewhere.

Coleridge introduces the example of his poetry, which has been criticized, he writes, for being too "devoted to metaphysics" (*BL* 2:240)—i.e. for not making sense to its readers. His specific example is *Christabel*, composed between 1797 and 1800 but not published until 1816, during which time the text existed in the half-life of its circulation via Coleridge's private recitations. Coleridge goes on to describe the effect of these readings as a psychosomatic suspension of reason inflicted by criticism turned back upon his audience,[21] "a species of Animal Magnetism, in which the enkindling Reciter, by perpetual comment of looks and tones, lends his own will and apprehensive faculty to his Auditors" to create the "excitement and temporary sympathy of feeling" (2:239). But this transference silences by mesmerizing the other within the "dilated sphere of [the Reciter's] intellectual Being" and infecting the other with the poet's "apprehensive faculty" (2:240). This sphere of instruction locates the text's identity in the absent psychosomatic space of the transference between author and audience, suggesting confusion rather than insight, the pathologizing effect of the other that Wordsworth's Prospectus resists.

The scene of philosophy's mesmerism, Coleridge suggests, is poetry. The "dilated sphere" of *Christabel*'s textual history is part of a larger metonymy for his poetic identity constituted by his texts as "an interpolation of heterogeneous matter." Poetry is the absent psychosomatic body of philosophy's contemplative discourse, the desiring other of its search for truth. The end of the *Biographia* seems to want to bring the psychoanalytical exploration of its philosophical unconscious into dialogue with its textual consciousness. The lyric totality of Coleridge's identity as Philosopher is unsettled by philosophy's narrative, which interpolates the autobiography or psychology—and therefore the self-difference—of philosophy as self-writing. This is the voice of transference as the "sound of [Kantian] rational thought," wherein reasoned meditation gives itself over to a self-observation of the truth that is potentially interminable. In *The Ancient Mariner* and *Christabel*, as we shall see, this hearing is experienced irrationally to produce something startling different from a Wordsworthian "language really used by men."

The Body of Mesmerism in Coleridge's *Notebooks*

For all that *Biographia* surrenders its rational self-sufficiency to tell its own story, let alone one without the desire for transcendental authority, the extent to which this shift is any more than symptomatic remains debatable. Coleridge's manuscript explorations of mesmerism, however, tell a different story. Wordsworth notes how in his youth the phenomenal world "sank down / Into [his] heart and held [him] like a dream" (*1799* 1:213–14) to mesmerize his senses, what he later describes as a "conflict of sensations without name" that resists interpretation.[22] By relaxing the discipline of his philosophical idealism, Coleridge's *Notebooks* suggest a cognitive response to this conflict. Between a psyche in motion and a mind musing in solitude at the boundary between mind and body, Coleridge attempts to broach a "dialectic of mind and spirit, the 'polar logic' of nature and mind, objective and subjective" (*BL* l:xxvi). Yet when the psychosomatic wanders with a mind of its own, this mind takes the spectral form of an identity outside yet uncannily linked to the subject, a form that is answered in the *Notebooks* with an emerging psychoanalytical inquiry. They constitute a monumental yet unstable *corpus* that multiplies and changes shape according to the heterogeneous proliferation of Coleridge's self-observations.[23] The notebook entries are what James McKusick, borrowing a term from Coleridge, calls "'scraps,'"[24] fragments of thought which Coleridge intended to work into a larger philosophical coherence but which, like the *Biographia*, stand in for a system his prose does not attain. Writing of history's "pursuit of the origin (*Ursprung*)," Foucault argues that "if the genealogist refuses to extend his faith in metaphysics, if he listens to history, he finds that there is 'something altogether different' behind things: not a timeless and essential secret, but the secret that they have no essence or that their essence was fabricated in a piecemeal fashion from alien forms."[25] The *Notebooks'* "alien forms" suggest a history of the subject that resists metaphysics. They exist between experience and theory, narrative and epistemology, the empiricism of self-analysis and its induction toward self-knowledge. Put another way, in the *Notebooks* psychoanalysis and philosophy, the psychological and the metapsychological, appear to coexist.

Coleridge uses the psychosomatic to think through the Cartesian "*contrariety* of Soul and Body, as Subjects absolutely heterogeneous, each partially definable by negativing the properties of the other," as in the "separation of Psychology from Physiology."[26] Between "the Organic & the Vital," Coleridge addresses "their shadings off & transitions into each other" (*CN* 1:1822) through the passions or feeling. He defines "Passion" as "a state of emotion which, whatever its object or occasion may be, in ourselves or out of ourselves, has its proper and immediate cause not in this, but in our Thoughts respecting it."[27] In this he differs from Wordsworthian feeling, which comprises a form of monumental self-writing, what David Miall, borrowing a term from cognitive psychology, calls an "affective script."[28] This writing operates beyond language to impress rather than to in-scribe a developmental matrix, as in the Infant Babe passage of *The Prelude.* Wordsworthian affect contains a "fundamental paradox," however, in that it is both anticipatory, "something evermore about to be," and atemporal, like memory or like the affective bond of man to the One Life of Nature.[29] Moreover, whereas anticipation can produce anxiety about a contingent future, memory can equally generate a contingency within thought. This pathology of feeling, for instance, arises symptomatically in the drowned man episode, suggesting how an indeterminate psychology of feelings remobilizes a psychosomatic body that Wordsworth cannot repress.

The mind-body complex of feeling is for Coleridge the self's fundamental nature: "By deep feeling we make our *Ideas dim*—& this is what we mean by our Life—ourselves . . . the Feeling is deep & steady—and this I call *I*" (*CN* 1:921). He proposes an Essay on the Passions, which would address the reciprocity of how "An Action in the Mind is a Passion in the Body: and Actions of the Body are reflected as Passions in the Mind,"[30] as in his 1804 desire to explore the skin as the "Terra Incognita in Medicine" because it marks the "intimate connection . . . of the Feeling & Consciousness of Volition" (*CN* 1:1827). But feeling is also indeterminately autonomous, a challenge to the body of scientific perception, "a *Feeling* of a Person quite distinct at all times, & at certain times *perfectly separable* from, the Image of the Person" (2:2061):

> All our Thoughts all that we abstract from our consciousness & so form the Phaenomenon Self is a Shadow, its whole Substance is the dim yet powerful sense that it is but a Shadow, & ought to belong to a Substance / but this Substance can have no marks, no discriminating Characters, no hic est, ille non est / it is simply Substance—& this deepliest felt during particular phaenomena with a consciousness that the phaenomenon is in us but it not in the phaenomenon. (2:3026)[31]

This psychosomatic suture of substance and shadow stages identity as something both essential and alien to the body: "all that is characteristic of his Nature as Man, is seated in the incommunicable part of his Being, of which we know that it is not his Body, nor of it; tho' it may well be, that his body is *of* it" (*CN* 3:3962).

In the early 1800s, the time of Coleridge's estrangement from Wordsworth and growing dependency on opium, he records the effects of a psychophysiological deconstruction of the subject that disturbed Locke and Hume:[32]

> Images in sickly profusion by & in which I talk in certain diseased States of my Stomach/Great & innocent minds *devalesce*, as Plants & Trees, into beautiful Diseases/Genius itself, many of the most brilliant sorts of English Beauty, & even extraordinary Dispositions to Virtue, Restlessness in good—are they not themselves, as I have often said, but beautiful Diseases—species of the Genera, Hypochondriasis, Scrofula, & Consumption! (*CN* 1:1822)

The mind's autonomous return to its bodily evidence suggests the pathology of imagination, which Coleridge experiences as a consciousness within the unconscious, or the consciousness of unreason, what he terms the "non-existence of Surprize in sleep" (1:1250).[33] Hence, 'falling' asleep constitutes a "real *event* in the body" that is also "in *excess*" of the physiological fact of sleep, so that a psychological "Disease from deficiency of this critical sensation" is created "when people imagine, that they have been awake all night/& actually lie dreaming, expecting & wishing for this critical Sensation" (*CN* 1:1078). Coleridge explains this phenomenon as "that curious modification of Ideas by each other" that creates the *feeling* of reason without rational understanding—"the Element of *Bulls*" (1:1620). This sensation of paradox is similar to the "irritability" of genius, which Coleridge associates, like Kant in the *Anthropology*, with *Schwärmerei* (*BL* 1:30–31), the 'swarming' or fanaticism of the mind's activity, an 'unreason' intrinsically disruptive to the work of imagination.[34] "The poetic PSYCHE, in its process to full development," reveals the faults of genius that are "as heterogeneous elements . . . carried off" by the "very *ferment*" which produced them, 'purified' by genius itself. They are as "some diseases, which must work on the humours, and be thrown out on the surface, in order to secure the patient from their future recurrence" (*BL* 1:78). The *Biographia* would 'purify' this pathology of experience to produce a philosophy of imagination as the therapeutic cure of the patient.[35] This pathology is sustained in the *Notebooks*, however, through a self-observation or narrative stream of consciousness that performs variations on the absent psychosomatic body.

The search beyond science to other phenomena leads to Coleridge's interest in mesmerism. Mesmerism helps Coleridge to explain, or at least describe, the obscure and mesmerizing body of perception that imagination becomes within the body of philosophy in the *Biographia*. At first Coleridge resists "the contemptuous rejection of animal magnetism before and without examination" because mesmerism conforms to "reproducible facts," like Galvanism, which contradicted Newton's laws, or the Copernican system, which contradicted the "apparent evidence of the senses."[36] Explaining the "power of the visual and its substitution for the conceptual," Coleridge maintains that people asserted an "eager belief of Electricity" only because it "exhibited a flash of Light."[37] He similarly holds that no one has "detected falsehood or delusion" in mesmerism because its psychosomatic effects, as recorded in the accounts of patients and eyewitnesses, constitute an irrefutable empirical body of evidence. Yet Coleridge ends up admitting that animal magnetism is too "strong and consentaneous" to be disproved, but too "fugacious and infixable" to support a theory of the "existence of a correspondent faculty in the human soul." Indeed, the soul seems to be the only hypothesis "adequate . . . to the satisfactory explanation of the facts—though that of a metastasis of specific functions of the nervous energy taken in conjunction with extreme nervous excitement, +some delusion, +some illusion, +some imposition, +some chances, and accidental coincidences might determine the direction in which the Scepticism vibrated." Having studied it for nine years, "collected a mass of documents in French, German, Italian, and the Latinists of the 16th century," as well as questioning eyewitnesses, especially of "literary or medical celebrity," he concludes, "I remain where I was . . . without having advanced an inch backward or forward."[38]

Coleridge's frustration is symptomatic of the resistance of science to mesmerism. Galvanism or gravity suggested the vitality and cohesion of bodies toward a common purpose. The absent psychosomatic body of mesmerism, however, demonstrated how the unconscious transgressed the *cogito*'s rational contours. Yet, paradoxically, while mesmerism appeared to suspend agency, like associationism, it simultaneously induced heightened consciousness.[39] For Coleridge this self-transcendence provided evidence that the "crass materialism" of mesmerism could acquire a "better spirit . . . from the Natúr-philosophy."[40] His account of mesmerism appears indebted to Schelling's 'intuition,' the unconscious of self-consciousness that is linked to the transcendental organic and dynamic principle of existence operating within and between subjects.[41] Coleridge's 'clinical' rather than scientific or philosophical assessment of animal magnetism, however, expresses a protopsychoanalytic *modus operandi* that appears to de-idealize the unconscious. Speaking of "the only position . . . asserted by all Magnetists as Magnetists," he describes an incipiently psychoanalytical scenario wherein magnetism, "under certain previously defined Conditions of distance and position, and above all of the relation of the Patient to the Agent and of the Agent to the Patient, is capable of acting and producing certain pre-defined Effects on the living human bodies external to it." "It" is "the will or . . . *vis vitae* of Man [which] is not confined in its operations to the organic Body," but yet works, like Schopenhauer's will, as a deterministic rather than transcendental force.[42]

Despite mesmerism's resistance to theory, it holds a certain fascination for Coleridge as a metonymy for the imagination: "if the zöomagnetic influx be only the influence of the Imagination, the active Imagination may be a form of the Zöomagnetic Influence" (*CN* 4:4806). As a sympathy or synthesizing agent between mesmerist and patient, mesmerism suggests the recreative, unifying, and idealizing power of the secondary or "active" imagination, which coexists with the "conscious will" (*BL* 1:304). Yet this is to distinguish mesmerism from the primary imagination, the "living Power and prime Agent of all human Perception" that operates beyond consciousness. Chapter Seven of *Biographia* explains the involuntary imagination as part of a symbiosis with the active or willing subject through an "intermediate faculty, which is at once both active and passive" and which Coleridge names "IMAGINATION" (1:124–25), thus dialectically resolving its primary and secondary modes into a higher unity, what Chapter Thirteen names as the synthesizing "tertium aliquid." This metaphysical principle is fundamentally at odds with mesmerism, however, which suggests between self and other, mind and body, consciousness and the unconscious, an *interpenetration* of positions that, like Jung's transference, destabilizes rather than unifies and thus suggests a lack of agency. Moreover, the free-associationism of the mesmerized body suggests a psychosomatic fluidity that, read against the grain of Coleridge's idealism, figures the tertium aliquid as a trans(pos)itional or transferential force—a fluid space—where the subject is neither subject nor object. This mobile identity is neither the mind-work of philosophy nor the body-work of science, both of which privilege a stable subject, but rather the psyche-work of imagination that perpetuates rather than resolves differences.

Transference emerges symptomatically in Coleridge's writing as a way of positing the subject's identity in the contingency between psychic determinism and self-making. The *Notebooks* attempt to mystify transference as imagination, which evolves in the *Biographia* as the product of both empiricism and metaphysics, but also then to read transference in conjunction with mesmerism. Yet transference haunts Coleridge's metaphysics in the form of a free-associationism that mobilizes the unconscious of both mesmerism and imagination. Freud's inability to decode transference at the end of his writing will repeat Coleridge's inability to theorize imagination as mesmerism in Romantic psychoanalysis.[43] Transference threatens the rationalism of Freud's metapsychology and the success of the analytical cure, upon the scientific credibility of psychoanalysis rested, in the same way that psychology disrupts the 'cure' of Coleridge's metaphysics as his transcendental system of Imagination in the *Logosophia*, upon which he hoped to rest his "reputation" (*CL* 4:589). Because transference repeats the conflicting effects of the unconscious as much as it resolves them, the psyche lies always beyond the ken of either the analyst or analysand. As Peter Brooks writes,

> the "truth" of psychoanalysis depends very much on the process of its articulation. Freud in the course of his career came to recognize more and more clearly that there is no final truth uncovered by this process—indeed, that psychoanalysis is inherently interminable, since the dynamics of the transference and the resistance to closure will always create new material to work on.[44]

This description reminds us of two converse situations for the subject in transference. On one hand, transference evokes the affective and psychic force moving from analysand to analyst as stable subject positions, so that countertransference from the analyst to the analysand marks the antistrophe to an essentially sympathetic process. On the other hand, transference signifies the *de*stabilization and circulation of subjects. In this sense transference is always already countertransference, the 'unreason' within the 'reason' of transference. Transference suggests how the 'psychology' of metapsychology and metaphysics, like the autobiography of philosophy, mutates a terminable epistemology of the subject into an analysis interminable.

The specific stumbling block of Coleridge's metaphysics, like that of Freud's metapsychology, is countertransference. Its spectral force, symptomatically present in mesmerism's resistance to theory, complicates the emergence of psychoanalysis in Coleridge's texts. By submitting *Christabel* for approval, Coleridge is unable to control the transference of audience response, just as this response—*our* response—can never make ultimate sense of its own transference with Coleridge and to a text that resists our appropriation. Countertransference reminds us that *neither* side has control. In mesmerism, the magnetizer would 'electrify' a divining rod with mesmeric 'fluid' and hold it out to one person, who then joined hands with others to form a type of circuit.[45] This instigated a cathartic crisis, the palliative effect of which depended on the illusion of an uninterrupted psychic path between subjects, a linear circuit conducted through the stability of the mesmerist as a subject presumed to know. Likewise, transference indicates the patient's desire for the analyst, who regulates or stabilizes the patient's wayward psychic 'energy.' The circuit of the analyst's desire for the patient in countertransference, however, creates a type of analytical short circuit that unsettles the illusion of the analyst's authority and disrupts the continuity of knowledge, complicating an already complex psychic and epistemological process. Operating in excess of reason, mesmerism unconsciously constellates (counter)transference, not as the linear circuit of electricity, but as something approximating the 'crisis' effects of nuclear fission, which is the negative side of the *rapport* or interpsychic and affective bond between subjects theorized by Puységur after Mesmer. Commenting on the shamanistic healing of diseases, Coleridge distinguishes between the mechanical or mediate agency of physics or medicine and its magical or immediate function, "not unlike the difference between conducted and radiant Heat." He contrasts the linear circuit with nonlinear fission, the latter meaning that an "effect passes from *a* to *b* without any known tangible, visible, or ponderable inter-agent. Thus the Act of the Will on the nerves and muscles of my Arm and Fingers I call 'magical' in the original and unsuperstitious use of the term."[46] Coleridge extrapolated a transcendental version of associationism that linked all elements of existence within a universal circuit both mobilized and organized by imagination. But this organicism itself suggested a type of free-associative fission incommensurable with the rationalism of philosophy. For Coleridge organicism's unconscious was 'unthinkable' because it suggested the relativity of associationism as madness or delirium—*the imagination firing away at will.*

(Counter)transference evokes a broad deconstructive transference that constitutes identity only as it is circulated between subjects as part of a narrative of self-making. This narrative, like the repetitive structure of *The Ancient Mariner*, is discontinuous and nonlinear, a temporal rather than transcendental dramatization of the absent psychosomatic body. Coleridge describes poetry as a "rationalized dream dealing" with the "manifold Forms of our own Feelings, that never perhaps were attached by us consciously to our own personal Selves" (*CN* 2:2086). Anticipating Keats's idea that the "poetical character, . . . [as] distinguished from the wordsworthian or egotistical sublime, . . . has no Identity" (*KL* 157), Coleridge dramatizes the feeling self through the psychic activity of dreams, poetry and imagination, a scene of psychoanalysis where the subject both experiences and loses himself as other.[47] As Coleridge writes, "it is an instinct of my Nature to pass out of myself, and to exist in the form of others."[48] He speaks of the

> mode in which our thoughts, in states of morbid slumber, becomes at times perfectly *dramatic*, . . . [and] the *form* of the vision appears to talk to us its own thoughts in a voice as audible as the shape is visible; and this too oftentimes in connected trains, and not seldom even with a concentration of power which may easily impose on the soundest judgments.[49]

For Coleridge poetry "does not require us to be awake and believe, . . . only to yield ourselves to a dream" (*BL* 2:218). But this "*dramatic* probability" discloses the irrationality of the psyche's multiple voices—hence Coleridge's '*rationalized* dream,' like Freud's dream interpretation.

The heterogeneous form of the *Notebooks*, however, exposes philosophy to its own contingency, a troubling interiority evoked by mesmerism. For while the evidence of mesmerism's individual cases confirms Coleridge's faith in the reality of the psychosomatic, this evidence disputes his metaphysics. The "Images" of clairvoyants who, during mesmeric trances, are able to describe the "inward parts and structure . . . of their own bodies or those of others *in report* with them," are, Coleridge offers, "clearly the Products of Sensations explained by the Fancy as in ordinary Dreams." By aligning mesmerism with fancy, however, this statement, written five years after *Biographia*, exhibits a Lockean paranoia about associationism that needs to be safely quarantined from and by the imagination. He thus proposes "that we ought to begin at the other end—namely, from the individual Cases" which record paranormal phenomena, applying to the inferences of these cases an inductive logic that will "simply generaliz[e] their import" (*CN* 4:4908). This approach allows Coleridge to accept but also to rationalize *away* the psychosomatic body, though it is unclear how he might extract metaphysics from the para-psychological, and thus move from *praxis* to theory. At the same time, and in a gesture radical in its implications for Romantic psychoanalysis, Coleridge not only shifts the burden of proof from physiological to psychological reality, but also moves epistemology within the sphere of narrative, where psychic determinism and imagination meet in the experiencing and self-making subject. This gesture reintroduces Coleridge's poetry, particularly *The Ancient Mariner* and *Christabel*, which signify early in his writing a preoccupation with telling the narrative of psychic reality. The vision of the dice game in *The Ancient Mariner*, for instance, like the narrative of a clairvoyant during a mesmeric trance, explores a psychic interiority transferring between the Mariner and the Wedding-Guest. Thus, Coleridge's later concern with mesmerism reads as a return to the phemonena of the unconscious of philosophy in Coleridge's poetry, an unconscious that is repeated in Coleridge's later attempts to bring these phenomena within the explanatory range of his metaphysics.

The Scene of Mesmerism in Coleridge's Poetry

The Rime of the Ancient Mariner

The *Notebooks*' exploration of mesmerism points to the supernatural, which Coleridge associates with "our inward nature." These "shadows of imagination" require the "willing suspension of disbelief for the moment" (*BL* 2:6). Coleridge distinguishes the supernatural "illusion" (2:134) of these shadows, which "constitutes poetic faith," from their "delusion," which is the work of fancy. His resistance to bringing metaphysics and psychology into dialogue with one another *as psychoanalysis*, however, lies precisely in the fact that it would read imagination psychically, as a mechanism of both poetic *illusion* and associative *delusion*, rather than transcendentally, and thus would introduce the imagination's unconscious as a foreign presence within the consciousness of the creative subject. Psychoanalysis remains a mesmerized and mesmerizing or *preternatural* presence within *Biographia Literaria* and the *Notebooks*, the (un)seen/scene of reason as the mesmerized body of philosophy.[50] Through various tropes and mechanisms *The Ancient Mariner* and *Christabel* explore this scene as an embryonic scene of psychoanalysis. The encounter between the Wedding-Guest and the Mariner or between Christabel and Geraldine figures a scene of interpretation that would speak trauma or read dreams. However, both encounters are unsettled by transference and by other factors: the dreaming or reverie within the encounter itself; the reading of these encounters *as if* within a dream; and in the case of Christabel, a crippling family romance. On one hand, these encounters tend to devolve into primal scenes and to turn psychoanalysis into trauma, as if the texts are unsure of what to do with their own psychoanalytical content. On the other hand, they emerge with at least limited cognitive potential to read the unconscious by which they function. They thus produce a symptomatic response to the disruptively interminable nature of psychoanalysis. Mesmerism comes to signify the dark potential of this interminability as a suspension of identity within transference. In the repetitive compulsion of this psychic motility, the texts evoke how the psyche resists philosophy/theory, the site where Coleridge's philosophy falters as a terminable project. According to a Wordsworthian schema, they are alien presences within the organic Gothic body of *The Recluse*, "sepulchral recesses" that the contemplative mind cannot expose.

Both *The Ancient Mariner*, written in 1798, and *Christabel*, written between 1798 and 1801, disturb the systematic integrity of Wordsworth's idea of *Lyrical Ballads*, psychic aberrances that do not fit its aesthetic whole.[51] The composition of *The Ancient Mariner* circumscribes this errancy: both poets planned the poem, inspired by a dream, to defray the expense of a November 1797 walking tour that germinated the idea for *Lyrical Ballads*, to which Coleridge was also to contribute *Christabel*. Shaped by a dialogue between the poets and between the Wedding-Guest and the Mariner, the text forms a type of transferential psychic organism that cannot be disciplined and that, even once Coleridge claims the texts as his own by publishing *Christabel* in 1816 and by publishing *The Rime* under his own name in the 1817 *Sibylline Leaves*, continued to disrupt Coleridge's *corpus*. The 1817 marginal gloss to *The Rime* especially attempts to terminate the repetition compulsion of the Mariner's tale or of Coleridge's revisions to the text.[52] Wordsworth's dissatisfaction with the poem and Coleridge's concession to his criticisms are attempts to discipline its *unheimlich* presence. But Wordsworth's reaction, especially to *Christabel*, also suggests the thorough occultation of the peripatetic *cogito* as a threat to the stability of his philosophical *anthropos*.[53]

Christabel and *The Ancient Mariner* suggest to Wordsworth the excess of a "spontaneous overflow of feeling," the subtext of an empirical subject who speaks the language of solitude *not* used by rational men, of emotion recollected in the trance-like suspension of reason rather than in the contemplative mood of tranquillity. His reaction, however, repeats a response that both texts already internalize in the form of subjects who observe the uncanny nature of their own psychic lives.[54] The solitude of wandering is thus a metonymy for the spectral form of psychoanalysis in Coleridge's writings, which read the Wordsworthian subject as conflicted between wandering and reclining. "The Ruined Cottage" resolves this conflict by preempting the *need* to tell one's story. But Margaret's absent psychosomatic body continues to wander in the form of Coleridge as a projection of Wordsworth's own self-alienation. This wandering form emerges as the pathology of *The Ancient Mariner* and *Christabel*, which suggest the *cogito*'s errancy, the unconscious of the transcendental imagination. Specifically, the Mariner's wandering and the phantom of Christabel's "wandering mother" are lurid figures of the absent psychosomatic body of the psychology or poetry of philosophy that both elicits and resists psychoanalysis. The Mariner is a specter of both the Pedlar and Margaret; the listener/therapist survives in the Wedding-Guest, but unlike the Narrator of "The Ruined Cottage," he is mesmerized rather than tranquillized.

The Mariner and Christabel are mesmerized by witnessing their psychic life so that conversation in Wordsworth becomes in Coleridge's texts symptomatic of what *cannot* be told or understood between subjects. Employing the compulsion to tell as its framing device, *The Ancient Mariner* places the solitary wanderer in process/on trial through the encounter between the Wedding-Guest and Mariner, thus reforegrounding the Pedlar's initial encounter with Margaret as an attempt to work-through psychic suffering.[55] Yet in doing so, Coleridge's text, refiguring the unreason of Margaret's tale as the preternatural unconscious of the Mariner's experience, must confront in this experience its power to suspend one's rational ability to understand it. Dialogue in the poem reproduces transference as mesmerism, constellating a scene of psychoanalysis that is simultaneously suspended by the text's inability to negotiate the psychic motility of the subjects it interrogates. In an 1818 entry in *The Friend* Coleridge, after *Hamlet*, defines reason as "'the mind's eye'" or "inward eye," "an organ bearing the same relation to spiritual objects . . . as the eye bears to material and contingent phaenomena."[56] In that it sees something neither spiritual nor physical, the Mariner's "glittering eye" (3, 17) is the eye of unreason within reason's sight. In the poem this comes to signify the mesmerizing force of the unconscious, whose form is an absent and alien psychosomatic identity that is the wandering form of the text's psyche.

The Mariner's "glittering eye" appears to link mesmerism solely to his supernatural agency, which suspends the Wedding-Guest's reason: he leaves the scene of telling as one who "hath been stunn'd / And is of sense forlorn," apparently infected by the Mariner's compulsive telling (668–70). The double sense of "sense" means both the mesmerism of the Lockean body of perception and the suspension of this body's reason. In a passage deleted after the 1798 text, the Wedding-Guest states: "'Marinere! thou hast thy will: / For that, which comes out of thine eye, doth make / My body and soul be still'" (372–74). Between "body" and "soul" hovers an indeterminate identity that Coleridge, by deleting the passage, represses, but that nonetheless persists within the text. From the beginning of the tale, the Mariner "holds" the Wedding-Guest physically "with his skinny hand" (13) *and* psychically with his "glittering eye," so that mesmerism is associated with the Mariner's touch and feeling. Hence his crew fear his increasingly spectral appearance: the Pilot "shriek'd / And fell down in a fit," and the Pilot's boy "doth crazy go" (606–7, 611). Moreover, the effects of the Mariner's presence are excessive, generating in the crew a type of *counter*mesmerism that is equally tenacious. Plagued "in dreams" by his shooting of the albatross, they impress in his psyche a look that "never [passes] away" (128, 258). After death, they rise again, and he falls in a "swound" (333, 406). When he awakens, "All fix'd on [him] their stony eyes" that, like his, "in the moon did glitter"; and he "could not draw [his] een from theirs," even once this spell is "snapt" (444, 450–56).

Mesmerism confronts the solitary imagination with an alien presence that exceeds consciousness. The Mariner describes himself as "one, that on a lonely road / Doth walk in fear and dread, / And having turn'd round, walks on / And turns no more his head: / Because he knows, a frightful fiend / Doth close behind him tread" (460–65). Again, in four stanzas deleted after 1798, this phantom exerts a more-than-psychic force: "Full many shapes, that shadows were" advance from the surface of the water like the "bodies," and their "dark-red shadows" reflect on his own "flesh" (490–507).[57] And they reappear three stanzas later in the same textual form ("Full many shapes, that shadows were" [519]).[58] The vision of the dice game stages this mobile psychosomatic otherness as a protean phantom. It emerges as "something in the Sky" that gradually assumes form ("A speck, a mist, a shape, I wist"), but whose "certain shape" also "plung'd and tack'd and veer'd" indeterminately (140–48). Within the ship are a "woman and her fleshless Pheere," although "she is far liker Death than he" (180, 199). In two passages included in the Bristol first issue of the 1798 *Lyrical Ballads*, but excluded in its London second issue and thereafter, Coleridge emphasizes the shape's/ship's interiority as a type of spectral organism: "a plankless Thing, / A rare Anatomy! / A plankless

Spectre—and it mov'd / Like a Being of the Sea!" (184–87). Although the "Woman" and Death sit *in* the ship together, she is also its "naked ribs," while he is a "fleshless Man"; she defines its exterior, while he signifies its exposed ("fleshless") interior, just as two stanzas later "*His* bones are black with many a crack" and "*Her* lips are red, *her* looks are free, / *Her* locks are yellow as gold: / Her skin is as white as leprosy" (177–98). As part of her "anatomy," he also thus suggests an otherness or alien presence *within her.* Removing both stanzas after 1798, however, Coleridge refigures the woman both within the ship and as the ship itself. He thus elides exterior with an interior that is completely evacuated by the 1817 gloss, which formalizes an allegorical relationship between "DEATH" and "Night-Mair LIFE-IN-DEATH," the latter become a demonic parody of the wedding feast's Christian Bride (189, 193).

Yet as figures of chance circulating within the economy of the dice game itself, death and life-in-death, both in earlier and later versions of the text, also function as tropes for the Mariner's psychosomatic body.[59] The undead movement of the "ghastly crew" silently working the Mariner's ship refigures the demonic motility of the "Spectre-ship" as part of the Mariner's own ship or body (341, 210). The crew's vitality, like the "strong wind" behind the ship, emerges as a "groan" or nonanthropomorphic force that also suggests semiotic potentiality: "Sweet sounds rose slowly thro' their mouths / And from their bodies pass'd. / Around, around, flew each sweet sound, / Then darted to the sun: / Slowly the sounds came back again / Now mix'd, now one by one" (329–55). This music echoes Nature's one life, a "sweet jargoning" that "makes the heavens be mute" (360, 364). But both connected to and dissociated from the body, the sound is also an autonomous associative or transpositional force that "swift as dreams" (600) keeps rising in the text, and by which the text appears to alter itself, both within and across individual versions. In 1798, for instance, the "Storm and Wind" that invisibly drive the Mariner's ship are natural forces, but they are also a singular omen of evil and, finally, parts of a monolithic and anthropomorphized spirit (45, 393). The 1817 text attempts to stabilize this indeterminacy by immediately both allegorizing the tempest as a "STORM-BLAST" (41) and anthropomorphizing it as "he." Whereas Wordsworthian anthropomorphism later tends to allegorical abstraction, Coleridge's allegory seems to replicate the Mariner's imagination as a phantasmagoria of textual forms, which, like the "personal forms" of Wordsworth's early version of the Prospectus, multiply and fragment the psyche as an array of diverse and semiautonomous voices and personalities.[60] The 1817 gloss refigures the two voices of the Mariner's dream, for instance, as "fellow-daemons" of the

"Polar Spirit" who hunt the Mariner for his crime, thereby aestheticizing the unconscious within the text's symbolism of supernatural forms. Yet by abstracting an identity for which the text offers little validation, the gloss seems oddly dissociative, a separately imaginary rather than recuperatively symbolic narrative, which in turn repeats rather than represses the imagination's pathology.

If subsequent alterations remain unable to discipline the content of the text's psychic narrative, they are equally baffled by its form.[61] The 1798 title, *The Rime of the Ancyent Marinere, in Seven Parts*, was changed to *The Ancient Mariner: A Poet's Reverie* (the title that stuck until Coleridge himself published the text in 1817's *Sibylline Leaves* under its original title). The shift displaces the Mariner as a subject presumed to know and discredits his tale's supernatural authenticity, foregrounding the uncanny encounter between the Mariner and the Wedding-Guest as the fever of a poet's mind, what Coleridge, speaking of "Kubla Khan," calls a "psychological curiosity" (*CP* 180). Yet "curiosity" also concedes that the reverie might have the force of the unconscious as the excess of rationality or morality. Moved to the end of *Lyrical Ballads*, *The Rime*'s multiple personalities are subsumed and thus marginalized by the professional *cogito* of the volume's now-named author, Wordsworth. Yet as "reverie" or mere daydream the poem remains suspended between consciousness and the unconscious so that, like Wordsworth's dream of the Arab, it signifies "neither" and "both at once." The title's shift from Mariner to poet draws the imagination's dis-ease closer to home at the same time that it defuses the story's importance.

This minimalization demonstrates how Wordsworth might discipline the text: ignore the problem, and it will go away. But the repressed returns, in that the poem follows the strange logic of psychoanalytic repetition. At the end of his story, the Mariner implores the Hermit to "shrieve" him.[62] The Hermit asks him to declare himself: "'I bid thee say / What manner man art thou?'" The question evokes a bodily response that only narrative can cure: "Forthwith this frame of mine was wrench'd / With a woeful agony, / Which forc'd me to begin my tale / And then it left me free." He continues: "Since then at an uncertain hour, / Now oftimes and now fewer, / That anguish comes and makes me tell / My ghastly aventure." Although it links the Hermit's question to the Mariner's tale, his "woeful agony," like his entire experience, erupts arbitrarily to exert a type of determinism within the body of the Mariner and the body of the text. The "agony" is both *of* the Mariner and foreign to his "frame" of being, for it determines, by overtaking, his identity—a psychosomatic trauma that tells him who he is by confronting him with what he is not.

The next stanza proves that trauma is constitutive: "*I* pass, like night, from land to land; / *I* have strange powers of speech; / The moment that his face *I* see / *I know* the man that must hear me; / To him my tale *I* teach" (620–36; my italics). But the telling makes selfhood a tenuous possession. The Hermit's question and the somatic response it provokes intertwine physiology and psychology in a de-personified and de-personifying narrative process that takes us back to the text's future as the work of the narrator's/poet's imagination: "*It* is an ancyent Marinere" (1; italics added). Marking his own voice by neutralizing the Mariner's identity, the speaker rationalizes the occasion of telling ("he stoppeth one of three" [2]) in a manner that contradicts the Mariner's own supernatural intuition: "The moment that his face I see / I know the man that must hear me." Moreover, the 1798 text does not use quotation marks to separate narrator from Mariner, so that the Mariner's tale is embedded within the speaker's telling, both supplementing and unsettling its narrative authority.[63]

The one reader who seems immune to the Mariner's influence is the Hermit. He is the first to interrogate the Mariner, and where the Pilot faints and the Pilot's boy goes mad, the Hermit "pray'd where he did sit" (609). He is the first subject presumed to understand the Mariner's traumatic experience by recognizing in his psychosomatic presence the history of his suffering. The Hermit poses the one question ("What manner man art thou?") that might unlock the meaning of the Mariner's life, thereby distilling his past to its essential paradox: that identity is based in a traumatic or "ghastly" lack of identity. The Hermit exhibits little professional finesse in conducting the Mariner to this self-knowledge: he addresses the Mariner's trauma *before* he sees in the patient a willingness to remember its catastrophic psychic effects, and so he *produces* symptoms before, or in lieu of, reading the symptom with which the Mariner presents him. He thus usurps the Mariner's identity before it is (re)formed, however ambivalently. Their encounter establishes an unwilling suspension of disbelief in the Mariner that predetermines his future telling as repetition rather than remembering. This initiates a psychoanalysis the text cannot carry out and generates a transference that suspends rather than actualizes the Mariner's unconscious life. Narrative reproduces rather than alleviates the psychosomatics of his suffering, so that he is trapped between the psychic determinism of his "woeful agony" and the self-making potentiality of his ability to "teach" his tale, his "strange powers of speech" suggesting both the wilful and the autonomous functioning of his psyche. As neither analyst nor analysand, the Mariner is spoken by a psychic language of the unconscious that the text *that speaks him* is unable to psychoanalyze.

One must instead speak of the free-associative narrative economy of the text's imagination. This economy circulates subject positions as aberrant or supernatural identities that cannot be attached to the subject who speaks them. The text attempts to read within the Mariner's tale a mesmerism peculiar to the dream-like economy of his experience. It locates this reality within the narrator's larger telling of the text as a scene of reason that places the text's autonomy under the narrator's creative will. That this attempt remains conflicted, however, is internalized within the scene in which the Mariner appeals to the Wedding-Guest to suspend his disbelief: "Listen, O listen, thou Wedding-guest!" To which the Wedding Guest replies: "'Marinere! thou hast thy will: / For that, which comes out of thine eye, doth make / My body and soul to be still'." And the Mariner again: "Never sadder tale was told / To a man of woman born: / Sadder and wiser thou wedding-guest! / Thou'lt rise to-morrow morn" (362–79). The passage figures between their separately bounded egos a communication wherein the Mariner predicts the hermeneutic outcome of their session. Yet his repeated appeal to the Wedding-Guest to "listen" undermines this authority by projecting it onto the Wedding-Guest. The scene of reason is infected by a transference that circulates agency by suspending the will of the other.

As readers we are ourselves caught in a countertransference that leaves us barely presuming to know where the text's subject lies. Removing the passage after 1798, Coleridge draws our attention away from transference-as-mesmerism to the dialogue between two disembodied voices that emerge at the end of Part Five. This scene reads the Mariner's interior life clearly by verbalizing the sound of reason that the Mariner is able to "discern" within his "soul" (410). That the beginning of Part Six allegorizes the distinction between "First Voice" and "Second Voice," however, also formalizes the self-divisions of reason within a scene of analysis, in which the second voice signifies a subject presumed to answer the first's questions. Moreover, this scene in turn reads the primal scene of the Mariner's crime as repeated in his future ("the man hath penance done / And penance more will do" [422–23]), so that the resolution of the past is subsumed within the ontologically undecidable intertextual event between original experience and future telling(s). The gloss attempts to renarrativize the text's repetitive psychic events as part of a case history of moral and spiritual development. It thus constructs the therapeutic apparatus of a terminable analysis, an intentional reading of the text that, like the conclusions to *Christabel*, reduces psychological complexity to empirical anecdote.[64]

Christabel

The Mariner both does and does not possess his body and thus both is and is not his tale's author. *Christabel* stages this traumatic dispossession as an inability to tell—both to articulate and to comprehend—who the subject was and is. Like *The Ancient Mariner*, *Christabel* seems trapped by a psychic determinism that it cannot bring into dialogue with self-making. But it stages this impasse with psychoanalysis differently. Whereas in *The Ancient Mariner* the relief from trauma offered by telling becomes in turn traumatic repetition, *Christabel* dramatizes, and so appears to recognize, how the history of trauma *cannot* be told—or rather, how telling becomes a traumatic displacement of this history.[65] That Coleridge does not finish the poem leaves the supernatural to wander within the text's narrative. The text's two-part structure is symptomatic of a *cogito* collapsed between Part One's unconscious night and Part Two's rational but equally divided day-world of dream interpretation. Marjorie Levinson suggests that as a "true fragment" the poem escapes "that quintessential Romantic bind: how to tell one's dream without hypostatizing and privileging one's peculiar, particular narration."[66] I would argue that the poem's fragmentation is a response to *Mariner*'s specter of interminability: the text hypostatizes a reading that implicitly suppresses the interminable prospect of countless others because it is unable to broach the interminable darkness of the psyche.

In Part One Christabel "had dreams all yesternight /. . . / . . . that made her moan and leap" (*CP* 27–29), but the text does not state that she *is* dreaming, although Bard Bracy's dream later figures her kneeling beside the oak outside the castle walls. The trope of dreaming both objectifies and abjects the disturbing nature of Christabel's psychic life, placing the unconscious at a safe distance by marginalizing its supernatural presence. Like Geraldine's body, Christabel's tale is "A sight to dream of, not to tell" (247), a way of dramatizing the text's traumatic inability to read the unconscious. Christabel is wandering, Mariner-like, in a forest, and she hears "It," which emerges, like the Mariner, as kind of nonentity: "It moan'd as near as near, as can be, / But what it is, she cannot tell" (41–42). The 'moaning' becomes a figure fetishized in parts (neck, feet, eye, breast), both sinking as a "weary weight" and rising "as [if] she were not in pain," simultaneously bodied forth and disembodied (126, 129). She appears to emerge from Christabel's unconscious to become, on one hand, a figure of how the unconscious cannot be read and, on the other, a figure of how consciousness represses this trauma. At first, then, she depends on Christabel as having engendered her. Her fuller identity begins to emerge in the traumatic telling of her own history, initiated by Christabel's questioning, "How cam'st thou here?" (74), which prompts only a preliminary assessment of facts ("Why have you come to me?") rather than an immediate confrontation with the subject's identity ("What manner man art thou?"). Geraldine's brief history recounts her own traumatic attack, by which she has been partly mesmerized: "I have no thought what men they be; / Nor do I know how long it is / (For I have lain in fits, I wis)" (88–90). Christabel's best analytical intentions, however, are no match for Geraldine, who devolves into a "frightful" psychosomatic presence that then becomes "lord of [Christabel's] utterance" (64, 256).

At first a figure of Christabel's unconscious, then, Geraldine emerges as an autonomous and alien presence, a projection of psychic life that in turn silences Christabel's analytical abilities. Part One stages their relationship as a suspended scene of psychoanalysis—a scene of mesmerism. Geraldine's transference with Christabel, as a figure who 'saves' her, mutates into a (counter)transference in which, as a figure of trauma, Geraldine reprojects trauma in Christabel. That is, the effects of Geraldine's tale in Part One (and especially as they are dramatized in Part Two) reduce Christabel to the trauma that this history is unable to tell. In doing so, Geraldine's story, by reducing the complexity and obscurity of her psychic experience to a brief and incomplete case history, produces in turn the interpretive trauma of reducing Christabel's identity to a singular diagnosis she is unable to refute: "For this is alone in / Thy power to declare, / That in the dim forest / Thou heards't a low moaning, / And found'st a bright lady surpassingly fair: / And didst bring her home with thee in love and in charity, / To shield her and shelter her from the damp air" (260–66). A particularly insidious version of the Hermit's authority, Geraldine's gaze is, like the stare of Apollonius's "cold philosophy" (*KP* 230) that reduces Lamia to a serpent, the discipline of reason that finds its symbolic power in the "custom and law" (*CP* 326) of Part Two.

Yet this discipline overcompensates for what threatens it by exerting a hyper-rationalism that becomes its own excess. Geraldine is thus also haunted by the "wandering mother" (199) who effects the "unsettled eye" of Christabel's consciousness in Part One, a reflection of the unconscious repressed within reason. This mother functions like Nicholas Abraham's concept of the "phantom," a "formation of the unconscious that has never been conscious—for good reason. It passes—in a way yet to be determined—from the parent's unconscious into the child's," but "*returns to haunt [to] bear[ ] witness to the existence of the dead buried within the other.*" The phantom is usually associated with a "parent's or a family's guarded secret, even though the secret's text and content are inscribed within the patient's own unconscious."[67] This unconscious returns in Part Two where, mesmerized by Geraldine's "spell," Christabel rises again, troubled by a "perplexity of mind / As dreams too lively leave behind" and repeating the wandering form of her mother as a metonymy for the text's own psychic aberrancy (*CP* 255, 373–74).[68] Looking "askance" at Christabel, Geraldine thus *again* represses the unreason of her own psychosomatic otherness by projecting it onto Christabel, who *again* falls in a "dizzy trance, / Stumbling on the unsteady ground" and "Shudder[s] aloud, with a hissing sound" (569, 577–79), having become what she beholds in the (m)other. It seems Geraldine knows the text of the unconscious that Christabel might interpret, and so steps in to model, rather fanatically, how it *should* be read.

Telling, then, allies Geraldine with Sir Leoline (the Baron), Christabel's father, who reads Christabel as an increasingly occult presence, first by restricting her interpretive freedom and then by abjecting her altogether from the text. Like Freud and Fleiss, Geraldine and the Baron offer the bitter parody of a cure. The Baron ritualizes his grief for his dead wife by sounding a melancholy "warning knell" (330) each dawn. Abraham and Torok note that "[t]wo interrelated procedures constitute the magic of incorporation: *demetaphorization* (taking literally what is meant figuratively) and *objectivation* (pretending that the suffering is not an injury to the subject but instead a loss sustained by the love object)."[69] Encryption is so complete in the Baron's case that he takes Geraldine, who has encrypted herself in Christabel's body, as the daughter who reminds him of his dead wife, so that he is twice removed from the real of death. When he meets Geraldine, she tells her story, he validates it, and between them they enforce a law of correct telling that forecloses another interpretation in which he might see that his 'cure' is in fact harming his own daughter.[70] Moreover, he sees in Geraldine the opportunity to resolve his conflict with Lord Roland, which left men a "hollow heart . . . paining," the "scars remaining" that can never be "wholly" forgotten (408–9, 413). Repeating Leoline's relationship to Geraldine, the two men are joined by a kind of melancholic homosocial bond predicated on keeping communication at bay.

Geraldine thus evolves to signify an absent psychosomatic body of grief that refuses diagnosis, a return of the repressed that will not be remembered. What is most disturbing is Christabel's consciousness of this body's symptoms: she knows—and *feels*—why things are wrong, but is denied access to any therapeutic strategy for fixing things. When the Baron embraces Geraldine, Christabel experiences a "vision of fear, the touch and pain," that falls upon her "soul" (440–41). The Baron can only see "his own sweet maid / With eyes upraised, as one that prayed" (449–50). When he asks what ails her, she can only answer according to "custom and law" (a rather bitter parody of Cordelia's "truth" in *King Lear*): "'All will yet be well!'" (460). Her mind is reduced to the "sole image" that "passively did imitate / [Geraldine's] look of treachery and hate," so she stands "With forced unconscious sympathy / Full before her father's view" (592–98). Like Margaret, she is both disclosed and repressed by a conversation that excludes her. This "full" picture is both the reduction of his Symbolic law and "full" *imago* he cannot comprehend: that she is his dead wife reconstellated *as* this *imago*. For a moment the "thoughts" of his "heart and brain" "swelled his rage and pain" to "work confusion there," and then "His heart was cleft with pain and rage" (624–28), as if the force of grief in his countertransference with his daughter has finally broken through and he is on the verge of admitting loss. Yet just as swiftly his wild eyes, the sign of her hysteria transferred to him, turns to a "stern regard" (636) and, arrayed in rational defense with Geraldine against Christabel, he turns away from his patient.

It makes sense that, as the voice of philosophical contemplation, the Baron is only a "Half-listening" (553) analyst when presented with Bard Bracy's dream, which offers what Abraham and Torok speak of as the "*means [by] which metaphors become possible*"[71] in order to introject or accept loss by revealing the unspoken trauma. The Baron misinterprets the dream's "gentle bird" suffocated by the snake as Geraldine rather than his daughter, and so vows *to Geraldine* to "crush" it, just as he vowed to dislodge the "reptile souls" from the "bodies and forms of [the] men" who abducted Geraldine (*CP* 520, 559, 430–31). Geraldine's imaginary place within the Symbolic order created by the Baron's violent hermeneutics turns his daughter into what Geraldine was (and still is). The Baron likewise displaces the Bard's interpretation. The Bard seems to read Geraldine's mutating and deterministic power of reason as part of the text's mobile allegory. His interpretation is thus metaphorical rather than analytical, Jungian rather than Freudian, as if to refigure this power as the self-making force of poetry. That his ability to tell dreams liberates speech in Christabel suggests how poetry both represents and reads the unconscious. Like Christabel, he threatens "custom and law" by speaking the poetry of the Baron's philosophy. And the Baron's "confusion" in turn suggests a hyper-rationalism or excess of reason, his mesmerized *in*ability to entertain anything but a monolithic interpretation of the Bard's dream.

If Geraldine and the Baron signify a reductive psychotherapeutic cure, Bracy and Christabel offer a potential scene of psychoanalysis that *imagines* rather than *reads* past trauma in the narrative of the unconscious and its present effects in the absent psychosomatic body. Christabel's bedroom in Part One tropes this site as a trance-like seduction of the creative consciousness. Like the sepulchral recess of Gothic philosophy in Chapter Thirteen of *Biographia Literaria*, the bedroom suggests a primal scene of imagination, a type of Keatsian maiden-chamber of the psyche in which the disturbing unconscious simultaneously opens and closes: a "chamber carved so curiously, / Carved with figures strange and sweet / All made out of the carver's brain" (172–74). This is "A sight [site] to dream of, not to tell." Its unreadability also marks it as a scene of trauma where the imagination confronts its autonomously pathological nature. The semiosis of this pathology is what Christabel initially hears but "cannot tell," a de-humanizing generation of affect that resists intellectual or textual containment: "It moaned as near as near can be" (41–42). This "moaning" wanders throughout the text to disturb "custom and law." As poet, Bracy utters this disturbance of imagination against the Baron's monolithic "warning knell." He interposes the heterogeneous echoes of "Three sinful sextons' ghosts . . . / Who all give back, one after t'other, / The death-note to their living brother" (341–43). Like Christabel speaking in "low faltering tones," he recounts his dream in "faltering voice," within which he hears Christabel "Fluttering and uttering fearful moan" (371, 509, 523). This faltering of the Symbolic indicates a semiotic potentiality associated with the wandering form of the mother's body. The Baron's reason is unsettled by this affective force when he gazes upon Christabel to remember momentarily his wife's plea that he not wrong his "only child" (621), and for a moment to experience the effects of Geraldine's mesmerism in Christabel transferred to him.

Mesmerized by the touch and gaze of Geraldine, Christabel, by remaining unable to tell what she knows, is also unable to speak what she does not know. The text internalizes this inability through the narrator's framing of events. He both tells and revises his telling ("Is the night chilly and dark? / The night is chilly, but not dark") as an attempt to understand as empirical reality supernatural phenomena that resist naturalization: "Is it the wind that moaneth bleak? / There is not wind enough in the air / To move away the ringlet curl / From the lovely lady's cheek" (14–15, 46–49). He appeals to the reader as part of a broader hermeneutic that is crystallized by Christabel's question to Geraldine, which initiates the text's search for origins. Yet in this textual dialogue between self and other the narrator's authority also falters. He asks twice "what can ail the mastiff bitch?" (144, 148), yet provides no response, so that he both narrates and is narrated by events. This ambivalence is reflected in the text's unstable subject positions. Ordering Bracy to travel to Roland's castle, Leoline at first addresses him in second person. The following verse stanza, however, shifts to third person, suggesting the voice of the narrator or an odd dissociation of voice in Leoline, who then speaks again in first person in the next stanza. Moreover, the text, like *The Ancient Mariner*, is careless with its use of quotation marks. The first speech of Bracy in Part Two, for instance, is left open, suggesting the faltering of his position within the text, as well as a larger inability to hypostatize the bounded *cogito* of the text.

These indeterminacies unsettle the Conclusions to Parts One and Two, which attempt to recuperate the poem's uncanny events by imposing symbolic narratives of psychic reparation. The Conclusion to Part One reads the encounter between Geraldine and Christabel "As a mother with her child," so that Geraldine, the bad mother encrypted within Christabel's psyche, is displaced by the good object or "vision sweet" of the wandering mother who waits for Christabel to embrace her: "What if her guardian spirit 'twere? / What if she knew her mother near?" (289, 314–16). The conclusion to Part Two triangulates maternal authority according to oedipal logic, so that Christabel, infantilized in Part One, is interpellated by Symbolic law: "Makes such a vision to the sight / As fills a father's eyes with light" (648–49). Derwent Coleridge's and James Gillman's hypothetical completions of the text thus suggest the denouement of a family romance that reads the child's development as alienated from the mother by the intercession of paternal desire, redomesticated within the social order through reconciliation with her father and properly assuming the role of mother through marriage to her lover. Yet, like the marginal gloss to *The Ancient Mariner*, the conclusions impose a terminable analysis the text itself resists at the same time that they resist their own closure. In the first, Christabel is figured at the margins between consciousness and the unconscious, "dreaming fearfully, / Fearfully dreaming," and "Dreaming that alone, which is—" (281–83). That the conclusion does not tell what she dreams marks the provisional nature of its hermeneutic. In the second conclusion, the father "Must needs express his love's excess / With words of unmeant bitterness" (652–53). Yet because this reprimand produces a "giddiness of heart and brain" that "Comes seldom save from rage and pain," interpretive *relief* instead reproduces the father's absent psychosomatic body, overdetermining through the conclusion the text's already overdetermined psychic content. Completing the text's broader hermeneutic, the conclusions interpellate instead a reading subject of interminable analysis (663–64).

In Chapter Twenty-One of *Biographia Literaria*, Coleridge describes the origins of meter as a symbiosis between a "state of increased excitement" and the artificial imposition of a "*voluntary* act, with the design and for the purpose of blending *delight* with emotion, so the traces of present *volition* should throughout the metrical language be proportionally discernible" (*BL* 2:65). This symbiosis cannot be a "partnership, but a union; an interpenetration of passion and of will, of *spontaneous* impulse and of *voluntary* purpose." The imaginations of both *The Rime of the Ancient Mariner* and *Christabel* do not obey this philosophy of poetry. Textual events appear oddly dissociated from their own epistemological moorings, grounded in a process of telling that the text is unable to master. The origin of telling's meter in the semiotic of rhythm marks an obscure determinism that functions autonomously to create identity as a presence alien to itself. The unreason of reason that suspends Christabel's ability to speak also dictates the Mariner's traumatic recounting of events. This repetition avoids working-through the past and thus avoids a psychic interiority that becomes, as Henderson notes of Romantic constructions of the "notion of a heart of core in either society or the individual," "the center of movement or circulation, a place of dangerous fluidity." In Coleridge's poems this fluidity is a subject in process/on trial between mind and body. Both texts stage the scene of reason as it is mesmerized by the unconscious, which unsettles philosophy's determinate terminability, and so offer a phantom scene of psychoanalysis that reads philosophy as the subject of its unconscious psyche. But the texts' inability to locate this subject as part of a terminable project abjects interminability as a threat equal to, if not greater than, philosophy's unreason. Put another way, the emerging subject of psychoanalysis is mesmerized by the thought of his own interminability, so that the scene of psychoanalysis is stalled as a scene of mesmerism.

The two texts respond differently to this paralysis. The scene of mesmerism in *The Ancient Mariner* circulates like the Mariner's body to suggest a psychoanalytical content disrupting the body of the text's hermeneutics. The text describes the Mariner's unconscious, but it subsequently fails to provide an apparatus adequate to an analysis of the psyche because its subjects become mesmerized by its contents before they ever get to its analysis. *Christabel* seems to provide this analysis by staging the scene of mesmerism circulating indeterminately within *The Ancient Mariner*. Whereas subject positions in that text are transposed according to an unmanageable narrative economy, *Christabel* capitalizes upon this economy's subtextual interpretive topoi: a reading of the effects of the unconscious, and thus of identity, *as indeterminate*. *Christabel* fixes the other text's mobile subject positions in order to place them in process/on trial within a de-idealized hermeneutic that asks questions for which there are no answers. *Christabel* thus also stages *The Ancient Mariner*'s absent psychosomatic body as a spectral presence constellated in the encounter between Christabel and Geraldine. It negotiates an ambivalence between psychotherapy as hermeneutic cure and psychoanalysis as narrative self-exploration, both variations of Coleridge's attempt to rework philosophy to accommodate its inherent poetry. But while *Christabel* unsettles the rationalism of the former, it attenuates the latter's potential. By a strange logic the text aborts its emerging scene of psychoanalysis by controverting it as trauma, thereby demonstrating how psychoanalysis is itself an abject presence within the text and how conventional psychoanalysis, as diagnosis and cure, does not work. In *Christabel* mesmerism exceeds narrative's explanation to become the case history of *The Ancient Mariner* as a potently missed encounter with psychoanalysis in Coleridge's writing.

That *Christabel* stages the trauma of reason in her most excessive mood returns us again to *The Recluse*, a 'feminine' sensibility that both Wordsworth's and Coleridge's texts seem, ultimately, unable to deal with except anxiously to contain this nervousness, like that of the woman's nervous fever in *Biographia Literaria*, through equally nervous textual reactions. "The Ruined Cottage," the Prospectus, *The Prelude*, *Biographia Literaria*, the *Notebooks*, *The Ancient Mariner*, *Christabel*—all inscribe a psychic potentiality that breeds as psychic excess within the finite paradigm of the larger idea's organic conception. This excess demands the invention of an alternative interpretive model in Romantic psychoanalysis. In Wordsworth and Coleridge this invention is conflicted. Psychoanalysis emerges in Wordsworth as a movable scene wherein the phenomenology of the social world becomes a vast projection of trauma overwhelming the subject, such that the patient cannot deal with the repressed's monumental return.[72] Wordsworth internalized this projection in childhood when he saw external existence as "not apart from, but inherent in, [his] own immaterial nature": "Many times while going to school have I grasped at a wall or tree to recall myself from this abyss of idealism to the reality." In later years, however, this tranquillizing effect produced a "subjugation of an opposite character" in which his psychic life had become all too lifeless.[73] Coleridge confronts this abyss of idealism *as reality*, an all too real symptom of the imagination's inner life, by observing the trauma of identity's indefinable empirical contours. The enlightenment of his prose attempts to render this indeterminacy clear and thus to sublimate the psyche within a vision of the transcendental imagination. This produces a conflicting Romantic impulse toward idealization conflicted by its desire to *know* the indeterminate subject. The failure to provide the *cure* of the Enlightenment subject through this knowledge produces a post-Kantian subject of transference. At the core of this transference, again, is the specter of a suspended absent psychosomatic body—Margaret's body—that refuses to go away, a body that induces much talk and much analysis between men, but no cure for or of its agitated, agitating, and often suffering presence.

The psychoanalysis that Wordsworth avoids and that Coleridge is simultaneously, if resistantly, drawn towards, constellates a control situation through which to investigate the psyche, a type of necessary swerve away from the sublime of the unconscious so that it may be observed. Within the dynamic movement of the sublime Neil Hertz installs the notion of blockage, before the mind's internal exertion of reason, as a way of preserving the self from total dissolution.[74] Romantic psychoanalysis attempts to construct the apparatus for exploring this moment as the site where the absent psychosomatic identity of the subject—the transferential body of identity—*is*, a site where the subject sees identity as always divided by a radical otherness it cannot know. This process demands, however, that the essentially itinerant apparatus of the psyche submit itself to an Enlightenment investigation that places the patient on the couch, the extreme negativity of the undead child analysand that Wordsworth constellates in the Intimations ode and that horrifies Coleridge. Attempting to escape from the materialism of science, Freud distinguishes the psychic reality of the dream, the abyss of its idealism, from its physiological functioning. Freud is wholly Coleridgean in this respect. Yet opening the contents of the dream to a surgical analysis that would offer an empiricism of the psyche, he is tempted by the materialism of the scientific method. He thus turns the tolerance of the poetic production of free association back into contemplation—finding the 'right' interpretation that would illuminate a psyche that can only be illuminated 'darkly.' Coleridge places a Wordsworthian Freud, for whom narrative and conversation serve a hermeneutic function, in process/on trial by reproducing poetry as what *cannot* be told or understood. That Coleridge reacts to this process as what he calls in the Preface to "Kubla Khan" a "psychological curiosity" indicates his own resistance to it. His is a mesmerized exploration of how the absent psychosomatic body of psychoanalysis will not be contained/repressed—will not be made to lie down. The session within the scene of analysis is, then, implicitly recognized by Coleridge as itself illusory/delusory, for the pathology of the imagination will submit to neither Enlightenment rationalism nor Romantic idealism. The psyche permits a dialogue between psychic determinism and self-making, but does not allow the latter to transcend the former. How to accept self-making as a provisional but necessary swerve in the face of psychic determinism is the topic of our next chapter.

FOUR

De Quincey Terminable and Interminable

> The mere understanding, however useful and indispensable, is the meanest faculty in the human mind and the most to be distrusted; and yet the great majority of people trust to nothing else; which may do for ordinary life, but not for philosophical purposes.
>
> —"On the Knocking at the Gate in *Macbeth*"

Autobiography, and the Confessions of Philosophy

Thomas De Quincey's 1821 *Confessions of an English Opium-Eater* attempts to tell what cannot be told, what he calls the "*burden of the Incommunicable*" (*WDQ* 2:170). It thus comprises a psychic anatomy of Wordsworth's and Coleridge's missed encounters with psychoanalysis in their struggle with the unconscious of Kantian reason.[1] Kant's physiological anthropology is the medicalized form of a psychology Kant acknowledges with some reluctance. De Quincey refigures this reluctance in terms of how a pragmatic anthropology, what man makes of nature through the shaping spirit of philosophy, is haunted by its own psychology. But De Quincey himself remains haunted by Kantian reason's resistance to enlightenment. Like Wordsworth's writing of *The Prelude*, in *Confessions* De Quincey attempts to give an explanatory, terminable shape to psychic self-exploration, to make a coherent connection between the physiology of addiction and the psychology of dreams. However, his 1856 revisions to *Confessions*, which I shall address at some length later in this chapter, disrupt this connection by expanding his autobiography. This expansion seems to exhaust the telling of the psyche, but inevitably it makes the psyche susceptible to further analysis. Between the 1821 and 1856 versions, the 1845 sequel to *Confessions*, *Suspiria de Profundis*, or "Sighs from the Depths," offers a different approach. *Suspiria* refashions the psychosomatic "body of [his] opium dreams" (*WDQ* 2:102) as a self-making response to their psychic autonomy. *Suspiria* offers a mythopoeic rather than scientific interpretation of dreams. Its Romantic psychoanalysis is deliberate rather than symptomatic and invites us to read De Quincey's confessional writings synchronously rather than teleologically, and to uncover his conflicted relationship to the psychoanalysis he helps to invent.[2] Understanding this relationship demands more than mere understanding: it demands from the reader no less than to follow De Quincey into the unconscious.

Confessions first appeared in two 1821 installments of *London Magazine*.[3] The first installment or Part One contained a preface "To the Reader" and "Preliminary Confessions," which briefly sketched the writer's life up to this 1803 impoverishment in London and the beginning of his addiction. Part Two continued with the last three paragraphs of "Preliminary Confessions," "The Pleasures of Opium," "Introduction to the Pains of Opium," and "The Pains of Opium," these later sections chronicling De Quincey's opium taking and its psychological effects. The work's immediate notoriety lead De Quincey to promise a third instalment to address moral charges against the work's moral laxity. De Quincey never wrote this third part, although to the 1822 publication of the text in book form by Taylor and Hessey he added an Appendix detailing his habit and how it had stalled his writing.[4] Already we see how the fragmentary and addictive relationship between life and life-writing shape De Quincey's *corpus* as what Coleridge, speaking of *Biographia Literaria*, calls an "immethodical miscellany."[5] De Quincey eventually responded to this aborted beginning when in 1856 he published a substantially revised version of *Confessions* as the fifth volume of his fourteen-volume collected works, entitled *Selections Grave and Gay, Writings Published and Unpublished*, which he began editing in 1853, the last volume appearing in 1860, the year after his death. This text begins as "Confessions of an English Opium Eater," a fourfold expansion of "Preliminary Confessions" that dilates the confessor's life to clarify its developmental chronology. This expansion shifts the text's epistemological center from "Pleasures" and "Pains" to that of the well-told life, as if to dissociate this life from its nightmarish addictions.[6] The psyche is now ordered in advance of its analysis, and the self-reflective, historiodescriptive mode of autobiography outweighs, if not preempts entirely, the psychoanalytical mode of confession.

De Quincey's writings between 1821 and 1856 signal this shift. In 1834 De Quincey published a series of seven articles for *Tait's Magazine* called "Sketches of Men and Manners from the Autobiography of an English Opium-Eater." These writings formed the kernel of what he called his Autobiography, which signaled a self-writing distinct from confession.[7] The Autobiography imposes the Symbolic pattern of a life history on De Quincey's early wanderings as if to terminate the disruptively chronic effects of addiction. As V. A. de Luca writes, these later recollections are "carefully edited and arranged to form a narrative continuum, . . . a kind of anthology of [De Quincey's] previous autobiographical writings."[8] The Autobiography confirmed De Quincey's later Victorian authority as a man of letters who, like Wordsworth or Walter Scott, collects the pieces of his psychic life under the rubric of the Great Man or Sage.[9]

The 1845 *Suspiria* elaborates this narrative differently. Published in four installments of *Blackwood's Magazine*, *Suspiria* focuses on *Confessions*' attempt to "reveal something of the grandeur which belongs *potentially* to human dreams."[10] It records De Quincey's "third prostration before the dark idol" of opium as a "final stage" or cure to addiction that "differ[s] in something more than degree" from his previous attempts (*WDQ* 15:129). By repeating the 1821 text's ambivalence, however, *Suspiria* goes on to explore a more radical approach to psychic indeterminacy. Whereas *Confessions* is narrative and diachronic, *Suspiria* is a hybrid between narrative and various symbolic episodes that offer synchronic versions of the self. These later sections stand outside the experiential to imagine a radically contingent and literary apparatus within which to anatomize a subject self-analyzed by the doubles, shadows, and phantasms of his own psychic interiority. *Suspiria* turns *Confessions*' empirical claims for the subject into cosmic and mythopoeic ones and is remarkably different not only from *Confessions* but from anything else in Romantic literature.

The 1821 *Confessions* promises the moral that De Quincey has "triumphed" over his opium addiction, making the text a "useful and instructive" (*WDQ* 2:9) record of his struggle. But the effects of addiction remain complicated by the unconscious, as his "dreams are not yet perfectly calm" (2:76). A closing 1821 paragraph goes back to the future of the text's opening ambivalence: "I . . . have untwisted, *almost* to its final links, the accursed chain which fettered me" (2:10; my italics). Later misquoting "untwisted" as "'unwound'" (2:74), a word which suggests 'coming unwound,' the statement becomes the symptom of an unconscious that the text repeats rather than remembers. 1821's *two* attempts to overcome addiction become *three* in the 1845 *Suspiria* and *four* in the 1856 *Confessions.* As Paul Youngquist argues, accounts of De Quincey frequently pathologize his "crazy body" for his intellect's inability to call this body to order. For Youngquist, De Quincey's body "has a mind of its own" that De Quincey, unlike Kant, decides to feed with opium and dreams. To "read him from [this] extramoral [Nietzschean] perspective would be to open ourselves, intellectually and bodily, to the full force of his physiological aesthetics and to the kind of life it affirms."[11]

But neither his body nor his mind is De Quincey's biggest obstacle. *That* obstacle is his struggle to come to terms with the symptomatic form that both mind and body take as psychosomatic phenomena. Yet to read De Quincey's body symptomatically is not necessarily to pathologize it. The mind of its own that De Quincey's body has is both disturbingly *and* potently psychosomatic, neither mind nor body but something radically other to both. This body's symptomal authority comes from a more constitutively traumatic repression than a Freudian attempt to explain these symptoms might suggest. For if the mind reproduces itself as body in the symptom, a body with a mind of *its* own that resists rational explanation, one must further ask: what embodied form does this second mind take? The psychosomatic symptom that takes on a life of its own evokes how identity is *always* symptomatic. Put another way, the body of perception produced by the mind is a psychosomatic body that haunts both the mind and body, is always symptomal because it must always already repress the mind's or body's existence as a phantasy to which its own phantasy responds. The only thing disturbing about opium is that it brings this point home to the subject with a ferociousness that the conscious mind can, when tranquil, frequently avoid. And most disturbingly, opium demonstrates with devastating clarity to the subject how this symptomology fundamentally resists interpretation. It is *this* absent psychosomatic body, the psychosomatic other of reason's body, that De Quincey recognizes within the primal scene of suffering around which his confessional writings hover. This other makes the subject both think with feeling intensity and feel with thinking intensity about his inability to know himself. But the anxiety produced by this inability is, for De Quincey, the axis of the subject's creative life—*is* the subject's life. The repetition of addiction in De Quincey's confessional writings, therefore, evokes the dark resilience of the psychosomatic body, an anatomy that calls out for psychoanalysis.

The 1821 text attempts to shape this psychoanalysis into a pragmatic form and the 1856 text attempts to counter it with a well-told autobiography. But we can read in De Quincey's texts a process of pathologization that they both internalize and resist. Divided between (later) Autobiography and (earlier) confession, De Quincey's *corpus* offers different responses to its own psychoanalytic content. The 1856 expansion of the 1821 text favors autobiography as an 'accomplished' life-writing, not unlike that of Mill's *Autobiography*, in advance of confession by conserving the social and moral character of a public persona who can both endure and resist later analysis.[12] The 1856 text demarcates public and private personae in order to indicate their conjunction, but also to maintain separate spheres of epistemological instruction. As if threatened by how confession will manifest the Autobiography's latent psychic meanings, the 1856 text balances itself as a pragmatic anthropology against the physiological anthropology of the 1821 text.[13] But the Autobiography cannot answer the need *to* confess. By attempting to exhaust the subject's social construction, the 1856 text is symptomatic of a broader interminability in De Quincey's confessional writings. The Autobiography marks in self-writing the interminable struggle between the narrative closure of the self (in terms of a finite plot with a beginning, middle, and end) and the unending narrative proliferations of its psychology (through multiplying characters and episodes). In short, the Autobiography is unsettled by its own autobiography, the confessional other of Autobiography that analyzes its own psychology.

Suspiria explodes tensions between confession and autobiography in order to negotiate the division between psychic determinism and self-making that threatens De Quincey's confessional project. In *Suspiria* confession provides the raw material from which the subject can fashion his identity as a Nietzschean aesthetic phenomenon. The radically indeterminate nature of *Suspiria* collapses the 1821 and 1856 *Confessions* into one another by anatomizing the psychoanalytical subject on trial/in process within the earlier text. But it also points forward to the later text's inability to move beyond its 1821 origin and thus to a larger conflict between terminability and interminability. In De Quincey terminability allows for the exploration of psychic dis-ease, but is drawn toward a cure by locating pathology within an interpretive framework—a Pathology *of* pathology. By naming dis-ease, this Pathology normalizes its own internal heterogeneity by defusing its psychic determinism. Interminability, however, explores the pathology *within* Pathology as a site of both negativity and potentiality and does not, indeed cannot, demand closure.

By transgressing the division of labor between confession and Autobiography, De Quincey explores a Wordsworthian/Coleridgean tension between a psychotherapeutic or philosophical cure of the psyche and a psychoanalysis that resists this cure. In its attempt to account for the unconscious, De Quincey's philosophy turns into a free-association that produces a split in philosophy itself. The majestic Wordsworthian intellectual pursuit of De Quincey's mind, its desire to bend his narrative toward philosophical closure, is unsettled by its Coleridgean body of psychosomatic evidence. This body of "excess, not yet *recorded*" (*WDQ* 2:10), reproduces itself through his dreams as a psychic determinism from which he cannot free himself, the Abyssinian plain of Wordsworth's transcendental imagination turned into the "Nilotic mud" (2:71) of De Quincey's unconscious. De Quincey attempts to provide his own overview of this unconscious, but is also compelled to give a deconstruction of its details. He thus explores the autobiography of philosophy at the site of its own self-making in the psyche of the philosopher himself. This autobiography does not order the conscious mind but rather confesses its own unreason as the poetry of philosophy that Wordsworth and Coleridge ultimately resist.

For De Quincey philosophy is the work of the "*subtle thinker*" who has "an inner eye and power of intuition for the vision and the mysteries of our human nature," besides "merely the possession of a superb intellect in its *analytic* functions" (2:12–13). But his exploration of the "incommunicable" leaves him alone with a mind/body singularly beyond his control. De Quincey's philosophy is thus conflicted between a Wordsworthian moral-contemplative mode and its more Coleridgean mode as endless subtlety, which in *Biographia Literaria* Coleridge defines as wandering in the labyrinth or "unwholesome quicksilver mines of metaphysic depths" (*BL* 1:17). Like Wordsworth, De Quincey is a philosopher-*infans* fascinated by his own reason. He writes, "from my birth I was made an intellectual creature. . . . [T]he opium-eater boasteth himself to be a philosopher; and accordingly, . . . the phantasmagoria of *his* dreams . . . is suitable to one who in that character, *Humani nihil a se alienum putat* ['He deems nothing that is human foreign to him']" (*WDQ* 2:10–12). For De Quincey, like Coleridge, reason, like the "sensual pleasure" of opium, holds him in "fascinating enthralment" (2:10). When in Stanza 8 of the Intimations Ode Wordsworth refigures the boy of Winander, who in *The Prelude* is "Mute, looking at the grave in which he lies" (*P* 5.422), as if mesmerized by the unconscious of his own psychic life, he reconceives the developmental child immaculately as "Philosopher" and "Mighty Prophet! Seer blest" (*WP* 110, 114). But he also *dis*figures his inner philosopher-child as lying awake in his own grave. This "place of thought where we in waiting lie"[14] is a type of abortion of the child's psyche as always already dead. The embalmed psyche—the *reductio ad absurdum* of the contemplative mind as a mind at eternal rest before it is even born—horrified Coleridge (Wordsworth subsequently removed the passage).

The child suggests the semio-type of a potential analysis of the psyche that Wordsworth, by foreclosing the 'couch' within the coffin, resists.

Coleridge's reaction to Wordsworth's child is part of his works' genotext of the psychoanalytical explored through the tension between philosophy and autobiography in the *Biographia.* In "Dejection: An Ode" this child becomes the abject of Wordsworthian vision, the "Reality's dark dream" of the "little child" lost "Upon a lonesome wild," who "now moans low in bitter grief and fear" (*CP* 95, 121–24). But where Coleridge stops short of exploring Wordsworthian interiority, De Quincey psychoanalyzes the suffering subject born into and borne through the world by the "dark dream" of its unconscious, the "poor, friendless child" (*WDQ* 2:199) who repeats the author's own suffering presence as if at the primal scene of childhood affliction. He focuses specifically on how the empiricism of the unconscious produces grief and suffering. In *Suspiria*, for instance, the trance in Elizabeth's chamber "remoulded itself continually" in De Quincey's "Oxford dreams" (15:170). *Confessions* explores the "case of poor Anne the Outcast," which "shaped, moulded and remoulded, composed and decomposed—the great body of opium dreams" (2:102). Like the Boy of Winander reviving as the drowned man of Esthwaite, De Quincey's decomposing body of dreams signifies a free-associating imagination that endlessly reproduces itself through the "*myriad*" (2:36) associations of his unconscious. Indeed, the face, a type of transcendental signified of the *anthropos*'s rational identity, comes to signify a perpetually lost, endlessly proliferating pathology of reason. In its most extreme form, De Quincey suffers the unmitigated grief produced by the "transition from the . . . unutterable monsters and abortions of [his] dreams, to the sight of innocent *human* natures and of infancy" in his children's faces, his Wordsworthian child within having become a "damned crocodile" (2:71–72).

That De Quincey's experience of his unconscious in *Confessions* suspends reason to expose his narrative to its own interminability necessitates in his writings a kind of generic revolution in which philosophy and narrative challenge the limiting epistemologies of established generic distinctions. *Suspiria* is most radical in this respect, philosophically shaping the poetry of its own self-observation without making the latter answerable to the former. In the 1853 General Preface to the first British edition of his collected works, *Selections Grave and Gay, Writings Published and Unpublished*, De Quincey places *Suspiria* as the third or "far higher class of compositions" above the first class of merely descriptive works such as "Autobiographic Sketches," which "[propose] merely to amuse the reader," and the second class of "ESSAYS," which "address themselves purely to the understanding as an insulated faculty." *Suspiria* "more emphatically" repeats *Confessions* as a form of "impassioned prose" (20:12–16). Different from Wordsworth, who transcendentalizes passion, or Joanna Baillie's "Introductory Discourse" to *Plays on the Passions*, which suggests a clinical taxonomy of feeling,[15] *Suspiria* addresses an impassioned range of suffering that speaks beyond and frequently *against* "understanding."[16]

This "impassioned prose" recalls Wordsworth's attempt to manage poetry as philosophy, conflicted by its own impassioned contemplation of reason, philosophy's unconscious of which Coleridge's poetry is symptomatic. But De Quincey's prose extracts the heterogeneous work of poetry from its conscious rhetoric both in philosophy and in poetry itself and submits this poetry to psychoanalysis.[17] De Quincey must then surrender narrative as a vehicle of logic and the *logos*—the ordering work of Autobiography—to the contingency of its own experiential other—the self-writing of the confessional imagination. That is, De Quincey drags the psychology of poetry onto the scene of its interrogation in narrative and so collapses poetry into a prose that must subsequently negotiate between philosophy and poetry, metaphysics and psychology, as part of a transitional psychoanalysis. The late nineteenth-century editor of De Quincey, Alexander H. Japp, called the *Suspiria* "Prose-poems," which are "deeply philosophical, presenting under the guise of phantasy the profoundest laws of the working of the human spirit in its most terrible disciplines."[18] But the psychosomatic effects of De Quincey's addiction confronts him with a phantasy that constitutes philosophy rather than disguises its "profoundest laws." What is supernatural threat in Coleridge's poetry, the return of fancy in his theory of imagination, is for De Quincey constitutive of imagination as the site of reason's or philosophy's self-making, a phantasmatic structure that becomes philosophy's profoundest law and that leaves unsutured the rift of the unconscious that the Kantian sublime opens yet subsequently glosses over. This means that, unlike Wordsworth's treatment of Margaret or Coleridge's of Christabel's mother, De Quincey identifies with the wandering figures of his text as projections of his own unconscious (Anne or Elizabeth, the Dark Interpreter, the apparition of the Brocken, Levana and the Ladies of Sorrow). This means that, at some level, women once again do the dirty psychic work for the male Romantic writer. However, in De Quincey, despite glaring blindnesses (the rabid imperialism of much of his sociopolitical writings, for one thing), can be also empathic to the situation of the other, often, as in the case of Anne, when the other is the woman as outcast from society. While Anne's voice, like Margaret's in Wordsworth's texts, is missing in De Quincey's, his sensitivity to and identification with her 'silence' constitutes a marked difference between men. As often as not, this means that he seems willing to inhabit his texts through the spectral form of his own autobiography as confession. In *Suspiria* this confessional persona stages in mythopoeic terms the shifting scene of philosophy's self-writing as the mobile hybrid of the psychoanalytic scene.

De Quincey's encounter with the excess of Kantian reason is not unlike Schopenhauer's interrogation of Kant's idealism, wherein the system Schopenhauer would construct unravels into an autobiography of philosophy.[19] De Quincey similarly offers a philosophy that confesses its own limits. Up to his addiction, his Autobiography follows a developmental pattern in which the body of suffering lies dormant within the mind's contemplative life. Opium disrupts this tranquillity by exposing the subject to the unconscious as the site of his absent psychosomatic identity. Confronting this identity, De Quincey is compelled to retrace its origins in the time before his addiction, and as a simple act of memory this process still conforms to a linear chronology. Yet its regressive thrust also reproduces a myriad of psychic forms that turn Aristotelian chronology into Nietzschean genealogy. Confession moves back to the future of a radically splintering self-exploration that unfolds toward the always receding terminus of *Confessions* and, most radically, toward *Suspiria*'s narration of the incommunicable. *Suspiria* revisits the earlier *Confessions* as the scene of its own psychoanalysis in order to remember its psychic effects. Yet the 1856 revisions suggest that these effects are more repeated than remembered. This takes us back to the future of this repetition in *Suspiria* itself, an intertextual struggle that betrays De Quincey's desire for system. In 1856 he recalls that he "had devoted the labour of [his] whole life . . . to the slow and elaborate toil of constructing one single work," to be named after Spinoza's unfinished *De Emendatione Humani Intellectus*:

> This was now lying locked up as by frost, like any Spanish bridge or aqueduct, begun upon too great a scale for the resources of the architect; and, instead of surviving me, as a monument of wishes at least, and aspirations, and a life of labour dedicated to the exaltation of human nature[,] . . . was likely to stand a memorial to my children of hopes defeated, of baffled efforts, of materials uselessly accumulated, of foundations laid that were never to support a superstructure,—of the grief and the ruin of the architect. (*WDQ* 2:63)

Addiction ruins the organic growth of De Quincey's imagination, the symptom of grief exposing an absent psychosomatic body of suffering that remains as unrealizable within the architecture of reason as *The Recluse* does in Wordsworth's writing. De Quincey names the primal scene of this body as the infant born into a suffering existence sutured psychosomatically between mind and body. This suffering forms the matrix of the psychoanalysis De Quincey then helps to invent.

Chronic Psychoanalysis: *Confessions of an English Opium-Eater*

The 1821 Text

David Wright calls *Confessions of an English Opium-Eater* the "prose counterpart of *The Prelude*."[20] Wordsworth's text ends up being "unprecedented" because talking never seems to suffice. "I have lengthened out / With fond and feeble tongue a tedious tale," he writes to Coleridge, in the hope that he "might fetch / Invigorating thoughts from former years" and "fix the wavering balance of [his] mind" (*P* 1.646–50). But his endless revisions mean that more talking determines the text's epic shape instead of the aesthetic imperative to cure the mind's "wavering balance." By exposing Wordsworthian interiority to psychoanalysis, *Confessions* seems to offer the mode of self-observation *The Prelude* suppresses. But De Quincey's "unprecedented" claim is not without its own resistances. Psychoanalysis in *Confessions* is a chronic response to interminability that uses interpretation to palliate rather than cure the psyche.[21] The confessional imagination's psychic determinism exposes the unconscious as the place where reason falters and where the text ends up skirting a psychic exhaustion of never being able to speak the "whole burthen of horrors which lies upon [De Quincey's] brain" (*WDQ* 2:61).

This exhaustion is not at first apparent in the 1821 text. Its opening address "To the Reader" apologizes "for breaking through that delicate and honourable reserve, which . . . restrains us from the public exposure of our own errors and infirmities." De Quincey says he will explore the "moral ulcers and scars" under the "'decent drapery,' which time, or indulgence to human frailty, may have drawn over them."[22] And unlike Wordsworth, De Quincey goes public, "hav[ing] for many months hesitated about the propriety of allowing this, or any part of my narrative, to come before the public eye, until after my death (when for many reasons, the whole will be published) . . ." (2:9). The decision to publish may not be Wordsworthian, but the passage's feint of reservation is. Moreover, De Quincey's pseudonym, "X.Y.Z.," protects his real self from the work of confession. His self-analysis "court[s] privacy and solitude" but also presents itself as a "useful and instructive record." Both daring and calculated, De Quincey exposes the text's unorthodox nature to public censure at the same time that he manages the other's response within this transference. He figures his audience as a subject "into whose private ear [he is] confidentially whispering [his] confessions" (2:61), both courting acceptance of his psychoanalytical authority and affirming the reader's ability to hear his confession.[23] De Quincey figures himself as a subject presumed to know and also submits to the reader as a silent screen upon which to project his unconscious.[24]

But we are thus never sure where to place the confessing *cogito*. "To the Reader" is followed by "Preliminary Confessions," which attempts to tie the confessor's internal life to his external history. This "introductory narrative of the youthful adventures which laid the foundation of the writer's habit of opium-eating in after-life . . . furnish[es] a key to . . . the dreams of the Opium-eater" and "creat[es] some previous interest of a personal sort in the confessing subject" (2:12). But it also recounts the "youthful sufferings which first produced [the] derangement of the stomach" that precipitated De Quincey's opium use as an "article of daily diet" (2:13). The text's conflict between mind and body isolates the somatic within De Quincey's psychic life, but also leaves the text divided against itself.[25] As De Quincey states in 1856, the immediate origin of his addiction was an *acute* physical ailment demanding a terminable medical cure. His chronic or "*habitual* use of opium" (2:109), however, resulted from the "misery" and "settled and abiding darkness" that can be traced presomatically to the sufferings of childhood repeated in his dreams. This *symptomatic* or *psychosomatic* life demands a different telling.

De Quincey thus distinguishes his earlier use of opium because of "excrutiating rheumatic pains" (2:42) associated with a toothache from his later 'regular' opium use, begun in 1813, as if to dissociate opium from the body.[26] He refutes the surgeon John Abernethy (1764–1831) who, by arguing that opium dulls the intellect, ties addiction "generically to all modes of nervous excitement" (2:46) and thus relies too heavily on the "materia medica" of science, which medicalizes the psyche as a physiological effect.[27] That is, De Quincey traces the psychogenesis of his "*habitual*" opium use not in nervous disorder but in the evidence of his "large and profound personal experience" (2:45). This reliance on narrative, however, presents other problems. For as De Quincey recounts his suffering, the retelling process itself, especially as the narrative of the psychosomatic body demands telling, increasingly leads narrative astray: "I dally with my subject because, to myself, the remembrance of these times is profoundly interesting" (2:32–33). What Part One is unable to tell in order to account for this body becomes in Part Two this body's resistance to narrative, or rather the uncanny effect of this body's dreamlike nature, a repetitive determinism that wrests narrative from its author's control.

The problem, of course, is the untenable connection between the external events of "Preliminary Confessions" and, as he states in *Suspiria de Profundis*, the "imagery of [De Quincey's] dreams, which translated everything into their own language" (15:132), largely alien to these events. The dreams are told briefly at the end of *Confessions* as if to dissociate them from earlier circumstances. Conversely, the preliminary scenes of the 1821 text seem to be only "interesting in themselves" (2:13), a mere preface to a more relevant later analysis of his life. "Preliminary Confessions" sketches De Quincey's life up to his destitution in London during the winter of 1802–1803 and focuses on his friendship with the prostitute Anne.[28] Certainly, because their separation produced his "heaviest affliction," his time pre-Anne pales by comparison with other events in his etiology of suffering. Yet because of this intensity the reader is compelled to retrace the text's earlier somatology for symptoms of a broader psychosomatic complexity. The missed encounter with Anne becomes a synecdoche for rather than origin of a broader circuit of loss that De Quincey is unable to narrate effectively. This encounter effects two changes: first, it displaces the chronology of De Quincey's suffering by propelling the text toward the indeterminate *telos* of its dreams; second, it evokes in the absence of an origin an insatiable desire to tell what is left untold of the past. The reader is thus caught in an untenable countertransference that, instead of locating the reader in a position of authority, draws her into the text's own circuit of moving back to a future meaning the text can never produce. *We* become the text's psychosomatic subjects.

This effect becomes increasingly apparent as we move into De Quincey's description of his opium pleasures, as when he analyzes the empiricism of the mind's 'other' addictive functioning while recounting his "Opera pleasures" and his London "rambles" (2:49, 50). Listening to music, De Quincey argues, constructs between the senses and the intellect a psychosomatic "pleasure." When heightened by opium, this experience can, through a "chorus . . . of elaborate harmony, [display] before [him], as in a piece of arras work, the whole of [his] past life—not as if recalled by an act of memory, but as if present and incarnated in the music, . . . its passions exalted, spiritualized, and sublimed" (2:48). Opium "introduces amongst [the mental faculties] the most exquisite order, legislation and harmony" and can "overrule all feelings into a compliance with the master key" (2:44, 50). But this figure for how we are to read the text's own ramblings intellectually turns into that of De Quincey's experiential wanderings through London's "*terra incognitae*." These "knotty problems of alleys, such enigmatical entries, and such sphinx's riddles of streets without thoroughfares" are reproduced in his unconscious as a return of past associations for which he "paid a heavy price in distant years, when the human face tyrannized over [his] dreams, and the perplexities of [his] steps in London came back and haunted [his] sleep, with the feeling of perplexities moral or intellectual, that brought confusion to the reason" (2:50). The pleasure of his faculties returns as a repressed free-associationism through which the absent psychosomatic body of De Quincey's unconscious reproduces itself as the suffering or "confusion" of reason, again leaving the reader confused as to where to situate the text's meaning or its author.

As if to systematize this experience, Part Two divides the imagination between "Pleasures" and "Pains." Part Two follows De Quincey's relatively benign use of opium in London in 1804 to his later addiction and nightmares, after his departure from Oxford, from 1812 to 1817. "Pleasures" explores opium's transcendence of bodily suffering and empirical reality through the visionary imagination: "in an hour, oh! Heavens! what a revulsion! what an upheaving, from its lowest depths, of the inner spirit! what an apocalypse of the world within me!" His physical "pains" reduced to a "trifle," De Quincey experiences "the abyss of divine enjoyment thus suddenly revealed," which refutes accepted medical knowledge as to opium's "bodily effects" (2:43). Opium is the "hero" of the tale, then, because, by casting on reality the "great light of the majestic [Wordsworthian] intellect," it anatomizes a mode of (Romantic) self-expression that is the essential embodiment of De Quincey's confessional imagination (2:74, 45). "Pains" explores this imagination's 'other' functioning as a kind of Coleridgean dejection encrypted within pleasures. Certainly in "Pleasures" De Quincey felt only "as if the tumult, the fever, and the strife, were suspended; a respite granted from the secret burthens of the heart" (2:51).[29]

Both "Pleasures" and the subsequent "Introduction to the Pains of Opium" anticipate the return of a free-associationism already present in the mind, as neither section entirely sublates the 'revulsive' and 'upheaving' excess of imagination. Early in "Pleasures" De Quincey describes the "grave and solemn complexion" that later becomes the "gloom and cloudy melancholy of opium" insulating the "brilliant water" of his reason (2:72, 55–56). The dis-ease of the *anthropos* confronted in "Pains" lies only dormant within the body of his purer intellectual or visionary splendors.[30] "Pains" finally shifts to the "history and journal of what took place in [De Quincey's] dreams," "the immediate and proximate cause of [his] acutest suffering" (2:65). Here narrative continuity and moral reticence go out the window: "I have not been able to compose the notes for this part of my narrative into any regular and connected shape" (2:61). Instead, the text becomes narrative free-association: "my way of writing is rather to think aloud, and follow my own humours, than much to consider who is listening to me" (2:62). Liberating the true force of confession from Autobiography, De Quincey now self-observes psychic phenomena. He identifies four common characteristics or "facts" of his dreams,[31] but this metapsychology's speculative nature becomes symptomatic of the unconscious mind's "palsying effects" on his "intellectual faculties" (2:66, 62). Rather than *theorize* the unconscious, De Quincey remains the unwilling spectator of its determinism, his suffering as analysand contesting his authority as analyst.

This determinism radically alters the interpretive thrust of confession. Describing the child's involuntary "power of painting . . . upon the darkness, all sorts of phantoms," De Quincey states that in his dreams "a theatre seemed suddenly opened and lighted up within [his] brain, which presented nightly spectacles of more than earthly splendour." But these "vast processions" also "passed along in mournful pomp" and "friezes of never-ending stories" (2:66). Like his dream of Coleridge's description of Piranesi's *Carceri d'Invenzione*, these tableaux proliferate in "endless growth and self-reproduction" (2:68) beyond De Quincey's ability to control them. Over his dreams "brooded a sense of eternity and infinity that drove [him] into an oppression as of madness," through which his unconscious mutates into the "thousand repetitions" of a "cursed crocodile" (2:71). This multiform pathology is the extreme physiological other of the pragmatic anthropological identity of his majestic intellect, the interminable or excessive functioning of the Wordsworthian "types and characters of the Infinite" (2:72). As he "lies under the weight of incubus and night-mare," his "intellectual apprehension of what is possible infinitely outruns his power, not of execution only, but even of power to attempt" (2:65). His "analytical understanding," while greatly expanded by opium, is overwhelmed by the "intellectual torpour" created by its own interminable "Circean spells" (2:63, 65). This intellectual torpor manifests the latent "disease" of solitude that was in De Quincey's early life a "natural inclination," which, but for his efforts to "counteract" it, would have made him "hypochondriacally melancholy" (2:50). The condition of being alone with one's own mind, the necessary prerequisite to psychoanalysis, is, then, the repetition of the very thing it seeks to avoid. On one hand, "solitude and silence," as the "indispensable conditions of those trances, or profoundest reveries, which are the crown and consummation of what opium can do for human nature," restore psychological equilibrium.[32] However, the exploration of psychic interiority that through opium "naturally seeks solitude and silence" exacerbates the pathology of "meditat[ing] too much," producing a psychosomatic "torpour" that increasingly comes to characterize the fundamental nature of De Quincey's identity (2:50).

The emergence and significance of this psychosomatic identity shifts the text's epistemological center of gravity, a shift focused in two scenes, both of which stage psychoanalysis in solitude. The opening of Part Two terminates De Quincey's London sufferings at the same time that he returns to London in the present, where he writes as a "solitary and contemplative man" who "walked" again in London "for the most part in serenity and peace of mind." De Quincey argues that "although it is true that the calamities of my noviciate in London had struck root so deeply in my bodily constitution that afterwards they shot up and flourished afresh, and grew into a noxious umbrage that has overshadowed and darkened my latter years," he has confronted "these second assaults . . . with a fortitude more confirmed. . . ." He uses a (Wordsworthian) "maturer intellect" to battle his suffering (Coleridgean) body of psychosomatic evidence and looks northward to the "consolation" and "sympathising affection" of Dove Cottage and his wife Margaret: "'*that* is the road to the north, and therefore to [Grasmere], and if I had the wings of a dove, *that* way would I fly for comfort'" (2:39–40).

Revisiting the scene of his London traumas brings De Quincey to his decision to connect later sufferings with earlier origins. But the *mise-en-scène* constructed between London and Grasmere follows a complex temporality that unfolds a more ambivalent response to a psychoanalysis the text both endorses and resists. London, "chief scene of [his] youthful sufferings," still leaves him "oppressed by anxieties that demand all [his] philosophy and the comfort of [his wife Margaret's] presence to support" (2:35, 41). He yearns toward Dove Cottage to avoid the return of the repressed. But the locus of consolation is also the site of the "second birth of [his] sufferings," a primal scene of the latter stages of his opium use: "There it was, that for years I was persecuted by visions as ugly, and as ghastly phantoms as ever haunted the couch of an Orestes" (2:40). His use of the metaphor is crucial. It situates his sufferings in the past, while in the present he conserves the future of the text's self-observation by invoking Margaret's analytical presence, his "Electra." Like Dorothy, she domesticates his dark imagination by rescuing him from the madness of solitude. De Quincey thus contemplates the textual future of the suffering he is about to recount as already worked-through: "these troubles are past: and thou wilt read these records of a period so dolorous to us both as the legend of some hideous dream that can return no more." Preempting analysis by suppressing his "hideous dream" as a story already told, however, De Quincey mobilizes a disruptive transference with Margaret as one whose "own peaceful slumbers had by long sympathy become infected with the spectacle of [his] dread contest with phantoms and shadowy enemies" (2:40–41). His psychic dis-ease contaminates the analytical authority he has thrust upon her. Moreover, he returns to Grasmere as the site of both therapy *and* trauma. An Orestes hunted by his own Furies, De Quincey places himself on the Romantic psychoanalytical couch as the site of an ongoing theater of suffering, just as his dreams open up a "theatre" of "never-ending stories" (2:66). Moving from Autobiography to confession, he formally inscribes psychoanalysis and then discloses its interminable suffering. Against this disclosure, one can read the text's subsequent gestures toward psychic closure as chronic responses to an interminability the text can never cure. It is as though Wordsworth's Margaret, whose nervousness Wordsworth uses his sister Dorothy to domesticate, returns in the form of De Quincey's transference with his wife Margaret (the woman/sister Wordsworth really marries), a marriage that mesmerizes as much as it harmonizes De Quincey's imagination.

As De Quincey "quit[s] the subject of happiness altogether" (2:58), his appeal to the reader grows more urgent. At the end of "Introduction to the Pains of Opium," in order to "save [himself] the trouble of too much verbal description," he invokes an imaginary painter to whom he gives "directions" for the "picture" of his final sufferings within the text (2:60). The shift from the verbal to the visual evokes the shift from narrative as a chronicle of events to narrative as the heuristic telling of the drama of experience. The passage foregrounds in the imaginary reconstruction of the past the temporal gap between experience and interpretation, practice and theory. It also ambiguously orchestrates both the reader's and the author's attempts to work-through this gap. De Quincey paints himself alone in his study with a "quart of ruby-coloured laudanum" and "a book of German metaphysics," thus juxtaposing between the "divine luxuries of opium" and the subtleties of philosophy a missed encounter with psychic revelation (2:60, 11). However, De Quincey also parallels the "fascinating enthralment" of opium and the mesmerizing influence of metaphysics as it discloses the unreason within reason that De Quincey interrogates within the subtext of philosophy: "I read Kant again; and again I understood him, or fancied that I did" (2:56). His opium religion ("the truth church on the subject of opium: of which church I acknowledge myself to be the only member—the alpha and the omega" [2:45]) is thus a variety of mesmerism through which he stages the mutating psyche of his dreams as it resists the philosophy of his analysis.

Tellingly, the passage displaces him to the periphery of his world:

> . . . I ought to occupy the foreground of the picture; that being the hero of the piece, or (if you choose) the criminal at the bar, my body should be had into court. This seems reasonable: but why should I confess, on this point, to a painter? or why confess at all? If the public . . . should chance to have framed some agreeable picture for itself of the Opium-eater's exterior, . . . why should I barbarously tear from it so pleasing a delusion—pleasing both to the public and to me? No: paint me, if at all, according to your own fancy . . . (2:61)

Like the earlier apostrophe to Margaret, De Quincey orchestrates in advance a picturesque reaction to a sublime reality. The hypothetical painter/reader mediates De Quincey's transference with the other by 'composing' its indeterminate effects and thus modeling an allegory of correct rather than dark interpretation. Moreover, by absenting himself from the scene and withholding his dreams ("why confess at all?"), he both protects the reader from confession and turns interpretation over to him, although in this maneuver one also senses the desire to anticipate and thus control the other's pathologizing conclusions. The deferral has a further dimension, however. The painter is also a Dark Interpreter to whose "fancy" De Quincey surrenders the "delusion" of a "pleasing" empirical reality that he less determines than is determined by: the unconscious paints the subject both in or out of his own picture as easily as the subject is able to reconstruct this picture's psychic perspectives. When De Quincey questions a child about his "power of painting" phantoms upon the darkness, the child replies, "'I can tell them to go, and they go; but sometimes they come, when I don't tell them to come'" (2:66). The 1821 *Confessions* remains in conflict about what to do when "they come" against the subject's will, an autonomy of the unconscious in his dreams in "The Pains of Opium," which indicate all too clearly the addictive excess of an absent psychosomatic body, a habit of being from which the subject can never escape.

The 1856 Text

The 1856 *Confessions*, as a response to this conflict, both alleviates and prolongs its ambivalence. De Quincey's expansion of *Confessions* appears more coherently to connect dreams with past suffering and thus to integrate the confessing subject's disparate identities: "in these incidents of my early life is found the entire substratum, together with the secret and underlying motive of those pompous dreams and dream-sceneries which were in reality the true object—first and last—contemplated in these Confessions" (2:110). The 1856 text attempts to contain the earlier text's symptomatic reproduction of the past in light of De Quincey's now much-prolonged addiction, the contingency of his life's experience having evolved separately from his self-writing effort to control it. "I trace the origin of my confirmed opium-eating to a *necessity* growing out of my early suffering in the streets of London," De Quincey now writes with an urgency precipitated by the fact that by 1856 he has "four several times" overcome his addiction only to [resume] it upon the warrant of [his] enlightened and deliberate judgment." Hence, although the 1821 text emphasizes his London experience, "what reasonably calls for sorrow" in 1856 is the "extravagance of childish folly which precipitated [him] into scenes naturally producing such hardships." He thus greatly expands these scenes as the "key to the proper understanding of all which follows," as now "indispensable" to his narrative (2:109–10). Furthermore, his recurring bouts with addiction make it that much more imperative that he find the psychic origins of his later suffering. The 1856 text uses its backward deductive momentum to stabilize the indeterminate inductive weight of the 1821 moral of De Quincey's Pyrrhic victory over opium. The symptomatic force of this balancing act, however, simultaneously pulls De Quincey toward the "Nilotic mud" of his unconscious, a process that in its determination to tell definitively what was left untold in 1821 succumbs to its own psychoanalytical compulsion to say more. The telling of the unconscious becomes the alpha and omega of his project in a way that De Quincey does not entirely anticipate.

In 1856 De Quincey acknowledges that Parts One and Two had "no link whatever to connect them, except the slight one of having both happened to the same person" (2:204), his fear being precisely that, both as child and adult and as mind and body, he is two different people at once. In the 1856 "Pains of Opium" he explains this "*causal* connection" in order to rationalize the earlier text's disparate narrative instructions and thus to clarify the backward temporality of the text's psychoanalysis at the precise point that in 1821 he sacrifices narrative continuity:

> The final object of the whole record lay in the dreams. For the sake of those the entire narrative arose. But what caused the dreams? Opium used in unexampled excess. But what caused this excess in the use of opium? Simply the early sufferings; . . . through the derangements which they left behind in the animal

> economy. On this mode of viewing the case, moving regressively from the end to the beginning, . . . there is one uninterrupted bond of unity running through the entire succession of experiences—first and last: the dreams were an inheritance from the opium; the opium was an inheritance from the boyish follies. (2:240–41)

To avoid the unraveling 1821 terminus, De Quincey, by a narrative sleight of hand, relocates the telos of his narrative in the text's beginning in the past, so that the more heterogeneous (Jungian) pathology of his dream-life is now tied to the biology of its (Freudian) ontogenesis. Accordingly, the 1856 text also streamlines the ambivalent divisions of the earlier text into three distinct sections to resolve suffering dialectically backward, the antithesis between 'pleasures' and 'pains' being synthesized regressively in the origin of suffering in the text's opening "Confessions."[33]

Yet the proliferating confession of 1856, intended to buttress the confessing subject's social Autobiography, unravels into its own interminability, the symptom of a past that the text's dream-life—the end of the text's other in its 'other' end—had already determined to be incommunicable. The 1856 *Confessions* returns to the original *Confessions* as the primal scene of its inability to work-through its own indeterminacy, the later symptom of which is De Quincey's recurring addiction. However, because the 1856 text attempts to read this scene as a textual unconscious amenable to enlightenment, this return involves a repetitive temporality that exceeds De Quincey's ability to name it in the above passage. In the 1856 Preface De Quincey speaks of the text's "own former self" whose "narrative had been needlessly impoverished." The 1856 text will now say what was in 1821 left unsaid: "not so properly correction and retrenchment were called for, as integration of what had been left imperfect, or amplification of what, from the first, had been insufficiently expanded" (2:100). By naming the earlier text's "*burden of the Incommunicable*," the later text raises from symptom to interpretation the subject's displacement by what he cannot tell. But, again, naming the unconscious also places it within a hermeneutic that claims to circumvent the very interminability to which, by virtue of the text's prolonged talking, it inevitably succumbs, the explanation of a symptom for which there can be no cure.

De Quincey's more significant 1856 additions reproduce more than they alleviate symptoms. Expanding the telling of his time at Manchester Grammar School, De Quincey calls his decision to leave a "fatal error" (2:138), which seems an "inexorable advance" and "rapturous command" (2:143) that is largely "*Inexplicable*" (2:138) except as it was "spoken from some hidden recess in [his] own will" (2:144) and through "forms of darkness shrouded within the recesses of blind human hearts" (2:153–54). The "deep deep magnet" of Wordsworth and the "enchanted land" (2:147) of his poetry draws De Quincey away, but this magnetism is only part of his departure's mystery that De Quincey would understand. To account for the hidden motivations of the experiential, he uses the example of rhabdomancy (which in its "ordinary physical" sense means the art of divining wells) as it evokes the "marvellous magnetism of Christianity." Within the context of Christianity's "magical power of evocation," rhabdomancy signifies the "[unveiling] or [deciphering] of what is hidden" in the exegetic sense of "gifts of interpretation applied to what is dark, of analysis applied to what is logically perplexed, of expansion applied to what is condensed, of practical improvement applied to what might else be overlooked as purely speculative." This exegetical power has "called up from the darkness sentiments the most august, previously inconceivable, formless, and without life," and "by incarnating these sentiments in images of corresponding grandeur, . . . has so exalted their character as to lodge them eternally in human hearts" (2:152–53, 152n). Such analysis is, De Quincey notes further, linked to the practice of *oneiromancy*, or the interpretation of dreams, deriving from the Greek word *oneiros* or "dream"—an explanation meant to contain the later disturbing recounting of his dreams in "The Pains of Opium."

The problem is that De Quincey cannot tell if he is agent or patient within this process. That this divination materializes sentiments where there were none, lodging them *as if* they were eternal "in human hearts," suggests the phantasmatic structure of the absent psychosomatic body called forth in mesmerism, which appears as if from the nonempirical, but to exert in indisputable empirical effect. Coleridge argues that "[t]he pith of [his] system is to make senses out of the mind—not the mind out of the senses, as Locke did."[34] Where Coleridge was looking for the SUM that 'makes' sense of things, De Quincey is oddly closer to the Lockean perspective Coleridge rejects: the senses produce a mind, to be sure, but one without any distinct control over its own body, a body that has a mind of its own not in any metaphysical sense. Like mesmerism, the effects of rhabdomancy produce evidence of a process that cannot be empirically validated except by these effects (as De Quincey quips, rhabdomanists are rejected for "[building] upon a long chain of induction, upon the uniform results of their lifelong experience," without attention to the result that "most of the tea-kettles in the vale of Wrington are filled by *rhabdomancy*" [2:152n]). De Quincey's implicit point seems to be that his confessing subjectivity likewise produces a suspect yet undeniable body of psychosomatic evidence that takes on a life of its own. The 1856 text uses rhabdomancy to give an explanatory shape within his opening "Confessions" to a psychic experience that the 1821 text had broached only in its later sections. In this way, the 1856 opening "Confessions" attempts to preempt the symptomatic interminability that unraveled the 1821 text. But this naming also formalizes a digressively interminable fascination with and by the unconscious. By focusing on the "blind sympathy of some unknown force" that defines the "interspace between religion and philosophy," De Quincey figures interpretation as a type of mesmerism wherein he is agent or patient—or neither at the same time (2:152n, 162).

Two further episodes reinforce this textual fascination. In his last hours before departing Manchester, De Quincey dreams with "eyes open" in a "sort of trance, a frost as of some death-like revelation." The reverie restages an earlier experience in the Whispering Gallery of St. Paul's Cathedral, in which the voice of one of his friends' "breathing in the softest of whispers a solemn but not acceptable truth" at one end of the gallery reaches De Quincey as a "deafening menace in tempestuous uproars" at the other. But in *this* reverie he is further "surprised" by *another* dream of the "great Roman warning, *Nescit vox missa reverti* (that a word once uttered is irrevocable), a freezing arrest upon the motions of hope too sanguine that [also] haunted [him] in many shapes" in later life (2:155–56). Each dream stages in turn the determinism of experience, which the subject then reexperiences as a psychic determinism that discloses the insight of his blindness as the reproduction of further blindnesses. This determinism returns a few pages later in De Quincey's description of the Bore. De Quincey describes walking along the Cop of the river Dee toward a woman "steadily advancing towards [him]—face to face," her "countenance naturally serv[ing] as a mirror to echo and reverberate [his] own feelings." He then hears a "sudden uproar of tumultuous sounds rising clamourously ahead," from some "passionate" and "mysterious" "unseen reach": "*Ahead* I mean in relation to myself, but to *her* the sound was from the rear. . . . Only this I felt, that blind, unorganised nature it must be—and nothing in human or in brutal wrath." The "proximate cause of this mystery declared itself to [their] eyes, although the remote cause (the hidden cause of that visible cause) was still dark as before," as a Bore of water "coming down upon [them] at the rate of forty miles an hour." He later asks her "how . . . she read the mystery?" She replies that the Bore is an "affection to which only some few rivers here and there were liable" (2:163–65). De Quincey then modifies this description to "nervous affection," as if nervously to medicalize or pathologize a spontaneous overflow of feeling beyond his control. Yet he also locates this force in a nervous or psychosomatic body that both materializes their response and sets this response deterministically beyond their bounds of reason as the nervous body of Nature itself.

Through the passages on rhabdomancy, the Whispering Gallery, and the Bore a scene of psychoanalysis emerges that seems to have more than symptomatic but slightly less than cognitive value within the text. The rhabdomanist is a medium conducting darker forces he can only presume to know; the Whispering Gallery reframes this process as the relay of this blind sympathy between two equally mesmerized subjects; in the final passage two subjects, either agent or patient, confront one another "face to face." Their traumatic encounter with a blind and causeless determinism functions transferentially to threaten their identities; from this crisis emerges dialogue that interprets the unseen motivation of their experience, but only to mark its fundamental mystery. The text conceptualizes the idea of psychoanalysis as a mobile scene of confrontation with the mesmerizing influence of the unconscious, but also as a psychoanalysis mesmerized by its own functioning. The Whispering Gallery and the Bore symbolize how the telling and thus the naming of psychic determinism within autobiography in 1856 reinforces this determinism as a textual figure for how interminability has not been overcome. Consequently, this determinism turns merely digressive passages into symptoms of an addiction to telling that displaces the purpose of confession altogether. The *very* long account of Manchester Grammar School, for instance, is now prolonged to the point of being pointless, leaving the reader mesmerized by so much telling.

De Quincey's revisions become especially conflicted at the end of the text. In 1821 De Quincey's telling of his "final specimen" dream evokes the ambivalence of Wordsworth's Arab Dream: "Somewhere, I knew not where—somehow, I knew not how—by some beings, I knew not whom—a battle, a strife, an agony, was conducting,—was evolving like a great drama, or piece of music; . . . I . . . had the power, and yet had not the power, to decide it." The free-associationism of his unconscious leaves De Quincey mesmerized by its psychic determinism at the same time that he remains aware of his position as a figure "central to every movement" within the scene of its unfolding. He is conscious of his identity, but as something he cannot possess. The dream's death-like "sense that all was lost" and that the unconscious shatters the illusion of his identity leaves De Quincey himself shattered: "I awoke in struggles, and cried aloud—'I will sleep no more!'" (2:73–74). The 1856 text describes the dream as "a battle, a strife, an agony" that "was travelling through all its stages—was evolving itself, like the catastrophe of some mighty drama" (2:264). Here De Quincey imposes "stages"to foreground the dream's internal logic within the external logic of dream interpretation, the simile evoking a crisis worked through by aesthetically framing the unconscious. The intensive "itself," however, stresses a different agency, depending on whether "to evolve" is treated transitively or intransitively. As a gerund, 'to evolve' offers the possibility of an outcome, while the simple infinitive suggests an actionless unfolding without termination. Despite the revision, the dream unfolds both within and autonomously from De Quincey's self-writing authority.

In 1821, having recounted this final dream, after which he vows to "'sleep no more!'," De Quincey writes: "I am now called upon to wind up a narrative which has already extended to an unreasonable length." Unable to relate "how this conflict of horrors was finally brought to its crisis," he shifts attention away from his own failure to a more "legitimate centre": "Not the opium-eater, but the opium, is the true hero of the tale . . . The object was to display the marvellous agency of opium, whether for pleasure or for pain: if that is done the action of the piece has closed." In the next paragraph, as if to evoke the crisis he cannot precipitate, he vows to "die throwing it [opium] off," but at the beginning of the next paragraph he writes: "I triumphed: but think not, reader, that therefore my sufferings were ended" (2:74–75). In 1856, to resolve this tension between closure and indeterminacy, he discards the previous two paragraphs and describes instead the (Victorian) social subject who, like Wordsworth and Mill, has triumphed over the (Romantic) ambivalence of this subject's interiority:

> Nothing short of mortal anguish, in a physical sense, it seemed, to wean myself from opium; yet, on the other hand, death through overwhelming nervous terrors . . . seemed too certainly to besiege the alternative course. Fortunately I had still so much of firmness left as to face that choice, which, with most of instant suffering, showed in far distance a possibility of final escape. (2:265)

To confirm this stoicism, at the start of the next paragraph De Quincey writes: "This possibility was realised: I *did* accomplish my escape." But the Preface to the 1856 text challenges this self-prescription. De Quincey speaks of curing the imperfection of the "very principle of change" in the 1821 text, but the battle has been "won at a price of labour and suffering" in the form of a "nervous malady, . . . which has attacked [him] intermittingly for the last eleven years" and has returned "almost concurrently with the commencement of this revision . . ." Reading beyond the end of the 1856 text, the Preface reactivates rather than alleviates the symptoms of the text's production: "The consequences have been distressing to all concerned. The press has groaned under the chronic visitation; the compositors shudder at the sight of my handwriting" and the "wearying siege of an abiding sickness" has tainted the "clearness of critical vision."[35] "[K]nowing the unintelligibility and the repulsiveness of all attempts to communicate the Incommunicable," De Quincey "attempt[s] no description of this combat," the burden of which leaves him in turn repelled, paralyzed (2:100–1). The 1856 revisions, rather than restoring the mind's control over the body, produce instead the return of a repetitive psychosomatic determinism that makes its own nervous revisions to the text. This "chronic" and "abiding" return of the somatic before the text even begins marks the implicitly interminable, repetitive, and deterministically psychoanalytic nature of De Quincey's revisions. This undertaking is rendered impossibly symptomatic in advance of the reader's entry into the text. His interpretive cure is immediately compromised in the way the text compromises its own philosophical integrity, to compose a psychoanalysis that collapses at the site of its own cure. By 1856, Nigel Leask argues, *Confessions* is "removed from the troubling no man's land of the elegant case-history or pathology" of both the personal and the cultural in the 1821 version and "settled comfortably into the genre of literary autobiography,"[36] wherein the reader can also more comfortably find his own bearings in the business of validating De Quincey's self-worth. But it is also true that the 1856 text is in many ways more Romantically heterodox than its predecessor.

Acute Psychoanalysis: *Suspiria de Profundis*

Both *Confessions* circumscribe a psychoanalysis compelled to cure interminability with more telling, more interpretation. Like addiction, this telling evokes a kind of exhaustion from living with the "burden of the Incommunicable," of never being able to say enough. Chronologically this exhaustion comes later in the author's life. Symptomatically, however, it suggests a response to psychoanalysis throughout his confessional writings. Rather than attempting to tell what cannot be told, *Suspiria de Profundis* stages De Quincey's perception of the unconscious at the *acute* moment where the suffering subject encounters the "*umbras* and *penumbras*" (15:569) of his radical otherness. *Suspiria* resituates the dream, the unconscious, repetition, trauma and the primal scene within an aesthetic metapsychology, an interpretation of dreams, as I suggested earlier, that is literary and aesthetic rather than scientific. It then deploys the imaginary nature of this apparatus at the site where psychic determinism and self-making deconstruct identity. Reading in his "unsearchable depths" the "creative agencies in every part of human nature" (15:569), De Quincey sees the dark reflection of his salvation, the self-making alterity of the *anthropos* that is the limit form of De Quinceyan Romantic psychoanalysis. Moreover, *Suspiria*'s repeated appeals to its reader makes her complicit in a transference different from that demanded by *Confessions*. If *Confessions* situates its reader ambivalently as both judge of its moral character and conspiratorial confessant, a role increasingly compromised by the text's psychoanalytical functioning, *Suspiria* seems to take this transference for granted as part of the text's being. The reader is positioned as spectator of but also actor within—both analyst and analysand—its scene of epistemological suffering.

De Quincey had ambitious plans for *Suspiria*, but what survives gives little sense of the work's structure.[37] He never revised *Suspiria* for his Collected Edition, an absence that seems to abject psychoanalysis from his *corpus*. Officially a "sequel" to the 1821 *Confessions*, *Suspiria* returns to the earlier text as a kind of primal scene of interminability. But it also interrogates in advance of the 1856 revisions an equivocal response to 1821 by staging the textual unconscious of both texts as its own. It offers an acute confrontation with the radical contingency of Romantic psychoanalysis as myth-making at the threshold between self-making and psychic determinism. Moreover, that De Quincey suffered the intensity of this experience as both "divine luxuries" and "cancerous kisses" (2:71) indicates that this psychoanalysis is an interminably *lived* rather than merely *interpretive* experience, inevitably impossible but existentially necessary to maintain. *Suspiria*'s lyric condensation and allegorical obscurity sublate interminability through a *bricollage* of heterogeneous psychic episodes—some autobiographical, some theoretical, some apocalyptic—which suggest the visionary sweep of the subject across the genealogy of his disparate parts. By both naming and staging its own psychoaesthetic apparatus as part of its self-making response to the unconscious, *Suspiria* marks the first determinate rather than symptomatic emergence of Romantic psychoanalysis traced by this study.

The larger structure of *Suspiria* thus emerges from its *un*systematic account of the psyche through its absent as well as existing parts. In this sense the work suggests the epic alterity of Wordsworth's unrealizable idea for *The Recluse*. *Suspiria* psychoanalyzes within the reflective identity of that text's Gothic body its sepulchral recesses, confronting there the "mutations that extend their sway" by breeding "fear and awe." If *Confessions* is tempted by Wordsworthian strictures, *Suspiria* stages the unseen/scene of reason as the dramatization of its unconscious.[38] De Quincey examines how the pathology of a free-associating imagination dehumanizes the *anthropos*. This anatomy is shaped, not by a philosophical disciplining of its interiority, but from the psychic determinism of interiority itself, from which the text's metapsychology emerges as a radically equivocal form. Unlike *Confessions*, *Suspiria* allows itself to be shaped by the "body of De Quincey's opium dreams," a body that mutates its own organic form as it develops.[39] Put another way, *Suspiria* dissociates the psychic functioning of organicism from its Coleridgean ideology in order to examine how organicism's mutating poetic content breeds within its aesthetic or philosophical form, the 1856 *Confessions*' "first and last" structure.

The English Mail-Coach, which De Quincey planned to include as part of *Suspiria*, describes this organicism as "the caprices, the gay arabesques, and the lovely floral luxuriations" that "betray a shocking tendency to pass into finer maniacal splendours." This "horrid inoculation upon each other of incompatible natures" demonstrates the pathology of imagination, through which the "dreamer finds housed within himself . . . some horrid alien nature" that "contradicts his own, fights with it, perplexes and confounds it." More disturbingly, this pathology proliferates into multiple forms which shake the "inviolable sanctuary" of the self (16:421–23).[40] The "Dream-Fugue" from *The English Mail-Coach* refigures Wordsworth's Gothic church as the "mighty mists" out of which arises an "infinite cathedral" containing a "vast necropolis" or "city of sepulchres." Within this vision unfolds a "rising, sinking, fluttering, trembling, praying" female "sinking down to darkness," one of the dream's "dreadful resurrections." This "female infant that rode in a carriage as frail as flowers" proliferates into a sea of "faces, which no man could count" (16:442–49). The passage recalls the sea of "innumerable faces . . . surged upwards by thousands, by myriads, by generations, by centuries" (2:70) in *Confessions*, but now as a cognate of the subject's multiple personalities. This anthropomorphization of the hidden mind genders the unconscious as a kind of infantile and infantalizing succubus devouring rational identity; yet it also represents a powerful locus of encrypted meaning—a radically generative semiosis—to which De Quincey is drawn as to a necessary psychoanalysis that leaves the masculinity of reason inadequate to the task.

De Quincey's hybrid organicism derives from the immanent errancy of its own form to challenge Romanticism's anthropomorphization of the post-Kantian subject.[41] The source of being is what Krell refers to as idealism's *contagion*. Krell's account evokes reason's lack of immunity to the "dire forces of nature."[42] Perceived as homogeneous, organicism functions against itself through the psychic divisions between consciousness and the unconscious, waking and dreaming, representation and will.

Coleridge's organicism exposes the "roots" of his system insofar as they "lift themselves above ground [and] are visible to the naked eye of consciousness." For Schopenhauer, as we have seen, the roots of consciousness, while "essential, original, perennial, and primary," are hidden by the will's blind determinism: the subject (dis)appears at the collum or intersection between the will's "root" and the "secondary" and "dying" corona of representation. De Quincey describes this indeterminate appearance in traumatic terms, through what John Whale describes as arbitrary or "anarchic" moments of "sudden revelation, in a crisis, of a hitherto unknown starting-point."[43] The subject's appearance is eruptive, as in *The English Mail-Coach*, marking the traumatic way in which identity becomes palpably present as part of the subject's experience of himself, the painful reminder that the psychosomatics of experience is the guarantee of identity that necessarily dispossesses us of this representation and its truth-value.

Suspiria's "Introductory Notice" explains this traumatic organicism as the free-association of narrative commensurate in the text with De Quincey's self-observation of this subjectivity, an account of the faltering narrative continuity that "The Pains of Opium" never quite supplies:

> the whole course of this narrative resembles . . . a *caduceus* wreathed about with meandering ornaments, or the shaft of a tree's stem hung round and surmounted with some vague parasitical plant. The mere medical subject of opium answers to the dry withered pole, which shoots all the rings of the flowering plants, and seems to do so by some dexterity of its own; whereas, in fact, the plant and its tendrils have curled round the sullen cylinder by mere luxuriance of *theirs*. . . . The true object in my "Opium Confessions" is not the naked physiological theme—on the contrary, *that* is the ugly pole, the murderous spear, the halbert—but those wandering musical variations upon the theme—those parasitical thoughts, feelings, digressions, which climb up with bells and blossoms round about the arid stock; ramble away from it at times with perhaps too rank a luxuriance; but at the same time . . . spread a glory over incidents that for themselves would be—less than nothing. (15:135)

Here De Quincey sets aside the "mere medical" physiology of opium for the imagination's "parasitical" and digressive effects, a telling of the psyche that continually leads narrative astray from the psyche, but whose digressiveness is integral to this account. This narrative economy becomes the model for *Suspiria*'s attempt to read between consciousness and the unconscious, its restless search for an apparatus for its own self-exploration. It revisits scenes and figures from *Confessions*, but now reads the past within the imaginary structure of the metapsychology it evolves for this reading.[44] This process is less a stable hermeneutic than a mobile tableaux of psychic perspectives, a shifting ontology of the scene of Romantic psychoanalysis that tells different versions of the subject, which both comment upon and contest one another. We are thus compelled to read the text in two ways: genealogically, as successive stages in a process of psychic development unfolding a radically *un*grounded *mythos* of the self; and palimpsestically, as the composite of this myth's disparate parts held synchronously within the psychoanalytical imaginary that the text urges its reader to construct.

"The Affliction of Childhood," by unfolding the paradigmatic form of the unconscious through the syntagmatic chain of narrative, offers the former model as a type of psychic reverie: a wandering of the mind that takes its meandering shape from the dictates of the unconscious. "The Palimpsest" offers the latter model of how to read the mind's deep structure (and thus the deep structure of the text) in order to expose its formation. "Levana and Our Ladies of Sorrow" names this structure as a "dream-legend" (15:182n) or visionary telling of identity between waking thoughts and dream thoughts. The unconscious, its "dream-legends" determined by past experience, becomes in turn the legend by which we are always reading the past toward a future present. *Suspiria*'s telling of identity is thus an infinite displacement of our conscious "uttering" into our unconscious past, transacted at the site of a finite present that infinitely escapes the subject's grasp. This "*virtual* time" (15:170) of the unconscious evokes the trance-like nature of the work's "impassioned prose." "Savannah-La-Mar" names this radical contingency as the "deep . . . ploughing of grief" by which "God," who alone is infinite, "sacrifices the human present" to the future:

> the present, which only man possesses, offers less capacity for his footing than the slenderest film that ever spider twisted from her womb. . . . The time which *is*, contracts into a mathematic point; and even that point perishes a thousand times before we can utter its birth. All is finite in the present; and even that finite is infinite in its velocity of flight toward death. (15:186–87)

This vanishing present is rooted in two complexly intertwined modes of experience, Apollonian dreaming and Dionysian suffering, as the locus of the absent psychosomatic body's "fear and awe." In dreams

De Quincey encounters the psychosomatic intensity of his suffering, which compels him to read his dreams to find the origins of suffering as the index of his future:

> The machinery for dreaming . . . , in alliance with the mystery of darkness, is the one great tube through which man communicates with the shadowy. And the dreaming organ, in connexion with the heart, the eye, and the ear, compose the magnificent apparatus which forces the infinite into the chambers of a human brain, and throws dark reflections from eternities below all life upon the mirrors of the sleeping mind. (15:130)

The "magnificent apparatus" of dreaming is both "machinery" and "organ," technological and intrinsic, mind and body. It seems the conduit of some greater visionary force except that this force is "shadowy," the "mystery of darkness." Moreover, it is intimately connected with the psychosomatic complex of "heart, eye, and ear" to in turn "compose" the machinery itself as the conveyor of darkness, a body of representation without which the darkness would be merely void. This composition radicalizes the Lockean model of the *camera obscura* to compose a picture of the unconscious as the site of a dream production that is also fundamentally constitutive of the subject's suffering anatomy. This anatomy casts its reflections darkly through the absent psychosomatic body of dreams, where the subject, by 'sensing' his "shadowy" otherness, senses also his inability to possess this identity.

Between dreaming and suffering, *Suspiria* locates an "intolerable grief" (15:133). Where *Confessions* ambivalently tranquillizes grief, the psychosomatics of grief in *Suspiria* mark the site where the subject is never at one with himself: "My pain is the hidden side of my philosophy, its mute sister," writes Kristeva; "melancholia . . . is not the philosopher's disease but his very nature, his *ethos*."[45] Like Schopenhauer's will, De Quincey's suffering imagination materializes the symptomatic body of reason. De Quincey explores the "endless growth and self-reproduction" of his psychic interiority as an interminable theatre of suffering where the identity of the subject never rests because "all things change or perish" (*WDQ* 16:420).[46] He describes grief as the process by which "Faces begin soon . . . to 'dislimn': features fluctuate: combinations of features unsettle. Even the expression becomes a mere idea that you can describe to another, but not an image that you can reproduce for yourself." Grief pathologizes anthropomorphism at the site where it is most recognizable—the human face—but grief is also the subject's constitutive affect. As De Quincey writes, grief marks the vanishing of the flesh at the same time that it works by "powers that were intellectual and moral—powers *in* the flesh, though not *of* the flesh"—like Merleau-Ponty's idea of the chiasmatic structure of flesh—which mark the subject's vanishing selfhood (15:153). Hence, the way in which De Quincey's unconscious reproduces the "lost features" of Anne or Elizabeth through a "myriad" of faces—the female infant sinking to darkness in *The English Mail Coach*—suggests how his suffering identity emerges "*in* the flesh" to take on a life of its own as the affliction of his identity from the earliest stages of his development. As the register of De Quincey's self-writing project in *Suspiria*, this psychosomatics of identity at the site of the subject's (dis)appearance in the flesh is the point between the semiotic and the Symbolic where "moods—and particularly sadness—are the ultimate reactions to our traumas." These are the "imprint of a humankind that is surely not triumphant but subtle, ready to fight, and creative. Literary creation is that adventure of the body and signs that bears witness to the affect."[47] The emergence of this "intolerable grief" is the primary mechanism of the scene of psychoanalysis unfolding through the different sections of *Suspiria*, which form, as it were, the palimpsest of the unfolding mythopoeia of the unconscious—perhaps De Quincey's.

"The Affliction of Childhood"

The confessional centerpiece of *Suspiria* is "The Affliction of Childhood," which revisits the "earliest incidents" (15:137) of the author's life, specifically his sister Elizabeth's death. Like the 1821 "Preliminary Confessions" or the 1856 "Confessions," "Affliction" is naturalistic and speaks in the empirical first person. But it also locates life traumas and the language of the unconscious in the same narrative to produce an organic decentering of identity between self-making and psychic determinism that had left *Confessions* fractured. The "Introductory Notice" prepares for this shift by describing the text's narrative model of errant organicism in conjunction with the machinery of dreaming discussed above. "The Palimpsest of the Human Brain," which follows "Affliction," then describes the psychic topography of the unconscious, a model that predates Freud by almost fifty years. Both sections offer a metaphorical metapsychology that collapses the boundary between the literary and the scientific or philosophical.

"Affliction" recounts the earliest "'passage'" or "nursery experience" of De Quincey's life as the "origin" or "key" that "harmonizes with" his current "record of a dreadful visitation from opium excess." "Was it opium, or was it opium in combination with something else, that raised these storms?" he asks the reader. This experience is, he argues, a "proper communication for a stranger's ear" and appeals to the reader's "sympathy" as analyst to connect the adult to the child: "An adult sympathizes with himself in childhood because he is the same, and because (being the same) yet he is *not* the same. He acknowledges the deep, mysterious identity between himself, as adult and as infant, for the ground of his sympathy" (15:133–34). By describing his confession as fit for strangers, De Quincey appeals to as wide an audience as possible, marking his experience as universal and therefore preempting moral censure. But "sympathy" also indicates a transference of feeling between subjects, which he models on the transference between himself and his past that constitutes his "identity." Getting the reader to agree to this sympathy then locates this identity within the circle of proper telling that makes the social sphere cohere. De Quincey is clear in a later note that "though a child's feelings are spoken of, it is not the child who speaks. *I* decipher what the child only felt in cipher. . . . I the child had the feelings, I the man decipher them. In the child lay the handwriting mysterious to *him*; in me the interpretation and the comment" (15:149–50n).[48] Here the authority of interpretation has a clear center in the adult author. Yet by relying on the kindness of strangers, De Quincey, like the Ancient Mariner, draws the reader into a transference with the unsettling grief of his psychoanalysis that also exists beyond comment. The "differences between his two selves," the "main quickeners of [this] sympathy," also entail a "move[ment] through a wilderness of natural thoughts or feelings; some in the child who suffers; some in the man who reports" (15:134). This "wilderness" consequently leaves both De Quincey and the reader bewildered as to the origin of De Quincey's selfhood.

The central episode of "Affliction" is the death of Elizabeth, a "moment of darkness and delirium," of "utter, utter misery" that "cannot be *remembered*": "Itself, as a remembrable [sic] thing, is swallowed up in its own chaos. Mere anarchy and confusion of mind fell upon me." But this trauma nonetheless generates an associationism to which De Quincey would give a cognitive form: "our deepest thoughts and feelings pass to us through perplexed combinations of *concrete* objects, pass to us as *involutes* (if I may coin that word) in compound experiences incapable of being disentangled." He incorporates the primal loss of the object through an infolding of the trauma of external experience that is simultaneously an externalization or unfolding of a dark psychic interiority. Moreover, this grief is reproduced through the imagination's free-associationism, which "moulds and remoulds" his later remembering of the event, especially the sudden "trance" at Elizabeth's deathbed. As De Quincey looks through the bedroom window, "A vault seemed to open in the zenith of the far blue sky, a shaft which ran up for ever," upon which De Quincey "in spirit rose as if on billows that also ran up the shaft for ever": "The billows seemed to pursue the throne of God; but *that* also ran before us and fled away continually. The flight and the pursuit seemed to go on for ever and ever. Frost, gathering frost, some Sarsar wind of death seemed to repel me . . ." This "Sarsar wind," like the grief associated with De Quincey's ruined Spanish aqueduct in *Confessions*, seems to fascinate De Quincey's senses through a type of mesmerism in which "Time became infinitely elastic, stretching out to such immeasurable and vanishing termini" (15:141–44). He is stunned by his inability to raise the psychic life of his dead sister, who lies on the couch as an analysand utterly resistant to interpretation.

Analyzing this moment fifty years hence, De Quincey imagines his own response to death at the time as an analyst turned inward to his own suffering, grief crippling his ability to return empathy to Elizabeth, who was both his guide and protector. But grief produces other effects. In the time just before the trance, De Quincey, confronting death's profound absence, writes that "awe, not fear, fell upon [him]." At this moment he hears a "solemn wind . . .—the most mournful that ear ever heard," which he describes as a "hollow, solemn, Memnonian, but saintly swell" that is "the one sole *audible* symbol of eternity." Both grief-ridden and "Aeolian," this sound fills the interspace between experience and the visionary as the site of trauma wherein the subject is simultaneously lost and reborn. This psychosomatic of grief figures at the intersection between life and death, consciousness and the unconscious, the "wandering or suspension of [the] perfect mind" that mesmerizes De Quincey while also releasing his psyche's potentiality (15:144–45).

This trance becomes one of the text's dream-legends, which both frame and generate the determinism of its "great abysses of grief" (15:155). Yet this determinism also produces the possibility of revelation and self-making: "Rapture of grief, that, being too mighty for a child to sustain, foundest a happy oblivion in a heaven-born sleep, and within that sleep didst conceal a dream, whose meanings in after years, when slowly I deciphered, suddenly there flashed upon me new light" (15:144). The movement of the psyche toward its own absence in the remembering of trauma generates the "new light" of the imagination. Hence, "intolerable grief" has a fundamentally productive side, for without "a bent for melancholia," Kristeva writes, "there is no psyche," for "there is no imagination that is not, overtly or secretly, melancholy." Like De Quincey, Kristeva speaks of this melancholy as "rapture," a "sad voluptuousness, a despondent intoxication," like the melancholic intoxication of the Dionysian.[49] The movement back to the subject's future works by the strange mourning of imagination to recreate the subject's lost identity. Grief's "rapture," that is, both suspends and transforms reason. De Quincey's Sunday morning reverie after Elizabeth's death stages this phantasy of mourning. Gazing at the stained-glass windows of apostles and saints, he sees in the "wide central field of the window where it was uncoloured" the far sky, which "grew and shaped itself into a [self-sustained] vision of beds with lawny white curtains" lifting to God "dying children, that were tossing in anguish." This reshaping of his earlier trance works by the "faculty of shaping images in the distance out of slight objects, and grouping them after the yearning of the heart," which "grew upon [him] at this time." "Deep grief" and "deep love ... ally themselves with religious feeling," De Quincey writes. In the next sentence, however, "religious feeling" becomes "the passion of reverie" and "the mystery of devotion" which, when allied with solitude, have "fascinations as of witchcraft" (15:148–49).[50] At this "subtle *nexus*" between psychic determinism and self-making, grief both suspends the subject and "itself [becomes] a fiery chariot for mounting victoriously above the causes of grief" (15:145, 149). The analyst both succumbs to a countertransference with a suffering that cripples his senses and is able to resurrect himself as analysand from the bed or couch of suffering, a transfiguration, as we shall see, that forms the pivotal episode of "The Daughter of Lebanon."

Reading between who he is and who he was, De Quincey follows the "labyrinthine infinity of curves" by which the "*primary* convulsions of nature ... come round again and again by reverberating shocks" (15:162–63). This is to ascribe the force of trauma to the "idealizing tendency [that] existed in the dream-theatre of [his] childhood," which has a "preternatural strength" and which leaves the "whole economy of his dreaming faculty ... convulsed beyond all precedents" (15:169). The inaccessibility of some traumas was to prove to Freud the compulsively repetitive nature of psychoanalysis, leaving both the analyst and analysand unable to speak with any certainty. Trauma, that is, always left more to tell. As Cathy Caruth argues, what is as traumatic as trauma itself or its traumatic forgetting is the fact that it can never be taken in at one go: "pathology consists ... solely in the *structure of its experience* or reception: the event is not assimilated or experienced fully at the time, but only belatedly, in its repeated *possession* of the one who experiences it."[51] Trauma comes with the 'not being able to know' that makes all experience, because it can never be taken in empirically, traumatic and that repeatedly possesses the subject. To exist and to perceive—*esse* and *percipi*—causes a traumatic bewilderment that necessitates perpetually making sense, perpetually telling more.

In "Affliction" Autobiography and confession merge to retell the 1821 *Confessions* in embryo, so that where *Confessions* "[tends] to externalize, often reductively, the data of inward experience,"[52] *Suspiria* enters into a dialogue with dreams. "Affliction" therefore recasts the reluctant analysand on Orestes' couch in *Confessions* as enduring a more sustained foray into the unconscious. This prolonged analysis suggests two shifts in De Quincey's writing: first, the couch becomes too limiting a vehicle for psychic exploration, and so Freudian analysis at the very least, is not an option; and second, the text demands the reader's involvement, at the very point that he turns the text over to this more radical psychoanalysis, in a way *Confessions* does not: "Here pause, reader! Imagine yourself seated in some cloud-scaling swing, oscillating under the impulse of lunatic hands" (*WDQ* 15:169). This swing's fluctuating temporal shifts evoke the movements of the analysand's imagination across the stage, and through the stages, of his psychoanalysis as if by some autonomous force that foregoes his possessing any ultimate knowledge of the process. This choric movement takes place on Nietzsche's "primal ground of tragedy," "the womb that gave birth to the whole of the so-called dialogue. This world of the stage, the real drama" (*BT* 65), marks the subject's (dis)appearance between Dionysus and Apollo. De Quincey similarly describes the palimpsest as the "chorus of the Athenian stage [which] unwove through the antistrophe every step that had been mystically woven through the strophe" and names the text's succeeding visions as different "choruses winding up the overture contained in Part 1" (*WDQ* 15:174, 177) of *Suspiria*. This choric utterance of affliction becomes a moveable drama of Dionysian suffering that stages as Apollo the text's shifting scene of psychoanalysis. This process shapes the giant form of its subject, "eternally suffering and contradictory" (*BT* 45), as the interminable dialogue of Romantic psychoanalysis.[53]

Such a traumatic state of things makes De Quincey's psychoanalysis as traumatic for the reader as it does for De Quincey himself. Twelve years hence in Oxford, opium has reawakened the "agitations of [his] childhood" through a series of visions that refashion themselves in his unconscious as if "upon some Grecian stage": "Dream formed itself mysteriously within dream" (138). Most traumatically, the trance in Elizabeth's chamber "remoulded itself continually" within "these Oxford dreams." At the point where the 1821 text can only describe the effects of this psychic autonomy, De Quincey now interprets an array of psychic tropes and figures that repeat the associations produced by trauma. Hovering above this involute network is "a gleaming host of heavenly beings surrounding the pillows of the dying children," the latter signifying the negativity of grief, the former suggesting its transformative potentiality.

Having worked chronologically back to its primal dream, the text now shifts forward to the future visions that comprise the retelling of this dream through the "gleaming host" of De Quincey's unconscious life. He rises from his couch in "Afflictions" toward the staging of his unconscious floating in and above his head. This self-making response to psychic determinism, the "cloud-scaling swing" of his confessional imagination yoked to the whim of "lunatic hands," requires from its reader a suspension of disbelief in the incipient madness of De Quincey's vision (15:170).

"The Palimpsest"

The palimpsest is "a membrane or roll [vellum] cleansed of its manuscript by reiterated successions," a chemical process that "[discharges] the writing from the roll . . . sufficiently to leave a field for the new manuscript, and yet not sufficiently to make the traces of the elder manuscript irrecoverable" (15:171, 173). The palimpsest works on many levels. As a metaphor for the human brain, it signifies a vast textual unconscious registering in successive layers the history of a single consciousness in its entirety. It thus describes the unconscious as a series of erased narratives potentially retrievable, but not in their original form. It therefore also models the associationism of what *Confessions* calls the "fierce chemistry of . . . dreams," through which the dreaming faculty unfolds its work "slowly like a scroll" (2:66). Through these "*diplomata* of human archives or libraries" one can read the composite scene of one's own making, the "grandeur of human unity" behind the "fleeting accidents of a man's life." De Quincey recounts from the 1821 *Confessions* his mother's near-drowning as a case study of this process:

> . . . in the twinkling of an eye, every act—every design of her past life lived again—arraying themselves not as a succession, but as parts of a coexistence. Such a light fell upon the whole path of her life backwards into the shades of infancy, as the light perhaps which wrapt the destined apostle on his road to Damascus. Yet that light blinded for a season; but hers poured celestial vision upon the brain, so that her consciousness became omnipresent at one moment to every feature in the infinite review.

De Quincey takes the occasion to remind his 1821 skeptics that the story has "since been confirmed by other experiences [or cases] essentially the same." What strikes him is not the "*simultaneity* of experience," but the "possibility of resurrection, for what had so long slept in the dust. A pall, deep as oblivion, had been thrown by life over every trace of these experiences; and yet suddenly, at the silent command, at the signal of a blazing rocket sent up from the brain, the pall draws up, and the whole depths of the theatre are exposed" (15:175–76).

The passage concerns us here, of course, because of the potent model of psychoanalysis it suggests, for De Quincey is not so intent on the brain's neurology as he is on the power of the mind to reproject or retell its own narratives, a power transferred through the text's dramatic power in articulating its own "dread line of revelation." The palimpsest is a series of "dream-legends" or layers of psychic encoding comprising a larger cultural narrative (a "knightly romance," a "monkish legend, a "Grecian tragedy") whose structure is unreadable except as the subject passes through and decodes its discrete moments (15:176). De Quincey describes as "brazen profligacy" the "modern magic" that permits chemistry to raise the dead from the palimpsest by restoring the layers of its successive narratives (15:174). But in the text's case study it is clear that he means the "modern magic" of a power, like rhabdomancy in the 1856 *Confessions*, that divines the psyche's secrets at the same time that it leaves them essentially untold.

As if to revisit the trauma of Wordsworth's Infant Babe passage, De Quincey reads, "lurking below all," and "lurk[ing] to the last," the "deep, deep tragedies of infancy, as when the child's hands were unlinked for ever from his mother's neck; or his lips for ever from his sister's kisses" (15:176). The "unity" of the subject revealed, then, is, paradoxically, the drama of primal separation, what in *Confessions* he calls the "*burden of the Incommunicable*" between himself and his mother and what Kristeva will call the "*impossible mourning for the maternal object*" that becomes a melancholia, not for the lost object, but for the "'Thing' as the real that does not lend itself to signification."[54] Reading intertextually backward from this scene, to his separation from Anne, or the death of Elizabeth, and even further to a pre-Symbolic cognate of the mother's absence (which her literal near drowning enacts metaphorically), De Quincey envisions the palimpsest of the psyche as a scene of suffering staged across the mind's "endless strata," "the countless . . . mysterious handwritings of grief or joy," Dionysus's "convulsions of dreaming or delirium" told darkly through its Apollonian representations (15:176–77). Moreover, the trauma persists in the attempt to tell what can still never be told in the text. De Quincey can never convey the "greater mystery" of the psyche's power to unfold itself to its reader through a type of "long *regressus*," except to say that the fundamental secret of this narrative "is repeated, and ten thousand times repeated by opium, for those who are its martyrs" (15:174, 176). The telling rests in its repetition yet never in its disclosure of a secret, a trauma made affectively visceral through the almost camp drama of De Quincey's writing. The reader is left with the texts' visionary performance of the possibility of psychoanalysis, and with a palpably psychosomatic sense of this performance's subject, but never with a sense of this subject's fundamental presence.

"Levana and Our Ladies of Sorrow"

As if to make its point about the profoundly theatrical nature of the palimpsest's monumental staging of the subject's personal and cultural history, "Levana and Our Ladies of Sorrow" narrates how this primal drama unfolds as the genealogy of psychic affliction staged as a chorus of "Sublime Goddesses" (15:181; Mater Lachrymarum, "Our Lady of Tears," the Madonna; Mater Suspiriorum, "Our Lady of Sighs"; and Mater Tenebrarum, "Our Lady of Darkness," the youngest). "Levana," and the following "Apparition of the Brocken" and "Savannah-La-Mar," are fantasized case studies of the psychoanalytical subject as dream mythopoeia rather than rational dream interpretations. Each stages a type of mythic encounter between what might be broadly termed an analyst's and analysand's psychic fields of experience as they intersect through a kind of global or mythic (counter)transference, what De Quincey calls an 'electric sympathy.' "Levana" describes a mythography of the psychoanalytic subject's giant form, and De Quincey even suggests in a note that the text would provide a kind of psychosomatic architectonic for the completed *Suspiria*.[55]

These "*Eumenides*" anatomize the "agencies of grief," the "mighty system of central forces hidden in the deep bosom of human life, which by passion, by strife, by temptation, by the energies of resistance, works for ever upon children" (15:181, 178); but they also "educate," that is, 'educe' and 'develop,' this suffering through a process of psychoanalysis that reads the trauma of suffering. As both symptom and scene, the Sorrows are delegates of Levana herself, a kind of archetype of the primal rift from the maternal, which orchestrates the mirror stage:

> either the paternal hand, as proxy for the goddess Levana, or some near kinsman, as proxy for the father, raised [the infant] upright, bade it look erect as the king of all this world, and

> presented its forehead to the stars, saying, perhaps, in his heart—"Behold what is greater than yourselves!" This symbolic act represented the function of Levana. (15:177)

The "symbolic act" of this "paternal hand" stages the lost autonomy of the *infans*, his radical self-dividedness, within the maternal. Levana is thus what Kristeva calls the "'imaginary father,'" the "phallic or symbolic [identification] . . . which insures the subject's entrance into the universe of signs and creation." Such an identification with this "father, form, schema," rather than with the lost object, makes "a triumph over sadness possible."[56] The "Sorrows" then stages the grief mobilized by Levana as the unfolding absent psychosomatic body of the subject's essentially melancholic identity. They "disdain the infirmities of language" and "utter voices through the organs of man when they dwell in human hearts," "mighty abstractions that incarnate themselves in all individual sufferings of man's heart." They are thus de-constitutively semiotic, "Mighty phantoms" whose "form . . . fluctuated in its outline," "abstractions presented as impersonations" (15:179). As anthropomorphism without form, they exist in the imagination as a body of suffering that resists language and reason.

Accordingly, they communicate by affect but via faces that refuse a full reading of the subject's identity, in a manner we shall see repeated between the poet and Moneta in Keats's *The Fall of Hyperion.* Levana "never revealed her face" except in dreams; Mater Lachrymarum's "eyes are sweet and subtle, wild and sleepy by turns," and she "[calls] for vanished faces"; Mater Suspiriorum's "story" cannot be read in her eyes because they are "filled with perishing dreams, and with wrecks of forgotten delirium." Only Mater Tenebrarum, whose identity is the most ambivalent, "*might* be hidden, . . . [but] cannot be hidden" as she is "the mother of lunacies." But the end of the text constructs the scene of suffering instruction by Madonna, who "spoke by her mysterious hand. Touching my head, she beckoned to Our Lady of Sighs; and *what* she spoke, translated out of the signs which (except in dreams) no man reads, was this:—". Educating by touch, she instructs the other Sorrows how the narrator "'shall . . . be accomplished in the furnace,'" wherein he will "'see the things that ought *not* to be seen—sights that are abominable, and secrets that are unutterable'" until their "'commission . . . from God'" is "'accomplished'": "'to plague [the subject's] heart until [they have] unfolded the capacities of his spirit'" (15:179–82).[57] This scene of mesmerism (the laying on of hands to bring about a crisis) produces the prophecy of secrets that can never be told. At the end of the text, the reader senses these spectrally anthropomorphized agencies of grief vanish into the text's unconscious.

"The Apparition of the Brocken" and "Savannah-la-Mar"

"The Apparition of the Brocken" offers an allegory of reading that seems to want to become a scene of psychoanalysis, or at least the impersonation of one, which is what makes the Specter—more particularly its allegorization as the Dark Interpreter—so challenging to interpretation in the first place. Directly addressing the reader, De Quincey describes the process of "uttering your secret feelings to him," the "reflex of yourself" and in doing so "making this phantom the dark symbolic mirror for reflecting to the daylight what else must be hidden forever" (15:184). This phantom spectrally embodies the unconscious to establish a potential dialogue between self and other through which representation becomes the only means by which we can know the self. The text describes this form as the Specter of the Brocken, an atmospheric phenomenon by which human shadows are writ large on mists both as a magnification and as a distortion of the human form (this phenomenon forms one of the central episodes of James Hogg's 1824 gothic novel, *The Private Memoirs and Confession of a Justified Sinner*). In a note De Quincey refers the reader to Coleridge's "Constancy to an Ideal Object," which uses the apparition to describe how "yearning Thought" is the only constant within a world of things that "veer and vanish" (*CP* 4, 2). The woodman in the poem's final apostrophe sees an "image with a glory round its head" advancing toward him in the "viewless snow-mist [that] weaves a glist'ning haze." Yet although the "enamoured rustic worships its fair hues," he does not know that "*he* makes the shadow . . . he pursues" (28–32; my italics). Moreover, this self-projection also marks his self-alienation, the *un*constancy of thought's "yearning" that deconstructs the *anthropos*, so that the "poem contains within itself an illusory self-projection through which it explores the duplicity of its own mode of being."[58] Where Coleridge's text does not confront this self-alienation as the specter's (dis)embodied form, De Quincey's text does. His Specter figures the unconscious as the subject's at once autonomous and sympathetic determinant, a "solitary apparition, in the sense of loving solitude," that is "not always solitary in his personal manifestations" (15:183). A note also ties the Specter to a collective or cultural unconscious of the "gloomy realities of Paganism" (15:183n), which rationalizes the Specter's threatening psychosis as the primitive substructure of a higher consciousness, but also sets aside this primitiveness. Either way, the Specter signifies a psychosomatic interiority where the subject is not one with himself, a mind left to confront its own solitude—the mythopathology Wordsworth could not confront in the Prospectus.

But De Quincey then anatomizes the Specter as the Dark Interpreter. By giving a face to the unconscious, De Quincey marks the otherness of the *anthropos* as truly *other* and thus anatomizes a Lockean/Humean fear of an autonomous associationism as the deconstructing reflection of selfhood. The Dark Interpreter emerges as a central feature of De Quincey's metapsychology in that he is both a figure for the mechanism of repetition within the unconscious and a formal trope for the unconscious itself, more particularly for a staging of the unconscious's reading of itself in which it speaks De Quincey's conscious identity for him.[59] The Dark Interpreter is "originally a mere reflex of [De Quincey's] inner nature," like the Specter, both conscious and in dreams. But as "the apparition of the Brocken sometimes is disturbed by storms or by driving showers, so as to dissemble his real origin, in like manner the Interpreter sometimes swerves out of [De Quincey's] orbit, and mixes a little with alien natures," both "anchored and stationary in [De Quincey's] dreams; but great storms and driving mists cause him to fluctuate uncertainly, or even to retire altogether" (15:184–85). The Dark Interpreter seems to allegorize the Specter as a figure of analysis for the free-associating imagination which the Specter merely tropes, while also indicating that this figure is itself subject to the mind's autonomy. The features of the Dark Interpreter both (dis)limn and are (dis)limned by the pathology of imagination.

On one hand, then, the Dark Interpreter is a subject presumed to know. Like the Greek Chorus, he tells the subject nothing "absolutely new," but "[recalls him] to [his] own lurking thoughts" (15:185n).[60] Yet within this hidden revelation he also "assume[s] new features or strange features, as in dreams always there is the power not contented with reproduction, but which absolutely creates or transforms": "Generally I believe . . . that he is a faithful representative of myself; but he also is at times subject to the action of the god *Phantasus*, who rules in dreams." Because in "these cases" De Quincey does "not always know [the Dark Interpreter] . . . as [his] own parhelion," the Interpreter also becomes an intertext for De Quincey's own self-analysis in *Suspiria* as the (missed) encounter of the *anthropos* with its own otherness (15:185). As a double who is also other, the Dark Interpreter both is and is not the subject who speaks (of) him, is both within and beside the self.[61]

What *is* clear is that, whether a figure for reading or an impersonation of a potential scene of psychoanalysis, the Dark Interpreter can neither be read nor analyzed himself. He is self-deconstructing, emphasizing a self-making interiority while at the same time foregrounding the phantasmatic nature of this imaginary projection as a narrativization of the Real (even the deep structure of the palimpsest is at least *potentially* readable). The Dark Interpreter figures the allegorical or mythopoeic representation of the subject's psychosomatic presence as being disturbingly *absent*. Neither analyst nor analysand, the Dark Interpreter writes De Quincey into his own text as the lurid figure of his own imagination, like the Sorrows, through which he uses the text's psychoanalysis to 'educate' the reader by telling the story of what we, like he, cannot learn. Here is how De Quincey describes the process in a passage on the Dark Interpreter most likely intended for *Suspiria* but never published in De Quincey's lifetime: "The truth I heard often in sleep from the lips of the Dark Interpreter. Who is he? He is a shadow, reader, but a shadow with whom *you must suffer me* to make you acquainted" (15:568). Recalling *Confessions*, De Quincey describes the Interpreter's influence as the "semi-voluntary" and "automatic" power of phantasy in children's imaginations, as when "in darkness they project a vast theater of phantasmagorical figures moving forward or backwards between their bed curtains and the chamber walls."[62] Suffering, De Quincey argues, possesses "a power of self-projection not unlike to this," so that 'suffering' De Quincey's self-analysis is also, for the reader, to suffer herself. Thus educating the reader through the voice of the Dark Interpreter, De Quincey writes that "Pain driven to agony, or grief driven to frenzy, is essential to the ventilation of profound natures" (15:568). But, it needs to be repeated, suffering comes with the Dark Interpreter's essential unreadability, which reminds the subject—the reader—of who he is by pointing to who he is not.

"Savannah-La-Mar" anatomizes the "Pain driven to agony" as a city "[buried], but not [concealed]," which "seems floating along the noiseless depths of ocean." Above this "ample cemetery," "mariners from every clime look down into her courts and terraces, count her gates, and number the spires of her churches" (15:185–86). Typologically, this metaphor refashions "Affliction"'s "general history of navigation, supported by a vast body of voyages," a monumental edition of historical narratives which De Quincey orders on speculation in childhood but then worries might "[tend] to infinity." This idea of the interminability of narrative parallels in his mind the metaphor of London, origin of the work's endless publication, as a "vast centre of mystery" that catches him like a "ghostly cobweb radiating into all the provinces from the mighty metropolis," a "vast systematic machinery" that "appal[s] a child's imagination" (15:165–66). As these images are condensed and displaced through the dream "machinery" of De Quincey's text, they reemerge as the "ample cemetery" of Savannah-la-Mar, which also "fascinates the eye with a *Fata-Morgana* revelation, as of human life still subsisting in submarine asylums sacred from the storms that torment our upper air." "Savannah" thus stages the potential reading of the unconscious by those who float over its depths as a scene of possibly apocalyptic semiosis, whereby in dreams the narrator and the Dark Interpreter "cleave the watery veil that divided [them] from her streets." But the Interpreter only whispers this knowledge to himself by reading the city's "silent nurseries" as "waiting for the heavenly dawn." For the narrator, he only reads the "'sad'" and "'piteous'" signification of how "'by infinite declensions the true and very present, in which only we live and enjoy, will vanish into a mote of a mote, distinguishable only by a heavenly vision.'" "'Upon the sorrows of an infant'," he states, "'[God] raises oftentimes from human intellects glorious vintages that could not else have been'" (15:185–87). Theirs is a transference that lays out, in the topography of the city itself, the almost tangible possibility of a comprehensive interpretation, only to have this possible 'cure' of knowledge drown at the chiasmus between surface and depth.

"The Daughter of Lebanon"

This suffering of an impossible psychoanalysis is what makes "The Daughter of Lebanon" the most telling yet perhaps inevitable summation of the evolution of *Suspiria*'s psychoanalysis. Intended for *Suspiria*, but published after the 1845 text as an appendix to the 1856 *Confessions*, "Daughter" takes us back to *Suspiria*'s future in the 1821 *Confessions*, at the same time that it reads *Suspiria*'s future ambivalently after the 1856 text.[63] De Quincey's psychoanalysis as an education in grief is formalized in "Daughter" as the encounter between the evangelist and the daughter, apparently anatomizing once and for all the scene of psychoanalysis haunting *Confessions*. This encounter imagines Anne as having been transfigured as the "Magdalen" (2:36) to become the redeeming archetype of De Quincey's unconscious.[64] On her couch the Daughter is now Anne as the analysand who at last revisits the primal scene of *Confessions* in a way that Wordsworth's Margaret was never allowed to tell her own story. Moreover, attended by the evangelist at her bedside, she is also the more profoundly missed encounter with Elizabeth. But she profits from her story only through a version of the Victorian separate spheres in which, as the carrier of a nervous reaction to her world, she must make the ultimate sacrifice in order to keep that world's Symbolic order intact.

The Evangelist seems to be a spiritual subject presumed to know, but his Symbolic power is both materialized and dematerialized. He emerges in the text through "sounds . . . that, from a postern gate, looking eastwards over secret paths that wind away to the far distant desert, break the solemn silence of an oriental night," the same Memnonian or Aeolian sound that precedes De Quincey's trance in "Affliction." The narrator addresses himself to "Damascus, first-born of cities, *Om el Denia*, mother of generations, that was before Abraham, that wast before the Pyramids," as if to address the sunken Savannah as a site of potential readability and thus of psychoanalysis. The Evangelist, Christ-like, emerges semiotically from this maternal matrix beyond the city's Symbolic boundaries. But he emerges more particularly through the narrator's interrogation of this power ("what sounds are those . . . whose voice is that . . . ?"), which then confirms the Evangelist's authority: "Thou knowest him, Damascus, and hast known him in seasons of trouble as one learned in the afflictions of man; wise alike to take counsel for the suffering spirit or for the suffering body" (2:266). In this way the text figures Damascus itself as a kind of cultural reader or analysand in whom the narrator confirms the acquisition of knowledge.

As the Symbolic "voice that breaks upon the [semiotic] night," the Evangelist emerges from the "mother." But, as both spiritual healer and physician, equipped to diagnose both mind or soul and body, he redeems her history. His case for this redemption is the daughter herself, who bears the marks of this history's trauma. She re-remembers this trauma as a type of psychic death that finds her translated into the "Paradise" of everlasting life, and so she is both "transcendent" and an outcast who "lost a princely station in Lebanon" through rejection by her father. She is the abject of a cultural body of knowledge for which the Evangelist speaks. Moreover, her identity emerges by his questions: "Was she born of woman? Was it perhaps the angel—so the evangelist argued with himself—that met him in the desert after sunset, and strengthened him by secret talk?" He reads her identity by touching her forehead, seeing in her "ruin" the transcendence of her "birth—glorified in such excess that no Solomon in all his pomp—no, nor even the lilies of the field—can approach [her] gifts." He says "secretly to himself" that he will "search this woman's heart" and implores her to be "wise on her own behalf." But while he speaks "half to himself, but half to her," he divulges nothing, while she exposes everything. Imploring him to "put [her] back in [her] father's house," she "came into [his] guardianship" with nothing of her own identity (2:266–68).

Their encounter from this point stages a scene of mesmerism as well as psychoanalysis in which they communicate by both word and by touch: she gets, as it were, the full treatment. Self-observational rather than contemplative, she "sought not to varnish her history, or to palliate her own transgressions." Her talking cure lasts thirty days (an appropriately Biblical time), "if she will not defeat it herself," a statement that marks the conflict between repetition and repression and remembering. As she comes closer to termination, her crisis is compounded by the psychosomatic recurrence of her symptoms, as the city itself falls under her "burning fever" and the terms of her 'cure' are waged ambivalently as both psychic renewal and spiritual transcendence: "And thus daily the doubt was strengthened—would the holy apostle suddenly touch her with his hand, and say, 'Woman, be thou whole!' or would he present her on the thirtieth day as a pure bride to Christ?". On the thirtieth day she lies "in blissful trance," the guardian at her bedside. Their dialogue—he beside her "couch," whispering into her ear—negotiates her working-through her final crisis, during which she "by intervals communed with him, and by intervals slept gently under the oppression of her fever." Then, he touches her "temples" three times with his "pastoral staff" in order to "rebuke" the "light clouds of delirium [which] were playing about her brain." First, he clears the "delirious clouds" of her mind to reveal the vision of her homeland; second, he clears away the "gloomy vapours" of this vision; and third, he clears the entire vision itself as "'but a mask'" in order to reveal "infinite revelations that can be made visible only to dying eyes." Out of this "infinite chasm," she meets the emerging vision of her departed "twin-sister": "Immediately in rapture she soared upwards from her couch; immediately in weakness she fell back; and, being caught by the evangelist, she flung her arms around his neck" (2:268–70). The scene resonates uncannily with Freud's story, barely fifty years later, of how one of his early female analysands, during a hypnotic trance, threw her arms around Freud's neck. After this, confronted by the excessive manifestation of transference he could not control, Freud abandoned hypnotic suggestion. De Quincey's text plays the specter of phallic control that Freud attempts to gloss over. During this moment, the Daughter is reunited with the double of herself in a moment of psychic reparation. This healing of the primal rift of the subject, both externally with her past history and internally with the otherness of her own identity, marks the site where, through the radical psychoanalytic mythopoeia of the text, the subject "stands single" by being "not the same."

Yet the meeting between therapist and patient, by both literalizing and theologizing the encounter with the unconscious, compromises the radically literary and aesthetic nature of *Suspiria*'s psychoanalysis. The daughter signifies the redemption of the semiotic "mother of all generations," whose potentiality has been vitiated by Symbolic power. By submitting herself to the evangelist's paternal guardianship, however, the daughter plays into the hands of this power in ways that seem to exceed De Quincey's intentions for the text. Her crisis suggests her sacrifice for the redemption of the Symbolic as much as the working-through of her own internal suffering, a return to "her Father's house" (2:270) from which only death can release her. That her mesmerism is facilitated by an agent of Symbolic power only repeats the trauma under which she first suffered. At a psychically archetypal or semiotic level, her trance signifies the productive phantasies of Levana's imaginary father, who represents the primal separation from the mother that marks the entry into the Symbolic at the same time that he marks the imaginary's power to locate the phantasy of (re)union in place of this rupture. Moreover, the "rapture" of her psychic regeneration, played against the defeat of her physical body, also suggests how the psychosomatic is both trauma and redemption, an *un*tangling of the psychosomatic complex of her crisis that works through the psychosomatic to release the potentiality of its suffering anatomy. But the Evangelist seems to mark Symbolic prescription more than thetic potentiality, and so turns the Nietzschean cast of the Dark Interpreter's imaginary theater into a Symbolic Drama that dictates the subject's identity.

That the scene is both radical and reactionary suggests clues to De Quincey's subsequent revisions to *Suspiria*. De Quincey placed the text at the end of the 1856 text, which, as Logan writes, resituates dreams as "purely imaginative products of [De Quincey's] intellectual sensibility" cut off from the body of the confessing subject.[65] "The Daughter of Lebanon" allegorizes this moment by dissociating the analysand's tainted body from her ascending spirit to become the angel in the Evangelist's house. "Affliction" celebrates an interminable yet imaginative melancholy that turns the negativity of grief—the psychosomatic determinism of the subject' s inability to cure, by telling definitively, what ails him—into a Romantic self-making that, as De Quincey comes to realize, *becomes* the fundamental condition of his life. His subsequent treatment of *Suspiria*, however, places *Confessions* and the *Autobiography* at the center of his *corpus* by displacing *Suspiria*'s Romantic melancholy.[66] In 1853 De Quincey evacuated "Affliction" from *Suspiria* and revised it as Chapter Two of his "Autobiographical Sketches," which comprised Volume One of his collected works. "Sketches" relocates "Affliction" within a *bildungsroman* that begins with the proper origins of "Parentage and the Paternal Home" in 1785 and ends in adolescence at St. John's Priory in 1803.

"Affliction" now ends with the apostrophe to the "burden of solitude" and omits the intervening passages about grief's mysterious effect on De Quincey's later unconscious life. He then moves to the last paragraph of "Affliction" ("Once again, after twelve years' interval"), retitled separately as "Dream-Echoes of These Infant Experiences." The division erases the complex connection between the suffering child and adult. In this new section's prefatory "Notice to the Reader," De Quincey merely summarizes what had previously introduced the interminability of the unconscious: "psychological experiences of deep suffering or joy first attain their entire fullness of expression when they are reverberated from dreams" (19:17). This recuperates as the "power and the grandeur of recovered life" how dreams "dislimn" identity. Accordingly, De Quincey anthropomorphizes "Affliction"'s "host of heavenly beings" as "a gleaming host of faces" (19:17), limning what had been dislimned and transforming into the pragmatic anthropology of dreams its psychosomatic other. As added insurance, he adds another section, "Dream-Echoes Fifty Years Later," a shortened version of "The Apparition of the Brocken," which offers a type of developmental closure to the unconscious fifty years earlier. This new version discards the psychoanalysis of the last four paragraphs, which materialized the Dark Interpreter, and so returns authority to the Social Autobiographer who reads instead of *being read*. The text closes with the image of the Specter as "Judea weeping under her palm-tree," giving a face to the "unutterable" affliction of childhood that in its earlier version was dislimned by the Dark Interpreter (19:21).[67]

De Quincey's third descent into the unconscious convinced him "profoundly" that terminating its "new and monstrous phenomena" "was impossible": "in the imagery of my dreams, . . . I saw through vast avenues of gloom those towering gates of ingress which hitherto had always seemed to stand open, now at last barred against my retreat, and hung with funeral crape" (2:132). The rest of *Suspiria* explores the unconscious through a series of extended aphoristic set-pieces written *beyond* Reason. This psychoanalysis refigures the empirical and teleological thrust of scientific or philosophical inquiry in *Confessions* as a literary or aesthetic genealogy of the self's dark mythopoeia, written in the face of its psychic determinism. Foucault argues that

> [w]here the soul pretends unification or the self fabricates a coherent identity, the genealogist sets out to study the beginning—numberless beginnings, whose faint traces and hints of colour are readily seen by a historical eye. The analysis of descent permits the dissociation of the self, its recognition and

> displacement as an empty synthesis, in liberating a profusion of lost events.[68]

Yet De Quincey's genealogical descent into the self constitutes for him an *authentic* subjectivity that is, by its dissociativeness, akin to the pathology of soul-making as a profoundly deconstructive/reconstructive psychosomatic experience. De Quincey thus refashions the ontology of Romantic self-expression by interrogating the limits of its idealism in order to mark in turn the limit form of his psychoanalytic inquiry.

But still, one has to contend with *Suspiria*'s fragmentation. The 1856 Preface to *Confessions* recounts how the kernel of *Confessions*, the journal of "a succession of some twenty or twenty-five dreams and noon-day visions, which had arisen under the later stages of opium influence," "disappeared: some under circumstances which allow me a reasonable prospect of recovering them; some unaccountably; and some dishonourably" (2:101–2).[69] Without this document, the dream interpretation that was to be the "crowning grace" of De Quincey's confessional project—the first epic about Romantic psychoanalysis—becomes another missed encounter. To fill this gap, De Quincey edits his collected works by foregrounding the Autobiography's incorporated selfhood, which in turn sets the tone for subsequent revisions to *Confessions* and for De Quincey's pirating of *Suspiria* to buttress the Collected Edition's ideal of the public man. Without the confessing subject in "Affliction," the mythic theorizations of *Suspiria*'s other sections are dissociated from the telling of the *anthropos*, whose psychic interiority they stage, thus undoing the text's radical engagement between psychic determinism and self-making and suggesting an abandonment of psychoanalysis. Ironically, the evacuation of "Affliction" returns this text to its former status as one of the initial 1834 writings toward the Autobiography.[70] This fact again suggests in De Quincey's *corpus* an early and ongoing ambivalence between a Romantic exploration of the subject's inner life and a Victorian buttressing of this life's external coordinates, a turning of psychoanalysis toward a social purpose that first demands from the subject psychic closure. But De Quincey's lost dreams also become a metonymy for how the 'writing' of life, which prevents him from proceeding with the business of writing, compels him nonetheless to return repeatedly to life-writing and thus to an unconscious that is perpetually lost to its subject, so that the conservation of the (Victorian) subject in his writings is always challenged by the contingencies of its confessing (Romantic) other.

Suspiria marks a critical juncture in the invention of Romantic psychoanalysis. The text is framed by the psychic trauma of *The Recluse* in the late 1790s and the psychic exhaustion that the 1856 *Confessions* barely overcomes. Wordsworthian contemplation is a missed encounter with the unconscious and thus with psychoanalysis itself. In Coleridge the imagination's organicism is mutated by its own unconscious, the return of the repressed poetry of Wordsworthian philosophy. Mesmerized by this poetry, however, Coleridge cannot accept its radically interminable, self-making potential. De Quincey's struggle with reason and philosophy is a struggle for the psyche's poetry, where reason confronts its own interminability. *Suspiria* evolves a mythopoeic psychoanalysis at a time when psychology—De Quincey's conflict with the "*materia medica*" of science in *Confessions*—was still entrenched in an Enlightenment discourse of the medical body. His theorization of the self's potentiality swerves away from this scientism toward aesthetic self-observation, whereby the self realizes itself as the product of its own self-making potentialities, but where the negativity of this mythopoesis refashions the imagination as the dark organicism of an analysis interminable.

De Quincey marks a transition from the terminable self-explorations of Wordsworth and Coleridge to the interminable aesthetic staging of identity in Keats's *The Fall of Hyperion*. De Quincey attempts to confront how the primal scene of Romantic psychoanalysis resists representation and, most disturbingly, leaves Romanticism without a subject, an absence marked by *Suspiria*'s spectral, allegorical shape. But De Quincey's sense of this absence also moves his confessional writings away from psychoanalysis. De Quincey Victorian*izes* his *corpus*, in which Victorianism comes to signify the consolidation of an otherwise heterogeneous Romantic psychoanalysis always in process within the paradigm of the moral and social subject whose external form embodies, and thus imposes empirical and epistemological conditions on, the Real of psychic interiority. The desire for terminability suggests a nostalgia for a therapeutic cure of the psyche's interminable functioning, a cure toward which De Quincey continually struggles. His attention to the 1856 *Confessions* and subsequent neglect of *Suspiria* is thus a conflicted Victorian gesture that neither fully represses nor fully recuperates Romantic heterodoxy. Rather, his later revisions constitute a type of *exhausted* Victorian response to Romantic interminability. The psychic intensity of Romantic myth-making that is in De Quincey the limit form of psychoanalysis requires the ability always to exist psychically where the subject is *not one*. Although interminability is the fundamental condition of a post-Kantian subjectivity, it becomes for De Quincey a psychically unendurable, if imaginatively productive, existential position.

FIVE

KEATS AND THE BURDEN OF INTERMINABILITY

An extensive knowledge is needful to thinking people—it takes away the heat and fever; and helps, by widening speculation, to ease the Burden of the Mystery: a thing I begin to understand a little . . .

—Letter to J. H. Reynolds

. . . I am gone
Away from my own bosom: I have left
My strong identity, my real self,
Somewhere between the throne, and where I sit
Here on this spot of earth.

—*Hyperion*

The Poetry of Poetry

De Quincey discloses within a Wordsworthian/Coleridgean imagination the parasitic function of Kantian reason. For our purposes he is thus a transitional figure between a first generation terminable and a second generation interminable Romantic psychoanalysis. He remains split between the psychomachia of a mythopoeic "I" in *Suspiria* and the epistemology of an empirical "I" in *Confessions*. Separating the suffering subject from his aesthetic anatomy in *Selections Grave and Gay*, De Quincey leaves the latter free of its self-writing author but now paradoxically hollow, as if to isolate Schopenhauer's "*world as representation* . . . whole and pure" from the will's contaminating "lack," "deficiency," and "suffering" (*WWR* 1:179, 196). De Quincey's confessional writings thus both disclose and conserve their most radical psychoanalytical insights. Certainly conservation becomes a necessity, for interminability leads to a kind of psychic exhaustion that comes with struggling with the "*burden of the Incommunicable*," what Keats, echoing "Tintern Abbey," calls the "Burden of the Mystery" (*KL* 92). Keats died the year after De Quincey published *Confessions*, but his psychoanalysis of the Wordsworthian "egotistical sublime" (157) works-through a De Quinceyan ambivalence between the chronic and acute forms of psychoanalysis. Comparing Milton to Wordsworth within the unfolding unconscious of poetry's "grand march of intellect" (96), Keats argues that Wordsworth ventures beyond Milton into the mind of the subject.[1] Asking "whether Wordsworth has in truth epic passion, and martyrs himself to the human heart, the main region of his song" (93), Keats points to the psychosomatic body of poetry that Wordsworth suppresses as "Reason in her most exalted mood." Wordsworth is a "Genius [who] is explorative of those dark Passages" that Wordsworth himself, although writing beyond the "resting places and seeming sure points of Reasoning" (95–96) of Milton's Protestant vision, dared not explore.

In Nietzschean fashion, Keats *does* dare to explore. He confronts poetry's radically self-making nature by reading within the giant forms of his unconscious the "hidden [Dionysian] substratum of suffering and of knowledge" revealed beneath the contemplative Apollonian surface of poetry's "beauty and meditation" (*BT* 46).[2] And he offers the sustained development of the clinical setting of the psychoanalytical scene as the dialogic encounter between two subjects who struggle to articulate this suffering as it is displaced transferentially between them. Their analysis brings them to what Shelley, in the essay "On Life," calls the "dark abyss of—how little we know" (*SPP* 508), the tragic insight gained from the Apollonian contemplation of the Dionysian "core / Of an eternal fierce destruction" ("To J. H. Reynolds," *KP* 96–97) that cannot be told ("I have a mysterious tale to tell, / And cannot speak it" [86–87]). Keats writes in *The Fall of Hyperion* that "Poesy alone can tell her dreams" (8). *Endymion* attempts to read the unconscious as transformative and transcendental, like "Adam's dream": the subject awakens to its immanent and essential "truth" (*KL* 37). *Endymion*'s traumatic realization that this dream exists "no more" (4.669) then becomes *Hyperion*'s epic about the struggle for self-awareness, except that Apollo's vision remains unsettled by the mind's "Creations and destroyings" (3.116). *The Fall*'s dream vision does not repeat the Real in a "finer tone" (*KL* 37) but exposes the "*principium individuationis*" (*BT* 36) to the abyss of its own unreason, at the same time that it defeats the "curse of individuation" (71), what Keats in *Endymion* calls the "habitual self" (3.276). Nietzsche distinguishes between Apollo and Dionysus as the difference between "*dreams* and *intoxication*" (*BT* 33). Apollo reads the unconscious through its symbolic appearance, whereas Dionysus surrenders to this symbolism's dark irrationality. *The Fall* distinguishes between Apollo as Poetry's dream and Dionysus as this dream's intoxication, which *The Fall* struggles to hold in a creative tension the poet is compelled to speak. To *not* tell one's dreams is to remain unconscious of their irrationality and to live one's life as if one's soul were a "clod" (2.13); *to* tell is to enter into the dream of life as a perpetual reading of its unconscious. *The Fall* figures this struggle between telling and not telling as the primal scene of poetry's self-making power. Poetry, as psychoanalysis, thus becomes for Keats, as art is for Nietzsche, both a "protection and remedy" (*BT* 98) against the tragic awareness of life's irrationality.

Keats's attempt to tell the psyche invokes the tension between poetry and philosophy that has been one of this study's important narratives.[3] Coming after Wordsworth's attempt to make poetry function as Philosophy, De Quincey attempts to psychoanalyze the psychic process of poetry within prose. Keats moves back into poetry to explore how this process functions firsthand. He psychoanalyzes within the contemplative form of Poetry its self-observational other—the poetry *of* Poetry. Moreover, this psychoanalysis plays out at a broader textual level the drama of gender that has been one of the subtexts of Romantic psychoanalysis in this study's previous chapters. As fancy (the fancy that Coleridge sets aside in his theory of imagination, for instance) becomes associated increasingly with romance and sensibility in the early nineteenth century, it comes to signify a wandering or interiorized discourse of the imagination feminized as the other to masculine writing, which is often concerned with strategies for containing this threat, or eradicating it altogether.[4] This emergence of the separate spheres of masculine and feminine posits gender as a force of signification mobilizing its own system of cultural prescription, one that comes to evoke a psychical as much as biological determinism or essentialism. But the gendered 'feminine' in Romanticism, as that which the gendered 'masculine' would marginalize, cannot be defined only by virtue of this marginalization.

The very positing of gender points to its implicit volatility and instability. Butler argues that the "constant repetition" of the "logic" or "metaphysics" of the "naturalized ontologies" of gender paradigms points to the "mechanism of the cultural reproduction of identities" that allows in turn for a "subversive repetition" of the "the regulatory practice" of identity itself": "the very multiplicity of [this practice's] construction holds out the possibility of a disruption of [its] univocal posturing."[5] Because "gender attributes . . . effectively constitute the identity they are said to express or reveal,"[6] they offer within their own essentialized and essentializing terms a force of speculation by unsettling and redistributing the terms of gender's own signifying economy. If identity is thus "phantasmatic, then it must be possible to enact an identification that displays its phantasmatic structure."[7] That gender's positing power of subjectivity has its fundamental locus in phantasy allows one in turn to disrupt, resist, and transform this power, a constitutive articulation of the subject as the other of gender's own constitution of identity.

Romanticism re-thinks gender's "phantasmatic structure," albeit with some ambivalence. Geraldine in *Christabel* or Margaret in "The Ruined Cottage" signify a feminized excess of reason haunting the masculinist *cogito* of Romantic imagination, just as the scientism of Freud's metapsychology is haunted by the alien psychology of 'woman.' Wordsworth aborts psychoanalysis by feminizing within it what threatens reason's masculinity. While Wordsworth signifies reason as a feminine subject presumed to know, "Reason in her most exalted mood," he also registers beneath her intellectual facade a psychosomatic complex or "mood" of thought that suggests radical doubt. As if implicitly to contain this threat, he also transcendentalizes the anthromorphized or 'embodied' feminine as allegorical abstraction so as to abject her as 'other.' Accordingly, the femininity of reason is placed beyond Wordsworth's control to more than one end. Coleridge repeats woman's dis-ease by emerging in *The Prelude* as an effete analysand in need of the phantasy of Wordsworth's heroic ability to overcome his own mental crisis. In both Wordsworth's and Coleridge's texts Margaret's absent psychosomatic body reproduces itself in the unstable negotiation of unreason between men, the telling symptom of a flaw in reason's narcissistic, masculine facade. And despite De Quincey's cognition of a feminine pathology that challenges the masculine self-confidence of reason to think itself on different terms, his "The Daughter of Lebanon" ultimately seems to close itself to this challenge, just as the deaths of various significant female figures in his life, while tragic, also ironically place women at a safe distance from his texts.

When Keats argues that Wordsworth had thought farther "into the human heart" (*KL* 96) than Milton, he uses the discourse of sensibility to psychoanalyze the patriarchy of epic and thus of the Romantic visionary tradition's powerfully masculine signification.[8] Keats reads within the gendered economy of Wordsworth's reason by opposing poetry to philosophy's "consequitive reasoning" (*KL* 37). Apollonius's reasoned gaze would "clip an Angel's wings, / Conquer all mysteries by rule and line" ("Lamia," *KP* 2.234–35) and eradicate the "gordian shape" (1.47) of Lamia's unreason because the reason of his "cold philosophy" (2.230) is haunted by its own unconscious. Keats instead explores this unconscious as the "speculation" (*KL* 157) of philosophy, its "Burden of the Mystery" or "*Negative Capability*, that is when man is capable of being in uncertainties, Mysteries, doubts, without any irritable reaching after fact & reason" (43).[9] Thus, when Keats names his paradigmatic theme in "Ode to Psyche" ("I will . . . build a fane / In some untrodden region of my mind" [*KP* 50–51]), it is " without a name" (61). To leave the feminine unnamed is to mark its resistance to signification, but also to mark this resistance as a transgression *of* masculine signification.

Favoring feminine fancy in "Ode to a Nightingale," "opening on the foam / Of perilous seas, in faery lands forlorn" (69–70), Keats seems to redress a Wordsworthian marginalization of the 'feminine.' Yet Keatsian identity is also perpetually 'tolled back' from its feminine "vision" (79) to the "sole self" (72) of the poet's egotistical consciousness. The sensibility of the speaker's absent psychosomatic body in "Ode to a Nightingale" mesmerizes masculine reason: "My heart aches, and a drowsy numbness pains / My *sense*" (1–2; my italics). He would thus pit the empirical autonomy of his "sole self" against the unreason of his imagination—"the fancy cannot cheat so well / As she is fam'd to do" (72–74)—as if to will the poem, almost against its own will, to return from Dionysian suffering to Apollonian calm. But Fancy both constitutes and transgresses the boundaries of masculine vision. Hence, when Keats feminizes melancholy as "dwell[ing] with . . . Beauty that must die" ("Ode to Melancholy," 21), he suggests the eradication of the feminine but also uses it to overturn the static aesthetic hegemony of Beauty associated with the kind of masculinist visionary tradition within which Wordsworth situates his Prospectus, for instance. The poet is caught in a no-man's-land of gender's ambivalent "waking dream" ("Ode to a Nightingale," 79). On one hand, gender allows the poet to distinguish reason from unreason, the real from phantasy, as the masculine from the feminine. On the other, however, he then succumbs to this distinction as a type of psychic determinism he is subsequently, out of his compulsion to repeat its prescription, compelled to resist and transform.

The speculation of gender also points to poetry's speculative nature, which discloses the psyche's immanent and interminable self-observational power. The ambivalence of "Ode on a Grecian Urn," for instance, arises not from the observation of its object but from the manner in which contemplation "dost tease us out of thought" (44).[10] The urn's marble brede depicts figures "For ever panting, and for ever young— / All breathing human passion far above" (27–28), a type of beautiful *end* to the work of being human. Within this stasis, however, contemplation also generates a sublime ambivalence, figured in the urn's subject as either "men or gods" (8). Contemplating immortality unravels into the search for an autonomous self-knowledge, the interminability of which is the unconscious of contemplation, signaled by the urn's metaphysical *coitus interruptus*, which perpetually suspends the ideology of a heterosexual union between men and maidens. A subtle yet profound shift in Keats's writings turns immortality into interminability to produce what Nietzsche calls the "clash of different worlds, e.g., of a divine and a human one" (*BT* 71). This is the clash of the subject with the "primordial contradiction" of his being: that to transcend reason's curse of individuation is to lose one's identity in a moment both liberating and terrifying, neither potently masculine nor cripplingly feminine.[11]

Despite their internal psychological complexities, however, the odes' shorter and elaborately overwrought form suggests a terminability that becomes compromised in Keats's longer works. As the fragment of a dream, *The Fall of Hyperion* figures interminability as part of its formal structure (*Hyperion* is also a fragment, but seemingly against its own will). Moreover, whereas *Hyperion* and the Odes express the terminability of poetry through consciousness and the *cogito*, *The Fall* follows the interminability of the unconscious. This difference evokes Keats's distinction between the "camelion" nature of the "poetical Character" and the determinate selfhood of the "wordsworthian or egotistical sublime." "A Poet," writes Keats, "is the most unpoetical of any thing in existence; because he has no Identity." The "unpoetical" has "no self" except as it is "continually in for—and filling in some other Body";[12] the otherness of "poetical" objects stand in for its contemplative identity, such as "[t]he Sun, the Moon, the Sea and Men and Women who are creatures of impulse" because they "have about them an unchangeable attribute" (*KL* 157). The "poetical" fixes poetry as a kind of mechanical reproduction of itself, wherein the "unpoetical" continually places this identity in process as part of an interminable search for identity. The word "impulse" points to the psychosomatic or *habitual* determinism of this process. The "I" defines its self-making in terms of the autonomy of what is "not I," so that identity is displaced through the autonomous alterity of its own imaginative processes. In *A Defence of Poetry* Shelley calls this poetry's "vitally metaphorical" (*SPP* 512) nature as it unfolds through the interminable reproductions of its own unconscious. Shelley and Keats offer a post-Schopenhauerian understanding of identity as a representation of psychic life deconstructed by the will, and both read this identity in terms of myth. Keats especially emphasizes the profoundly literary nature of psychoanalysis, which dramatizes the psyche's complex subjectivity through the multiple, mythopoeic forms of its unconscious. The psychoanalysis of the Greek pantheon in Keats's writings is, in this respect, Nietzschean, staging the self-less and "unpoetical" Dionysian subject who can only be named darkly through his "poetical" Apollonian representations.[13]

We have already explored how the psyche resists mastery by the authoritarian ego of Wordsworth's Prospectus. For Hillman the psyche unfolds through the irrational perspectives of its own experience, a "dehumanizing" process of pathology and personification that suggests the productive forms of the *cogito*'s unreason. On one hand, *Hyperion* attempts to follow the developmental trajectory of Greek mythology from the Titans to the Olympians. But this history is displaced by the unresolvable case study of Hyperion/Apollo, whose analysis is interrupted apocalyptically because Keats cannot yet concede that immortality is interminability. Hillman cites Addison on the dangers of imagination by way of noting how before Keats's "[p]ersonifications were the result of a special state of the psyche, when it was not its usual rational mechanical self." Keats encounters this process in the Greek pantheon as a type of multiple personality disorder, a gigantic mythopoeic case study of the psyche as what Hillman calls "the myth in the mess."[14] In his preface to *Endymion* Keats expresses this anxiety about the personifications of Greek mythology by damning his obsession with paganism as a state of unreason between "the [healthy] imagination of a boy" and "the mature [and healthy] imagination of a man" the "space of life between, in which the soul is in a ferment, the character undecided, the way of life uncertain, the ambition thick-sighted" (*KP* 64).[15]

Keats seems to put aside this mutation in consciousness within an organic movement from Romantic adolescence to Victorian adulthood. However, read against the Preface's canonization, which too vehemently rejects the poem's flaws, this middle ground is also immanently transgressive. Alan Bewell argues that reviews of Keats's 1817 *Poems* and 1818 *Endymion* are early responses to the poetry's "gender conflict": an attention to sensuous and luxuriant imagery, associated with an effete literature of sensibility, that points to a Romantic excess not fitting (of) a heterosexist Victorian paradigm of social duty and self-control. As a male poet, that is, Keats is either too libidinous or not potent enough. However, Keats "enact[s this conflict] within the later poems . . . as a matter for revision. In these poems, Keats consistently rewrites the conflict between women's literature and the male visionary tradition as a conflict between his earlier and later self."[16] *The Fall of Hyperion* thus distinguishes between the poet as the picture of masculine health and as the carrier of a femininized and pathologized fanaticism. Keats's "stylistic cross-dressing"[17] borrows from "women's" romance and sensibility at a time of Regency culture's rising anxiety about its own masculinity. Yet Keats also exploits the labor of the feminine within the larger project of constructing his own later persona as a more potently masculine writer. However, Keats's transformation at the expense of the feminine does not accrue wholly to the masculine. The economy of Romantic psychoanalysis mobilized between *Endymion*, *Hyperion*, and *The Fall of Hyperion* unfolds within its identity its own "phantasmatic structure," dramatized by an internalized "subversive repetition" of gender that this identity comes to confront within itself. These texts constellate an unfolding scene of gender in the Romantic psychoanalysis we have studied to this point. This psychoanalysis reads its masculine science or model of the mind as a feminine phantasy of reason, but in order to confront the 'masculine' and 'feminine' as both constitutive *and* destabilizing categories within this process.

In a letter of May 1818, four months before starting *Hyperion*, Keats "compare[s] human life to a large Mansion of many Apartments, two of which [he] can only describe," the "infant or thoughtless Chamber" and the "Chamber of Maiden-Thought" (*KL* 95). The second apartment "becomes gradually darken'd and at the same time on all sides of it many doors are set open—but all dark—all leading to dark passages." In his progress into the mind of Man, Keats argues Wordsworth had got this far in "Tintern Abbey." Beyond this indeterminate 'maiden' stage, one expects a later shift into masculine experience. A year later, however, having abandoned *Hyperion*, Keats describes life as a "vale of Soul-making" (249), a site of both negativity and potentiality. Here the "Soul or Intelligence [is] *destined* to possess the sense of Identity," soul-making is "where the heart must feel and suffer in a thousand diverse ways" in "a world of Circumstances" that perpetually delay this destiny (250–51; my italics).[18] Both descriptions provide metaphors for later Freudian paradigms, but are also fragmented by a psychic contingency that finds the second metaphor revising the first. Whereas Wordsworth's Gothic church organizes the psyche metapsychologically and syncretically, Keats humanizes the suffering of philosophy as a large Mansion that the subject inhabits developmentally. Yet because it is a rem(a)inder of Wordsworth's architectonic, and because of Keats's increasingly tragic awareness that life is a place where "the thought that we are mortal makes us groan" (*KL* 33), he *de*humanizes this model by exposing it to its own pathology. For the developmental logic of reason Keats now substitutes the psychosomatic field or "Vale" of the psyche's dark internal functioning, staged indeterminately between the masculine and the feminine.

Endymion and *Hyperion* express an essentially gendered interiority; yet they also treat this interiority with some ambivalence. By feminizing unreason, *Endymion* would colonize romance—its tendency to wander in its own mazes—in the service of building Keats's masculine identity as Poet. But the text unravels into a wandering scene of psychoanalysis constituting the unstable hegemony of Romance. Keats calls this romance's "uncertain path" (1.61), just as Endymion is "wandering in uncertain ways" (2.48).[19] The epic cast of *Hyperion*, however, is similarly unsettled by a subtext of psychoanalysis in which gender figures prominently. By staging the *mise-en-scène* of the gendering of these genres as if returning to the first *Hyperion* as the second text's primal scene, *The Fall* is equally ambivalent about its own gendered nature. Psychoanalysis and gender thus emerge as mutually contested and contesting forces in all three texts. The prototype of this struggle occurs in *Endymion*, where Peona, to help Endymion read the "troubled sea of the mind" (1.454), places him "On her own couch" (1.438). Here the woman is the feminine unreason of Romanticism as well as its female analyst, both compromised by and resisting a masculine analytical authority the text would presume to know. Yet Peona also facilitates in the poet a confrontation with the pathology of his visionary imagination—a confrontation with Margaret's madness as the projection of his own masculinist *cogito*. The feminine, that is, resists the philosophical confidence of gender's prerogatives, dragging them to the phantasmatic scene of their own authority, a place of "no Identity" that is both absence *and* potentiality. The feminine discloses the phantasy of reason, opening reason to its own internal psychic determinism but also displaying/mobilizing its performative or self-making potentiality as a constitutive resistance to this determinism.

Wandering Psychoanalysis in *Endymion*

Endymion appears to be more Apollonian than Dionysian, but there is already trouble in its protagonist.[20] Endymion is a "very contemplative sort of a Person [who] lived solitry [sic] among the trees and Plains *little thinking*" (*KL* 18; my italics), a figure of "solitary thinkings" (*KP* 1.294) who contemplates things, but without self-awareness.[21] The stating of the poem's theme—"A thing of beauty is a joy forever" (1.1)—is meant to signify the goal at the heart of romance's labyrinth in the 'heart' of the poet's soul, where beauty will register the journey's lasting effects. However, these effects are more incessant than transcendental as Endymion becomes intoxicated by a vision of the autonomy of his mortal self as his "sweet dream" (1.677) of Diana. 'Forever' comes to represent a painfully uncertain time. *Endymion* explores the anatomy of eternity as the interpretation of this dream as it perpetually "[falls] into nothing—into stupid sleep" (1.678). Stuart Sperry argues that the poem gradually shifts its allegiance from Pan, "the symbol of a form of *thinking*" that is "inscrutable" and "unimaginable," to Apollo, who symbolizes "prescience and control."[22] Pan's pagan unreason reflects his unstable position as a sprite between body and spirit, mortality and divinity.[23] Keats thus shifts from a "mortal" hero who "is led on, like Buonaparte, by circumstance," to Apollo, "a fore-seeing God [who] will shape his actions like one" (*KL* 51). The shift is not that straightforward, however. *Endymion* searches for the self-knowledge to cure its protagonist's burden of "secret grief" (*KP* 1.539); but his dark dream comes to explain why Apollo, ultimately conceived against the grain of his godlike "Knowledge enormous" (3.113) at the end of *Hyperion*, dies into life. The intoxication of Endymion's desire for omniscience, and so for the telos of romance, becomes addiction, a melancholic dis-ease of "secret grief" which the text's therapy cannot overcome. This dis-ease is contingently figured in Diana, who haunts the text as mythology's Protean mutation into the multiple tellings of the Greek pantheon. She suggests a free-associationism, both in Endymion's mind and in the form of the text's narrative, and thus in the psyche of romance itself, which the text would resist. As myth's pathology, she signifies the psychic dis-ease of Endymion's own contemplation, "Reason in her most exalted mood" as a radical psychoanalysis of Wordsworthian vision: "where / Are those swift moments? Whither are they fled?" (1.970–71). That Endymion never possesses Diana suggests a masculine anxiety toward feminine vision. But this rupture within the text's *cogito* is also its own resistance to a masculine mastering of the feminine and thus to colonization by romance (and Romantic) prescriptions. If uncomfortable with feminine unreason, the text appears equally uneasy about a masculine reason that would gender away what seems integral to its own identity.

Subtitled "A Poetic Romance," the poem is more concerned with a romance of poetry that functions, as Sperry argues, as "allegory in its broadest and most general sense." Sperry refers to a pre-Romantic conjunction of allegory and romance in which the text's "prodigality and confusion of detail" is symptomatic of the struggle to disclose beneath its literal veneer an immanent denotation.[24] Keatsian allegory, however, lends itself also to post-Coleridgean or de Manian allegory, which responds to temporality rather than transcendence. Andrew Bennett addresses "the dilatory, the digressive, the delaying" narrative tactic of

Endymion, the "solecism" by which the text, "lost within textual mazes and labyrinths," is "overwhelmed by narrative."[25] This overwhelming telling is the symptom of a psychic interminability that the text cannot overcome. The text's composition betrays this wandering.[26] Keats wrote *Enydmion* in order to attempt, like Wordsworth, "things unattempted yet in prose or rhyme," so that he might, as the poem's preface tells us, "[fit himself] for verses fit to live" (*KP* 64).[27] He describes the poem as "a trial of my Powers of Imagination and chiefly of my invention which is a rare thing indeed—by which I must make 4000 Lines of one bare circumstance and fill them with Poetry" (*KL* 27).[28] This aesthetic calculus suggests that each of the four Books occasions a precise *duration* of talking—a 1,000-line session—that treats its subject matter incidentally and is more concerned to evoke the free-associationism of romance's "uncertain path" that follows Endymion's "wandering in uncertain ways." This stock reflection on the poet's imaginative powers is offset by Keats's repeated interventions as an ongoing register of his affective state. Most notably, Book Four's Invocation describes the "lowliness of heart" with which Keats "move[s] to [the text's] end" (4.29). He later writes: "Endymion! unhappy! it nigh grieves / Me to behold thee thus in last extreme" (4.771–72). Here the text confesses a melancholy about its own inability to cure itself, the failure of poetry to transform "our dull, uninspired, snail-paced lives" (4.25).[29]

Endymion's wandering through the Greek pantheon becomes the psyche's endless search for its own narrative self-possession. Again, the signifier of this tendency is Diana, who mutates into a variety of both divine and sublunary forms and whose "Protean flexibility"[30] reflects mythology's tendency to fragment into multiple tellings. Moreover, her indeterminate presence, the reflection of Endymion's own ambivalent identity, discloses within her immortal frame a psychosomatic interiority described at the beginning of Book Three as "How chang'd, how full of ache, how gone in woe" (3.80). She suggests the embodied pathology of mythology itself, the psychic dis-ease of Endymion's contemplation that perpetually turns to self-observation, hence the text's perpetual mourning for the lost *telos* of Endymion's desire: an end to the uncertain wandering of self-observation itself. *Endymion* proceeds through a series of episodes that find its central character unable to maintain his opening meditative stance.[31] Within the "sober ring" of philosophy, he is supposed to "discourse" with an "aged priest" "upon the fragile bar / That keeps us from our homes ethereal" (1.356–61). Instead, he "[flings] / Himself" (2.95–96) or "[throws] himself" (2.711) on the ground, on couches, or on beds (1.436–38; 2.95–96; 2.440ff; 2.711ff; 3.107–9) in order "to ponder / On all his life" (2.886–87) and to tell his dreams, or he falls into dreams that prefigure his future fate (4.376ff). These are also scenes of "entrancements" and "ravishment" in which his "soul deceives / Its powerless self" (2.704, 715, 701–2). What are potentially moments of self-revelation simultaneously conduct to a mesmerism of Endymion's faculties, which undergo a type of frenzied catharsis without any therapeutic results.

This resistance to psychoanalysis is embodied in Endymion, who can make no connection between the telling of his dreams and the retelling of his life. Although everyone in Book One's Festival of Pan is "ripe for high contemplating," talk turns out to be cheap. They "wandered, by divine converse, / Into Elysium, vying to rehearse / Each one his own anticipated bliss," and "all out-told / Their fond imaginations." This wandering 'rehearsal' for immortality, however, suggests both anticipation and an excessive lack of fulfillment, while "out-told" suggests both apotheosis and excess. While this group mesmeric crisis is circuited through Endymion and the "aged priest," their "sober ring" is also a "fragile bar / That keeps us from our homes ethereal," as though philosophy is the curse preventing the *cogito*'s transcendence (1.355–93). Everyone "feelingly could scan" Endymion's "lurking trouble," but remains susceptible to its psychic dis-ease (1.178–79). Endymion's "senses . . . [swoon] off" (1.398), as though reason itself becomes the feminine suspending his 'sense.' Peona removes him from the opening scene of masculine philosophy to one of feminine interrogation (1.407ff) and lays him "On her own couch." Where he and the priest discourse as if of one mind, Peona addresses Endymion as part of a dialogue. A singing analyst, Peona plays on her lute "A "lively prelude, fashioning the way / In which her voice should wander," as if to recall Endymion from this self-division. Yet she "can trace / Something more high-perplexing in [his] face" which she cannot read. Morever, her music's "deep intoxication" is both curative and infectious. That it carries the wandering of her voice suggests the threatening influence of gender that she embodies/bodies forth, a contagion unsettling her "self-possession." This countertransference uncannily repeats Endymion's trauma, so that he must himself turn therapist: "'Tell me thine ailment: tell me all amiss! / Ah! thou hast been unhappy at the change / Wrought suddenly in me.'" Gradually Endymion begins to "ease [his] breast / Of secret grief" (1.479–539). The source of his agitation is his dream of Diana as a "second self" that resists assimilation within what the text will later call his "sovereign vision" (1.659, 3.183), a feminine penetration of the masculinist *cogito*.

As if responding to the gender ambivalence of psychoanalysis as a threat to romance, Peona then shifts to speak as romance's superego. Here the text exemplifies 'woman' as having internalized cultural restraint by loathing her own dreams as the province of feminine sensibility: "*Shame / On this poor weakness*!" (1.717–18). Dismissing psychoanalysis in favor of behavioral therapy, she would cure Endymion's feminized melancholy by appealing to his sense of duty: "'wherefore sully the entrusted gem / Of high and noble life with thoughts so sick?'" (1.757–58). Tellingly, it is Endymion who would persist in romance ("No merely slumberous phantasm, could unlace / The stubborn canvas for my voyage prepared" [1.771–72]) as equal to social action: "My restless spirit never could endure / To brood so long upon one luxury / Unless it did, though fearfully, espy / A hope beyond the shadow of a dream" (1.854–57). He reads his dream's reality metaphysically within a developmental vision of the *anthropos* (1.769–842) as a "Pleasure Thermometer" (*KL* 60).[32] The passage appears to signify imaginative redemption, the "Idea of all our Passions as of Love [as] all in their sublime, creative of essential Beauty" (*KL* 37). Yet this "Life of Sensations rather than of Thoughts" (37) remains unsettled by the mind's "entanglements, enthralments far / More self-destroying" (*KP* 1.798–99). Thus, as the potentially transformed *anthropos* "Full alchemized, and free of space," he remains "knit" by an "under-darkness" that becomes the symptom of the abstract *cogito* as if divided from its inner life (1.780, 701–2). Endymion settles upon "demurest meditation" (1.975), which suggests a feminine empowering of masculine contemplation that would resist normative gender prescriptions. But the 'demure' discourse of sensibility also suggests capitulation, so that both the feminine and masculine are 'compromised.' Endymion "Bear[s] up against [Sorrow]" and would show a "more healthy countenance" (1.974, 986). Yet he rises from his couch only "faint-smiling" (1.990). In Book Two, "Brain-sick," his "old grief" returns immediately and the text continues to unfold as an avoidance of "coming madness" played out as Endymion's compulsion to repeat the text's psychoanalysis (2.42, 47, 218).

Books Two, Three, and Four retell the text's own mythopoeia as its repeated attempt to fashion a scene of psychoanalysis that would account for Endymion's wanderings. Two specific episodes seem to bring this psychoanalysis to fulfillment. Book Two's union of Venus with Adonis in his "Bower" (2.387 ff) figures the cure of Endymion's transference with Peona, and thus the end to self-division as the consummation of his desire for Diana. Book Three similarly recuperates Endymion's truncated 'discourse' with the priest as the fulfilled psychoanalysis of Endymion's "discoursing" with Glaucus, who "know[s Endymion's] inmost bosom," so that they become "twin brothers in this destiny" (3.723, 293, 713). Endymion revises Glaucus's "lifeless" identity and hears the "secret [of his own destiny] all display'd" in Glaucus's story (3.314–711), the uncanny repetition of Endymion's unfulfilled desire for Diana (3.220, 308). At the end of this narrative, Glaucus tears the "scroll" (3.670) that prophesies the consummation of his own fate in Endymion's. In a moment of homosocial bonding, as if to buttress the masculinist ideology of reason, he asks Endymion to scatter its fragments on both of them as on the "files of dead," whose reason has, like that of Glaucus, been slain by Circe, "arbitrary queen of sense" (3.770, 459). Thus reanimated, these 'dead' turn Glaucus's "mumblings funeral" into a "noise of harmony," so that the melancholic dis-ease of the feminine within reason is overcome (3.748, 791). Here the gender ambivalence of previous attempts at psychoanalysis is reclarified in terms of the visionary trope of apocalypse negotiated between men, just as the union between Venus and Adonis confirms the text's heterosexual matrix.

Yet the parallel between Circe and Diana in Book Three unsettles these negotiations by suggesting that the release from unreason is instead a missed encounter with its radically transgressive feminine power. By destroying the scroll, as if to transcend language, Glaucus also eliminates any record of the feminine's murderous designs on reason. The elimination itself, however, confirms the feminine's constitutive power within the Symbolic as the occulted repetition of this order's instability, the flaw within its masculine narcissism. The most potent symptom of this trauma is Book Four's Cave of Quietude, "Made for the soul to wander in and trace / Its own existence" (4.514–15). As the analytical office of the text's pantheon, the Cave anatomizes as if from the text's unconscious its wandering scene of psychoanalysis. As a "native hell," "Happy gloom," or "Dark paradise," where the soul is made by both "buried griefs" and "new-born woe," the cave seems adapted to internalize the text's ambivalence toward psychoanalysis (4.517–38). A spectral and imaginary rather than productive clinical response to the text's psychic dis-ease, the cave suspends the cognition of psychoanalysis. Like the mythopoeic form of De Quincey's *Suspiria*, it exists without analysts or analysands to embody its suffering spirit, although it prefigures the Poet's encounter with Moneta in *The Fall of Hyperion*, as though Keats is already imagining the future case study of *Endymion*'s missed encounter with its own trauma. Partly this suspension implicitly rejects what Butler calls the "disembodiment of the abstract masculine epistemological subject."[33] This abstraction is a type of Kantian *epoché* that privileges self-awareness only by bracketing it off from the volatile economy of gender by which subjectivity is constituted. Endymion refuses to take on Glaucus's identity and thus to reject entirely the 'embodiment' of this identity's 'other' gender. As the poem ends, Peona blesses Endymion and the Indian maiden as they "vanish'd" (4.1002) into the text's now defunct romance topography. Awkwardly expedient, this resolution repeats Book Two's union between Venus and Adonis, but by staging a compulsory heterosexuality that the text would no longer defend.

The psychoanalytic scenes of Books Two, Three, and Four appear to release the mythopoeic power of Peona's rather limited therapeutic cure in Book One. But they hold no cognitive value for Enydmion. When he "shuts his eyes in vain / Imagination gave a dizzier pain" (3.1008–9). Feeling the psychosomatic burden of his imagination's mystery, where he is unable to read the encrypted "fragments of the dead" (3.784) that people and haunt his unconscious, he once again misses the self-making potentiality of his encounter with the unconscious. Again "sad and lost" (4.51) and "full of grief" (4.107), he confronts his lost autonomy in a statement that becomes the epistemological kernel of *Hyperion*:

> What is this soul then? Whence
> Came it? It does not seem my own, and I
> Have no self-passion or identity.
> Some fearful end must be: where, where is it?
> By Nemesis, I see my spirit flit
> Alone about the dark— (4.475–80)

Able at last to "scan" the tragedy of his lost contemplative identity, Endymion appears to have begun a process of soul-searching that *Hyperion* picks up in the opening figure of Saturn. When Endymion awakes for the final time, he discovers that he has "clung / To nothing, lov'd a nothing, nothing seen / Or felt but a great dream" (4.636–38). He is left to realize that "there never liv'd a mortal man, who bent / His appetite beyond his natural sphere, / But starv'd and died" (4.646–48). And so he says he will have "no more of dreaming" (4.669).

Realizing his "kingdom's at its death" (4.940) Endymion discards the masculinist illusion of immortality and autonomy. Instead, he "inwardly began / On things for which no wording can be found" (4.961–62). This music, echoing Peona's "intoxication" and Glaucus's "harmony," yet left darkly unprescribed by the ideology of masculine vision ("Deeper and deeper sinking, until drown'd / Beyond the reach of music" [4.963–64]), suggests Kristeva's idea of the semiotic *chora.* Kristeva associates the *chora* with the mother's body as a primal matrix of biological, cultural, and patriarchal regulation from which the (de)constituted subject emerges, a form of theoretical essentialism against which Butler herself famously reacts.[34] Refusing to identify the semiotic with the 'feminine,' however, Kristeva uses the semiotic to posit within any symbolic economy its constitutive instability or repetitive marginality as (to return to Butler, albeit in a way she might not welcome) the very mechanism of its cultural reproduction. The semiotic thus suggests within the text's prescribed economy of gender alternate identities facilitated by the feminine as it signifies, although does not essentialize, a productive ambivalence within this economy. However, that these identities are left unexplored suggests finally that the text cannot overcome what it perceives to be flaws within its own gendered schema. Endymion remains "lost" (4.51) between masculine and feminine, reason and unreason. He awakens to his world's ineffectual psychoanalysis by pointing toward *The Fall of Hyperion*, where Moneta is the carrier of a radically temporal disposition or "immortal sickness which kills not; / It works a constant change, which happy death / Can put no end to" but is instead "deathwards progressing / To no death" (1.258–61). The "immortal sickness" of romance betrays the melancholy of a self-exploration without terminus or cure, utterly immune to poetry's therapy. The text is prone to psychoanalysis, yet only as a specter haunting the stubborn structure of romance, which, despite its tendency to wander, resists psychoanalysis's alien feminine presence.

Hyperion and the Anatomy of Titanic Melancholy

Four months after completing *Endymion*, Keats was compelled to "Take refuge" from "detested moods in new romance" (*KL* 111–12). *Hyperion* recasts *Endymion*'s uncurable serial pathology as epic as if to monumentalize the psyche by tracing its archetypal parentage. But *Hyperion* manifests the previous text's latent psychoanalysis of the Greek pantheon, figured in Saturn's trauma, which places a monumental psychic burden on the text. Apollo's entry in Book Three is meant to alleviate this burden, but the text's Olympic succession cannot cure its own Titanic neurosis.[35] *The Fall of Hyperion* then psychoanalyzes as a scene of trauma the first text's inability to ease the burden of compulsive self-observation. Here, Keats invents the scene of Romantic psychoanalysis as a dream vision, through which the subject imagines the Apollonian appearance of his life as his own self-making encounter with the Dionysian irrationality of his imagination.

Hyperion dramatizes the autonomy of masculine vision as if moving through the mirror stage of its own identity into its Symbolic ambivalence. Saturn's opening speech to Thea, his female interlocutor, refigures Endymion's mortal doubt as the trauma of Titanic selfhood: "I am gone / Away from my own bosom: I have left / My strong identity, my real self, / Somewhere between the throne, and where I sit / Here on this spot of earth" (1.112–16). The statement locates Saturn's "strong identity" between immortality and mere existence but also in his heart and thus in a locus of feeling that seems authentic but that, because it is not self-present to Saturn, cannot be named. Subsequent encounters repeat this self-alienation and describe a once-constitutive selfhood as a purgatorial, transitional "vale of soul-making" between self and other, which makes Saturn painfully aware of his subjectivity by making him traumatically aware it is not in his possession. Kristeva calls this process abjection, "the first authentic feeling of a subject in the process of constituting itself as such." The abject is that which "disturbs identity, system, order . . . the in-between, the ambiguous, the composite." It is both/neither within and/nor outside of the symbolic boundaries of the subject, although by rupturing these boundaries, the abject marks the subject's (dis)appearance. She further defines the psychoanalytical process as an "indefinite catharsis" characterized by abjection: "One must keep open the wound where he or she who enters into the analytic adventure is located. . . . [It is] a heterogeneous, corporeal, and verbal ordeal of fundamental incompleteness."[36]

Abjection suggests the ambivalence between mourning and melancholia. Laplanche and Pontalis, quoting Daniel Lagache, write that the "work of mourning consists in 'killing death.'" Melancholy, however, results from an inability to "'sever [one's] attachment to the object that has been abolished.'"[37] Saturn's melancholy results from his inability to 'kill' the *imago* of his archaic patriarchal divinity, for the past, while utterly alien, is also integral to who he was/is. Mourning produces contemplative composure, the end of psychic interminability via a "poetical" cure of the unconscious. However, mourning is always unsettled by melancholy, the psyche's inability to tell its psychic dis-ease in full—that is, to tell the unconscious—and thus to bring the subject to psychic completion. Saturn's struggle thus stages as a more overt scene of trauma the homosocial narcissism of patriarchy in *Endymion*. Where in *Endymion* romance seems regressively melancholic, as if unable to accept the "phantasmatic structure" of its own gendered economy, *Hyperion* struggles to account for melancholy as this structure's constitutive and constituting nature. Without "a bent for melancholia," Kristeva writes, "there is no psyche," for "there is no imagination that is not, overtly or secretly, melancholy," an "*impossible mourning*" for an inaccessible—and inaccessibly lost—object."[38] As a version of this impossible mourning, Saturn's patriarchal vision is internalized within the text as the feminine sensibility of melancholy, as if in an attempt to transpose these categories beyond their own essential terms. The unconscious emerges beyond gender in the text as a source of both negativity and potentiality, and the prospect of a melancholic interminability, despite its regressive cast, produces tragic insight, even imaginative power.[39]

The psychosomatic condition of Titanic selfhood as it finds itself at the margins of its own identity marks the "in-between" subjectivity of abjection caught between mourning and melancholia. Judith Little argues the Titans' meditative self-examination marks *Hyperion* as a "poem of contemplation, not of action," a text "working itself into a statement of evolutionary development"[40] between the Titans and the Olympians, but never getting there. More projected than accomplished, however, Olympic succession is also delayed by this self-examination. It is not so much a question of Titanic melancholy displacing the Apollonian mo(u)rning of Olympian contemplation as it is that one is always immanent within the other. Thea refers to the poem's "aching time," and there is a "listening fear in her regard" (1.64, 37). Her "Sorrow more beautiful than Beauty's self," read against the grain of her "Memphian" stature, signifies within the poem's beautiful monumental form its sublime absent psychosomatic body, which includes the suffering of Saturn, Hyperion, and Apollo within its "unsecure" anatomy (1.36, 31, 168). Hyperion compares his fallen state to Saturn's, his "eternal essence thus distraught," and "melancholy numbs [Apollo's] limbs" (1.232, 3.89). Melancholy infects these dependent subjects who search for their cultural identities as part of an unconscious past they can no longer read. They are mesmerized or "Amazed" between "alternate uproar and sad peace," anxious self-observation and resigned contemplation (3.1–2). Hence, *Hyperion* begins as the monologic exegesis of the fall of the Titans but, like *Endymion*, unfolds as a series of fallings within the Greek pantheon, raising the specter of patriarchal immortality, and thus of the *cogito* of epic, as a multiple personality without cure unfolding interminably against the grain of the text's epic desire. Accordingly, this sociocultural movement of the text's subjectivity unsettles the apparatus of the epic ego. The gods are monolithic entities that convey an epic, if tragic, grandeur; yet as textual figures they are also fluid metaphors of an indeterminate self. The former constitutes identities as an array of bounded egos within a fixed symbolic tableau; the latter suggests a semiosis that destabilizes identities and foregrounds the differences both within and between them.

These 'unstable' subjects read their identities through the discourse of the other, and the most powerful intratextual mechanism of self-observation—and the most powerful threat to epic contemplation—becomes *dialogue*. The text unfolds as a series of encounters through which Saturn, Hyperion, and Apollo are mirror images of an analysand who transfers his psychic dis-ease onto various analytical figures: Thea (1.23–71; 2.89–100), Coelus (1.306–48), Oceanus (2.163–246), Clymene (2.247–303), Enceladus (2.107–10; 2.303–55), and Mnemosyne (3.46–79). *Hyperion* is a powerful intertext with Shelley's *Prometheus Unbound* in this regard.

Panthea, who in Act 1 visits the bound Prometheus, in Act 2 returns to Asia, who reads Prometheus's psychic interiority in Panthea's face, now a site of potential recognition and communication between Asia and Prometheus: "Lift up thine eyes, / And let me read thy dream" (*SPP* 2.2.55–56). Eventually Asia reads Prometheus's "written soul" through a "wordless converse" (2.2.110) that imagines transference interpsychically. As Rajan argues, these scenes construct a dialogic "model" that presents "reading as a psychological and not just a semiological process,"[41] so that Shelley's poem tropes the potentiality of social apocalypse as a psychological process of trauma both repeated and remembered as the reading of 'dreams' and 'written souls.' *Hyperion*'s scenes of reading similarly focus on a questioning subject who requires the other's face and affect to validate his own identity. In Book One, for instance, Saturn *feels* Thea's presence before he sees her face, which he then asks her to lift (as Asia does Panthea), so that he might "see [their collective] doom in it": "Look up, and tell me if this feeble shape / Is Saturn's" (*KP* 1.97–99). Although he can "see his kingdom gone," however, he is still left asking "where is Saturn?" (1.90, 134). He still yearns to repossess his lost autonomy: "cannot I fashion forth / Another world, another universe, / To overbear and crumble this to naught?" (1.142–44). Thea responds in Book Two by observing "direst strife" after "*sidelong* [fixing] her eye on Saturn's face" (2.91–92; my italics), thus confirming his melancholy. But her indirect confrontation suggests an inability to deal with her own countertransference and thus to read his affect productively. Moreover, the intensity of his transference onto Thea and thus of his inability to understand his own identity seems almost pathological. When he addresses the "fallen tribe," he says "Not in my own sad breast, / Which is its own great judge and searcher out, / Can I find reason why ye should be thus" (2.100, 129–31).[42] But even as the psychology of trauma is both remembered and repeated in these scenes, communication remains more projected than fulfilled. Thus more part of the text's subconscious, they comprise a psychoanalytical allegory in which the subject confronts, but cannot seem to move beyond, the narcissistic construct of its own epic autonomy. Like Endymion, Saturn can "see his kingdom gone," but still yearns to repossess it.

As a desperate subject presumed to know, then, Saturn has a "nervous grasp" (1.105) on reality. In the literature of sensibility, Peter Melville Logan notes, "the female body, though victimized by confinement, is also the contagious source of the nervous epidemic; the nervous mother, in her debility, infects her offspring with a constitutional nervous temperament."[43] Here, however, the father's body is infected by a nervous contagion that is passed on to the text's two suns/sons, Hyperion and

Apollo. Although a mirror image of Saturn's melancholy (in the pantheon, he would be Saturn's brother, and in the text, he signals the Titans' own internal hope for redemption), Hyperion suggests an ambivalent identity between a "shape majestic" and a "vast shade / In midst of his own brightness" (2.372–73). His "horrors, portion'd to a giant nerve, / Oft made [him] ache" (1.175–76). He signifies the anatomy of the text's *anthropos* dying into the life of his own psychosomatic interiority: "through all his bulk an agony / Crept gradual, from the feet unto the crown" (1.259–60). In this respect he assumes the text's archetypal psychoanalytical pose between Saturn's downward gaze "couchant on the earth" and Apollo's upright stance "Full ankle-deep in lilies of the vale" (3.35) and gazing at Mnemosyne (1.87, 3.35).

As the *imago* of Apollo, the rising sun/son who Saturn would become, Hyperion emerges as key to the family romance of the text's patriarchy. The transition to Apollo is partly negotiated through Hyperion's transference with Coelus. As god of the heavens, he is both Hyperion's and the text's Father. Hyperion "[stretches] himself in grief and radiance faint" (1.304) on the earth and talks upward to Coelus, the melancholic son having placed himself on the couch. Hyperion seems able to confront the unreason of an interiority that Saturn cannot: "'O dreams of day and night! / O monstrous forms! O effigies of pain! / . . . / Why do I know ye? Why have I seen ye? . . . / . . . / Saturn is fallen, am I to fall too?" (1.227–34). Just as Thea recognizes in Saturn a "supreme God / At war with the frailty of grief" (2.92–93), Coelus also sees in Hyperion "an evident God" struck with mortal "grief" (1.338, 335). He would place Hyperion "in the van / Of circumstance" (1.343–44) so that the Titans' ascension can be realized. By the end of Book Two, however, Hyperion remains "dejected" (2.380), so that the father's therapy is ineffectual. As an abstract or "Ethereal presence" that is "but a voice," Coelus demands that the patriarchy's 'sons' must embody the melancholic disease it has denied and thus confront the text's "sad feud" of "son against sire" (1. 340, 321–22). By turning Hyperion toward his outward duty, however, Coelus would avoid Saturn's melancholy, just as Saturn only addresses his adversarial son Jupiter through Thea, Oceanus, and Enceladus. Although speaking "from the universal space" (1.307) that also bodies forth Apollo, Coelus remains the disembodied signifier of reason's masculinist, yet 'nervous,' desire for release from its internal dis-ease, a patriarchal psychoanalysis that does not work.

By "leav[ing]" (3.3,7) the Titans behind, Book Three appears to fulfill this truncated therapy. Book Three recasts dialogue as Apollo's encounter with Mnemosyne who, as Memory, asks Apollo to "Show [his] heart's secret" (3.76) and thus to overcome the Titans' self-forgetting. After Apollo reads a "wondrous lesson" in her face, he feels a god-like "Knowledge enormous" within himself (3.112–13). Fixing a "stedfast" and "level glance" on her features, he experiences "wild commotions," "Most like the struggle at the gate of death" (3.121–26). He then "Die[s] into life" (1.130), as if to work-through Titanic trauma and thus to enter the psychosomatic body of feeling (Saturn's "nervous grasp") from which the Titans seem hysterically suspended. "During [this pain] Mnemosyne," a kind of Delphic psychoanalyst, "upheld / Her arms as one who prophesied" (3.133–34). The gesture is complex, for it suggests a visionary suspension, as well as a transforming 'contamination,' of Apollo's Olympian body. On one hand, Apollo's "commotions" suggest confusion, covered over by the trope of apocalypse, which pretends to remove any need for mediation and thus dismisses Mnemosyne's female presence, whose feminine 'confusion' stems from the fact that, as a Titan goddess, she has 'shifted' her allegiance to the Olympians. On the other hand, gender productively displaces a detached Olympian "knowledge enormous" by bodying forth in Apollo a confrontation of reason with its own signifying economy of gender.

It is thus significant that Apollo says to Mnemosyne, "Thy name is on my tongue, I know not how" (3.83). This inability to name Titanic 'madness' is also its resistance to Symbolic prescription and thus to the containment of madness by gender. *This* ambivalence suggests within the text's melancholic anatomy a subversive immanence. In Thea's "listening fear," which repeats Saturn's opening stance of "bowed head . . . list'ning to the earth, / His ancient mother, for some comfort yet" (1.20–21), resides a semiotic potentiality related to the mother's body, although not grounded in it (significantly, 'Terra' remains *un*named in the text). Replayed more consciously in Thea's anxious readiness, this potentiality signifies a pre-Titanic "infant world," elsewhere referred to as the "murmurs" of "[Oceanus'] first-endeavouring tongue" (1.26, 2.171).[44] These "mourning words" translate the text's "feeble tongue / . . . like accents . . . frail / To that large utterance of the early Gods" and thus signal both the negativity and potentiality of the text's melancholy (1.49–51). An apotheosis of this melancholy is played out in Clymene's transmutation of Saturn's grief. She recounts how she "took a mouthed shell / And murmur'd into it, and made melody" (2.270–71), just as in Shelley's *Prometheus Unbound* Asia breathes into the "many-folded" and "curved shell which Proteus old / Made [her] nuptial boon," "Loosening [within] its mighty music" a "voice to be accomplished" (*SPP* 3.3.65–81).[45] This "new blissful golden melody" eventually anatomizes the "morning-bright

Apollo" (*KP* 2.280, 294). The trope of apocalypse again suppresses differences within an economy of vision. Yet this new 'new' vision is productively melancholic without suppressing melancholy's ambivalence ("each gush of sounds" was a "living death" [2.281]). Melancholy registers the text's flawed interiority, the constitution of the text's identity only through its endless iteration. This ghost in the machine of the text's cultural reproduction, however, also offers the possibility of authentic, albeit suffering, voices.[46]

This readiness to grieve is both regressive and recuperative within the text's family romance. Book Two alludes to a feminine muse (2.89). But Book Three, which invokes an unnamed muse, also calls upon the "Father of all verse," presumably Apollo, to "Flush everything that hath a vermeil hue," a color associated in Book One with Hyperion's entrance into the poem (3.13–14). Leaving behind the Titans, the text apparently moves from a maternal muse to a paternal music, and from a now-archaic origin in the Titans' own birth to the text's more productive Olympian progeny. Yet *to flush* vermilion from the sky also suggests the rising of the sun as Hyperion/Apollo, so that the text both overcomes and repeats Hyperion's ascension. Moreover, that Apollo is "*once more* the golden theme" (3.28; my italics) of Book Three favors eternal recurrence over teleology, the repetitive rising of the text's imagination from the ruins of its past accomplishments rather than the apotheosis of imagination itself. Moving from "his mother fair / And his twin-sister sleeping in their bower" to the "awful Goddess" Mnemosyne, Apollo is thus his own paternal hybrid engendered between two feminine strains, one signifying his genealogical past and the other signifying his creative ability to re(-)member this past (3.31–32, 46). Moreover, where Endymion awakens to nothingness after his dream of Diana, Apollo awakens to find a "lyre all golden by [his] side" (3.63). Mnemosyne reads his dream for him and tells a version of his own genealogy ("From the young day when first thy infant hand . . ." [3.73ff]) that fulfils Clymene's prophecy. Yet the lyre signifies in turn Apollo's own self-making ability and thus, unlike the influence of Peona's music, the ability to counter the other's mesmerizing influence. Hence, as the "Father of all verse" who is guided by the Mother of all muses, Apollo is the prototype of a poet who parents himself darkly within the economy of a destabilized subjectivity. He holds the text's potentially (r)evolutionary insight that we are "not the beginning nor the end" (2.190) freed from Oceanus's politics of power.

Another factor signifies here, however. While Mnemosyne is a therapeutic witness to the patriarchy's confrontation with its own gendered other, she also merely reflects back to the patriarchy its own inner disease. That is, Apollo's "commotions" also demonstrate how Saturn's contagion might be passed on to his son, for the male Titans, like Mnemosyne herself, are equally capable of shifting identities and allegiances. That one cannot tell from whom the contagion comes in the encounter between Apollo and Mnemosyne, then, also suggests the symptom of a patriarchal nervous disorder that Apollo, by recontaminating the feminine, would expel. Thus, Apollo, like Saturn, remains outside the transpositional economy of melancholy, so that the text's desire for psychoanalysis, like that of *Endymion*, seems again oddly suspended. Apollo's own strength remains "unsecure." Within *Hyperion*'s transposition between the gods as shifting metaphorical selves, Saturn, Hyperion, and Apollo must be read together as versions of the abject along a paradigmatic narrative axis that arranges them according to a teleology of desire rather than history, just as those who precede Mnemosyne are rem(a)inders of a prior analytical identity infected by Saturn/Hyperion's melancholy as "King," "god," and "father" (1.52, 2.184, 2.110, 2.252). Within this teleology Saturn is the abject or discarded rem(a)inder of Apollo that already disrupts the stability of his emergent domain.[47] Hence, although all three are palimpsestic versions of one another, one can also read through these versions for the narrative of the text's psychoanalytical subject who moves ambivalently "in-between" Saturnine melancholy and Apollonian mourning.[48] The melancholic cast of Hyperion's "Regal" (3.372) presence most closely defines the emergent Nietzschean anatomy of this subject's nebulous ontology. Nietzsche names the cure of the Apollonian after its "glance into the inside and terrors of nature" as "dark-colored spots" on our eyes after attempting to gaze at the sun, "luminous spots to cure eyes damaged by gruesome night" (*BT* 67). Apollo emerges to transform this deadly stasis of contemplation. Yet he is also unstably positioned between regression and recuperation as the abjective rem(a)inder of Hyperion. As an "indefinite catharsis" of the first two Books, Apollo's dying into life appears to manifest the text's latent psychoanalytical subjectivity; but the text, as if not knowing what to do with this subject, fragments itself in a moment of trauma: "Apollo shriek'd—and lo! from all his limbs / Celestial . . ." (3.135–36).

The Fall of Hyperion and the Dream of Psychoanalysis

Confronting this trauma as an inability to remember the original text as its own identity, *The Fall of Hyperion* turns to psychoanalyze *Hyperion*'s abandoned identity. *Hyperion*'s Apollonian anatomy is rather reluctantly sustained by its "suffering and contradictory" (*BT* 45) Dionysian interiority, an Apollo who is less Nietzschean than unstably Olympian, so that the text's abandonment is symptomatic of a melancholy that cannot be recognized. *The Fall of Hyperion* attempts to analyze this symptom by reading *Hyperion* as the product of a dream in which the poet confronts the unconscious of his imagination. Yet *The Fall* is itself a dream and thus a product of its own unconscious and of the textual unconscious of poetry. Exposing the interiority of poetry's contemplative identity, *The Fall* is a poem about the poetry of Psychoanalysis, the psychology within its metapsychology. *The Fall* reads within *Suspiria*'s metapsychology the suffering experiential process of its own making within the subject who imagines it. Through this psychoanalysis of poetry, the text confronts poetry's interminability as the burden of its Dionysian mystery, of which the text's, as well as the narrator's, Apollonian identity is an "inchoate, intangible reflection." In Nietzsche's words, the "image" through which *The Fall* "shows the artist his identity with the heart of the world is a dream scene that embodies the primordial contradiction and primordial pain, together with the primordial pleasure, of mere appearance" (*BT* 49). The dream of the subject—both as an event of his unconscious life and, more broadly, as the manner in which his existence *appears* to him—discloses the "mere appearance" of the empirical "I," the arbitrary and indeterminate phenomenology of the *cogito*. Yet the dream also figures identity as an aesthetic phenomenon, through which the subject's self-making potentiality redeems mere appearance from *dis*appearance. With the dream, the scene of Romantic psychoanalysis emerges in *The Fall* as the "indefinite catharsis" of the philosophical *anthropos*, whose progressive destabilization we have traced through Wordsworth, Coleridge, and De Quincey.

The Fall thus interrogates *Hyperion*'s ambivalent attempt to discipline unreason within the 'egotistical sublime' of poetry's properly masculine self and thus to make poetry submit to the essentialism of gender. Moreover, cast as a dream vision, *The Fall* enacts the phantasmatic structure of gender and thus performs the earlier texts' wandering psychoanalysis as the constitutive instability of the cultural reproduction of identity. *Endymion* and *Hyperion*, that is, attempt to prescribe a metaphysics of psychoanalysis. As metaphysics, this process depends on the reproduction of an array of gendered figures who also reproduce the nervous contagion of melancholy as the inability of this metaphysics to accept its own psychoanalysis. *The Fall*, however, focuses on the singular confrontation between the narrator (presumed to be masculine) and Moneta and so stages definitively within the text of Romantic psychoanalysis, albeit in a radically ambivalent form, its crisis of gender.

The Fall of Hyperion encrypts *Hyperion* as part of a revisionary site wherein *The Fall* reads its past—the past of *Hyperion*—as a site of trauma.[49] *Hyperion* is unable to remember the Titans' traumatic defeat by the Olympians, which the text repeats through the mediation of *Paradise Lost*, revisioned as the Greek theogony. By transferring analytic responsibility onto Milton, Keats thus displaces the trauma of the Greek pantheon within the apparatus of epic. That Book Three then discards epic as a form of authoritarian and terminable psychoanalysis suggests at the boundaries of the text's fragmentation the climax of a transference between Milton and Keats. Confronting as trauma poetry's inability to re(-)member itself, *The Fall* then psychoanalyzes *Hyperion* as the *imago* of an abandoned identity that Keats attempts to remember and work-through. *Hyperion*'s fragmentation, and its subsequent rewriting as *The Fall*, thus attempts to account for the countertransference of Milton as a subject presumed to know poetry's "resting places and seeming sure points of Reasoning." *The Fall* displaces Milton as the signifier of a poetry of contemplation that tames the free-association of imagination by making poetry remember its self. Milton, like Peona condemning Endymion's dreaming, is, in short, the wrong analyst for Keats's exploration of the poetic psyche. We can now read through the figures of Peona, Thea, and Mnemosyne in *Hyperion* the search for a post-Miltonic analyst, which is the counter-text to *Endymion*'s wandering scene of psychoanalysis. The result of this search in *The Fall* is Moneta. Through Moneta's interrogation of her own prescriptive authority as "Sole priestess of [Saturn's] desolation," the "pale Omega of a wither'd race" of Titans at the end of Miltonic authority, Keats interrogates his own identity as a subject presumed to know (1.227, 288).

The text's opening separates poets, those who can "tell" their dreams, from fanatics, who "live, dream, and die" without having spoken the "visions" that are the nature of "every man." Poetry's "fine spell of words alone can save / Imagination from the sable charm / And dumb enchantment" of its own psychic determinism. Where poetry speaks the dream's unreason, fanaticism is the symptom of its suppression by "weav[ing] / A paradise for a sect" and thus perpetuating the visionary tradition's false consciousness. Whether the "dream now purposed to rehearse" be poet's or fanatic's, the narrator says, can only be decided at the text's margins, "When this warm scribe [his] hand is in the grave." As rehearsal rather than performance, the dream signifies the most indeterminate staging of identity through which the poet subverts the cultural prescription of his own identity as a model for his future readers. Moreover, the text challenges the poet to undertake his own psychoanalysis as a process only terminated by death: "Who alive can say, / 'Thou art no Poet—mayst not tell thy dreams'?" (1.1–18).[50]

Responding to this interminability, *The Fall* manifests the complex temporality of narrative repetition latent within Titanic melancholy. The psychoanalytic narrative, according to Dominick La Capra, is the metonymic trajectory of "serial events which one tries to integrate through [a metaphorical] concordance of beginning and end," but which resists "full narrative closure and theoretical totalization."[51] By dreaming *Hyperion* as its primal scene, *The Fall* refigures the earlier text's anatomy of arrested episodes as part of a repetitive temporality that confirms the trauma of Oceanus's view that the Titans are "not the beginning nor the end." Like the Titans as they move back to the future of an indeterminate identity that always repeats but never remembers who they were, *The Fall*, while moving forward through the telling of its dream as if to retell and thus move beyond the earlier text's psychic determinism, also moves archaeologically back through its own textual past to encounter the encrypted form of *Hyperion* at 1.294, which exists, like Saturn as the abject rem(a)inder of Apollo, somewhere "in-between" the text's present telling—or its future telling—and its textual unconscious. *The Fall* reads its unconscious in *Hyperion* as what Peter Brooks calls a "structure of undecidability," whose "strange logic" of "suspicion and conjecture . . . can offer only a framework of narrative possibilities rather than a clearly specifiable plot."[52] Yet through its narrative possibilities, *The Fall* also exploits the earlier text's narrative *insistence* on making sense of things, the temporal destiny of the gods as having *to* confess and so reveal their human natures.[53] Like *Endymion*, the text unfolds as the displacement and condensation of a series of palimpsestically layered dreams and trances, as if to stage each movement through history according to its phantasmatic structure, yet so to challenge the narrator to read this structure. The text stages a series of struggles with the curse of the "habitual self," each of which he experiences as if, as Moneta tells him, "to die and live again before / [His] fated hour" (1.141–42) outside of his own identity. Yet each dying into life, opening him to another encounter with his unconscious, also exposes him to his imagination's self-making potentiality, so that he also flies "As if with wings" or "As once fair angels on a ladder flew" outside of his "habitual self" (1.59, 135). This process of individuation differentiates the psychic determinism of who he was and is from the imaginative possibilities of who he might yet be.[54] As Nietzsche states, the dream, by exposing the subject to its Dionysian indeterminacy, also refashions the subject: "the Apollonian state of dreams in which the world of the day becomes veiled, and a new world, clearer, more understandable, more moving than the everyday world and yet more shadowy, presents itself to our eyes in continual rebirths" (*BT* 66).

Within the text's larger dream, the narrator recounts his first trance as an encounter with *Paradise Lost*, the "refuse of a meal / By angel tasted, or our mother Eve" (1.30–31). Here the text revisits a kind of primal forgetting of the feminine, which then becomes the "domineering potion" as "parent of [his present] theme" (1.54, 46). The feminine's influence is both traumatically debilitating and genealogically productive: the story of his mesmerizing encounter with the pathology of poetic tradition in the form of Greek mythology which, he now suggests, was *Hyperion*'s subtext. This "draught" or Apollonian dream lulls rather than intoxicates the dreamer, in the way that he reads the mesmeric influence of Miltonic epic as an Apollonian appearance divorced from a dialogue with its own Dionysian intoxication. From this trance the narrator awakens into a Dionysian dream that signifies this original trauma as "the carved sides / Of an old sanctuary with roof august," to which "grey cathedrals, buttress'd walls, rent towers, / The superannuations of sunk realms, / . . . / Seem'd but the faulture of decrepit things / To that eternal domed monument" (1.61–71). The scene recalls Christabel's "chamber carved so curiously" from the "carver's brain," the primal scene of imagination that is a "sight to dream of, not to tell." That he "could not know" what any of these "remnants" now signify, marks in the text's present semiosis an irreparable epistemological rupture beyond which the narrator must surrender himself to the phantasy of reason (1.33–34). Toril Moi argues that Kristeva's semiotic, because it "can never take over the symbolic," works by "*expulsion* and *rejection*," a "*negativity* masking the death-drive" yet "analyzable as a series of ruptures, absences and breaks in the symbolic language."[55] By expressing its own identity negatively rather than essentially, the text 'parents' the poet's identity from "refuse," from the poet's specular identification with the past.

The narrator's "eternal domed monument" seems the unconscious of poetry itself. By staging the cultural reproduction of its past traumatically, *The Fall* suggests in the masculine remembering of poetry its overwhelming confrontation with the feminine, although the poem does not presume to read its gender essentially, that is to say outside of the prescriptive terms of its own culture. The devastated landscape of *The Fall* as "imageries" in a "mingled heap confus'd" is a partial recovery of *Hyperion* and of a larger poetic tradition centered in Milton (1.77–78). Both have been jettisoned into a cultural past the traces of which the present text would read potentially as what in *Hyperion* the narrator calls "hieroglyphics old" (1.277). However, the luxury of this primal scene of poetry, despite its 'confusion,' suggests a profuse Victorian commodification or staging of poetry's 'domestic' space. Alan Bewell suggests that

Keats's poetry "arises from an urban middle-class context" that "very much belongs to an incipient Victorian culture."[56] And so the scene of *The Fall* is the "Chamber of Maiden-Thought" in Keats's Victorian "Mansion" of the mind gendered by the ideology of the 'separate spheres'—yet in traumatic disarray. This is Wordsworth's Gothic church turned Victorian living room in Wordsworth's 'home at Grasmere,' yet *anti*-domesticated by the 'sepulchral recesses' of Margaret's/Dorothy's madness it would hide in the profuse details of its interior.

As the narrator approaches the altar of "An image, huge of feature as a cloud," a voice challenges him with the "Prodigious" burden of finding his identity in the midst of this trauma: "'If thou canst not ascend / These steps, die on that marble where thou art" (1.88, 121, 107–8). In a passage that mirrors in embryo the rising "mist" of Hyperion's transubstantiation into Saturn's absent psychosomatic body, the narrator undergoes a death-like catharsis or "a palsied chill" that "put cold grasp" on his ability to speak, as if to signify the killing effect of reason. Like Apollo dying into life, he "shriek'd" and, "[striving] hard to escape / The numbness," regains his sense(s), as if at least to read beyond *Hyperion*'s fragmentation in the textual unconscious and thus into its suspended economy of melancholy (1.125–28). In a type of *Matrix*-like gesture, the poet now finds himself on the far side of poetic tradition, as if within the 'other' consciousness buttressing its phantasmatic facade. Here, the voice takes up the text's opening interrogation of identity: "'Art thou not of the dreamer tribe?'" The dreamer "vexes" the world, whereas the poet "pours out a balm upon" it. Calling upon "faded, far-flown Apollo," as if to claim his place among poets rather than fanatics, the narrator in turn asks Moneta to interpret the landscape around him: "'Majestic shadow, tell me where I am: / Whose altar this; for whom this incense curls: / What Image this, whose face I cannot see, / . . . and who thou art?'" (1.198–215). Moneta is unable to defeat her curse of individualism, but she would facilitate the poet's understanding of his fate in order to avoid the psychic determinism of his past. How he chooses to read his dreams, that is, will determine the extent to which he can reimagine the aesthetic phenomenon of his own identity.

The poet's encounter with Moneta models dialogue, not between two full-fledged subjects, but as the circulation of subjectivities that manifests the *possibility* of a (dis)embodied subject, but without crystallizing this subject's identity within a metapsychology. *The Fall* betrays no desire for system, even in the way that *Suspiria* systematizes as aesthetic phenomena the anatomy of the mythopoeic psychoanalytic subject. Through dialogue the analysand/poet of *The Fall* struggles to understand his own self-divided identity by reading darkly in the mirror of an analytical other the de-stabilization of her own identity. In the same way that Saturn, Hyperion, and Apollo are versions of *Hyperion*'s emerging analysand, Thea, Mnemosyne, and Moneta are an intertextual composite of the Keatsian analyst who facilitates the poet's dark self-knowledge. Infected by the Titans' melancholy in *Hyperion*, Thea and Mnemosyne are now figured within Moneta's retelling of Saturn's fate, as if superseded by her ability to know the narrator's history. As it registers this history's radical temporality, however, Moneta's face is "Not pin'd by human sorrows, but bright-blanch'd / By an immortal sickness which kills not; / It works a constant change" that is "deathwards progressing / To no death . . ." (1.257–61). Tied to the previous text's melancholy, but now conscious of its effects, Moneta carries the pathology of gender as it infects the masculine visionary apparatus of poetry itself. She is the dis-ease of the text's psyche as the sickness of its immortality, figured in her fatal attachment to the mythology of Saturn's world. Hence her "power," although "Holy," is a "curse" (1.243, 136). As the "pale Omega of a withered race" of Titans who mark the end of Miltonic authority, Moneta signifies how reason is cursed by its own attempt to feminize unreason. She is the pathology of gender itself installed at the core of Romantic psychoanalysis as the attempt to occult Margaret's madness.

Moneta would also help the narrator enter into this cultural reproduction as a force of transgressive articulation against its hegemonic effects. She notes that her 'curse' "Shall be to [him] a wonder" (1.244). In the affect of her eyes he can read his own emerging subjectivity. These eyes are both "visionless" and "benignant"; they hold a "blank splendor" that mirrors/reflects both her own and the narrator's own blank identities as both absence *and* potentiality (a *tabula rasa*). Through her interpretation of his dream, which he reads as "high tragedy" being acted in "the dark secret chambers of her skull," he is able "To see as a God sees" (1.267–304). Different from Apollo's "knowledge enormous," the narrator's ability emphasizes a suffering imaginative vision rather than an abstract epistemological autonomy. He thus is able to 'see' within the interminable melancholy of her immortality the "electral charging misery" of the "scenes / Still swooning vivid through [her] globed brain" (1.244–46). This semiotic negativity offers a perpetual resistance to the symbolic language poetry—and the poem itself—would use to regulate the poet's identity. Moneta appears mesmerized by these scenes and thus is figured as part of a paralyzed and specular statuary (1.382–88) that the previous text has now become in the textual unconscious. The narrator struggles both to resist and to read this unconscious in order to subvert its power. This subversion is provisional, for his "lofty theme" is a "half-unravel'd web" (1.306, 308). He both stages and is staged by the psychic determinism of his "high tragedy," its "eternal quietude" and "unchanging gloom" (1.390–91). He thus pauses at the end of Canto 1, to "perhaps no further dare" (1.468), as if to resist an economy from which he can find no release. Canto 2 proceeds beyond the dream's "antechamber" (1.465) to Hyperion's "clear light" (2.49), but fragments "in-between" Saturn and Apollo as if to abandon altogether the false consciousness of Olympian ascendancy. Here the text rehearses its most radical contingency by progressing "deathwards" towards Keats himself and beyond, where gender is reproduced in the ambivalence of a time long after his 'warm scribe is in the grave.'

Where Apollo reads Mnemosyne's "lesson" as if in the "hollow" of his own brain, the poet of *The Fall* reads his identity "enwombed" within Moneta's "hollow brain" (1.276–77). He thus reads the unconscious *as if* possessed by another at the site of his own self-alienation. By finding his interiority in the discourse of the other, he marks gender distinctions as mobile and unstable. He (re)possesses himself through this autonomous production of gender as it discloses his selfhood to him, a radical staging of identity that subsumes the poet within its "mingled heap confused." Alexander Gelley argues that the 'scene' of narrative, like the analytic or primal scene, involves the ambivalent work of phantasy, through which the subject is both witness to her internal drama and projected as a (de-) constituted subject within this scene's dramatic effects.[57] This splitting is at the heart of Shelley's "The Triumph of Life," when Rousseau enjoins the narrator to "from spectator turn / Actor or victim in this wretchedness" (*SPP* 305–6). Similarly, the stages of the narrator's various catharses in *The Fall* enact the instability of his position between "actor" and "spectator." In Chapter One we explored how the staging of Dionysus by Apollo constitutes the "primal ground of tragedy," the moment of theater before Drama. Here the subject is not yet a subject, a space where identity *is* the stage of the subject experiencing (in Kristeva's words) "the first authentic feeling of a subject in the process of constituting itself as such." This imaginary theater exists within the outward 'drama' of the subject's symbolic identity as a 'stage' both facilitating and unsettling identity's constitution. In Keats' writings, this 'stage' is psychoanalysis as the articulation of gender's 'phantasmatic structure' within identity's formation. In *Endymion* the narrator attempts to read this process like "Adam's dream": the subject awakens to the realization of the dream's "essential Beauty" (*KL* 37) as the truth of the male visionary tradition. Disillusioned of this truth, Endymion says "no more" (*KP* 4.669) to this type of dreaming.[58] *Hyperion* repeats *Endymion*'s traumatic realization through the finer tone of epic, yet remains disrupted by the "Creations and destroyings" of a gendered psychoanalysis, so that neither epic nor psychoanalysis offer viable options. Casting this process as dream vision, *The Fall of Hyperion* stages the "abstract masculine epistemological subject" as the trauma of gender. Moneta's dark education of the narrator about his own unreason unsettles the patriarchal authority of the egotistical sublime, figured in the ruins of an epic identity over which she presides. In Moneta's ruined sanctuary, the madness of Margaret in Wordsworth's ruined Gothic church, as the ruined cottage or domestic space of gender Wordsworth would avoid, comes home to roost in the body of the male Romantic poet.

Within this "high tragedy" of psychoanalysis, the Apollonian and the Dionysian emerge as diverse psychic modalities of the subject, but also as separate subjectivities inhabiting the stage of the *cogito*, the pathology of the imagination's mythology as two of the multiple personalities of the subject's psyche.[59] Reading 'beyond' the Wordsworthian egotistical sublime, Keats encounters in *Hyperion* and *The Fall of Hyperion*, as they emerge from the wandering romance of *Endymion*, the (dis)continuous progress of his psychic history as this pathology of the imagination. As we have traced in earlier chapters, this pathology is the imagination's free-associationism, its ability to mutate beyond the control of the *cogito*. By establishing a dialogue with these 'mutations'—the radical otherness of the unconscious—Keats traces the dark anthropomorphism of the subject within the theater of its other subjectivities, staged at the intersection between its psychic determinism and its self-making potentiality. This moment of the subject's encounter with the "Burden of the Mystery" is the moment when the subject both finds and loses his identity in poetry, a moment that defines the distinctly heterogeneous and dark empiricism of the Romantic psychoanalytic scene. At this moment poetry *becomes* psychoanalysis as "high tragedy." Where the encounter between the narrator and the Dark Interpreter has a virtual quality (the Dark Interpreter himself is a projected phantasm of the narrator's unconscious), then, the *Hyperion*s inscribe the dying into life of this mythopoeic De Quinceyan subject as the dialogue between two full-fledged subjects who (mis)recognize the (disc)losing of their identities. This scene, like that of *Suspiria*'s mythopoeia, appears to be a determinately acute rather than tenuously chronic response to interminability.

Yet, as the repetitive temporality of *The Fall of Hyperion* suggests, the acuteness of this moment, as a *missed* encounter with the interminability of the unconscious, continually (d)evolves into a chronic version of itself as part of a perpetual struggle to move beyond the curse of individuation. The fragmentation of the text at the point that it appears about to enter another chamber of the narrator's dreamwork, gestures proleptically toward what De Quincey calls in the "Introductory Notice" to *Suspiria* "vast avenues of gloom" and "towering gates of ingress." In *Suspiria* De Quincey imagines the approach to these gates, despite their remaining barred to his entry, as a moment of acute astonishment at the power of interminability. The subject of *The Fall* suffers the psychic struggle of moving through each acute moment as if through the interminability of his life. Thus, the text's series of acute episodes, at each moment of transition to the next episode, becomes a moment of chronic fatigue, a "palsied chill" that reminds the dreamer, through the absent psychosomatic body of his imaginative life, of the interminably lived experience of his psychoanalysis. The repetitive temporality of psychoanalysis in *The Fall* follows the narrator's acute encounters with his Dionysian unconscious along the chronic axis of his Apollonian contemplation of Dionysus. Yet *The Fall*'s Nietzschean world traces the chronic *within* the acute, the (anti)strophic movement of the contemplative mind of Poetry gazing repetitively on its own eternally suffering and contradictory dream. As chorus, Moneta glosses this world darkly for the narrator's benefit. In this sense, one can read Moneta's "immortal sickness," not only as tied to the dead Symbolic of poetry's contemplative identity signified by Saturn's lost world, but also as the pure intoxication of this world's suspended Dionysian energy unredeemed by the Apollonian image that only the narrator/dreamer, through a will to power, can give it. Through the dreamer, poetry imagines its own psychoanalysis as the tragedy of its interminable suffering.

The *Hyperion*s negotiate Romantic psychoanalysis through the mirror stage of its own "high tragedy." They trace a complex narrative from poetry's ambivalent sense of its own narcissistic and contemplative autonomy in *Endymion* and *Hyperion*, to *The Fall of Hyperion*, in which poetry's reading of its own unconscious discloses poetry's interminable project. This contingency forestalls Keats's own attempt to read developmentally from the Titans to the Olympians, and thus to establish the apparatus of a progressive evolution empowered by its own internal authority. *The Fall* reinscribes this authority within a structure of desire that subdues the subject's master narrative to the "service of the time being." Keats's texts struggle *beyond* the Freudian ken of a therapeutic cure to explore identity's interminable pathology: the aesthetic residue of the subject's unconscious life perpetually recycled, the abject of the subject which *is* the subject. This trauma of the unsayable turns Romantic psychoanalysis into "Soul-making," but infected by a melancholy which, in one of Keats's dark personifications of the absent psychosomatic body, "dwells with Beauty . . . that must die." Keats's psychoanalysis is the interminable exploration of the psyche's darkness as the negative capability of what the subject cannot say or know about himself. This insight allows him to look into the "human heart" of a subject who suffers the Nietzschean awareness of his own unilluminable nature. The "Grand march" of Romantic psychoanalysis in Keats's poetry struggles toward the Nietzschean awareness of identity as the perpetual Apollonian staging of his Dionysian suffering. The interminable scope of this theater is an abject universe lacking "seeming sure points of Reasoning." Modern psychoanalysis describes this territory within its own metapsychology. It was Romanticism, however, that first thought to place the subject—precariously, fearfully—on her own couch in order to gaze upon a psychic world that was disappearing before her eyes.

NOTES

Introduction

1. I cite from MS. D of "The Ruined Cottage," as given in James Butler's Cornell Wordsworth edition of *The Ruined Cottage* and *The Pedlar*. See Chapter Two, note 9.
2. See Quinney, "Wordsworth's Ghosts."
3. On the history of mesmerism, or the place of Mesmerism within the emergence of psychiatry and psychological science, see Crabtree, *From Mesmer to Freud*; Ellenberger, *The Discovery of the Unconscious*; Forrest, *Hypnotism*; on the specific influence of mesmerism on British Romantic culture, see Fulford, "Conducting the Vital Fluid"; on mesmerism's later impact on the Victorian period, see Kaplan, *Dickens and Mesmerism*; Tatar, *Spellbound*; Winter, *Mesmerized*; on the emergence of mesmerism from the Enlightenment, see Darnton, *Mesmerism and the End of the Enlightenment in France*. See also Chapter One below.
4. This is not to say that the phenomenon *of* Romantic psychiatry has been overlooked. See Shorter, *A History of Psychiatry*; Porter, *Mind-Forged Manacles* and *Madmen*.
5. Borch-Jacobsen, "The alibis of the subject," 79.
6. See Coburn, *Experience into Thought*, 4. See McKusick, "'Living Words'," whose source for the provenance of the term in the *OED* is Schapiro, "Neologisms in Coleridge's *Notebooks*." The term did not appear in the *OED* until 1857. It entered common parlance at the end of the nineteenth century. In 1894 Freud used both *psychische analyse* and *klinischpsychologische analyse* (in *Neurologisches Centralblatt*, 15:364) and in 1896 first used the term *psychoanalyse* (in *Revue neurologigue*, 4:166). In *An Autobiographical Study*, Freud

recalls how, once repression, resistance, transference, and infantile sexuality had become the foundation of his treatment of neuroses, as opposed to the 'abreaction' of "an affect which had got on to the wrong lines," he "showed [his] recognition of the new situation by no longer calling [the] method of investigation and treatment *catharsis* but *psycho-analysis*" (*SE* 20:30).

7. Shamdasani and Münchow, "Introduction," *Speculations after Freud*, xv.
8. Derrida, *Resistances of Psychoanalysis*, 86, 118.
9. Rajan, *Dark Interpreter*, 25.
10. Arnold, "The Function of Criticism at the Present Time," 240.
11. Borch-Jacobsen, "The alibis of the subject," 79.
12. The problem of the transference haunted Freud throughout his writings, in 1913's "On Beginning the Treatment," for instance, but right to the end of Freud's career, as in the posthumously published "An Outline of Psycho-Analysis." In both Freud cites the necessity of isolating, deciphering, and thus controlling transference phenomena from those unrelated to the therapeutic situation.
13. Bloom, *Agon*, 93; Trilling, "Freud and Literature," 34. Trilling admits that the disciplines are interdependent, but suggests that the theoretical homogeneity of psychoanalysis cures literature's heterogeneous dis-ease: "The Freudian psychology is the only *systematic* account of the human mind which . . . deserves to stand beside the *chaotic mass* of psychological insights which literature has accumulated" ("Freud and Literature," 34; my italics). See also "Freud: Within and Beyond Culture," first presented by Trilling in 1955 as the Freud Anniversary Lecture of the New York Psychoanalytical Society and the New York Psychoanalytical Institute—the first time they had been addressed by a "speaker from the profession of letters" (90).
14. Bloom, *The Western Canon*, 375.
15. Lukacher, *Primal Scenes*, 15.
16. See, for instance, Faas, Williams and Waddell, or Thomas. Somewhat differently, Edmundson reads dialectically between the normative/therapeutic Freud and a 'Romantic'/creative Freud, who revises his metapsychology through "imaginative acts of self-destroying self-invention" (22). Edmundson parallels Freudian revisionism to Romantic self-fashioning and its contrary gravitation toward self-oppression in order to analyze Freud's seduction by his own normative thinking. Yet by preserving the mind's poetry-making function against the threat of science, Edmundson simply reverses the privileging of science and theory over literature.
17. Felman, "To Open the Question," 10. This shift was signaled in two issues of *Yale French Studies*: 1972's "French Freud: Structural Studies in Psychoanalysis" and 1977's "Literature and Psychoanalysis: The Question of Reading: Otherwise," which Felman introduced in "To Open the Question." See, for instance, Felman, "Turning the Screw of Interpretation"; Brooks, *Reading for the Plot*; and Hertz, *The End of the Line*. The intersection between psychoanalysis and narrative theory has been particularly fertile. See, for instance, Rimmon-Kenan's anthology, *Discourse in Psychoanalysis and Litera-*

ture, which begins with Brooks, "The Idea of a Psychoanalytic Literary Criticism," which can be read as a companion piece to Felman's "To Open the Question."

18. Bloom, "The Internalization of Quest Romance," 26. See Frye, "The Drunken Boat," 14–15, and *A Study of English Romanticism*; Abrams, *Natural Supernaturalism*, 29; Wasserman, *The Subtler Language*; Bloom, *The Visionary Company*; "Romanticism and Anti-Self-Consciousness."
19. de Man, "The Intentional Structure of the Romantic Image," 16. See also de Man "The Rhetoric of Temporality," and *Allegories of Reading*; Cynthia Chase, *Decomposing Figures.*
20. Litvak, "Back to the Future," 145.
21. See McGann, *The Romantic Ideology* or *The Beauty of Inflections*; Levinson, *The Romantic Fragment Poem*; Liu, *Wordsworth: The Sense of History.*
22. Siskin, *The Historicity of Romantic Discourse*, 13.
23. Jacobus, *Psychoanalysis and the Scene of Reading*, 18.
24. Butler, *The Psychic Life of Power*, 29.
25. Henderson, *Romantic Identities*, 9.
26. Smith, *Gothic Radicalism*, 7.
27. See also Massé, *In the Name of Love*; Bruhm, *Gothic Bodies.*
28. Castle, *The Female Thermometer*, 139. See also 120–39 and 184–89.
29. One model for this approach is Rajan's *The Supplement of Reading*, which historicizes the phenomenology of reading within a nineteenth-century hermeneutic tradition and reinscribes the question of the *subject* absent from a rhetorical poststructuralism associated with de Man. Although not overtly psychoanalytical, *Supplement* reinserts the subject of the psychological back into the often exclusively sociohistorical or cultural domain of more recent work in Romantic studies.
30. Felman writes: "literature, by virtue of its ironic force, fundamentally deconstructs the fantasy of authority in the same way, and for the same reasons, that psychoanalysis deconstructs the authority of the fantasy. . . . [The] reversal of the usual perspective is here intended to displace the whole pattern of the relationship between literature and psychoanalysis from a structure of rival claims to authority and priority to the scene of this structure's deconstruction" ("To Open the Question," 8). Felman is concerned with how psychoanalysis and literature intersect in contemporary criticism, however, not with the historical/genealogical relationship between them.
31. For a comprehensive historical account of the emergence of psychoanalysis out of a long history dating back to the earliest forms of shamanism, see Ellenberger, *The Discovery of the Unconscious.*
32. Philippe Lacoue-Labarthe and Jean-Luc Nancy argue disapprovingly that Romanticism has become the "*unconscious* . . . in most of the central motifs of our 'modernity'" (*The Literary Absolute*, 15), in the sense that "romanticism is our *naiveté*" (17) and that we have thus projected our critical desire onto the screen of 'romanticism' without always reading the blindnesses created by these insights.

33. Foucault, *The Order of Things*, 327–28.
34. Freud's desire for scientific credibility can be discerned in his early grounding in the physiological analyses of neurological disorders; in his early translation of Charcot's *Lectures on the Diseases of the Nervous System* (1893); in his relationship with the physiologist, Wilhelm Fleiss, which he protected at all costs for the scientific/medical legitimation it afforded (see Masson, *The Assault on Truth*); and in the fact that Freud calls his earliest sustained theoretical account of his research *Project for a Scientific Psychology* (1895). Steven Marcus argues that Freud "remained a materialist without going over to some kind of positivism or systematic reductionism" (*Freud and the Culture of Psycho-analysis*, 11).
35. Mehlman, "French Freud," 5. Lacan holds that the 'truth' of Freud's initial discovery is enacted in Freud's later repression of his first topographic model (conscious/preconscious/unconscious) by his second, more systematic paradigm of id/ego/superego. Ego psychology, which Lacan reviled, favored this latter model of a self conflicted between its instinctual drives and its desire to transcend its own biological determinism. According to Mehlman, a Lacanian reading of a Freud's metapsychology expresses the discontinuity between a "biological, genetic, adaptative, or functional scheme" and "one which finds its place in the context of an articulation of the specific modes of negativity (censorship, repetition, displacement) of a transmissible unconscious structure. It is a discontinuity then between a metaphorics of continuity (genetic gradualism) and one of discontinuity" (6).
36. Althusser, "Freud and Lacan," 179.
37. Jameson, "Imaginary and Symbolic in Lacan," 386–87.
38. A very different account of Lacan's mastery is Borch-Jacobsen, *Lacan: The Absolute Master*.
39. Lacan, *Four Fundamental Concepts*, 232.
40. Dufresne, *Tales from the Freudian Crypt*, 25, 17, 182, 11.
41. Psychoanalysis historicizes its own origins early in its history, thus immediately placing Freud's preeminence under erasure. Freud himself initiates this erasure in "On the History of the Psycho-Analytic Movement," in which he responds to Arthur Adler's and Jung's defections. See Jones, *The Life and Work of Sigmund Freud.* On Jung's split from Freud, see Jung, *Memories, Dreams, Reflections*, 146–69; Woodman, "Freud and Jung"; Donn, *Freud and Jung*; and Steele and Swinney, *Freud and Jung*. For a recent theoretical recuperation of Jung, see Clarke, *In Search of Jung* and especially Shamdasani's seminal *Jung and the Making of Modern Psychology*. It is a fascinating irony that Lacan, as Mikkel Borsch-Jacobsen notes, "in 1930 had done an internship at Jung's famous Burghölzli clinic" (*Lacan*, 23).
42. See as well Jung, "Psychology and Literature," *CWJ* 15:100–1, on the neurosis of the artist.
43. The unconscious, writes Jung in "The Psychology of the Transference," is "capable of infinite variation and can never be depotentiated" (*CWJ* 16:178). As such, its potency threatens the conscious mind with impotence,

so that consciousness is "the last stronghold against the threatening embrace of the unconscious," which in serious cases evokes "the secret fear of going mad" (16:181). One can read an immanent Lacanianism in Jung's individuation, in that it marks the subject's difference from his image, which appears as an *imago* and which suggests the Lacanian subject's empty schema, just as the collective unconscious, structured like a Lacanian symbolic language, generates the individuated 'text' of the psyche as determined by its cultural signifiers.

44. Lacan, *Ecrits*, 2, 4.
45. Ibid., 97.
46. Kristeva, *Revolution in Poetic Language*, 24–25.
47. Kristeva, "Psychoanalysis in Times of Distress," 16. Jung writes that "unconscious material" is something "*alive*," but "the language of body-cells and bacteria" cannot gauge its motility: "we need another language commensurate with the nature of the psyche" (*CWJ* 15:190) by which Jung suggests a language between the somatic and the psychic. Kristeva's semiotic, inflected both physiologically and imaginatively, also evokes Jung's unconscious, which both reveals and hides its "depths and potentialities" in the symbolic "meaning, effects, and characteristics" (15:178) of its contents.
48. Kristeva, *In the Beginning was Love*, 61.
49. Kristeva, "The Adolescent Imaginary," 8–11.
50. For instance, Kristeva herself uses the discourse of her analysands' case histories to gloss the presuppositions of her theoretical discourse. These histories foreground a semiotic level of affect registered within the analytic theory and thereby disrupt the symbolic schema of her discussion, allowing the 'literary' nature of narrative self-writing to encroach upon and coexist within the 'scientific' discourse of her theory. See Kristeva, *Black Sun*, 3–68; *Tales of Love*.
51. Kristeva, *Revolution in Poetic Language*, 22.
52. Richardson, *British Romanticism and the Science of the Mind*, xv.
53. See Freud, "Remembering, Repeating and Working-Through" (1914). Transference radically shifts both the subject's ontology and the empirical grounds upon which the subject comes to understand his being. "By postulating the death drive," writes Ned Lukacher, "Freud attempts to account for the absolute resistance to recollection that he meets in the transference" (*Primal Scenes*, 87). Transference, especially as complicated by countertransference, radically decentred the epistemology of psychoanalysis. See, for instance, Freud, "Analysis Terminable and Interminable" (1937). As Lacan argues, "transference is the means by which the communication of the unconscious is interrupted, by which the unconscious closes up again. Far from being the handing over of powers to the unconscious, the transference is, on the contrary, its closing up" (*Four Fundamental Concepts*, 130). Psychoanalysis is thus an "essential encounter [*tuché*]—an appointment to which we are always called with a real that eludes us" because it is *always beyond* signification (53). Displacing Freud's transference from the personal psychology of

patient or analyst, or as a force to be controlled by the analyst, Jung, in "The Psychology of the Transference," very much in the manner of Lacan, saw the unconscious as unreadable: "the unconscious is by definition not amenable to direct observation and can only be inferred" (*CWJ* 16:170). Transference is based on the "mutual unconsciousness" (16:176) between doctor and patient, in which the "*persona medici*" of analytical understanding cannot shield the analyst from "unconscious infection." Transference challenges "not only our understanding and our sympathy, but the whole man" and is "what happens when the check normally exerted on the unconscious by the conscious mind is disrupted" (16:178, 187).

54. For the extended story of the Wolf-Man's ongoing analysis, first with Freud, then with Ruth Mack Brunswick, as well as the Wolf-Man's own response to his case, see Freud and Brunswick, *The Wolf-Man by the Wolf-Man.* In "On the History of the Psycho-Analytic Movement" (1914), Freud writes: "If hysterical subjects trace back their symptoms to traumas that are fictitious, then the new fact which emerges is precisely that they create such scenes in *phantasy*, and this psychical reality requires to be taken into account alongside practical reality" (*SE* 14:17). On narrative and the primal scene, see Peter Brooks, "Fictions of the Wolf-Man." See Lukacher, *Primal Scenes*, 13–14, 42, 87. Marjorie Levinson writes, "the *originality* of an event—its status *as* an event in a psychic narrative (that is, as traumatic) and as *originary*, in the sense of engendering and, thus, explanatory—is constituted retrospectively both through its 'real life' repetition and, in a third phase, by the displaced repetition precipitated through the analysis" ("Introduction," 13).

55. Peter Brooks writes that transference is characterized by "complementarity and uncertainty, . . . to which Freud has recourse when he finds there is no centred and authoritative explanatory history. Analysis constitutes itself as inherently dialogic, a perpetually reversing counterpoint of closure and opening, origin and process, self and other, centerless and never finally terminable" ("Fictions of the Wolf-Man," 80). While transference in Freud and Lacan is strictly a force of darkness and negativity, for Jung it also mobilizes an imaginative potency at the matrix of psychic determinism from which identity is generated.

56. See, for instance, Abrams, *Natural Supernaturalism*, 123, and "The Correspondent Breeze," 52.

57. Where the Horatian ode is largely regular in form and public in nature, the irregular structure of the Romantic ode suggests the Pindaric ode, the formal structure of which derives from the chorus of ancient Greek drama. Hence the etiology of the Romantic ode as a latently dramatic form that implicitly projects the interiority of the subject onto a psychic stage. Nevertheless, the ode's dramatic or performative potential is not exploited psychoanalytically by Romantic discourse in the way it exploits this potential in the analytic scene.

58. For this idea I am indebted to Karen Weisman, who explores a lyric consciousness repressed within lyric formalism and, reading after Theodor Reik, speaks of the "*sound* of Romantic lyric [which] . . . plays a role in the cultural history of psychoanalytic formalism" ("Romanticism, Kant, and the Pre-History of Psychoanalysis," 2). She thus addresses the "sound" of analytic modes of engagement, of rhythm as repetition, and thus of an affect within the discourse of psychoanalysis which, against the diachronic structure of the psychoanalytic narrative, indicates the synchronous affective structure of subjectivity. Weisman expanded upon these ideas in a later paper, "Strange Silence."
59. On the destabilization of lyric by narrative in Romantic discourse, see Rajan, "'The Web of Things': Narrative and Identity in *Alastor*" and "Romanticism and the Death of Lyric Consciousness." Rajan speaks of a "[lyric] self as constituted by and not deconstructed by its differences from itself" ("Romanticism," 207).
60. Ellman, "Introduction," 6.
61. Lacan writes that the analysand looks to the analyst as a "subject who is supposed to know" (*Four Fundamental Concepts of Psycho-Analysis*, 233) what the analysand wishes to find and where he can find it. The analyst's 'absolute knowledge' is itself an illusion, however, as the unconscious remains always the "discourse of the other" (*Ecrits*, 55), both the discourse of the unconscious as the subject's otherness *and* the discourse or dialogue with the other in whom the subject always hopes to find this otherness and through whom the subject's identity is thus (dis)placed.
62. Borch-Jacobsen, *The Freudian Subject*, 1–9.
63. Rieff, *Freud*, 356, 347, 333, 334, 357.

Chapter One: The Psychology of the Romantic Subject

1. Coburn, *Inquiring Spirit*, 29.
2. Žižek, "Cartesian Subject versus Cartesian Theater," 258–59.
3. La Capra, *Soundings in Critical Theory*, 34. La Capra continues that psychoanalysis is "a process of repetition with change on all levels, from the drives to the attempt of the analyst to control repetition (both through its limited enactment in the analytic situation and through the effort to 'work through' repetition in transference)" (34).
4. Keats observed that Coleridge's thought "lets go by a fine isolated verisimilitude caught from the Penetralium of mystery," the result of being "incapable of remaining content with half knowledge" (*KL* 43). Keats describes Coleridge's conversation in similar terms in his long 14 February–3 May 1819 letter. See *KL* 237. This thought insists upon pursuing its goal of full knowledge. But the pursuit is restless, because it is endlessly deferred through the "Penetralium *of* mystery" that catches only the 'similitude' of

truth. Coleridge draws attention to this fact in a passage immediately after the one cited above: "Having as usual, thro' a Labyrinth of Parentheses wandered out of the P*ossi*bility of connecting my sentence grammatically tho' logically I have never *let go* of the Thought . . ." This con-fusion between the passage's drift of thought and its tortuous syntax evokes the free association of psychoanalysis. But this evolution pursues ("isolates") its unthought meaning at the same time that it confounds interpretation.

5. Knight, "Romanticism and the Sciences," 13–14.
6. Locke, *An Essay Concerning Human Understanding*, 2:104.
7. Hume, *A Treatise of Human Nature*, xvi, 646; my italics.
8. Hume, *Enquiry Concerning Human Understanding*, xiv, 7.
9. Barrell, *Imagining the King's Death*, 7.
10. Two views of imagination are Addison's and Johnson's. Unlike Coleridge, who will elevate imagination above fancy, Addison, in a 1712 essay for *The Spectator*, places the imagination-as-fancy therapeutically between perception and understanding. Imagination is "conducive to Health" and has a "kindly influence on the Body" different from understanding, which is often "attended with too violent a Labour of the Brain" (Tillotson, *Eighteenth-Century Literature*, 335). Even when it apprehends the "rude kind of Magnificence" suggesting the sublime, imagination "[flings the subject] into a *pleasing* Astonishment at such unbounded Views" (336; my italics). For Johnson the imagination is symptomatic of the very dis-ease it cures in Addison. In his 1765 Preface to Shakespeare, Johnson speaks of the pun as "the fatal *Cleopatra* for which [Shakespeare] lost the world," and in his life of Cowley, he speaks of the metaphysical conceit as a "*discordia concors*" by which the "most heterogeneous ideas are yoked by violence together" (Tillotson, 1072, 1077). Both descriptions disparage an imagination run riot, more specifically suggesting a reason that has lost control of the imagination's power of mutation, and thus also evoking a later eighteenth-century anxiety toward the imagination.
11. Locke, *Essay Concerning Human Understanding*, 2:395, 397, 161.
12. Ibid., 1:43. "What in me is dark / Illumine" (*Poems*, 1.22–23), writes Milton at the beginning of *Paradise Lost*, anxious about the usurpation of divine reason by the satanic thrust of the individual mind. In "Locke and the 'Dissolution of the Ego,'" Ernest Tuveson suggests that how the mind contemplates its own functioning, apart from receiving ideas from sense experience, troubles Lockean empiricism and prefigures the Freudian unconscious.
13. Ellenberger, *The Discovery of the Unconscious*, 197.
14. Locke, *Essay Concerning Human Understanding*, 2:109, 116, 110, 113, 45–46.
15. Cooper, "On Enthusiasm," 93, 95.
16. Engell, *The Creative Imagination*, 24; Smith, *An Inquiry into the Nature and Causes of the Wealth of Nations*, 22.
17. Wright, "Growing Pains," 224. Wright continues that there was an increasing "pathologizing of 'self-feeling'" that "was part of a larger Victorian program in which the subjection of the self to the national good supplanted

earlier formulations of the nation as a body which coheres through feeling" (224). On the relationship between sensibility and Romanticism, see McGann, *The Poetics of Sensibility*; Todd, *Sensibility: An Introduction*. On the nervous body see Logan, *Nerves and Narratives*; Bruhm, *Gothic Bodies*; and Youngquist."De Quincey's Crazy Body."

18. Caruth, *Empirical Truths and Critical Fictions*, 34, 37.
19. Hume, *A Treatise of Human Nature*, 1:251–54, 262, 9. Where going out of the self suggests that identity still resides within the power of the sympathetic subject, the German inflection of sympathy as empathy or *Einfuhlung* suggests a dislocation of the sympathetic identity entirely into the sphere of the other, which Keats will explore in his letters as "*Negative Capability*" (*KL* 43).
20. Hobbes, *Leviathan*, 1:8; Hume, *A Treatise of Human Nature*, 1:265, 257
21. Hume, *A Treatise of Human Nature*, 254.
22. Hume, *Enquiry Concerning Human Understanding*, 31–32.
23. Hume, *A Treatise of Human Nature*, 1:253.
24. Engell, *The Creative Imagination*, 103.
25. Krell, *Contagion*, 5.
26. Engell, *The Creative Imagination*, 6; Cunningham and Jardine, "Introduction," 3.
27. Deleuze, *Kant's Critical Philosophy*, 71, 2.
28. Deleuze, ix. The economy of the sublime emerged to account for the discontinuity between the obscure or indeterminate and the intelligible and determinate within the *cogito*, as in Kant, or for the affective experience generated by this discontinuity, as in Burke. The sublime, writes Thomas Weiskel in *The Romantic Sublime*, "comes to be associated both with the failure of clear thought and with matters beyond determinate perception" and so "is not a radical alternative but a necessary complement to a psychology that stressed its own limits" (17). But Weiskel also argues that the Enlightenment empiricism's self-imposed discipline generated the sublime as an antidote to boredom. "Boredom," Weiskel continues, "masks uneasiness, and intense boredom exhibits the signs of the most basic of modern anxieties, the anxiety of nothingness, or absence" (18). If boredom is the face that rationalism puts on empiricism's troubled interior, then post-Enlightenment theories of imagination and the sublime respond to Locke's emptying out of the soul as unknowable: "The soul [in Locke] is a vacancy, whose extent is discovered as it is filled. Inner space, the infinitude of the Romantic mind, is born as a massive and more or less unconscious emptiness, an absence" (15). In this way the sublime "dramatized the rhythm of transcendence in its extreme and purest form, for the sublime began where the conventional systems, readings of landscape or text, broke down, and it found in that very collapse the foundation for another order of meaning" (22).
29. Ibid., xii.
30. The editors of the *Anthropology*, however, note that Kant "had regularly lectured on this subject since the fall semester 1772–73 at the Albertus

University of Königsberg" (*A* viii), which suggests how a concern with the unconscious forms a subtext in all of his work (see note 33 below). The product of this philosophical/psychological ferment, argues Brown, is the Gothic novel; Gothic writers are "repressed philosophers," just as Kant is a "repressed mystic" ("From the Transcendental to the Supernatural," 163).

31. Brown, "From the Transcendental to the Supernatural," 151, 162.
32. Kant's definition of genius in *Critique of Judgment* is likewise situated precariously at the threshold between the containment of the imagination and its free play. Kant writes that the spirit of genius is its ability to "express the ineffable element in the state of mind implied by a certain representation and to make it universally communicable." To communicate this representation "requires a faculty of seizing the quickly passing play of imagination and of unifying it in a concept," except that this concept must be "communicated without any constraint of rules" (*CJ* 1:180).
33. Kant associates fanaticism with Swedenborg, who claimed "that the actual phenomena of the world, which present themselves to the senses, are merely a symbol of an intelligible world hidden in the background" (*A* 84). See Kant's first work, *Dreams of a Spirit-Seer*, a parodic and cynical reaction against Swedenborg, whom Kant revered as an elder sage of German scholarship, but who largely ignored Kant's overtures. In *Dreams* Kant moves away from a mystical toward a rational conceptualization of the mind and imagination, a move that signifies a fear of what the dream represents unconsciously. This fear of the dream returns, as it were, at the end of Kant's career in the *Anthropology*. The parallel between this shift from theology to science and scientism and that from Gassner and Mesmer in the history of mesmerism is also worth noting.
34. In Kant's description one can anticipate Schopenhauer, who yokes the subject's discord within himself to his suffering of a will beyond his comprehension. And beyond Schopenhauer, Freud, who defines how the unconscious re-stages the subject's identity as a radical discontinuity from his empirical self: "*a dream is a (disguised) fulfilment of a (suppressed or repressed) wish*" (*SE* 4:160).
35. Mesmer, *Mesmerism*, 67, 62, 44, 70. Mesmer articulated his theory of animal magnetism in his 1779 treatise, *Mémoire sur la découverte du magnétisme animal,* to which he appended twenty-seven postulates.
36. See Darnton, *Mesmerism and the End of Enlightenment*, 3–45, esp. 39. Darnton writes that mesmerism arose during a century of "'systems' as well as one of empiricism and experimentation": "The progressive divorce of science from theology in the eighteenth century did not free science from fiction, because scientists had to call upon the imagination to make sense of, and often to *see*, the data revealed by their microscopes, telescopes, Leyden jars, fossil hunts, and dissections" (11–12). Tatar makes a similar point: "Mesmerist doctrines, in part because of their eclectic nature, . . . furnish an ideal index of psychological, scientific, and philosophical issues in the nineteenth century" (*Spellbound*, x).

37. Here is Darnton's description of a mesmeric session in *Mesmerism and the End of the Enlightenment in France*:

> Mesmer and his followers put on fascinating performances: they sat with the patient's knees enclosed between their own and ran their fingers all over the patient's body, seeking the poles of the small magnets that composed the great magnet of the body as a whole. Mesmerizing required skill, for the small magnets kept shifting their positions. The best method of establishing 'rapport' with a patient was to rely on stable magnets, such as those of the fingers and the nose (Mesmer forbade taking snuff because of the danger of upsetting the nose's magnetic balance), and to avoid areas like the north pole at the top of the head, which usually received mesmeric fluid from the stars, and the south pole in the feet, which were natural receptors of terrestrial magnetism. Most mesmerists concentrated on the body's equator at the hypochondria, on the sides of the upper abdomen, where Mesmer located the common sensorium. This practice stimulated gossip about sexual magnetism but not about hypochondriacs, whose unbalanced humours elicited sympathy, not the scorn reserved for *malades imaginaires*. . . . Gossips also found inspiration in Mesmer's apparatus, especially his mattress-lined "crisis room," designed for violent convulsives, and his famous tubs. These were actually filled with iron filings and mesmerized water contained in bottles arranged like the spokes of a wheel. They stored the fluid and transmitted it through movable iron rods, which the patients applied to their sick areas. Sitting around the tubs in circles, the patients communicated the fluid to one another by means of a rope looped about them all and by linking thumbs and index fingers in order to form a mesmeric 'chain,' something like an electric circuit. Mesmer provided portable tubs for patients who wanted to take mesmeric 'baths' in the privacy of their homes, but he generally recommended communal treatments, where each individual reinforced the fluid and sent it coursing with extraordinary power through entire clinics. In his outdoor treatments, Mesmer usually mesmerized trees and then attached groups of patients to them by ropes in daisy-chain fashion, always avoiding knots, which created obstacles to the fluid's harmony. Everything in Mesmer's indoor clinic was designed to produce a crisis in the patient. Heavy carpets, weird, astrological wall-decorations, and drawn curtains shut him off from the outside world and muffled the occasional words, screams, and bursts of hysterical laughter that broke the habitual heavy silence. Shafts of fluid struck him constantly in the sombre light reflected by strategically placed mirrors. Soft music, played on wind instruments, a pianoforte, or

> the glass "harmonica" that Mesmer helped to introduce in France, sent reinforced waves of fluid deep into his soul. Every so often fellow patients collapsed, writhing on the floor, and were carried by Antoine, the mesmerist-valet, into the crisis room; and if his spine still failed to tingle, his hands to tremble, his hypochondria to quiver, Mesmer himself would approach, dressed in a lilac taffeta robe, and drill fluid into the patient from his hands, his imperial eye, and his mesmerized wand. Not all crises took violent form. Some developed into deep sleeps, and some sleeps provided communication with dead or distant spirits, who sent messages by way of the fluid directly to the somnambulist's internal sixth sense, which was extraordinarily receptive to what would now be called extra-sensory perceptions. Many hundreds of Frenchmen experienced such marvels, but few if any fully understood them, for Mesmer always kept his greatest doctrinal secrets to himself. (4–10)

38. Tatar, *Spellbound*, 22. Tatar writes, "[p]atients without much imagination . . . simply imitated the behavior of others. 'The imagination works wonders; magnetism yields no results,' read [the commission's] final verdict" (22).
39. See Leask, "Shelley's 'Magnetic Ladies': Romantic Mesmerism and the Politics of the Body." The practice, as opposed to cultural influence, of mesmerism "became popular in England in the late 1830s, reaching its height with the 'mesmeric mania' of 1851," notes Sally Shuttleworth ("'The malady of thought,'" 48). See also Kaplan, *Dickens and Mesmerism*, 3–33. Kaplan explores England's resistance to mesmerism until the time of Dickens. Dickens was influenced by John Elliotson, a spiritualist who popularized mesmerism in mid-nineteenth century England and the United States. On Mesmerism's emergence in France, see Darnton, *Mesmerism and the End of the Enlightenment in France*, 3–81.
40. Fulford, "Conducting the Vital Fluid," 58.
41. Ellenberger, *The Discovery of the Unconscious*, 72.
42. Here Ellenberger is paraphrasing Charles Richet's *L'Homme et l'intelligence. Fragments de philosophie* (1884), who believed, as Ellenberger continues, that Puységur's influence "equals or even exceeds the importance of Mesmer's own work" (70). The fortunes of mesmerism rose and fell several times during the nineteenth century. Mesmer himself disputed the advent of hypnotism, and a "polemic developed between the fluidists, who explained it in terms of the alleged magnetic fluid, and the animists, who contended that it was a psychological phenomenon" (113). As Ellenberger notes, Braid himself was determined to develop a new theory based on "brain physiology" (82) and thus to align the phenomena of mesmerism with empirical research into the nervous body. 'Hypnotism' could accordingly be tied to a scientific materialism through which could be traced the production of a cure. Hyp-

notism was used, for instance, to anaesthetize patients during surgery. See Ellenberger, *The Discovery of the Unconscious*, 82, 112–120.

43. He was especially concerned after one female patient during hypnosis threw her arms around Freud. Freud dismisses the suggestion of erotic attraction in the episode, although the rise—and fall—of mesmerism in the eighteenth century can be attributed to the threat of sexualism and seduction. See Masson, *The Assault on Truth*.
44. Two very divergent explorations of this haunting are Crabtree, *From Mesmer to Freud* and Dufresne, *Tales from the Freudian Crypt*, esp. 164–182. The history of mesmerism and its role in the development of dynamic psychiatry up to Freud is documented in Ellenberger, *The Discovery of the Unconscious*, 53–253. According to Ellenberger, 289–90, 'dynamic psychiatry' emerged in neuropsychiatry in the last twenty years of the nineteenth century. He traces the idea of the dynamic etiologically to Leibniz, who distinguishes the dynamic from the "static" and the "cinematic." Although Ellenberger coins five different usages of the term in the late nineteenth century, very generally it can be traced through the latter term of a set of distinctions: organic vs. dynamic; static vs. dynamic; material vs. immaterial; seen vs. unseen; inertia vs. motility. Although the terms remained grounded in the materialism of psychiatry, the dynamic becomes a moniker for the absent psychic cause as distinguished from the present physiological effect. With this in mind, we can understand "dynamic psychiatry" to indicate specifically the therapeutic as opposed to medical treatment of psychical problems. In medicine the body is an object of scientific study to which the physician administers medical treatment. In this sense psychiatry likewise medicalizes the mind as a physical organ. Medicine and psychiatry therefore situate the doctor hierarchically as a subject presumed to know over against the (inert) body as the locus of disease. A dynamic approach to psychical problems inflects the medical treatment of the mind in terms of the interpsychic interaction of the patient with the physician. This sense of the dynamic has parallels with Freud's dynamic conception of the psychic apparatus, which reconfigures the libidinal motility of his economic model in terms of a geography of interactive if warring psychic factions (id/ego/superego; the unconscious/preconsciousness/consciousness). This idea of the dynamic has its genealogy in the shaman as psychic healer/exorcist and the priest as exorcist/confessor.
45. Leder, *The Absent Body*, 5, 2.
46. Descartes, *Meditations on the First Philosophy*, 69, 118.
47. Coburn, *Inquiring Spirit*, 68.
48. Leder, *The Absent Body*, 5, 7. Although neither Merleau-Ponty nor Leder speak of the psychosomatic, Merleau-Ponty speaks of "flesh" as a chiasmatic structure, the suture between body and spirit, a point of "fission" where subject and object meet but never merge. As Leder writes, the "lived body is necessarily chiasmatic, a perceiver/perceived" (*The Absent Body*, 63). See also 62–68.

49. McKusick lists Coleridge's first use of the term in 1812, predating its 1863 entry in *OED*. McKusick's source is Coburn, who notes another usage of the term in Coleridge: "Joy and Grief, Hope and Fear, & c. have slipt out their collars, and no longer run in couples, under my whipping-in or from the kennel of my Psycho-somatic Ology . . ." (*Inquiring Spirit*, 67).
50. Shorter, *From Paralysis to Fatigue*, 14, 19. Theories of the relationship between mind and body before the rise of research into neurophysiology tended to center around three theories, one stressing an imbalance of the four humors, another seeing the mind as controlled by a master organ (as in theories that tied hysteria in women to the uterus), and a final theory asserting rather crudely that "the nerves control the mind" (Shorter, *From Paralysis to Fatigue*, 18).
51. As Shorter writes in *From Paralysis to Fatigue*, "defining certain symptoms as illegitimate, a culture strongly encourages patients not to develop them or risk being thought 'undeserving' individuals with no real medical problems. Accordingly there is great pressure on the unconscious mind to produce only legitimate symptoms." Shorter's thesis is that the "unconscious mind desires to be taken seriously and not be ridiculed. It will therefore strive to present symptoms that always seem, to the surrounding culture, legitimate evidence of organic disease" (x). Among the recent manifestations of such symptoms are those of chronic fatigue syndrome.
52. Ibid., 165.
53. Coleridge, *Lectures 1808–1819 on Literature*, 5.1:495.
54. The letter's narrative inscribes the Kristevan genotext of the imagination that both supplements and unsettles the phenotext of its later philosophical exposition. In Kristeva's account of how discourse determines subjectivity, the genotext organizes a semiotic "space" or process within language "in which the subject will be *generated*" and precedes the arrival of signification in the form of the Symbolic phenotext, which is "restricted to the two poles of univocal information between two full-fledged subjects" and which obeys the structural rules of grammar and logic (*Revolution in Poetic Language*, 86). Put in Lacanian terms, the letter's divided Symbolic subject stands in a specular relationship to a philosophy of the imagination and can only possess an imaginary identity within this philosophy.
55. In their "Introduction" to *Empathy, Form, and Space*, Harry Francis Mallgrave and Eleftherios Ikonomou argue that von Hartmann's unconscious "might better be viewed (that is, better than either Hegel's 'spirit' or Schopenhauer's 'will') as the ultimate metaphysical reality" (24). Von Hartmann's *The Philosophy of the Unconscious*, they argue, uses the idea of the 'Unconscious' as a kind of apotheosis of eighteenth- and nineteenth-century philosophical idealism. Laying claim to the term as the province of philosophy as if for the first time, Mallgrave and Ikonomou argue, von Hartmann sees the Unconscious as "achiev[ing] the solution of problems which, to adopt the common language, would be said to belong to the province of metaphysics." His approach reads like a Hegelian manifestation of the

unconscious through historical consciousness, wherein the Unconscious signifies both those modes of negativity which hide the Absolute and, finally, the Absolute itself revealed: "all unconscious operations spring *from one same* subject, which has only its phenomenal revelation in the several individuals, so that 'the Unconscious' signifies this One Absolute subject." Thus von Hartmann's concept, "expanded to *all-unity*, . . . embraces the Cosmos, and at last is suddenly revealed as that which has formed the core of all great philosophies, the Substance of Spinoza, the Absolute Ego of Fichte, Schelling's Absolute Subject-Object, the Absolute Idea of Plato and Hegel, Schopenhauer's Will, & c." (3–5).

56. See, for instance, the essays in Bernheimer and Kahane, *In Dora's Case*.
57. See Jacobus's reading of Eakins's painting in *First Things*, 235–49, especially her attention to the sole female spectator in the painting, the nurse.
58. On Schopenhauer's anticipation of Freud, see Gardner, *Schopenhauer*; or Gupta, "Freud and Schopenhauer." On Nietzsche's, see Copleston, "Schopenhauer and Nietzsche"; Chapelle, *Nietzsche and Psychoanalysis*.
59. Schopenhauer, *On the Fourfold Principle of Sufficient Reason*, 42, 115.
60. Lacan's imaginary and Symbolic suggests Schopenhauer's will and representation, the will being the unconscious that drives representation, although the will is also the Real that resists being represented. The will is also like the drives or instincts, finding their immediate representation in the body's corporeality and motility, like Kristeva's semiotic; but it is also like Lacan's unconscious, because it operates beyond physiology as desire mobilizing representation.
61. Terry Eagleton, "Schopenhauer and the Aesthetic," 19. Eagleton reads Schopenhauer's text as immanently Marxist, a type of cautionary tale against the specter of a bourgeois appropriation of the 'subject' as the privileged category exploited by a capitalist ideology championing the simulacrum of 'individuality' while all the while manufacturing its sameness.
62. In "Schopenhauer and the Aesthetic," Eagleton writes that an "idealist philosophy which once imagined that it could achieve salvation through the subject is now forced to contemplate the frightful prospect that no salvation is possible without the wholesale abnegation of the subject itself, the most privileged category of its entire system" ("Schopenhauer and the Aesthetic," 17). For Schopenhauer it is as "absurd to desire the continuance of our individuality, which is replaced by other individuals, as to desire the permanence of the matter of our body, which is constantly replaced by fresh matter" (*WWR* 1.277). He shatters identity's permanence in the way that Freud, in *Beyond the Pleasure Principle*, marks the death drive as a "matter of expediency" always returning the subject to a primal inertia: "an unlimited duration of individual life would become a quite pointless luxury" (*SE* 18:46). "We have," Freud continues, "unwittingly steered our course into the harbour of Schopenhauer's philosophy. For him death is the 'true result and to that extent the purpose of life,' while the sexual instinct is the embodiment of the will to live." Freud continues: "In later years I have denied myself the

very great pleasure of reading the works of Nietzsche, with the deliberate object of not being hampered in working out the impressions received in psychoanalysis by any sort of anticipatory ideas" (*SE* 18:49–50). Schopenhauer is as much in the tradition of Malthus and Darwin as he is in that of Nietzsche or Freud in his attempt to explain how the mind and body, irrevocably determined in blind concert with one another, coexist in a type of dynamic determinism that links the lowest functions of the organism to the highest theorizations of the intellect. As Eagleton argues, Schopenhauer writes as a "scathing Juvenilian satirist" for whom "[c]omedy is the will's mocking revenge on the representation, the malicious strike of the Schopenhauerian id against the Hegelian superego," except that "the source of hilarity is also, curiously, the root of our utter hopelessness" ("Schopenhauer and the Aesthetic," 4–5).

63. As Rajan and Clark argue, "Schopenhauer is himself divided on the nature and goal of aesthetic representation, at once affirming art as a metaphysically independent category, a triumph over life, *and* demystifying art as a subliminatory fiction projected upon the abyss" ("Speculations," 31).
64. Eagleton, "Schopenhauer and the Aesthetic," 13.
65. Kristeva, *Black Sun*, 12.
66. The 1819 first edition of *The World as Will* is a repetitive philosophical narrative that returns upon the discontinuity between will and representation. In 1844 Schopenhauer produced a second edition that is a fifty-chapter "supplementary" commentary upon the 1819 text, for "it would not do to amalgamate the contents of the second volume with those of the first into one whole" (*WWR* 1:xxii). The second edition signalled the recuperation of Schopenhauer's reputation after 1850, culminating in Nietzsche's reply to Schopenhauer's text in *The Birth of Tragedy*. The earlier text, now Volume One, calls forth the second Volume, which more than doubles the work's length, as both cure and symptom of its own chronic nature. The first edition emerges behind the 1844 excursus as a kind of trauma to which the second edition anxiously responds. So much *more* talking mourns the failure of an Enlightenment empiricism whose crowning achievement is Kant's transcendental idealism. But this mourning turns profoundly melancholic, as the subject's encounter with his willing body produces a chronic philosophy addicted to its own psychoanalysis, just as De Quincey becomes addicted to confession. The text's repetition compulsion turns hermeneutics into what Stanley Corngold calls a "prolonged meditation on death" (364). Mourning, which marks the terminable limits of philosophy's identity as the triumph of its idealism, becomes melancholy, philosophy's iterated response to the will's death drive. The text masters and is mastered by its melancholy, evoking a psychoanalysis of idealism that cannot presume to know the limits of its enlightenment as absolutes, although it is repetitively compelled to speak them. Within this fate the text tells another story of this melancholic loss as the constitutive moment of the subject's identity. For a fuller account of the

text's affinity with psychoanalysis, by comparison to De Quincey's *Confessions of an English Opium-Eater*, see Faflak, "Schopenhauer's Telling Body."

67. Rajan makes this point in "Language, Music, and the Body," 151, 154–67. Of the shift from Schopenhauer to Nietzsche, Rajan writes, "where Schopenhauer collapses the binary opposition between will and representation to reveal how all representation is contaminated by the will, Nietzsche collapses it to concede that all will is complicit in the order of representation, thus preserving only as desire the metaphysical thrust of his precursor's philosophy" (151).
68. Ibid., 150.
69. In his preface to the second edition of *The Gay Science*, Nietzsche argues that the "unconscious disguise of physiological needs under the cloaks of the objective, ideal, purely spiritual goes to frightening lengths" to hide the fact that they are all "hints of symptoms of the body," so that philosophy has been "merely an interpretation of the body and a *misunderstanding of the body*" (34–35). On Nietzsche and the body, see Woodman "Nietzsche, Blake, Keats and Shelley."
70. See Kubiak, *Stages of Terror*, 1–25, esp. 11–13.
71. Nietzsche's demon of eternal recurrence speaks in *The Gay Science*, aphorism 341:

    > What, if some day or night a demon were to steal after you into your loneliest loneliness and say to you: "This life as you now live it and have lived it, you will have to live once more and innumerable times more; and there will be nothing new in it, but every pain and every joy and every thought and sigh and everything unutterably small or great in your life will have to return to you, all in the same succession and sequence—." (273)

    See also aphorism 285, *The Gay Science*, 229–30.
72. Chapelle, *Nietzsche and Psychoanalysis*, 111.

Chapter Two: Analysis Terminable in Wordsworth

1. Lukacher, *Primal Scenes*, 24. Paraphrasing Althusser, Lukacher writes: "[*There*] *is no subject to the primal scene; it is the primal scene itself which is a subject insofar as it does not have a subject*" (13–14).
2. In *Wordsworth and* The Recluse, Kenneth Johnston argues that *The Recluse* is a "coherent though incomplete body of interrelated texts" (xi), suggesting Wordsworth's inability to respond to Coleridge's plea to "write a poem, in blank verse, addressed to those, who, in consequence of the complete failure of the French Revolution, have thrown up all hopes of the amelioration of mankind" (*WL* 1:289). Abrams writes that in *The Prelude* Wordsworth "organizes his life around an event which he regards as the spiritual crisis not of

himself only, but of his generation" (*Natural Supernaturalism*, 77). *The Recluse*, then, indicates the failure of Romanticism to realize the "possibility of universal human freedom and perfectibility" (Johnston xv), to convert contemplation (read: solipsism) into social concern.

3. Coleridge writes in "To William Wordsworth": "thou hast to tell / What may be told, to th' understanding mind / Revealable; and what within the mind / May rise enkindled" (*CP* 6–9).
4. Freud's dream interpretation tries to rationalize the dream's logic, or as Wordsworth writes, to articulate the significance of the dream "in the language of the dream" (*P* 5.87). Freud writes, "The restoration of the connections which the dream-work has destroyed is a task which has to be performed by the interpretative process" (*SE* 4:290). The dreamwork produces an overdetermination—a dream content—of primal dream thoughts, which are themselves beyond signification, "hidden" in the unconscious' "endless home / Among the depths of time" (*P 1805* 5.197–98). This content disfigures the dream thoughts as "another mode of expression" of the same meaning, a "pictographic script, the characters of which have to be transposed individually into the language of the dream-thoughts" (*SE* 4:277). What appears "nonsensical" in the content "may form a poetical phrase of the greatest beauty and significance" (4:278), the principle of the dream thoughts' integrity that interpretation then restores. Censorship and resistance, then, are essential to the formation of the dream structure, whose illogical nature interpretation clarifies. Paradoxically, to produce the dream structure that interpretation can then decode, dream thoughts must evade this censorship; yet without it, they would exist as part of an endless free association or white noise of the unconscious like Nietzsche's Dionysus without Apollo or Schopenhauer's will without representation. "Strictly speaking, then," Freud writes, "it is impossible to determine the amount of condensation" (4:279). Hence the 'tolerance' of self-observation, which remobilizes the dream thoughts' poetry of the psyche disfigured by these contents' representation, must ultimately be tempered, so that the most coherent expression of the dream thoughts can be obtained. My debate in this chapter is not with Wordsworth versus Freud but with the extent to which Wordsworth (and by implication Freud after him) asserts interpretive mastery, as contemplation rather than self-observation, over the 'dream of the subject' as a means of defending against the alternative: the subject's absence.
5. Johnston, *Wordsworth and* The Recluse, 10. Coleridge left for Malta with a manuscript copy of the first five books of *The Prelude*. Wordsworth wrote shortly thereafter, "I am very anxious to have your notes on the Recluse. . . . I cannot say how much importance I attach to this, if it should please God that I survive you, I should reproach myself for ever in writing the work if I had neglected to procure this help" (*WL* 1:452).
6. This poem was to follow an evolutionary trajectory from the physical sciences through to Anatomy and Medicine to "the *mind of man*—then the

minds of men—in all Travels, Voyages and Histories" (*CL* 1:320). Moving from science to history through the mind parallels the progression from the natural, to the human, to the social that in 1797 structures Wordsworth's "*views of Nature, Man, and Society*" as he examines, in the "Prospectus" to *The Recluse*, "our minds" and "the Mind of Man" (*WP* 41). Johnston argues that Coleridge's epic was likely conceived well before 1797. "Religious Musings" (written 1794; published 1796) appears as one version of this effort, and by 1798 Coleridge was also contemplating another version, to be called *The Brook*. See Johnston, *Wordsworth and* The Recluse, 10–12. Coleridge gives a brief account of this work: "I sought for a subject, that should give equal room and freedom for description, incident, and impassioned reflections on men, nature, and society, yet supply in itself a natural connection to the parts, and unity to the whole" (*BL* 1:195–96).

7. Coleridge partly adumbrates this focus on the personal. In the same letter cited above, in which he enthuses passionately about Wordsworth's poetic abilities, Coleridge writes that *The Recluse* would still be "the first & finest philosophical Poem, if only it be . . . a Faithful Transcript of his own most august & innocent Life, of his own habitual Feelings & Modes of seeing and hearing" (*CL* 2:1034). Yet this statement still focuses on the philosophical, rather than psychological, importance of a Wordsworthian ethos.
8. Wordsworth first mentions the poem in March 1798: "I have written 1300 lines of a poem which I hope to make of considerable utility" (*WL* 1:214). Four poems comprise the initial 1,300 lines of *The Recluse*, "all subsequently published in revised form" (Johnston 5): 1) "The Ruined Cottage," written in the spring/summer of 1797, eventually published as Book One of *The Excursion*; 2) "The Old Cumberland Beggar," begun at an unknown date, finished in 1797, published in the 1800 *Lyrical Ballads;* 3) "A Night Piece," written in 1797, published in the 1815 collected poems; and 4) "The Discharged Soldier," the concluding episode of Book Four of *The Prelude*. See Johnston, *Wordsworth and* The Recluse, 3–52; Finch, "*The Ruined Cottage* Restored"; Darlington "Two Early Texts"; Butler, The Ruined Cottage *and* The Pedlar, ix–xiii and 3–24.
9. MS. A includes "Argument for Suicide," "Old Man Travelling; Animal Tranquillity and Decay," "Description of a Beggar," "Yet Once Again," "The Baker's Cart" fragment, "Incipient Madness," and the first partial manuscript version of "The Ruined Cottage." The Racedown Notebook contains work on "The Ruined Cottage" from between March and June 1797. These passages correspond to the conclusion of MS. B (499–513) and MS. B (321–325), in which Margaret finds the money left by her husband. I use Butler's edition of the Cornell Wordsworth's *The Ruined Cottage* and *The Pedlar* for references to "The Baker's Cart," "Incipient Madness," and MSS. A, B, and D of "The Ruined Cottage" and MS. E of "The Pedlar." Unless otherwise specified, all references to "The Ruined Cottage" are from MS. D.
10. See *The Poetical Works of William Wordsworth*, 5:365.

11. Without these elements, John Alban Finch writes, "Wordsworth cannot meaningfully be said to have started work on *The Ruined Cottage*" ("*The Ruined Cottage* Restored," 32). In "The Baker's Cart" Wordsworth leaves a gap in place of the woman's name.
12. The former finds the subject lost in the interiority of a mental distraction that places her at the margins of the social order, as in "The Thorn" or "Her Eyes are Wild." Because of these fears in solitude, Wordsworth cultivates the meditative stance of reclusiveness, which places the psyche within the public sphere, yet at a distance, through a type of melancholy that pretends to be mourning. From this stance, social stability is invoked through psychic change, only because this change emerges as a suspended exploration of psychic interiority. I paraphrase Geoffrey Hartman, who writes that in Wordsworth's poetry "mourning and memory converge as an infinite task" ("Touching Compulsion," 361). "The Old Cumberland Beggar," among Wordsworth's earliest writings for *The Recluse*, cultivates this melancholic stance of solitude, directed toward a social end in later revisions of the poem, where the Beggar's life signifies the larger moral example of "a spirit and pulse of good, / A life and soul, to every mode of being / Inseparably linked" (*WP* 77–79). Although the Beggar exists within "that vast solitude to which / The tide of things has borne him," and although "he appears / To breathe and live but for himself alone," Wordsworth argues that, "Unblamed, uninjured," he should be allowed "to bear about / The good which the benignant law of Heaven / Has hung around him" (163–68). The peripatetic, central to the Wordsworthian ethos, thus evokes a subtextual repetitiveness, a melancholic return to scenes or objects that the psyche is unable productively either to incorporate as part of itself or to abandon (thus, in Freudian terms, to mourn successfully). According to the taxonomy of Wordsworth's *Poetical Works*, "Beggar" is included under "Poems Referring to the Period of Old Age," thus equating solitude with wisdom and maturity. "Animal Tranquillity and Decay," however, which ends the section and which contains extraneous passages associated with the first composition of "Beggar," describes a different solitude. On one hand, the wanderer is all intellect and no body or affect, "A man who does not move with pain, but moves / With thought." On the other hand, he is "*insensibly* subdued / To settled quiet," as though the sublimation of his physical existence into the life of the mind also produces intellectual torpor. Moreover, the "little hedgerow birds / That peck along the road" and thus define the boundary where the natural meets the social, "regard him not," so that the moral stance of solitude also produces alienation, his "one expression" evoking a pathological dissociativeness not unlike the narrator's temper in "Incipient Madness" (1–8).
13. Abraham and Torok, "The Lost Object," 142.
14. Bishop, "Wordsworth and the 'Spots of Time,'" 51.
15. Caruth, *Unclaimed Experience*, 8.
16. This ambivalence is also indicated by the word "Incipience," which suggests the liminality of a psychic condition that is neither sane nor insane.

17. Bollas, *The Shadow of the Object*, 28, 14.
18. Abraham and Torok, "Mourning *or* Melancholia," 128.
19. Ironically, the second half of line 14 and the first half of line 15 are missing in the manuscript, a gap which mirrors the narrator's dissociative state and divides the text between a preliminary melancholic statement of grief and a later attempt to work-through this melancholy.
20. Rajan, "Coleridge, Wordsworth, and the Textual Abject," 62. Rajan offers a cogent account of how Kristevan abjection implies a destabilization of identities both within and between subjects. She continues:

> [Abjection] is most often associated with waste material or threshold substances that are neither inside nor outside, with things or states that lack boundaries. Threatening the power of (self) definition, it must be expelled so that the subject can define himself in relation to what is now other. The very term "abjection" confuses boundaries, referring uncertainly to both self and other, to an act, a thing or an experience. "Abjection" indicates, from the point of view of the subject, the violent expulsion of what is constructed as "other." But the "abject" also refers to that which is cast out. Finally "abjection" refers to a feeling not dissimilar to what Coleridge calls dejection. But it is unclear whose feeling this is: that of the subject who responds to a threat by abjecting it, or that of the other whose abjection prevents it from being a subject. (62)

21. Wordsworth writes in *The Prelude*: "I would give, / While yet we may, as far as words can give, / A substance and a life to what I feel: / I would enshrine the spirit of the past / For future restoration" (11.338–42)
22. Butler, The Ruined Cottage *and* The Pedlar, x.
23. After "Two blighting seasons" (134) Margaret's husband Robert falls ill from a fever. Left financially and psychologically destitute by misfortune, and thinking his family better off without him, Robert eventually joins "a troop / Of soldiers going to a distant land" (268–69), leaving Margaret "Unutterably helpless," distracted between "fervent love" and "grief" (254–55). Unable to care for her children, Margaret sinks into despair and madness and eventually dies.
24. The narrative of the Pedlar evolved in drafts of "The Ruined Cottage" and in other writings associated with the poem, so that in 1801–2 Wordsworth created a separate text titled "The Pedlar," into which he reincorporated Margaret's story in 1803–4. In this version (MS. E) the Pedlar's history takes up part 1, while Margaret's is told in part 2, establishing his developmental authority before rehearsing her decline. Yet this symmetry also produces a spectral mirroring between the case studies, as Margaret's decline is anticipated symptomatically in the Pedlar's perception of a "wasting power / In all things which from [nature's] sweet influence / Might tend to wean him" (253–54). "The Ruined Cottage" and "The Pedlar" were eventually merged to produce Book One of *The Excursion*, wherein the Pedlar is renamed to

give the text its title, "The Wanderer." The Pedlar's philosophical authority is here secure, and his story is framed metaphysically as that of a man who, by virtue of his moral education by Nature, assumes a "vision and faculty divine" akin to that of "Poets" (*WP* 1:79, 76). The Pedlar and his life decidedly overtake the story of Margaret, who does not emerge as a figure in Book One until it is more than half finished. The initial lines related to "The Pedlar" are surplus material culled from the Alfoxden Notebook and MS. D (*R* 1–147), written between January and March, 1798, and first published by Jonathan Wordsworth in *The Music of Humanity*. The Pedlar evolved through several texts associated with Wordsworth's earliest writings for *The Recluse*, most significantly "The Old Cumberland Beggar," but also "Old Man Travelling; Animal Tranquillity and Decay" and "Description of a Beggar" from MS. A. The Pedlar's reclusiveness from society is also suggested in the figure of the Discharged Soldier. Implicit in the identity of the narrator of "The Baker's Cart," the Pedlar can also be associated with the narrator of "Incipient Madness," whose ambiguous position within the social order is similar to that of "Old Man Travelling."

25. Later revisions to "The Pedlar" in MS. E mark the relationship less arbitrarily, as a type of shared genealogy: "We were dear Friends: I from my childhood up / Had known him" (40–41), and later, "As I grew up, it was my best delight / To be his chosen comrade" (50–51).
26. MS. E ties the histories of the Narrator and the Pedlar closer to Wordsworth's own, yet now as a means of working out the genealogy of epic poet that Wordsworth was also about this time working-through in *The Prelude*. The Pedlar lives in Hawkeshead and, although his mother lives, is fatherless. However, his stepfather is a Schoolmaster who enforces paternal law as "Stern self-respect, a reverence for God's word, / And piety scarce known on English Land" (112–14). Most importantly, the Pedlar has "gaz'd upon that mighty Orb of Song, / The divine Milton" (239–40).
27. Butler, The Ruined Cottage *and* The Pedlar, 119.
28. He knows "not what to do / Or how to speak to her"; he "cannot tell how she pronounced [his] name"; she has a "face of grief / Unutterably helpless"; when "she spake / A strange surprize and fear came to [his] heart," and he "had little power / To give her comfort" (251–77).
29. The earliest version of the Prospectus is MS. 1 (Dove Cottage MS. 45). Beth Darlington argues that the Prospectus was probably composed between spring 1800 and early spring 1802 (22). See Darlington, 3–32, in the Cornell *Home at Grasmere*. Although MS. 1 is a separate entity, a close version of it concludes MS. B. of *Grasmere*, adding the lines describing the wedding of the mind of man to nature (1002–14 in MS. B; 56–71 in 1814), which, Darlington conjectures, were likely added in 1805 or 1806 (22). *Grasmere*, not published until 1888, is a type of prelude to the Prospectus and was subtitled "Part First, Book First, of *The Recluse*." MS. D includes the Prospectus version closest to its first 1814 publication. References to

the 1814 Prospectus are from *Poetical Works*, except where I cite from MS. 1 in Darlington's edition.

30. Abrams argues that the end of *The Prelude* marks the beginning of *The Recluse*, which is *The Prelude* itself, "an involuted poem which is about its own genesis—a prelude to itself. Its structural end is its own beginning; and its temporal beginning . . . is Wordsworth's entrance upon the stage of his life at which it ends" (*Natural Supernaturalism*, 79). Abrams also suggests that the Prospectus itself takes us back to *The Prelude*: it outlines the "subject, plot, and implicit argument of the story that Wordsworth has just finished telling in *The Prelude* and in its continuation, *Home at Grasmere*" (598). For Abrams, of course, the Prospectus *is* Romanticism's 'high argument': "faith in apocalypse by revelation had been replaced by faith in an apocalypse by revolution, and this now gave way to faith in an apocalypse by imagination or cognition" (334). With the writing of *Home at Grasmere*, Wordsworth had completed his archetypal journey 'home' to his imaginative resting place, and there was, in essence, nothing left to say.
31. In *Wordsworth's Revisionary Aesthetics* Theresa Kelley calls this Wordsworth's attempt to "'out-sublime'" Milton (44).
32. Jacobus, *Romanticism, Writing, and Sexual Difference*, 270, 292. Jacobus reads Wordsworth's canceled Book Thirteen passage on the analogy between the mind and nature through Derrida's re-reading of Kantian analogy as an abyssal structure and through de Man's use of prosopopeia as the trope of autobiography. Wordsworthian analogy is anthropomorphic because it naturalizes the externalization of the psychic interior, the self-alienating constitution of Wordsworth's identity between self and other. Analogy "arrest[s] the play of figuration with a name or personification" (286), marking the (Kantian) aesthetic imagination's usurpation of the empirical world as a 'natural' function. Reading this figural Wordsworth through Kristeva, Jacobus sees anthropomorphism as a defence against, rather than a repression of, difference. For Kristeva, the making of metaphors is both a natural and a saving function of the human psyche, the symptom of a primal repression that Kristeva calls the "zero degree of imagination" (*Tales of Love*, 24). Subjectivity arises from a primal self-differentiation inherent in the split between self and (m)other in preoedipal development. This split defines an "archaic, paternal space" (Jacobus, *Romanticism, Writing, and Sexual Difference*, 271) that is the precedent for the subject's later inscription by Symbolic authority, a (primal) metaphoricity that Kristeva calls 'love' or *eros* as opposed to metonymic desire mobilized by *thanatos*. Hence the affective destabilization of identities during transferences creates "not a narcissistic merger with the maternal container but the emergence of a *metaphorical object*," which means that the "very splitting that establishes the psyche, . . . bends the drive toward the symbolic of an other" (*Tales of Love*, 31). Wordsworth's deployment of the aesthetic after the sublime, traumatic suspension of the ego in the crossing of the Alps or the ascent to Snowdon "surfaces as a retrospective defence

against the threat to subjectivity" (Jacobus, *Romanticism, Writing, and Sexual Difference*, 291–92). I argue that this Wordsworthian salvation of identity, while it may inscribe the post-Kantian, poststructural tendencies of Romantic anthropomorphism and analogy, can also be read as an *avoidance* or missed encounter with the psychoanalytical impulses of Wordsworth's poetry. See also Kelley, *Wordsworth's Revisionary Aesthetics*, 23–42; de Man, "Anthropomorphism and Trope in the Lyric," "Autobiography as De-Facement"; Chase, *Decomposing Figures*, 3–31, 82–112.

33. As a response to Coleridge's distinction, Wordsworth's explanation of fancy and imagination in his Preface to the Edition of 1815 prompted Coleridge's reply in *Biographia* two years later. Wordsworth ascribes the power of fancy "to aggregate and to associate, to evoke and to combine" (*WP* 755) both to fancy and to imagination, whereas Coleridge ascribes this function only to imagination. The distinction for Wordsworth is that "Fancy does not require that the materials which she makes use of should be susceptible of change in their constitution," implicitly evoking the associationism Coleridge fears. Whereas "Fancy depends upon the rapidity and profusion with which she scatters her thoughts and images," caring "not how unstable or transitory may be her influence," imagination "is conscious of an indestructible dominion": "Fancy is given to quicken and to beguile the temporal part of our nature, Imagination to incite and to support the eternal." Immediately afterward, however, Wordsworth admits how the functioning of the two are combined, thus symptomatically evoking the return of the imagination's repressed instability, its self-mutating power. Miller argues that the function of the Wordsworthian imagination is to "[bring] something new into existence, something not present in the original experience" ("The Stone and the Shell," 126) and reads this logic of displacement in the dream of the Arab through Wordsworth's discussion of the imagination in the 1815 Preface. See Miller, "The Stone and the Shell," 136–38. On the gendering of fancy in British Romanticism, see Carlson, "Fancy's History." In "Suffering and Sensation in *The Ruined Cottage*," Karen Swann argues that, "the technical innovations in *The Ruined Cottage* allow Wordsworth to deploy a popular, feminine narrative machinery without becoming identified with a popular audience." This audience was an already constructed public of extravagantly passionate, feminized readers" to whom Wordsworth appeals in order to "simultaneously create[ ] the readers-to-be of high Romantic poetry" (84).

34. Keats's letters do not mention the Prospectus, but likely Keats read it along with *The Excursion*. Certainly he adopts its rhetoric when he asks "whether Miltons [sic] apparently less anxiety for Humanity proceeds from his seeing further or no than Wordsworth" (*KL* 93).

35. Hillman, *Re-Visioning Psychology*, 173, xviii, 32, 57, 174. Hillman calls this the subject's "subtle body," a term that suggests the absent psychosomatic body as it is tied to the work of the imagination. The "subtle body" is a helpful gloss on how Coleridge and especially De Quincey will come to see imagination as destabilizing rather than inspirational.

36. Comparing Freudian and Jungian dream interpretation in light of Hillman's rereading of Jung, Michael Adams writes that both Freud and Jung see interpretation as a type of allegory of the mind. One can think of allegory here in its Coleridgean rather than de Manian sense, so that the free associationism of Freudian interpretation and the comparative Jungian method of amplification are both "attempt[s] at demystification" ("Deconstructive Philosophy and Imaginal Psychology," 241). They close off that which exceeds consciousness (the dreamwork, the imagination, fantasy) within a rationalist conception of identity as the conscious ego containing excess. Whether grounded in Freudian infantile sexuality or Jungian archetypalism, interpretation reduces the dream to consciousness. See Woodman's distinction between metaphor and allegory in "Wordsworth's Crazed Bedouin."
37. In *Biographia Literaria* Coleridge defines "admiration of a great poet" as a "continuous *under-current* of feeling," thus implicitly foregrounding an unconscious of feeling that a Wordsworthian 'overflow' sublimates. Poetry has a "logic of its own, as severe as that of science; and more difficult, because more subtle, more complex, and dependent on more, and more fugitive causes," the latter once again exposing the fugitive unconscious of poetry (*BL* 1:23, 9)
38. Cited from Jonathan Wordsworth's reading text of "The Pedlar" in *The Music of Humanity*, l. 354. In Book 3 of *The Prelude*, "Residence at Cambridge," Wordsworth reapplies the phrase to his own mental development.
39. Bollas, *The Shadow of the Object*, 236.
40. Of the two-part *Prelude* Alan Richardson writes, "As an exploration of the role of early childhood experience in shaping the psyche, *The Prelude* offers its own tropes for representing psychic process, tropes which the language of psychoanalysis can help elucidate" ("Wordsworth at the Crossroads," 15). He reads dialogically between psychoanalysis and Wordsworth, so that *The Prelude* forms part of the prehistory of psychoanalysis, although his analysis is informed solely by object-relations theory and deals only with the spots of time. For a reading of Locke's influence on Wordsworth in the prehistory of psychoanalysis, see Quinney, "Wordsworth's Ghosts and the Model of the Mind." On the poem's parallels with psychoanalysis, see Bishop, "Wordsworth and the 'Spots of Time,'" 50; Wilson, *The Romantic Dream*, 168; Onorato, *The Character of the Poet*; Ellis, *Wordsworth, Freud, and the Spots of Time*. As Richardson notes, these last three studies treat the "author as analytic subject and the critic as lay analyst, establishing a post-mortem psychobiography in lieu of treatment" ("Wordsworth at the Crossroads," 15). A sophisticated Lacanian reading of the text is Robert Young's, which reads within the text a "logic of repetition, desire, the quest for the *object a*" ("The Eye and Progress of His Song," 79).
41. Frederick Pottle notes that "*The Prelude* is the first 'stream of consciousness' poem in European literature. Its organization is more associational than logical: its organizing metaphor is not a building but a river" ("Wordsworth in the Present Day,"128). The earliest draft also begins in lower case, suggest-

ing that the text begins in midthought. MS. E of "The Pedlar" describes its protagonist as having "trac'd an ebbing and a flowing mind, / Expression ever varying" (155–56).

42. Stephen Gill notes how at the end of longer text "the relative position the two poets had at the beginning of the poem is completely reversed. Then Wordsworth has looked to Coleridge as a monitor, who, both by example and by loving support, would assist him in his life's work—ultimately *The Recluse*. Now at the end of *The Prelude* it is Wordsworth who is encouraging and implicitly admonishing Coleridge" (*William Wordsworth*, 17).
43. Borrowing Mill's aphorism, Frye distinguishes between lyric as overheard rather than heard. Lyric represents the "concealment of the poet's audience from the poet" (*Anatomy of Criticism*, 249), where in *epos* the "author confronts his audience directly." The difference is that between "prayer" and "sermon." Paraphrasing McConnell's idea of Wordsworth's "confessional imagination," I note in passing how *The Prelude* functions confessionally as prayer, in which Wordsworth "turns his back on his listeners" (*Anatomy of Criticism*, 250), although Wordsworth would use this prayer to sermonizing effect: he *needs* to know the audience is behind him, just as the process of analysis would be pointless without the presence of the analyst 'behind' the analysand.
44. Rajan, "'The Web of Human Things,'" 87, 90. See also Rajan's "Romanticism and the Death of Lyric Consciousness," specifically her discussion of the absorption of "There was a boy" from MS. JJ into Book 5 of *The Prelude* (198–200): "Wordsworth's decision to absorb 'There was a boy' into *The Prelude* is a paradigm for what happens throughout the prehistory of the longer poem, as the still unwritten lyrical voice is situated in the prose of the world" (200).
45. Weisman, "Romanticism, Kant, and the Prehistory of Psychoanalysis," 6, 8–9.
46. Rajan, "'The Web of Human Things,'" 96, 104–5. Rajan notes how in *Alastor* Shelley distinguishes between narrative as episodic and lyric as epipsychic (92). On the episodic in *The Prelude*, see Bialostosky, *Making Tales*, 183.
47. In "Wordsworth and the 'Spots of Time,'" Bishop calls the spots of time "fragments of a drama, moments in a single action which has retired beyond the reach of direct expression" (41), although I would contest that they lead to a "single action."
48. Wordsworth suppresses this ambivalence in later versions by appealing through epic simile to a stable and unifying transcendental imagination: "The mind of man is framed even *like* the breath / And harmony of music. There is a dark / Invisible workmanship that reconciles / Discordant elements, and makes them move / In one society" (*P* 1.351–55; my italics). As if to further suppress the imagination's ability to 'frame' the mind, in *1850* Wordsworth speaks of the "immortal spirit" that spontaneously "grows / Like harmony in music," its influence now "inscrutable" and gnostically beyond comprehension rather than threateningly dark and unseen

(1.340–42). By making heterogeneous elements "cling together" rather than "move in one society," this power thus also makes them conform to a stable and conscious identity.

49. See Hartman, *Wordsworth's Poetry*, 16–17.
50. Wordsworth outlines the rationality of this system most clearly in his 1815 Preface, where in Kantian fashion he categorizes the six "powers requisite for the production of poetry" (*WP* 752), fancy and then imagination being the penultimate expressions of the last category, judgment.
51. On the reproduction of the excess of Lockean empiricism as a haunting within Wordsworth's psyche, see Quinney, "Wordsworth's Ghosts and the Model of the Mind."
52. See Jacobus, *Romanticism, Writing, and Sexual Difference*, 271–73 and note 33 above. Jacobus uses Kristeva to gloss the implications of the Wordsworthian natural sublime in the Mount Snowdon passage of *1805*'s Book Thirteen. I would use this account to gloss in turn the infant babe passage. Addressing the specific lines "and lo, / The moon stood naked in the heavens at height / Immense about my head" (13.40–42), Jacobus writes:

    > In a gesture of infinite regress, nature installs in the abyss of its own subjectivity something (a soul) that ought not to be there, a supernumary presence or noise in excess of the visible. "Imagination" stands for both man and moon, both mistscape and nature. The other of both, it is for ever displaced ("homeless"), constituted by its divided identification with the desires and images of another (the moon-mother). For Kristeva, it is this constitution in self-alienation, the earliest form of which is separation from the mother, that allows the most rudimentary form of signifying subject to come into being. Her account of the Oedipal as the overlay of an already triangulated pre-Oedipal elaborates a structure which might be called not simply the natural Sublime, but (doubly naturalized) the maternal Sublime. (173)

53. Walking suggests the anthropology of a bounded subject at large in society and in harmony with Nature, but also marginality and aimlessness. Reclining facilitates the contemplative form of the walking tour, the mind at rest within its mental landscape. Yet this mode can encounter the return of a repressed psychic peripateticism, the free-associationism of a subject-in-process.
54. I am not concerned to examine the significance of the dream's content to the larger thematic structure of the text or the significance of *Don Quixote* and thus of literature to the dream, especially in light of other convincing readings. See Hartman, *Wordsworth's Poetry*, 227–31; Jacobus, *Romanticism, Writing, and Sexual Difference*, 97–125; Miller, "The Stone and the Shell"; Smyser, "Wordsworth's Dream of Poetry and Science,"; Wilson, *The Romantic Dream*, 168–91; Woodman "Wordsworth's Crazed Bedouin"; Robert Young, "The Eye and Progress of His Song," 90–92.

55. Wilson reads the dream as nightmare, Wordsworth functioning as a "waking interpreter": "As a poet, he faces the conditions of deluge—the revolutionary bloodbath and its tidal ruin. Yet . . . Wordsworth can emerge from the shards of ruin to pursue his story, the poet energized by threats of destruction to pluck the fruits of his vocation" (*The Romantic Dream*, 177). Wordsworth's identification with the madness of the dream, however, is more complete and less recuperative than Wilson allows. Again, see Woodman's "Wordsworth's Crazed Bedouin."
56. Woodman, "Wordsworth's Crazed Bedouin," 118, 26.
57. Wordsworth first uses the spots of time passage to frame the text in this manner in the five-part *Prelude*. Although Wordsworth appears to have worked on this version for little more than eight weeks, Jonathan Wordsworth argues that the "five-book poem is the most formally rounded of the *Preludes*, beginning and ending in the early memories that were the source of Wordsworth's power, and attempting to define *en route* the nature of their restorative effect. . . . Wordsworth is not yet elegiac about his loss, . . . but he makes a positive effort to *explain*" ("The Five-Book *Prelude*," 20–21). Hence placing the passage at the beginning of the 1799 text marks it as a provisional apparatus, which later passages used to exemplify it might then dispute, a psychotextual conflict that Wordsworth later attempts to avoid.
58. As Wilson points out, Wordsworth, following Locke's, Stewart's, and Hartley's associationist theory of dreams, troped different levels of consciousness, each according to the suspension of the individual will, and thus of individual identity. These varying states of hypnagogic power were daydreams, reveries, trances, and finally dreams, the most threatening usurpation of the will. See Wilson, *The Romantic Dream*, 12–16.
59. Robert Young, "The Eye and Progress of His Song," 85.
60. For a discussion of the phenomenology between surface and depth as part of an analytic hermeneutic, see Kneale, "Symptom and Scene in Freud and Wordsworth." See also Young, who argues that the 'trouble' of Wordsworth's dreams "suggests the primary process that Freud identified in the dreamwork. . . . The 'huge and mighty forms' of the dreamwork subvert the signification of images—dissolving them into non-meanings, the (mythic) state where the signifying chain comprises a dazzling drift of the signified under the signifier—a discharge of the primary process, and, ineluctably, the death drive" (88).

Chapter Three: Analysis Terminable in Coleridge

1. In *Biographia Literaria* Coleridge alludes to a proposed treatise "on the Logos or communicative intellect in Man and Deity" as a "great book on the CONSTRUCTIVE PHILOSOPHY" (*BL* 1:302).
2. The letter continues: "The title is: Christianity the one true Philosophy—or 5 Treatises on the Logos, or communicative Intelligence, Natural, Human,

and Divine." In 1815 he describes it as a "work, which has employed all my best thoughts & efforts for the last twelve years and more, on which I would ground my reputation. . . . This work will be entitled LOGOSOPHIA: or on the LOGOS, divine and human, in six Treatises" (*CL* 4:589). One notes in the expansion from five to six treatises the changing and nebulous shape of the work.

3. As a cautionary figure of moral reproof, Dorothy is a type of benign domestic superego who "chastened, stemmed, / And balanced" the "deep enthusiastic joy" or "rapture" of Wordsworth's psyche (*1805* 13.261–64). He addresses the madness in solitude as "that beauty, which as Milton sings / Hath terror in it" and notes how Dorothy "didst soften down" the "oversternness" of his soul: "thou didst plant its crevices with flowers, / Hang it with shrubs that twinkle in the breeze, / And teach the little birds to build their nests / And warble in its chambers" (13.225–36). Here the unfinished Gothic church of Wordsworth's psyche is refashioned as a modest bungalow in the suburbs of Wordsworth's mind, and Dorothy replaces Urania as the muse of the Wordsworthian epic of domesticity. "Home at Grasmere" thus refashions *The Recluse* as a proto-Victorian paradigm of domestic stability. Chapter Five will explore the issue of gender in Romantic psychoanalysis at greater length.
4. In "Tintern Abbey," written in 1798, six years before the bulk of Book Thirteen of *The Prelude*, Wordsworth assumes sole therapeutic authority against Dorothy and Coleridge, who are a psychic distraction that Wordsworth redeems in them by way of abjecting it within himself. Wordsworth feels a "presence that disturbs [him] . . . / . . . a sense sublime / Of something far more deeply interfused" that exists in nature, but also within the "mind of man: / A motion and a spirit, that impels / All thinking things, all objects of all thought, / And rolls through all things." That this force seems to *exceed* his simple perception of nature means that he remains "still / A lover" of nature, but only because of its power, like the "still sad music of humanity," to "chasten and subdue": "for she can so inform / The mind that is within us, so impress / With quietness and beauty." He is now "well pleased to recognise / In nature and the language of the sense / The anchor of [his] purest thoughts." Were he not "thus taught," he would not (as opposed to *could* not) "Suffer [his] genial spirits to decay." The potential for *that other* process to enact itself—the *free*-associationism of his psyche—means that he must project this "language of [his] former heart" onto Coleridge, the "shooting lights / Of [whose] wild eyes" now hold the taint of psychic madness safely contained from Wordsworth's 'pure thoughts.' Wordsworth then consigns Dorothy to a similar solitude, blessing her according to the dark 'lunacy' of the moon: "Therefore let the moon / Shine on thee in thy solitary walk." Yet even when *her* "wild ecstasies shall be matured / Into a sober pleasure," even "If solitude, or fear, or pain, or grief, / Should be [their] portion," Wordsworth submits that she will remember him with "healing thoughts." Whereas Wordsworth suggests that Dorothy is contained within the sphere of his therapeutic authority, however, he must project the same

influence in Coleridge "after many wanderings, many years / Of absence" and appears rather more desperate to demand Coleridge's "warmer love—oh! . . . far deeper zeal / Of holier love." Where Dorothy figures more as a narcissistic extension of Wordsworth's own identity, then, Coleridge signifies the potential return of Wordsworth's own distraction in solitude, the possibility of reading in the "past existence" of Coleridge's "wild eyes" a *reflection* of Wordsworth's unconscious (*WP* 91–156).

5. This is also to resist the psychoanalytic dimension of their dialogue in *The Prelude* and of their conversations about *The Recluse*. Through their texts Wordsworth and Coleridge are engaged in an analysis of and transference with the other. One can say that *The Recluse* does not get written because the poet cannot terminate their discussion about it. Because neither poet's "literal conversation" nor its "moving spirit" are recoverable, Paul Magnuson, following Bakhtin, reads their dialogue as a site of difference rather than identity, by "[tracing] the variations in apparently similar statements [between the writers] to account for the discontinuities by which such a dialogue generates poetry" (*Wordsworth and Coleridge*, 10). Dialogue is paradoxical for both poets because their 'fear of amalgamation' necessitates both the separate identity of *genius* as a lyric totality or pure individuality and the presence of the other to authenticate *genius*.
6. The phrase "may be told" also inscribes the idea of the propriety of what can be told within the arena of letters. Wordsworth's embarrassment that he has told *too much* in *The Prelude*, like De Quincey's *Confessions of an English Opium-Eater*, foregrounds how the exposure of the psyche to public self-analysis is not only "unprecedented" (to borrow Wordsworth's term) but violates social and epistemological codes: saying too much indicates knowing too much, which indicates a subject that might not fit within the social order.
7. In "Coleridge, Wordsworth, and the Textual Abject" Rajan argues that Coleridgean dejection indicates how subjectivity is simultaneously self-reparative and self-alienating, the subject both alienated by what is alien within and constituted by the spectral identification with this abject.
8. The anecdote is recorded in *Memoirs of William Wordsworth*, published in 1851; cited in Wallen, *Coleridge's* Ancient Mariner, 94.
9. Rajan argues that Wordsworth "denies Coleridge's difference by using the latter as a source of antithetical confirmation for his own identity." Although Coleridge himself accepts this identity, "it is also the dialectical stimulus for Coleridge's attempt to accomplish in the *Biographia* the task he had set Wordsworth in his poetry, by recasting German philosophy not as a turning away from Wordsworth but as the very path of his redemption into High Romanticism" ("Coleridge, Wordsworth, and the Textual Abject" 64).
10. In a letter of May 22 Wordsworth solicited Coleridge's remarks on Wordsworth's 1815 edition of poems and *The Excursion*. About "To William Wordsworth" Wordsworth writes: "Let me beg out of kindness to me that

you would relinquish the intention of publishing the Poem addressed to me after hearing *mine* to you. The commendation would be injurious to us both, and my work when it appears, and would labour under a great disadvantage in consequence of such a precursorship of Praise" (*WL* 2:669). Coleridge was partly confused by Wordsworth's plan: "In order therefore to explain the *disappointment* I must recall to your mind what my *expectations* were. . . . *This* [*The Prelude*] I considered as 'the EXCURSION'; and the second as 'THE RECLUSE' I had (from what I had at different times gathered from your conversation on the Plan) anticipated as commencing with you set down and settled in an abiding Home, and that with the Description of that Home you were to begin a *Philosophical Poem*, the result and fruits of a Spirit so fram'd & so disciplin'd, as had been told in the former" (*CL* 4:573–74). His expectations were great indeed:

> Of course, I expected the Colours, Music, imaginative Life, and Passion of *Poetry*; but the matter and arrangement of *Philosophy*—not doubting from the advantages of the Subject that the Totality of a System was not only capable of being harmonized with, but even calculated to aid, the unity (Beginning, Middle, and End) of a *Poem*. Thus, whatever the Length of the Work might be, still it was a *determinate* Length: of the subjects announced each would have it's own appointed place, and excluding repetitions each would relieve & rise in interest above the other—. I supposed you first to have meditated the faculties of Man in the abstract, in their correspondence with his Sphere of action, and first, in the Feeling, Touch, and Taste, then in the Eye, & last in the Ear, to have laid a solid and immoveable foundation for the Edifice by removing the sandy Solipsisms of Locke, and the Mechanic Dogmatists, and demonstrating that the Senses were living growths and developments of the Mind & Spirit in a much juster as well as higher sense, than the mind can be said to be formed by the Senses—. Next, I understood that you would take the Human Race in the concrete, have exploded the absurd notion of Pope's Essay on Man, Darwin, and all the countless Believers—even (strange to say) among Xtians of Man's having progressed from an Ouran Outan state—so contrary to all History, to all Religion, nay, to all Possibility—to have affirmed a Fall in some sense, as a fact, the possibility of which cannot be understood from the nature of the Will, but the reality of which is attested by Experience & Conscience—Fallen men contemplated in the different ages of the World, and in the different states—Savage—Barbarous—Civilized—the lonely Cot, or Borderer's Wigwam—the Village—the Manufacturing Town—Sea-port—City—Universities—and not disguising the sore evils, under which the

> whole Creation groans, to point out however a manifest Scheme of Redemption from this Slavery, of Reconciliation from this Enmity with Nature—what are the Obstacles, the *Antichrist* that must be & already is—and to conclude by a grand didactic swell on the necessary identity of a true Philosophy with true Religion, agreeing in the results and differing only as the analytic and synthetic processes, as discursive from intuitive, the former chiefly useful as perfecting the latter—in short, the necessity of a general revolution in the modes of developing & disciplining the human mind by the substitution of Life, and Intelligence (considered in it's different powers from the Plant up to that state in which the difference of Degree becomes a new kind (man, self-consciousness) but yet not by essential opposition) for the philosophy of mechanism which in every thing that is most worthy of the human Intellect strikes *Death*, and cheats itself by mistaking clear Images for distinct conceptions, and which idly demands Conceptions where Intuitions alone are possible or adequate to the majesty of the Truth.—In short, Facts elevated into Theory—Theory into Laws—& Laws into living & intelligent Powers—true idealism necessarily perfecting itself in Realism, & Realism refining itself into Idealism.—(*CL* 4:574–75)

In an 1836 contribution to *Table Talk* he offers a much simpler version: "Then the plan laid out, and I believe, partly suggested by me, was, that Wordsworth should assume the station of a man in mental repose, one whose principles were made up, and so prepared to deliver upon authority a system of philosophy." Coleridge is explicit about who owned *The Recluse* as intellectual property: "Something of this sort was, I think, agreed on. It is, in substance, what I have been all my life doing in my system of philosophy" (*Table Talk*, 14.2:177).

11. Jerome Christensen locates this poetry at the level of rhetoric, as a "hypopoesis" that is the "enabling figure that makes fiction as well as philosophy conceivable—subfiction [as opposed to supposition] of the fact and position of an original standpoint of an author who must ultimately speak the truth or tell a lie" (*Coleridge's Blessed Machine of Language*, 19–20). The hypopoesis of language in Coleridge's prose, both early and later, proves the persistence of Hartley in Coleridge's thought, wherein rhetorical (free-)associationism proves that language has a will of its own. Christensen argues that Hartley's influence, "even on the superficial level of what 'Hartley' meant to Coleridge, was more complex than is widely supposed" and that "Coleridge never successfully completed the overthrow of association which he proclaimed in 1801" (17). See also Christensen, 58–95. The trope powering Coleridge's "machine of language" is chiasmus, the paradoxical and autonomous construction of identity between "the logic of self construction [and] the logic of self destruction" (184): "Eddy rather than bridge, the chi-

asmus in Coleridge's text tropes method as the indefinitely reproducible, always liminal traverse between consciousness and unconsciousness, will and willfulness, writer and text" (27). In "Philosophy/Literature: The Associationist Precedent for Coleridge's Later Poems," Christensen reads Hartleyan associationism as a protodeconstructive maneuver: "Hartley's doctrine renders the human as a dynamic nexus of representations ungrounded by a subject ever present to itself" (28). For a view contra Christensen, see Miall, who argues that associationism produces a self through feelings, albeit a "conflicted self" who must deal with the "equivocal nature of feeling itself" ("Coleridge's Debt to Hartley," 162).

12. Smith, *Derrida and Autobiography*, 18, 23.
13. Ibid., 18, 19.
14. As Coleridge wrote later in life (recorded in *Table Talk*, 21 July 1832), "The pith of my system is to make senses out of the mind—not the mind out of the senses, as Locke did" (14.1:312).
15. On the form of the *Biographia*, see Buell, who argues that the text is the "unfolding of the mind in the act of self-definition," yet disorderly to the point of subverting Coleridge's idea of aesthetic form ("The Question of Form in Coleridge's *Biographia Literaria*," 407).
16. The situation recalls the conflict of the psychosomatic body of writing in Wordsworth's famous statement to De Quincey: "I have a kind of derangement in my stomach and digestive organs which makes writing painful to me, and indeed almost prevents me from holding correspondence with any body: and this (I mean to say the unpleasant feelings which I have connected with the act of holding a Pen) has been the chief cause of my long silence" (*WL* 1:453).
17. Coleridge's criticism of Wordsworth's poetic theory focusses upon its "accidentality," its grounding in situations and characters of real life, which runs counter to Coleridge's essentially Aristotelian idea of poetry as the "noblest and most philosophical form of writing" (*BL* 2:126n), and therefore as an ideal rather than real form. Coleridge reacts against "accidentality," then, as a form of associationism wherein the text gets lost in the 'delirium' of minute particulars.
18. Rajan notes the irony of a Coleridgean refashioning of Kant as a post-Kantian idealist, which thus removes the taint of empiricism, and thus the threat of associationism, from the Critical Philosophy ("Coleridge, Wordsworth, and the Textual Abject," 62).
19. The friend's alteration of "To William Wordsworth" is also telling. Coleridge's poem reads "A song divine of high and passionate thoughts / To their own music chaunted!" (*CP* 46–47). *Biographia*, however, takes the lines' transcendental thrust and places them within the "obscure" and "strange" psychoanalytical space of the present text's ambivalence.
20. Foucault, *The History of Sexuality, Volume One*, 12.
21. For accounts of *Christabel*'s circulation as a semipublic document between composition and publication, see Swann, "Literary Gentlemen and Lovely

Ladies." For a similar account of "The Rime," see McGann, "The Meaning of The Ancient Mariner."

22. Upon finishing *The Prelude* Wordsworth wrote that "look[ing] back upon the performance it seemed to have a dead weight about it, the reality so far short of the expectation" (*WL* 1:594). The poem is still haunted by its conception, its writing suspending life in a kind of affective interspace that Wordsworth calls a "texture midway between life and books" (*P* 3.613), suggesting that aesthetics cannot sublimate the burden of the text's psychology. In a passage deleted from the 1817 *Sybilline Leaves* version of "To William Wordsworth" (entitled "To a Gentleman"), Coleridge describes the effect of hearing *The Prelude* as "thoughts [that] became / A bodily tumult" (*CP* 202). In a later published passage Coleridge appears to accept *The Prelude*'s vision of his imaginative life according to the forensic effects of the Intimations ode: "all which patient toil had rear'd, and all / Commune with thee had open'd out––but Flowers / Strew'd on my corse, and borne upon my Bier, / In the same Coffin, for the self-same Grave!" (*CP* 72–75). Wordsworth's "advancing" is both prophetic and crippling, for Coleridge finds himself "In silence listening, like a devout child," the strength of the Wordsworthian ego having reduced Coleridge to infancy (82, 95). His "soul lay passive" (96) on the couch of its own analysis, figured as a grave in which Wordsworthian analysis would place Coleridge's psyche. At the end of the poem, Coleridge attempts to rise from this grave "Absorb'd, yet hanging still upon the sound" (111) of Wordsworth's voice, an image of Coleridge caught in death-like contemplation ("Scarce conscious, and yet conscious of its close" [108]), sustained by the other's music and suspended in corpse-like awe by its autonomous strength. Coleridge thus figures the 'end' of *The Prelude* as both a benediction upon Wordsworth's greatness and a blessing that Coleridge might be released from its hold, the text finished literally before psychically it finishes off its auditor.
23. Commenting on the ongoing publication since 1969 of the Bollingen/Princeton *Collected Coleridge*, Jon Klancher writes:

> A magisterial product of the modern critical institution, these volumes ironically have helped open up English Romanticism to the historical, political, and epistemological critiques with which Coleridge's cultural authority was supposed to settle accounts. *The Collected Coleridge* displays a decidedly uncollectable Coleridge whose "texts" are enmeshed with those of his radical, mass cultural, middle-class, political, religious, skeptical, and literary interlocutors. ("English Romanticism and Cultural Production," 86)

24. McKusick, "'Living Words,'" 7.
25. Foucault, "Nietzsche, Genealogy, History," 78.
26. Coburn, *Inquiring Spirit*, 63, 65.
27. Ibid., 67.

28. Miall, "Wordsworth and *The Prelude*," 249.
29. Miall stops short of seeing this paradox as fundamentally threatening to the Wordsworthian cogito in the manner of my reading of anticipation and memory as disruptive. He nonetheless offers an interesting reading of the nonlinear, episodic structure of *The Prelude* as "the sequencing of . . . various episodes . . . so that their affective implications in forming the self that [Wordsworth] has become are allowed to emerge" ("Wordsworth and *The Prelude*," 247).
30. Coburn, *Inquiring Spirit*, 63.
31. Miall notes that Coleridge's observation of feeling up to the latter part of 1803 operates at a "descriptive, phenomenal level," where afterwards he displays a more "dynamic understanding" ("Coleridge on Feeling," 36–37). See also Vallins, "The Feeling of Knowledge."
32. Proposing an entire work devoted to the "subject of dreams, visions, ghosts, and witchcraft" the primary evidence for which would be drawn from the "facts and data" of "personal testimony," Coleridge argues that such phenomena could provide "valuable materials for a theory of perception and its dependence on the memory and imagination" (Coburn, *Inquiring Spirit*, 52–53).
33. Miall argues that Coleridge's writings "illuminate the relation between normal and pathological emotions, and . . . suggest the significant contribution that both make to an understanding of the imagination" ("Coleridge on Feeling," 36).
34. Coleridge writes later in the *Biographia*, "how restless, how difficultly hidden, the powers of genius are. . . . I conclude that POETIC GENIUS is not only a very delicate but a very rare plant" (*CN* 2:132).
35. Coleridge's later definitions of imagination in the *Biographia* resist the experience of feeling that is recorded in the *Notebooks*. See Miall "Coleridge on Emotion," 35–36. Miall compares two notebook drafts of 1809 and 1811 that were later revised for the *Biographia*.
36. Coburn, *Inquiring Spirit*, 45–46.
37. Ibid., 50.
38. Ibid., 57–58.
39. Coleridge extrapolates philosophical idealism from mesmerism perhaps through the writing of C. A. F. Kluge, who defined the magnetic state in terms of six degrees of consciousness, beginning with simple waking, sinking to half-sleep, and eventually leading to an inner darkness or full sleep that awakens within the subject inner clarity, a self-contemplation of the interior of both his own body and that of the magnetist with whom he is in rapport, leading to universal enlightenment through the abolition of time and space. See Ellenberger, *The Discovery of the Unconscious*, 78. Coleridge found the parallel between mesmerism and Schelling in Christian Wolfart's commentary on Mesmer's "Système des influences." Wolfart reacts against what Coleridge calls Mesmer's "crass materialism" (*Marginalia*, 3:873). The editors of Coleridge's marginalia to Wolfart write: "Wolfart claims that it is a gross

error to regard Mesmer's system as materialistic, arguing that the magnetic fluid is not a substance but a field of interaction between various bodies, and that Mesmer conceived of matter not as an independent entity but as a manifestation of an original unity in the absolute" (3:867n).

40. Coleridge, *Marginalia*, 3:387.
41. See F. W. J. Schelling, *The Ages of the World* (1815 text), 65–72.
42. Coburn, *Inquiring Spirit*, 47.
43. See Freud's "Constructions in Analysis" (1937) and "Analysis Terminable and Interminable" (1937).
44. Brooks, *Troubling Confessions*, 53; see Freud's, "The Dynamics of Transference" (1912).
45. See Chapter One, note 37.
46. Coburn, *Inquiring Spirit*, 55.
47. Keats, writing of Shakespeare, will call this a "life of Allegory" (*KL* 218), a radically different concept from Coleridgean allegory as "but a translation of abstract notions into a picture-language which is itself nothing but an abstraction from objects of the senses; the principle being more worthless even than its phantom proxy, both alike unsubstantial, and the former shapeless to boot" (Perkins 503).
48. Coburn, *Inquiring Spirit*, 68.
49. Ibid., 52–53.
50. Wordsworth reacts against this supernaturalism. *The Prelude* argues that Coleridge is no longer a poet according to Wordsworth's contemplative standard. By comparison Coleridge is an erstwhile seeker of truth, a prophet and seer both blessed and cursed by the dis-eased imagination of his poetry. This fuels the catastrophic image of Coleridge, as when Edward Bostetter states that "[t]he failure to complete *Christabel* marks the collapse of Coleridge as a significant poet" (*The Romantic Ventriloquists*, 118). This in turn sets the tone of metabiographical readings of Coleridge as troubled by neurotic or oedipal complexities. See McFarland, *Coleridge and the Pantheist Tradition*; Fruman, *Coleridge*. This view also reads an unbalanced symbiosis between Wordsworth and Coleridge, Wordsworth being stronger and more creative. Against this attempt to 'synonymize' their relationship, see Galperin, "'Desynonymizing' the Self in Wordsworth and Coleridge." Coleridge himself attempts to refashion his self-image, in *Biographia Literaria* and *The Statesman's Manual*, and later in *Aids to Reflection*, as a proto-Victorian man of letters who has transcended his radical/Romantic/poetic past.
51. In *Coleridge's* Ancient Mariner, Martin Wallen writes: "Wordsworth, finding in *Lyrical Ballads* a poetic voice which appealed to the public sufficiently to found a poetic vocation, felt he had more at stake in the volume than Coleridge did, and so he made it his own" (99). This story is already well told: it is clear that Wordsworth's 'idea' of the volume emerged more clearly *after* the success of the first edition. At that time Wordsworth prompted Coleridge to modernize *The Rime*'s archaisms and to remove its more sensa-

tionalist passages, and so he moved the text to the end of the 1800, 1802, and 1805 editions. *Christabel* was to be included in the expanded second edition, although it still lacked the conclusion to Part Two; and Wordsworth wrote the publishers to request that the poem, even if already printed for binding, be replaced by his own "Michael." One answer to Wordsworth's decision to retain *The Rime* was that, signifying the desire behind the poets' creative coupling, it was half Wordsworth's child, albeit unwanted. Accordingly, *Christabel* is aborted or stillborn in Wordsworth's mind because, although it was written during the flower of their friendship, it was wholly Coleridge's own. The homosocial and conjugal implications of this relationship are suggested by *The Rime*, in which the wandering Mariner cruises for his trick: "The moment that his face I see / I know the man that must hear me" (634–35). See Ault in Wallen, *Coleridge's* Ancient Mariner, xiii. All references to *The Rime* are from Wallen, *Coleridge's* Ancient Mariner, cited by line number from the 1798 version, except where indicated.

52. In his note to "We are Seven," Wordsworth notes how the text's autonomous growth eluded the organicism of his joint labor with Coleridge: "As we endeavored to proceed conjointly . . . our respective manners proved so widely different that it would have been quite presumptuous in me to do anything but separate from an undertaking upon which I could only have been a clog. . . . *The Ancient Mariner* grew and grew till it became too important for our first object" (Perkins, *English Romantic Writers*, 196).

53. Coleridge takes this abjection to heart. In a passage eventually deleted from "To William Wordsworth" he argues that in *The Prelude*'s version of his creative pathology, he has been left "to die, / A wanderer with a worn-out heart forlorn, / Mid strangers pining with untended wounds" (*CP* 202). "Far art thou wandered now in search of health" (*P* 6.249), writes Wordsworth, suggesting that Coleridge has "wandered" in search of a cure, but that his imagination has also "wandered" from the path of reason. According to *The Prelude*, the breeding/breding of Coleridge's imagination is improper. Because he "pine[s] / As one in cities bred might do," his is a "wilful fancy," "in endless dreams / Of sickness, disjoining, joining things, / Without the light of knowledge" (3.584–610). Because Wordsworth is bred by Nature, this "adulterate power" (8.592) is tempered by "pure Imagination" (*1850* 8.423) and his "thoughts did oft revolve / About some centre palpable, which at once / Incited them to motion, and controlled [them]," so that "At all times [he] had a real solid world / Of images about [him]" (*1805* 8.599–605). While this 'breding' disciplines the imagination's 'breeding,' however, it is tainted by its absent psychosomatic body. Where imagination leads from Nature to "love of human-kind," it then "[turns] itself / Instinctively to human passions" (8.588–91), which refashion Nature as a *palpable* or psychosomatic presence and which thus locate thought within a mobile rather than stable psychic space. Later repressing this motility, Wordsworth adopts (and enforces the Cartesianism of) the metaphysical conceit of purifying the psychic 'matter' of things into psychic abstraction ("each airy thought revolved /

Round a substantial centre" [*1850* 8.430–31]), so that the intellect resubstantializes the mind as a "real solid world" of things.

54. Speaking of the text's broader history as a commodity of Romantic criticism, Ault, in his Forward to Wallen's edition of *The Ancient Mariner*, notes that "incessant revisions" by Coleridge, Wordsworth, printers, and editors throughout the text's history are now part of "the ontological domain of the tale itself—that is, by its very nature the tale questions its own identity and tempts its readers and interpreters to retell or recreate that lost identity (that never was) in a way that completes it or gains access to its ever-receding origin" (Wallen, *Coleridge's* Ancient Mariner, vii). Wallen writes, "Viewed as the ensemble of revisions in which the poem actually embodies continual reenactment, the narration now unfolds in a changing context, one less susceptible to a determinate meaning" (*Coleridge's* Ancient Mariner, 110). My reading is indebted to both Ault's Forward to Wallen and to Wallen's extensive commentary on the texts in his critical edition of the poem, which prints parallel versions of the 1798, 1800, and 1817 texts, and variants from 1802, 1805, and 1828. See also McGann, "The Meaning of the Ancient Mariner."
55. Magnuson argues that the failure to coauthor "The Ancient Mariner" marks the start of a "lyrical dialogue" that, in the absence of real collaboration, creates a textual exchange of ideas through which either poet attempts to shore up creative capital. Thus Wordsworth's Salisbury Plain poems, written and revised between 1793 and 1797, inspire Coleridge's "The Ancient Mariner," which in turn prompts Wordsworth's "The Discharged Soldier," both of which were written in the winter of 1797–1798. Magnuson traces another sequence from Wordsworth's "The Ruined Cottage," first drafted in the summer of 1797, to "The Pedlar," drafted in late winter/early spring 1798, to April 1798, when Coleridge began "Christabel." Magnuson's reading suggests a wandering scene of analysis that circulates between the poets and that each invests in to different degrees. See Magnuson, *Wordsworth and Coleridge*, 33–138.
56. Coleridge, *The Friend*, 4.1:155–7.
57. Without these passages the text proceeds instead to the resurrection of the crew (517–50) as a foreshadowing of moral and spiritual rebirth.
58. Significantly, the Mariner is confronted by this otherness in the "harbour-bay" (486) of his "own countrée" (481). The harbour safely contains the potentially illimitable and alien expanse of the sea. The mobile tropes of sea/harbour and moon in the text thus suggest the work of the unconscious, the depths of which can only be read across the surface of consciousness as a mutable tableau of psychic life. *The Prelude* 4.247–304 ("As one who hangs down-bending from the side / Of a slow-moving boat") reads as an attempt to aestheticize Coleridge's mutating sea as a place of "beauteous sights" (4.252), although there is for Wordsworth still "Something . . . that perplexed / Th' authentic sight of reason" (4.295–96). Ongoing revisions to Part Three of "The Rime," which also includes the Mariner's vision of the "Spectre-ship" and the dice game, thus reveal an attempt to repress the absent psychosomatic presence of the unconscious as it is signified in the interplay between

sea and moon. Once the dice game is over, "With never a whisper in the Sea / Oft darts the Spectre-ship" (209–10). Yet the "horned Moon, with one bright Star / Almost atween the tips" (212–13), remains as an uncanny repetition of the ship's form and thus of the Mariner's solitary imagination. In a passage drafted between 1806 and 1811 but never used, this description foregrounds the psychosomatic presence of the "ghastly crew" as mesmerized by the Spectre-ship's silent disappearance into the unconscious sea: "And stifled words & groans of pain / Mix' on each ~~trembling~~ murmuring lip / And / we look'd round, & we look'd up, / And fear at our hearts, as at a cup, / The Life-blood seem'd to sip" (*1800* 207–11). In *1817* Coleridge minimizes this psychosomatic presence, attempting instead to naturalize the ship's uncanny disappearance: "The sun's rim dips, the stars rush out, / At one stride comes the dark; / With far-heard whisper, o'er the sea, / Off shot the spectre-bark" (203–6). Wallen then notes at least five different drafts of a marginal gloss, never used in *1817*, that attempt to provide empirical proof for what still appears as a supernatural phenomenon: "Within the Tropics there is no Twilight. At the moment, the second, that the Sun sinks, the Stars appear all at once as if at the word of a command announced by the evening Gun, in our W. India Islands." As if to suggest the inability to contain the mutating work of the unconscious, the gloss eventually used in *1828* reads simply, "No twilight within the courts of the sun."

59. That the stanzas on the ship's anatomy do not appear consistently in the text's first edition establishes a pattern of revisions to the dice game passage, which further confuse as much as they clarify the relationship between Mariner and crew. See Ault's description of these changes, which demonstrate the blurring "between *textuality*—indeterminate, apparently random or 'accidental' textual occurrences (features which 'show up' in the process of production)—and *intentionality*—determinate, necessary, presumably conscious meaning" (Wallen, *Coleridge's* Ancient Mariner, viii).
60. This indeterminacy infects the 1817 gloss most traumatically at two points where the text describes the influence of the "horned Moon" (*1817* 214) and the "moving Moon" (267).
61. The poem was published as "The Rime of the Ancyent Marinere, in Seven Parts" for the 1798 *Lyrical Ballads*. It was thereafter titled "The Ancient Mariner: A Poet's Reverie" in the 1800, 1802, and 1805 editions. It was published for the first time under Coleridge's name as "The Rime of the Ancient Mariner in Seven Parts" in the 1817 *Sibylline Leaves*. This edition includes the marginal gloss, but Wallen notes that it may have been written much earlier, perhaps even shortly after the poem's composition (*Coleridge's* Ancient Mariner, 105). *Sibylline Leaves* was to have been Volume Two of *Biographia Literaria*, then Volume Three as *Biographia* grew to two volumes itself. *Biographia* and *Sibylliline Leaves* are thus spectral images of one another, the former reflecting a philosophy troubled by its own poetry, the latter constituting a poetry that does not conform to the *Biographia*'s philosophy. The text's last publication in Coleridge's lifetime was in the 1828 *Poetical Works of Samuel Taylor Coleridge* in two volumes.

62. This is the only time in the 1798 text that the Mariner's voice is enclosed by punctuation, and even then only by an opening quotation mark.
63. Ault notes that other characters in the 1798 text, such as the Wedding-Guest and the Hermit, "are marked by open quotation marks only and are rarely closed (indeed, close quotation marks are the anomaly and call attention to themselves)" (Wallen, *Coleridge's* Ancient Mariner, ix). The 1805 edition "unequivocally stabilizes all vocal distinctions," but *Sibylline Leaves*, after placing quotation marks around "There was a ship," reopens the Mariner's tale at (21) and doesn't close it until (621), "technically sub-embedding all subsequent statements . . . in the Mariner's own voice (which in turn is embedded within the narrator's voice)." The most striking disruption of narrative identities occurs in the 1828 and posthumous 1834 editions, where the Mariner's tale is closed at (621), but never opened at (21).
64. Early in the text, for instance, the Wedding-Guest hears the "loud bassoon" (*1817* 32) announcing the bride's entrance, and the "Wedding-Guest here beat his breast" (31), an affective gesture of his suspended will. The gloss reads: "The wedding-guest heareth the bridal music; but the mariner continueth his tale," thus providing a factual emplotment of psychic phenomena that glosses over the scene's mesmeric potential.
65. Derwent Coleridge and James Gillman indicate that Coleridge intended to complete the text as a four-part construction. This whole would have dialectically recuperated Christabel through the antithetical abjection of Geraldine and then through the synthesis of Christabel's subsequent reconciliation with her father (and thus with the social order) via her marriage to her lost lover. As Gillman writes, "Thus defeated, the supernatural being Geraldine disappears" (cited in House, *Coleridge*, 128).
66. Levinson, *The Romantic Fragment Poem*, 96.
67. Abraham, "Notes on the Phantom," 173–75.
68. According to Karen Swann, a feminist reading of the triangulation between Christabel, Geraldine, and the Baron would charge the "Law with producing hysterics, women who 'cannot tell' what ails them because the Law legislates against every voice but its own" ("'Christabel,'" 549). Swann overdetermines this reading in two ways: first, by arguing that "hysteria produces the Law" in the first place; second, by arguing "that the Law is just one form of hysteria." See also Charles Rzepka's reading of the Lacanian (m)other in the text in "Christabel's 'Wandering Mother.'" The poem lends itself easily to psychoanalytic approaches. See Durham, "The Mother Tongue"; Paglia, "Christabel"; Schapiro, *The Romantic Mother*; Welch, "Coleridge's *Christabel*."
69. Abraham and Torok, "Mourning *or* Melancholia," 126–27.
70. They thus form twin sides of a hermeneutic that appears dialectically to resolve the trauma of Geraldine's abduction by recuperating the breach between Leoline and Lord Roland. This reading sacrifices Geraldine for the sake of patriarchal law by in turn silencing Christabel, and in turn reads various versions of the text as family romance. See esp. Levinson, *The Romantic Fragment Poem*; Welch, "Coleridge's *Christabel*."

71. Abraham and Torok, "Mourning *or* Melancholia," 132.
72. In *The Romantic Unconscious* David Punter argues that the French Revolution unleashed unconscious forces for which Romanticism struggles to find a representation lest it be overwhelmed by the unconscious.
73. Curtis, *The Fenwick Notes of William Wordsworth*, 61.
74. See Hertz, "The Notion of Blockage in the Literature of the Sublime," 40–60.

Chapter Four: De Quincey Terminable and Interminable

1. De Quincey's desire for Wordsworthian validation has been a mainstay of De Quincey biography and criticism, the image of a life lived in the shadow of greatness and stalled by addiction, what John Beer calls a "slow reenactment of Coleridge's career" ("De Quincey and the Dark Sublime," 172). Another version is that De Quincey, also like Coleridge, was divided on Wordsworth. In an 1803 letter he praises the Great Man for the "transcendency of [his] genius" and continues that "to no man on earth except yourself and one other (a friend of yours [Coleridge]), would I thus lowly and suppliantly prostrate myself" (*Recollections*, 385–87). De Quincey met both writers in 1807 and rented Dove Cottage from 1809 until 1821, but by 1820 both friendships were finished. Wordsworth's reply to De Quincey's 1803 letter was polite but distant: "My friendship is not in my power to give: this is a gift which no man can make, it is not in our power: a sound and healthy friendship is the growth of time and circumstance. . . . How many things are there in a man's character of which his writings however miscellaneous or voluminous will give no idea" (De Quincey, *Recollections*, 388–89). On De Quincey's published reminiscences as a case study of Wordsworth that deconstructs De Quincey's own self-representation, see Russett, *De Quincey's Romanticism*, 178–222; Cafarelli, "De Quincey and Wordsworthian Narrative." Of course, De Quincey published on Wordsworth and Coleridge long after 1821. He describes Coleridge as the "largest and most spacious intellect, the subtlest and most comprehensive . . . that has existed among men," but also as "overthrown or threatened with overthrow, . . . by the treachery of his own will" (*WDQ* 10:287, 304). Wordsworth's "attachment to nature," although it "grew out of solitude and the character of his own mind, . . . was indirect and unconscious" in "its mode of growth" (11:77). In the expanded preface to the 1856 *Confessions*, De Quincey corrects Coleridge's premise—that De Quincey took opium largely for pleasure—by turning the tables on Coleridge, even though elsewhere De Quincey states that he "began the use of opium, not as a relief from any bodily pains or nervous irritations, . . . but as a source of luxurious sensations" (10:318).
2. Many writers have suggested the parallel between De Quincey and modern psychoanalysis. See Corrigan, "Interpreting the Uncitable Text," 163; Clej, *A Genealogy of the Modern Self*, 16; Thomas, *Dreams of Authority*, 101; Proud-

fit, "Thomas De Quincey and Sigmund Freud," 89; Maniquis, "The Dark Interpreter and the Palimpsest of Violence," 111.

3. The installments were September and October. They were signed "X.Y.Z."
4. Dated 30 September 1822, the Appendix was reprinted in the December 1822 *London Magazine*.
5. It is also important to note that the bulk of De Quincey's writings appeared in periodicals, a form of publication necessitated by his frequently transient, debt-ridden, and addictive existence. On the tension between serial publication and book-market authorship in the production of *Confessions*, see Russett, *De Quincey's Romanticism*, 92–134.
6. Part One of the 1856 text is commonly titled "Introductory Narration," a title given by David Masson, the editor of the 1890 *The Collected Writings of Thomas De Quincey*. De Quincey himself only appended subtitles to Parts Two and Three, "The Pleasures of Opium" and "The Pains of Opium" respectively. See Masson, *The Collected Writings of Thomas De Quincey*, 3:223n.
7. Most of the pieces that became the Autobiography were written between 1832 and 1841 and expanded upon up to 1852. In 1834 De Quincey also began his recollections of Westmoreland and the Lake District, more broadly focused biographical and autobiographical studies of key intellectual figures in his life. The core of these pieces are the four Lake Papers, which include "Early Memorials of Grasmere," "Samuel Taylor Coleridge," "William Wordsworth," and "William Wordsworth and Robert Southey." Aside from *Suspiria*, De Quincey initiated another two-part series entitled "A Sketch of Childhood," published in 1851–52 in *Hogg's Weekly Instructor*. For *Selections Grave and Gay*, the impetus for which was an earlier Boston edition published with Ticknor, Reid, and Fields (1851–59; 20 volumes), De Quincey reshuffled and recollected these writings as his formal Autobiography. This comprised the first two volumes as "Autobiographic Sketches" and "Autobiographic Sketches, with Recollections of the Lakes." Volume One began with "The Affliction of Childhood—Dream-Echoes of these Infant Experiences—Dream-Echoes Fifty Years Later," reworkings of *Suspiria*'s "The Affliction of Childhood" and "The Apparition of the Brocken." These two volumes now formed part of a larger autobiographical rubric that anticipates De Quincey's expanded version of *Confessions* in Volume Five of the edition. In the 1871 revised edition of sixteen volumes, *Confessions* became the first Volume, usurping the place of the Autobiography, but followed by a revised version of the original Volume Two, now retitled "Recollections of the Lakes and the Lake Poets." The title of the original Volume One was lengthened to "Autobiographic Sketches (the Autobiography in Fifteen Chapters)" and was moved to the penultimate Volume Fourteen before the two supplementary volumes, the last of which opens with *Suspiria*, which had not appeared in the original collected works. Expanded British editions appeared in 1862–63, 1871, and 1878. Masson's *Collected Writings* was the standard, albeit incomplete, edition in fourteen volumes (1889–90) until the recent appearance of *Works of Thomas De Quincey*.

8. De Luca, *Thomas De Quincey*, 118–20.
9. Masson adds one of De Quincey's original 1834 *Tait's Magazine* articles, "Parentage and the Paternal Home," to the beginning of the Autobiography, thus enforcing its Symbolic pattern. He resituates "Autobiographic Sketches" as the first two volumes of the edition, retitled chronologically as "Autobiography from 1785–1803" and ". . . from 1803 to 1808." He calls the new title "less ragged" (*The Collected Writings of Thomas De Quincey*, 1:2) than the original and thus consolidates at the end of the nineteenth century a reaction against the heterogeneity of life-writing initiated in De Quincey's own self-revisions. On the implications of De Quincey's collecting his thoughts by collecting his works, see my "De Quincey Collects Himself."
10. The four instalments were March, April, June, and July 1845. The work begins with an "Introductory Notice" (later titled "Dreaming"). Part 1 includes "The Affliction of Childhood," "The Palimpsest," "Levana and Our Ladies of Sorrow," "The Apparition of the Brocken," the Finale to Part 1, "Savannah-La-Mar," and a few extraneous paragraphs. Part 2, left unfinished, consists of what was later called "The Vision of Life." Alexander H. Japp's 1891–93 edition of *The Posthumous Works of Thomas De Quincey* (4–5) included from De Quincey's manuscript papers his proposed list of sections for the complete work, the bulk of which were never written or have been lost. The recent *Works of Thomas De Quincey* (15:567) transcribes a more modest version of this list.
11. Youngquist, "De Quincey's Crazy Body," 356–57.
12. In "De Quincey Revises His *Confessions*" Ian Jack argues that in 1856 De Quincey "has moved too far in the direction of ordinary autobiography" (146), when it is clear that De Quincey's central desire is to tell the "crowning grace" (*WDQ* 2:101) of his dreams.
13. Against earlier opinions that the 1856 text dilutes the artistic merit of 1821, De Luca argues that the "new material becomes a kind of commentary on the old" (*Thomas De Quincey*, 122) and brings to a manifest conclusion meanings that were only latent in the original text. Jack argues conversely that 1856 digresses too much from the startling effect of 1821, which "[a]s a work of art . . . is much superior to its successor" ("De Quincey Revises His *Confessions*," 145). De Luca valorizes 1856 for its artistic maturity, while Jack recuperates 1821 for its strength of focus. Yet Jack also notes that the 1856 text renders "more marked" the earlier work's "uncertainty of intention" (124) about its own moral instructiveness.
14. Wu, *Romanticism: An Anthology*, 123.
15. Elizabeth Bruss argues that De Quincey's confessional writings transform autobiography into the "transcendental passion of the lyric" (*Autobiographical Acts*, 96), releasing the lyric essence of experience and burning off the dross of the "factual and the individual" to reveal out of "the expressionistic force of autobiography" its "purer subjectivity" (94). Something like *Autobiographical Sketches* is thus "derivative" and "secondary in literary importance" (93) to *Confessions* or especially *Suspiria*. Conversely, see Cafarelli, "De Quincey and Wordsworthian Narrative."

16. This deconstruction is immanent within the 1853 Preface. The second class marks the intermediate ground of reason between the merely historio-descriptive first class and the profoundly visionary third class. However, the excessive or "impassioned" psychosomatic substructure of this classification, which centers around the incommunicable primal scene of the "solitary infant, and its solitary combat with grief—a mighty darkness, and a sorrow without a voice," functions repetitively to unsettle the dialectical remembering and working-through of De Quincey's hierarchical pattern. Autobiography, understanding, and impassioned prose are thus separate signifiers of the subject's identity, yet also collapse into one another by force of the unconscious:

> It is because a man cannot see and measure these mystical forces which palsy him, that he cannot deal with them effectually. If he were able really to pierce the haze which so often envelops, even to himself, his own secret springs of action and reserve, there cannot be a life moving at all under intellectual impulses that would not, through that single force of absolute frankness, fall within the reach of a deep, solemn, and sometimes even of a thrilling interest. (*WDQ* 20:12–13)

17. De Quincey writes: "scarcely one effect in a thousand of all the memorable effects produced by poets, can, upon any theories yet received amongst us, be even imperfectly explained." He continues by stating that poetic identity emerges from the "antimonies of passion—cases of self-conflict, in which the understanding says one thing, the impassioned nature of man says another thing" (11:76–77). Critics have read De Quincey's response to poetry in terms of his inability to surmount Coleridge's and especially Wordsworth's example. See Clej, *A Genealogy of the Modern Self*, 123, 163ff.
18. Alexander H. Japp, *The Posthumous Works of Thomas De Quincey*, 2.
19. De Quincey notes the atavistic nature of Kant's intellect and parallels the dis-ease of his pragmatic anthropology to the disruptive physiological anthropology of the stomach: "The fact is, that, as the stomach has been known . . . to attach not only whatsoever alien body is introduced within it, but also . . . sometimes to attack itself and its own organic structure—so, and with the same preternatural extension of instinct, did Kant carry forward his destroying functions" (*WDQ* 10:299). As I've already discussed in Chapter One, Kant's fascination with mesmerism suggests at the boundary between empiricism and Romanticism the occult presence of material that does not fit our view of either a Kantian or post-Kantian Kant (see Brown, "From the Transcendental to the Supernatural").
20. David Wright, *Recollections of the Lakes and the Lake Poets*, 9.
21. Clej writes, "More like an 'interminable' self-analysis than a rigorous confession, De Quincey's discourse constantly transgresses its own boundaries and meanders away from its course, obliging the interpreter to follow what is often a vanishing trail" (*A Genealogy of the Modern Self*, 20).

22. Ronald R. Thomas writes, "these apologies are also recognitions that his writing is itself a symptom and that his text is the presentation of a case study that requires a kind of talking cure. . . . It records the history of a self inventing the language to describe its private life" (*Dreams of Authority*, 102).
23. Michael Cochise Young writes that De Quincey "seems simultaneously to welcome and divert a dialogue with his implied readers, recognizing in them both a necessary device in the conduct of such interchange and a threat to his narrative and personal autonomy" ("'The True Hero of the Tale,'" 56).
24. De Quincey reads this inability to get beyond the self in Wordsworth's "extreme, intense, unparalleled *onesidedness, (einseitigkeit)*," hence the "defective sympathy in Wordsworth with the universal feelings of his age" and his peculiar lack of empathy (*WDQ* 11:96, 258). *Einseitigkeit* is the antithesis of *Einfuhlung*, which Chapter Two explored as Shaftesburian sympathy. Whereas in this sympathy identity still resides with the sympathetic subject, the German *Einfuhlung* suggests a dislocation of the sympathetic identity into the sphere of the other.
25. De Quincey also establishes a somatic cause of suffering to refute charges of "self-indulgence" (*WDQ* 2:10) that Coleridge most notably levied against him. De Quincey answers this charge at greater length in "Coleridge and Opium-Eating" (1845) and at the beginning of the 1856 "Introductory Narration." For an overview of nineteenth-century cultural constructions of opium see Logan, *Nerves and Narratives*, 76–85; Leask, *British Romantic Writers and the East*, 170–87. John Barrell uses the addictive paradox of opium as both cure and infection—the palliative incorporation of the toxic other to keep one inviolable from its deeper subversion—to read within the historical/cultural/geopolitical imaginary of De Quincey's writings the spiraling tension between narratives of trauma and of reparation. At the center of this struggle is the "synchronic myth [of an uncertain and unspeakable horror] whose different versions are not themselves easily susceptible of narrativization, or not of that sort of narrativization which can distinguish the stages of a case history or the phases of a neurosis" (*The Infection of Thomas De Quincey*, 22–23). See also Leask, who explores how the "anxieties of empire could empower as well as disable the functioning of the imperial will" (*British Romantic Writers and the East*, 222), and Rzepka, *Sacramental Commodities*, which reads De Quincey's authorial struggle for what Foucault calls 'transcendental anonymity' as the sublimation of the materiality of commodity exchange in the dynamics of textual transmission. The sociocultural focus of all four studies either explicitly or implicitly evokes a medicalization of De Quincey as critical subject and, especially in Barrell, Logan, and Leask, a concern with the materialism of medical discourse and thus with the material effects of opium.
26. I read this resistance against the grain of Thomas's insistence that De Quincey, like Freud in *The Interpretation of Dreams*, aligns himself with the "medical profession . . . and presents himself as a case study in which he is both doctor and patient, the 'medical writer' who corrects and augments the

prevailing views of dream experience by writing his own life story into an inquiry about the 'extensive power of this drug' and the meaning of the dreams it provokes" (*Dreams of Authority*, 100–1). Treating Foucault's exploration of the "medicalization of the effects of confession" (67) in *The History of Sexuality* historically rather than genealogically, as part of a Hegelian *Geistesgeschichte* rather than the function of repressive discursive practices, Thomas reads the De Quinceyan "medicalizing [of] the soul" (103) in the mirror of a later Freudian apotheosis of Romantic insights.

27. Peter Logan discusses the de-somatization of De Quincey's narrative as a symptom of nervous narrative, the rising need of the nervous body to talk about itself as a way of transcending itself. In the 1821 *Confessions*, Logan argues, De Quincey claims a false independence from his addictive body. This attempt to "[make] over his *suspiria de machina* into a *suspiria de profundis*" (*Nerves and Narratives*, 75) is complete in 1856, where "De Quincey's new and expanded lectures on the physical properties of opium form a separate [medical] discourse interspersed within the autobiography" (107). This expanded autobiography means that "two-thirds of the narrative elapses before opium comes onto the stage," and the dreams, now wholly aestheticized, "at last float free from the materiality of the body" (108). See Logan 73–108, especially his discussion of the gendering of a conflict between a "'masculine' independence from the physiology of the body and a 'feminine' or 'effeminate' incarceration within it" (93). The issue in De Quincey, I believe, is only one part of the subject's heterogeneous identity. Where Logan reads the aestheticization of the dream as its dissociation from the body, I read how the dream reconceptualizes rather than transcends the mind/body's darkness. For a position sympathetic to Logan's, see Youngquist, "De Quincey's Crazy Body."

28. One sentence outlines De Quincey's life up to 1792: "My father died when I was about seven years old, and left me to the care of four guardians." Three long paragraphs then outline his life up to his departure from Manchester Grammar School in 1802, "from which my whole succeeding life has, in many important points, taken its colouring." Another four paragraphs about his wanderings in North Wales lead to a "latter and fiercer stage" of life that begins in London (*WDQ* 2:13, 15, 21)

29. Beer argues that the pains of opium are an intertext with Coleridge's "The Pains of Sleep" ("De Quincey and the Dark Sublime," 167). See also De Luca's distinction between Wordsworthian pleasure and Coleridgean pains (*Thomas De Quincey*, 16–17).

30. It is likely for this reason that in 1856 De Quincey removed this passage as well as the above description of "Pleasures" as both *l'Allegro* and *Il Penseroso,* the stoic demeanor of the Victorian social subject now untainted by his romantic melancholy.

31. First, his ability voluntarily to imagine things "upon the darkness was very apt to transfer itself to [his] dreams" and "immediately shaped themselves

into phantoms of the eye." Second, all "changes in [his] dreams, were accompanied by deep-seated anxiety and gloomy melancholy, such as are wholly incommunicable by words." Third, the "sense of space, and in the end, the sense of time, were both powerfully affected" and "amplified to an extent of unutterable infinity." Finally, the "minutest incidents of childhood, or forgotten scenes of later years, were often revived," but not so much as to "recollect" them as to "[*recognize*] them instantaneously" or intuitively. This last fact convinces De Quincey that "there [can be] no such thing as *forgetting* possible to the mind," despite the "thousand accidents [that] may, and will interpose a veil between our present consciousness and the secret inscriptions of the mind," a potential remembering of the entire contents of the unconscious that, while impossible, overwhelms De Quincey (*WDQ* 2:66–67). On the parallels between De Quinceyan and Freudian dream theories, see Clej, *A Genealogy of the Modern Self*, 90–111; Maniquis, "The Dark Interpreter and the Palimpsest of Violence," 117–35; McDonagh, "Writings on the Mind"; Proudfit, "Thomas De Quincey and Sigmund Freud," 95–100; Thomas, *Dreams of Authority*, 71–81, 105.

32. "Habitually to dream magnificently, a man must have a constitutional determination to reverie," De Quincey writes in *Suspiria*, and "No man ever will unfold the capacities of his own intellect who does not at least chequer his life with solitude. How much solitude, so much power" (15:130). Later in the text he speaks of the "burthen of solitude, that cleavest to man through every stage of his being" and is "mighty and essential," the "echo of a far deeper solitude through which already he has passed, and of another solitude deeper still, through which he *has* to pass" (15:151).
33. This resolution responds to two circumstances: De Quincey had lost many of his opium dreams, which were to be the "crowning grace" of his narrative, and in the 1821 text he had promised a "revised and enlarged" second edition that would more clearly connect the "necessity" of opium to his "youthful sufferings." He promises this edition just as a "most appalling irritation of the stomach, in all respects the same as that which had caused [him] so much suffering in youth, [was] accompanied by a revival of all the old dreams." Not wanting to "exhaust the reader's patience, by such a detail of my malady . . . as might suffice to establish the fact of my inability to wrestle any longer with irritation and constant suffering," he simply asserts that he again began to take opium daily (2:53–54). This second edition was never written.
34. See Chapter Three, note 14.
35. For Wordsworth the "act of holding a Pen" creates "unpleasant feelings" that evolved from a "derangement" (*WL* 1:453) of his stomach.
36. Leask, *British Romantic Writers*, 172.
37. For brief accounts of De Quincey's writing and publication of *Suspiria*, see Eaton, *Thomas De Quincey*, 427–28n; Lindop, *The Opium-Eater*, 353–358. As Eaton writes, "It is very confusing indeed" (428n). Except for "The Daughter of Lebanon" and *The English Mail-Coach*, intended for *Suspiria*

but published separately (the former as an appendix to the 1856 *Confessions*, the latter in an 1849 issue of *Blackwood's*), De Quincey published nothing of the text after the four 1845 *Blackwood's* installments, and it never appeared in his first collected edition, although it exists in various later incarnations, all truncations of the original. *Suspiria* next appeared in the revised (1871) collected edition (see Note 7). There it included six separate segments: 1) "Dreaming" (previously the "Introductory Notice"); 2) "The Palimpsest of the Human Brain" 3) "Levana and Our Ladies of Sorrow"; 4) "Savannah-la-Mar"; 5) "Vision of Life"; and 6) "Memorial Suspiria." Preferring this later collection to the "clotted confusion" of the original *Blackwood's* text, Masson argues that in "De Quincey's reduction of that heterogeneous [1845] original these pieces are rescued into impressive independence and stand on their own merits" (*The Collected Writings of Thomas De Quincey*, 13:333).

38. Toward the end of *Confessions*, De Quincey, in order to describe what he "saw frequently in sleep" (2:69), cites from *The Excursion* the Solitary's vision of the New Jerusalem: "The appearance, instantaneously disclosed, / Was of a mighty city—boldly say / A wilderness of building, sinking far / And self-withdrawn into a wondrous depth, / Far sinking into splendour—without end!" (*WP* 2.834–38). Where in Wordsworth the passage describes "an appearance actually beheld in the clouds," in De Quincey it suggests a darker imagination.
39. Martin Wallen writes that "De Quincey's body, as the narrative of opium-dream, follows its own architectonic" and, noting how in De Quincey the "fantastic is identical to the somatic," argues that De Quincey's impassioned prose "[emphasizes] the radiance of the body into linguistic spirit," so that through the "*jouissance* of rhetoric [his] body becomes metaphor" ("Body Linguistics in Schreber's *Memoirs* and De Quincey's *Confessions*," 101–5). On the intersection of the psychosomatic with the metaphorical in nineteenth-century philosophy and Romantic poetry, see Woodman, "Nietzsche, Blake, Keats and Shelley: The Making of a Metaphorical Body."
40. De Quincey explains the hybridity of dreams at the end of his much longer vision of Fanny of the Bath Road in 1849, wherein the text psychoanalyzes its own unconscious phenomena. Editing *The English Mail-Coach* in 1854 for Volume Four of *Selections Grave and Gay*, De Quincey removes this passage, replacing the earlier "mighty dial, sculptured with the hours, and with the dreadful legend of TOO LATE" (*WDQ* 16:421) with "sculptured with hours, that mingle with the heavens and the heavenly host" (16:733n). The shift from lost unconscious phenomena to a more contemplative religious frame subdues the disturbing psychic phenomenon of the "vast emblazonry . . . [of] unutterable horrors of monstrous and demoniac natures" to the text's patriotic heraldry of "One heart, one pride, one glory [connecting] every man by the transcendant bond of his English blood" (16:424). Here, the dissenting voices of Romantic interiority's multiple personality are silenced/cured by the monolithic (and Imperialist) ego of the Victorian social subject. See my comment below on the psychic hybridity of De Quinceyan organicism.

41. As Wallen writes of *Confessions*, "we find that what seems temptingly like organicism is actually something that threatens organicism by continually disclosing the dreaminess, the fantasy which must be accepted as the dominant force of this rhetoric" ("Body Linguistics in Schreber's *Memoirs* and De Quincey's *Confessions*," 104). See Snyder, "'The Loom of *Palingenesis*,'" 353 on De Quincey's writing as a critique of Romantic organicism. Barrell describes hybridity in De Quincey as follows: "there is *this* here, and it is different from *that* there, but the difference between them, though in its own way important, is as nothing compared with the difference between the two of them considered together, and that third thing, way over there, which is truly *other* to them both" (*The Infection of Thomas De Quincey*, 10). Thus he explains failed "inoculation" in De Quincey's geopolitical schema: "It never *immunizes* against the infections of the East; at best it enables the patient to shake them off for a time, or gives him the illusion of having done so, but always with the fear that they will return in a more virulent form" (16). Here De Quincey is afraid of the imagination's pathology, which Barrell views negatively. After Hillman, I would argue that pathology is a fundamentally productive psychic condition, which means "the psyche's autonomous ability to create illness, morbidity, disorder, abnormality, and suffering in any aspect of its behaviour and to experience and imagine life through this deformed and afflicted perspective" (Hillman, *Re-Visioning Psychology*, 57). See also Whale's distinction between Wordsworth's spots of time and De Quincey's "anarchic moments," wherein autobiography suggests an "aberrant organic principle" in which a "review of past experience may uncover threads of experience leading out from a seemingly insignificant event" ("De Quincey's Anarchic Moments," 282–89).
42. Krell, *Contagion*, 28.
43. Whale, "De Quincey's Anarchic Moments," 283.
44. De Luca argues that in the "oblique and unpredictable procedures" of the 1821 *Confessions* function "like the displacement technique of dreams, [keeping] the contours of the work's inner life at some distance below its shifting surface" (*Thomas De Quincey*, 13).
45. Kristeva, *Black Sun*, 4,7.
46. Kristeva writes: "if loss, bereavement, and absence trigger the work of the imagination and nourish it permanently as much as they threaten it and spoil it, it is also noteworthy that the work of art as fetish emerges when the activating sorrow has been repudiated" (*Black Sun*, 9).
47. Ibid., 22.
48. Jacobus writes of this passage, "It is as if Wordsworth had broken off from a spot of time to footnote the existence of two consciousnesses" ("The Art of Managing Books," 239).
49. Kristeva, *Black Sun*, 6, 9, 5.
50. When De Quincey moves "Afflictions" to the *Autobiography* in 1853, he removes "the passion of reverie," thus dissociating "religion" and "reverie," "religious feeling" now uncontaminated by the free-associationism of grief that is its phantastic other (15:746n).

51. Caruth, "Introduction," 4.
52. De Luca, *Thomas De Quincey*, 12.
53. De Luca reads in the "multifoliate" forms of De Quincey's visionary writing "the common denominator" or "sensed presence of a giant composite form, at once human and divine, like Blake's universal man, Albion" (*Thomas De Quincey*, 74). Where De Luca reads the "open-endedness of Romantic myth-making" (58) transcendentally, I would explore *Suspiria*'s psychoanalysis as a process of discontinuity and defamiliarization. By attempting to decipher the "mystery of darkness" (88) of his psychic interiority, the text's subject discovers that he is a stranger to himself, forever displaced by the Real of who he is (not).
54. Kristeva, *Black Sun*, 9, 13.
55. These "present Confessions," he writes, follow the pattern of "Levana"'s "dream-legend," which itself "rehearses or prefigures their course. This FIRST part belongs to Madonna. The THIRD belongs to the 'Mater Suspiriorum,' and will be entitled *The Pariah Worlds*. The FOURTH, which terminates the work, belongs to the 'Mater Tenebrarum,' and will be entitled *The Kingdom of Darkness*. As to the SECOND, it is an interpolation requisite to the effect of the others; and will be explained in its proper place" (*WDQ* 15:182n).
56. Kristeva, *Black Sun*, 23.
57. These "capacities" are what in "The Dark Interpreter" De Quincey calls the "creative agencies in every part of human nature" (*WDQ* 15:569).
58. Rajan, *Dark Interpreter*, 244.
59. De Quincey uses the Dark Interpreter on three separate occasions: in "The Apparition of the Brocken," in "Savannah-La-Mar" (which follows "The Apparition" as the Finale to Part One of the original 1845 *Suspiria*), and in a section entitled "The Dark Interpreter," another *Suspiria* text not published until 1891.
60. He is also associated with crime and the will's autonomy. In this respect, the Specter can also be read intertextually with Hogg's *Justified Sinner*, wherein George Colwan is haunted by his anthropomorphized (br)other Robert Wringhim, who leaves Colwan "confounded between the shadow and the substance" (42). De Quincey had met Hogg in 1814 and, like Hogg, published extensively with *Blackwood's*. See my "'the clearest light of reason': Making Sense of Hogg's Body of Evidence."
61. On this point I agree with Maniquis's account of the analytical encounter between the Spectre and the Dark Interpreter. Maniquis reads in this scene the "mirror game" of the "patient as self-interpreter whom the psychoanalyst must interpret," during which the "psychoanalyst must often witness a *cogito* observing some version of his own ego, resisting, testing, accepting its own reflections." The goal of this encounter, for both Freud and De Quincey, argues Maniquis, is the "ideal transparency each interpreter aims at," wherein the "'hidden' in De Quincey and the 'unconscious' in Freud disappear, its spatiality given over to the mirrored self in dialogue with

itself." The clearing of the mists from the Spectre imitates this moment of "imagined transparency," whereas the Dark Interpreter can then "speak the question of whence the violence cast upon the sufferer" ("The Dark Interpreter and the Palimpsest of Violence," 117–19). Revisioning the terms of Maniquis's account, I argue that by remaining interpolated through the representative "mists" of narrative, the Dark Interpreter, as the analyst reading the analysand's suffering, also repeats this suffering as analysand through the pathology of an imagination that reproduces rather than alleviates suffering in new forms.

62. In "The Affliction of Childhood" De Quincey describes this power in adulthood through the metaphor of the "aerial composing stick" of his unconscious as it functions, in "darkness and solitude," both within and against his will (*WDQ* 15:153).

63. In the Preface to the 1856 text De Quincey calls "The Daughter of Lebanon" the only dream to survive the "sudden conflagration" in his study. He has "intentionally placed it at the end [of the revised *Confessions*], as appropriately closing a record in which the case of poor Ann the Outcast . . . , more than any other, coloured—or (more truly I should say) shaped, moulded and remoulded, composed and decomposed—the great body of opium dreams" (*WDQ* 2:102).

64. Ironically, the 1856 text allegorizes Anne as "poor Anne the Outcast," now a stable and objectified figure of interpretation, which curtails the repetitiveness and interminability of her psychosomatic presence in the earlier text.

65. Logan, *Nerves and Narratives*, 108.

66. Joel D. Black argues this "*decomposition*" of *Suspiria* "seems to have been motivated by a desire to refine and crystallize both his confessional narrative and his digressive prose fantasies into the pure, irreducible form of dream fantasy, . . . opening up a space for a radically different discourse without subject matter and without subjects (speakers, thinkers, even dreamers)—in short, a pure discourse of dream" ("Confession, Digression, Gravitation," 318–19).

67. De Quincey's 1853 ordering of the Autobiography itself suggests an inability to make self-writing conform to a developmental structure. The three subsections of Chapter Two are meant to form a coherent unity under the general title of "Affliction," the termination of which is confirmed in the opening line of the next chapter, "Introduction to the World of Strife": "So, then, one chapter in my life had finished" (*WDQ* 19:22). The isolation of the dream-text, however, only serves to highlight the disruption between autobiography and confession. Here the dream exists against the heterogeneous work of psychoanalysis as empirical evidence within an instructive or pragmatic anthropology of the moral/philosophical subject.

68. Foucault, "Nietzsche, Genealogy, History," 81. Foucault's reading of Nietzschean genealogy is central to Clej's study of De Quincey as a post-Romantic "modernist *avant la lettre*" (*A Genealogy of the Modern Self*, 1). Clej draws upon Foucault's idea of the self's "empty synthesis" as moving beyond

Romantic self-expression to evoke a palimpsestic or "literary self" who emerges purely from the "network of discursive practices behind this formation" (115).

69. "Five or six," De Quincey continues, ". . . were burned in a sudden conflagration which arose from the spark of a candle falling unobserved amongst a very large pile of papers in a bedroom, when I was alone and reading" (*WDQ* 2:102).
70. "Affliction" was written in 1834 and later appropriated for *Suspiria*. De Quincey suggests in his 1853 General Preface that the Sketches have a "mixed character" (*WDQ* 20:12).

Chapter Five: Keats and the Burden of Interminability

1. Keats moves quickly beyond Wordsworth. In February 1818 he writes: "are we to be bullied into a certain Philosophy engendered in the whims of an Egotist . . . We hate poetry that has palpable design upon us. . . . I will have no more of Wordsworth" (*KL* 60–61). He does not appear to shed Milton's influence until September 1819, when he gave up writing *The Fall of Hyperion*: "I have given up Hyperion [for *The Fall*]—there were too many Miltonic inversions in it" (292). In another letter he writes, "I prefer the native music of [Chatterton's language] to Milton's cut by feet I have but lately stood on my guard against Milton. Life to him would be death to me. Miltonic verse cannot be written but [in] the vein of art—I wish to devote myself to another sensation" (325–26).
2. I am indebted here and elsewhere in this chapter to Rajan's account of the dialogue between Apollo and Dionysus in Keats. See *Dark Interpreter* 97–142, 143–203.
3. Transgressing the boundary between poetry and prose, description and psychoanalysis, the writing of poetry and the writing of prose are frequently collapsed as part of the same self-writing discourse in Keats's letters, most famously in his letter to J. H. Reynolds of 25 March 1818. The letters, through which Keats self-observes his imaginative life, have a cognitive value for his poetry different from the abortive relationship between Coleridge's published prose and his poetry. The letters comment directly upon, or often develop insights in advance of, his poetry. Keats talks to himself through the silent mediation of the addressee, and the letters offer a case study of the development of his psychic interiority as he confronts the psyche within his poetry itself.
4. Julie Carlson argues that "Romanticism . . . narrates English literary history in the form of romance, through a renunciation of romance . . ." Fancy "propels English literary history on its march toward enlightenment through renunciation of the magic, excess, and wonder of romance" while also "identif[ying] part of what we desire from art—less the transport out or transcendence of time associated with romantic aesthetics than access to the

lawlessness of infancy, the lack of distinction between person and thing, wish and reality" ("Fancy's History," 8).

5. Butler, *Gender Trouble*, 31.
6. Ibid., 141.
7. Ibid., 30–31.
8. On 'masculine' Romanticism and the masculine *in* Romanticism, see Mellor, *Gender and Romanticism*; Ross, *The Contours of Masculine Desire*.
9. Although, early in his letters Keats also expresses a nostalgia for the resolutions of philosophy: "What a happy thing it would be if we could settle our thoughts, make our minds up on any matter in five Minutes and remain content—that is to build a sort of mental Cottage of feelings quiet and pleasant—to have a sort of Philosophical Back Garden" (*KL* 77).
10. "O, never will the prize, / High reason, . . . / Be my award! Things cannot to the will / Be settled, but they tease us out of thought," Keats writes in "To J. H. Reynolds" (*KP* 74–77).
11. As Nietzsche writes, "Apollo [is] the transfiguring genius of the *principium individuationis* through which alone the redemption in illusion is truly to be obtained; while by the mystical triumphant cry of Dionysus the spell of individuation is broken" (*BT* 99). And again, "Thus the Apollonian tears us out of the Dionysian universality and lets us find delight in individuals, . . . the Apollonian *illusion* whose influence aims to deliver us from the Dionysian flood and excess" (128–29).
12. Keats defines this radical de-centering of self as a type of negative empathy:

    > When I am in a room with People if I ever am free from speculating on creations of my own brain, then not myself goes home to myself: but the identity of every one in the room begins to to [sic] press upon me that, I am in a very little time anhilated [sic]. (*KL* 158)

13. In "Ode to Psyche," written in the same month that he finally put aside *Hyperion*, Keats enshrines Psyche, the "latest born and loveliest vision far / Of all Olympus' faded hierarchy" (24–25), in "some untrodden region of [his] mind" (51), thereby staging the psychic determinism of the mind of mythology as the self-making potentiality of its own "working brain" (60).
14. Hillman, *Re-Visioning Psychology*, 7, 101.
15. Hillman explains between allegory and psychology the difference between seeing myths as "the instruments of reason rather than the very forms that organize reason." This is the tendency to "poeticize" the pathology of the god expressed by myth. Myths, treated allegorically, are the "*defensive reaction of the rational mind against the full power of the soul's irrational personifying propensity*" (*Re-Visioning Psychology*, 8). Endymion's endless search for his dream's beautiful truth is precisely this reaction against the dream's sublime "propensity." In *Endymion* Keats comes to understand how allegory, as the instrument of reason, is deconstructed by its own psychology or poetry. Keats reconceives allegory *un*poetically. Life, he writes, is a "continual allegory," the

"Mystery" of which "very few eyes can see": "Shakspeare [sic] led a life of Allegory; his works are the comments on it" (*KL* 218). Keatsian allegory suggests, at the intersection between self-making and psychic determinism, an interminable process through which the "poetical" nature of one's works "organize," to use Hillman's word, the "figurative" nature of the "unpoetical" process by which allegory unfolds as part of a broader life experience. Hillman writes, "myths offer the multiplicity of meanings inherent in our lives, while theology and science attempt singleness of meaning. . . . Polytheistic consciousness is ever reminded by myth of the ambiguity of meanings and the multiplicity of persons in each event in each moment" (158).

16. Bewell, "Keats's 'Realm of Flora,'" 92. In "Keats and the Manhood of the Poet," Susan Wolfson writes: "More than any other male Romantic, Keats writes from an intense intersection of creative genius and adolescent uncertainty. The result is to disrupt any unified syntax of 'masculine'" (2).
17. Ibid., 91.
18. Psychoanalysis, writes Jung, is an "intense suffering, a passion of the soul, but not a disease of the mind" ("The Psychology of the Transference," 187).
19. Keats is looking past *Endymion*, written April–November 1817 and published in May 1818, the idea of which he abandoned even before completing the poem. In September 1817 he writes, "I am tired of it and think the time would be better spent in writing a new Romance" (*KL* 25).
20. Keats wrote *Endymion* between April and November 1817. He wrote *Hyperion* between September and December 1818 and had abandoned the poem altogether by April 1819. *The Fall of Hyperion* was written between July and September 1819 and subsequently abandoned. That Keats wrote prolifically and brilliantly during this time is commonplace. His rapid acquisition of a competent poetic vocabulary suggests an equal desire to move rapidly beyond or *beneath* poetry's vernacular.
21. Baldwin's *Pantheon* (1806), one of Keats's early nineteenth-century sources for Greek mythology, describes Endymion as a "great astronomer . . . [who] passed whole nights upon mount Latmos contemplating the heavenly bodies" (cited in Barnard 705).
22. Sperry, *Keats the Poet*, 98, 116.
23. The editor of Keats's *Poems* notes how the account of Pan in Lemprière's *Bibliotheca Classica*, another of Keats's sources on mythology, "reflects Pan's uncertain position in classical mythology" (*KP* 713).
24. Sperry, *Keats the Poet*, 95.
25. Bennett, *Keats, Narrative, and Audience*, 72, 73, 78.
26. Although it is Keats's one completed long poem, *Endymion* is, Sperry notes, "labyrinthine and overgrown" (*Keats the Poet*, 90).
27. Rajan notes that Keats's "early poems almost programmatically sketch out instructions for the poet to follow: subjects to cover (in "I Stood Tip-Toe") and career paths to pursue (in "Sleep and Poetry")" ("Keats, Poetry, and the Absence of the Work," 336).

28. On Keats's use of 'invention' as distinct from 'imagination, see Bennett, *Keats, Narrative, and Audience*, 72–73.
29. In *Keats the Poet* Sperry notes that the plot of the story is predetermined by the Endymion myth itself, so that Keats's imaginative pursuit of his theme, the allegory of his self-analysis while pursuing the story's plot, defines the text's progress (100).
30. The term is Patricia Parker's. Parker writes:

> romance, while it intensifies one aspect of place—its numen or mystery—also unfixes the boundaries and clear dividing lines between places, creating, paradoxically, a heightened sense of the possibility of trespass. Keats's concept of Negative Capability unfixes the boundaries of the self, and, paradoxically, makes the possibility of trespass more terrifying. Filling other bodies is part of a delightful *Einfuhlung*, a wandering at will, but it also involves a trespass upon outer space which may invite, as part of a deadly compact, a violation in return. . . . *Einfuhlung* in Keats is a need as well as a capacity, and his preoccupation with the housing of the imagination continues a deep romance fear, that this Protean flexibility—the ability to assume identities at will—implies a more threatening absence of identity, its—complete dissolution. ("Keats," 115–17)

Here "need" suggests an unconscious desire different from "capacity," which measures the subject's more conscious "Protean flexibility." Hence, the *Einfuhlung* of Negative Capability threatens stable boundaries, while it also comprises within this disintegration a type of imaginative potentiality.

31. Responding to readings of the text's incoherencies as erotic fantasy, Sperry asks: "is it rather a chain of daydreams and reveries, best interpreted as a psychiatrist interprets the free associations of a patient and useful primarily for what it reveals concerning the quality of Keats's unconscious life?" (*Keats the Poet*, 93).
32. The Pleasure Thermometer moves from the physical sensations of nature to the "chief intensity" of "love and friendship," which "sits high upon the forehead of humanity" (802) and makes "Men's being mortal, immortal" (1.800–2, 844).
33. Butler, *Gender Trouble*, 11.
34. See Butler's critique of Kristeva's 'body politics' in *Gender Trouble*, 79–93.
35. Readers locate the text's dissatisfaction with epic in its generic or narrative stasis. Figured as monoliths in ruin, the Titans "encumber the text itself . . . and immobilize the undeviating march of narrative" (Aske, *Keats and Hellenism*, 92). Or, moving from epic in the first text to dream vision in the second marks the shift from a narrative of sculptural classical blindness to one of picturesque Romantic insight, *The Fall*'s "scenic education" organizing "the education of the narrator" (Goslee, *Uriel's Eye*, 98). One view sees

epic obstructing the temporality of narrative, while the other sees it offering the wrong narrative vehicle to express the temporality of self-discovery. Between the idea of *Hyperion* as an "epitaph to its own fragmentation" (Aske, 94) or a "static and stony" (Goslee, 96) frustration of narrative, I read the Titans as contemplative subjects destabilized by trauma, a contemplation that in *The Fall* turns to psychoanalysis.

36. Kristeva, *Powers of Horror*, 47, 4, 208, 27.
37. Laplanche and Pontalis, *The Language of Psycho-Analysis*, 486.
38. Kristeva, *Black Sun*, 6, 9.
39. In "Mourning and Melancholia" Freud does not see melancholy as productive and sees mourning as necessary to the healthy ego, for melancholia, in its most extreme form, can lead to psychosis, the retention of the lost object as if it were alive. Kristeva revises this position in *Black Sun* to see melancholy's productiveness. Rajan argues that the work of melancholy in *The Fall* is part of its "cultural responsiveness" ("Keats, Poetry, and the Absence of the Work," 349), its attempt to signify that which escapes the use-value of history.
40. Little, *Keats as a Narrative Poet*, 140.
41. Rajan, *The Supplement of Reading*, 308.
42. Oceanus similarly asks the "fallen tribe" if they have seen their conqueror's face, which forced Oceanus to "bid sad farewell / To all [his] empire" (2.238). That his question is both interrogative and rhetorical, however, leaves the process undecided.
43. Logan, *Nerves and Narratives*, 24.
44. Coelus will later also implore Hyperion to return "To the earth!" (1.345).
45. Endymion hears "echoing from these shells" (*KP* 2.913) his "silent thoughts" that are also the "dying swells / Of noises far away" (2.914–15).
46. Like Hyperion as he pejoratively names "the rebel Jove" (1.249) an "infant thunderer," Enceladus calls Clymene's speech "baby-words" (2.314). Both phrases implicitly disclose a semiotic potency that the Titans defend against recognizing. Enceladus's statement is especially telling as he is, according to Lemprière, "'the most powerful of all the giants who conspired against Jupiter'" (cited in Barnard 705).
47. Similarly, the figures who precede Mnemosyne are also rem(a)inders of a prior analytical identity always already destabilized by its countertransference with Saturn/Hyperion as "King" (1.52; 2.184), "god" (2.110), or "father" (2.252).
48. Books One and Two, for instance, alternate between their narratives "in the self-same beat" (2.1).
49. An earlier criticism treats the fragments as privileged artifacts or elides them into twin supplements of the same project, the failure of one antithetically justifying the success of the other. See Wasserman, *The Subtler Language*, 10; Muir, "The Meaning of 'Hyperion'"; Bostetter, *The Romantic Ventriloquists*, 8–9. See Levinson, *The Romantic Fragment Poem*, 167–73 for a deft critical

history of the poems. She locates the poems prosthetically within a postorganicist "system of revision" (174). Many readers, both explicitly and implicitly, adopt the rubric of psychoanalysis and read the poems through the narrative of a loss of (textual) omnipotence, moving from the illusion of narcissism toward a later shattering of this illusion. See Levinson, *The Romantic Fragment Poem*, 107–87; de Man, "Keats"; Parker, "Keats"; Schapiro, *The Romantic Mother*, 54–60; Bloom, *Poetry and Repression*, 112–42. Recent critics such as Levinson (in *Keats's Life of Allegory)* and Roe (*Keats and History*) attempt to return the poet to his original social and cultural milieu. See Scott, "Introduction." As Rajan argues, however, this trend "historicizes [Keats] without crediting Keats himself with any understanding of the poet's relationship to 'history'" ("Keats, Poetry, and the Absence of the Work," 334).

50. In *Keats, Narrative, and Audience*, Bennett reads this figure symptomatically through Keats's "anxiety of the audience" (12), so that the "'posthumous life of writing'" (8) becomes inextricably bound up with the "'posthumous life of reading'": "*Hyperion* figures death as a pre-condition for inspiration, . . . a mortal creativity, . . . [whereas *The Fall*] is crucially concerned to figure *reading* as an activity irreducibly bound up with death" (151). See Bennett 1–14, 144–158. Rajan's *Supplement of Reading* reads Keats's 'life of writing/reading' as a more productive process. See also Rajan's review of Bennett. Both are prefigured in Woodman's reading of the negativity/productivity of the future reader:

> In his revision of *Hyperion* [Keats's] hand holding a pen becomes the conscience of the reader. "Whether the dream now purpos'd to rehearse," Keats writes addressing his future readers, "Be poet's or fanatics will be known / When this warm scribe my hand is in the grave." It will be known, that is, when the reader reaches out to take hold of Keats's "scribe" to make a writing of his or her reading, constructing or deconstructing in the process a revisionary text. ("Romanticism and Reading," 7)

51. Dominick La Capra, *Soundings in Critical Theory*, 35. Offering a somewhat different version of narrative in psychoanalysis, Peter Brooks argues that the text submits to the "timelessness of the unconscious," which it contains but "cannot wholly subdue" (*Psychoanalysis and Storytelling*, 156).
52. Brooks, "Fictions of the Wolfman," 77.
53. Within the larger revisionary site of the *Hyperions*, this insistence is mobilized by the temporal contingencies of their narrative disruptions, by Keats's attenuated revisions, and by the indeterminate status of the text's future reader. Bennett, paraphrasing Gerald Prince, accounts for the textual unconscious of *Hyperion* through the trope of the "'disnarrated'" (147), through which the text's narrative suggests in a "'negative or hypothetical mode'" (147) what it has the potential to say but must suppress at the moment of its present telling.

54. I am here paraphrasing Jung's distinction between individuation and individualism, where the former means the "gradual differentiation" of the subject's "functions and faculties," while the latter valorizes the particularity of the ego's selfhood (*CWJ* 17:174). As Hillman paraphrases Jung, "*If the fundamental principle of psychological life is differentiation, then no single perspective can embrace psychological life*" (*Re-Visioning Psychology*, 88).
55. Moi, *Sexual/Textual Politics*, 170.
56. Bewell, "Keats's 'Realm of Flora,'" 73.
57. See Gelley, *Narrative Crossings*, 159–68. 'Scene' involves the idea of the Lacanian gaze, in which visibility does not coincide with consciousness and the *cogito*, and the Heideggerian notion of *Schein* or "showing," which is simultaneously revelatory and illusory. On the tension between illusion and reality, surface and depth in Keats, see Rajan, *Dark Interpreter*, 97–142. Rajan argues that Keats puts forth "an art that recognizes itself as simultaneously the projection of a realm of appearance and beauty, and (in Nietzsche's words) the 'annihilation of concrete semblances' through the disclosure of what lies behind them" (127). Hence Keats "points toward an art in which knowledge of the depth does not overwhelm the surface, but in which the surface is no longer a barrier to such knowledge" (142).
58. The fuller passage speaks of "Idea of all our Passions as of Love [as] all in their sublime, creative of essential Beauty" (*KL* 37). While the context suggests the redemptive, transcendental power of Beauty, that 'Ideas' and 'Love' 'create' Beauty, rather than express its essential being, suggests a subversion of essentialism that will play out in Keats's later poetry.
59. Nietzsche writes,

> the Apollonian illusion reveals itself as what it really is—the veiling during the performance of the tragedy of the real Dionysian effect; but the latter is so powerful that it ends by forcing the Apollonian drama itself into a sphere where it begins to speak with Dionysian wisdom and even denies itself and its Apollonian visibility. Thus the intricate relation of the Apollonian and the Dionysian in tragedy may really be symbolized by a fraternal union of the two deities: Dionysus speaks the language of Apollo; and Apollo, finally the language of Dionysus. (*BT* 130)

BIBLIOGRAPHY

Abraham, Nicholas. "Notes on the Phantom: A Complement to Freud's Metapsychology." In *The Shell and the Kernel: Renewals of Psychoanalysis*. By Nicholas Abraham and Maria Torok. Vol. 1. Edited and translated by Nicholas T. Rand. Chicago: University of Chicago Press, 1994. 171–76.

Abraham, Nicholas, and Maria Torok. "Mourning *or* Melancholia: Introjection *versus* Incorporation." In *The Shell and the Kernel*. 125–38.

———. "'The Lost Object–Me': Notes on Endocryptic Identification." In *The Shell and the Kernel*. 139–56.

Abrams, M. H. "The Correspondent Breeze." In *English Romantic Poets: Modern Essays in Criticism*. Edited by M. H. Abrams. London: Oxford University Press, 1960. 37–54.

———. *Natural Supernaturalism: Tradition and Revolution in Romantic Literature*. New York: Norton, 1971.

Adams, Michael Vannoy. "Deconstructive Philosophy and Imaginal Psychology: Comparative Perspectives on Jacques Derrida and James Hillman." In *Jungian Literary Criticism*. Edited by Richard P. Sugg. Evanston, Ill.: Northwestern University Press, 1992. 231–48.

Althusser, Louis. "Freud and Lacan." In *Lenin and Philosophy and Other Essays*, translated by Ben Brewster. London: New Left Books, 1971. 177–202.

Arnold, Matthew. "The Function of Criticism at the Present Time." In *Poetry and Criticism of Matthew Arnold*. Edited by A. Dwight Culler. Boston: Houghton Mifflin, 1961. 237–58.

Aske, Martin. *Keats and Hellenism: An Essay*. Cambridge: Cambridge University Press, 1985.

Barnard, John, ed. *The Complete Poems*. By John Keats. 2nd. ed. Hammondsworth: Penguin, 1973; rpt. 1977.

Barrell, John. *The Infection of Thomas De Quincey: A Psychopathology of Imperialism*. New Haven, Conn.: Yale University Press, 1991.

———. *Imagining the King's Death: Figurative Treason, Fantasies of Regicide, 1793–1796*. Oxford: Oxford UP, 2000.

Beer, John. "De Quincey and the Dark Sublime: The Wordsworth-Coleridge Ethos." In *Thomas De Quincey: Bicentenary Studies*. Edited by Robert Lance Snyder. Norman: University of Oklahoma Press, 1985. 164–98.

Bennett, Andrew. *Keats, Narrative, and Audience: The Posthumous Life of Writing*. Cambridge: Cambridge University Press, 1994.

Bernheimer, Charles, and Claire Kahane, eds. *In Dora's Case: Freud–Hysteria–Feminism*. 2nd edition. New York: Columbia University Press, 1990.

Bewell, Alan. "Keats's 'Realm of Flora'." In *New Romanticisms: Theory and Critical Practice*. Edited by David L. Clark and Donald C. Goellnicht. Toronto: University of Toronto Press, 1994. 71–100.

Bialostosky, Don. *Making Tales: The Poetics of Wordsworth's Narrative Experiments*. Chicago: University of Chicago Press, 1994.

Bishop, Jonathan. "Wordsworth and the 'Spots of Time'." *English Literary History* 26 (1959): 45–65.

Black, Joel D. "Confession, Digression, Gravitation: Thomas De Quincey's German Connection." In *Thomas De Quincey: Bicentenary Studies*. 308–37.

Bloom, Harold. *The Visionary Company: A Reading of English Romantic Poetry*. Ithaca, N.Y.: Cornell University Press, 1971.

———. "The Internalization of Quest Romance." In *The Ringers in the Tower: Studies in Romantic Tradition*. Chicago: University of Chicago Press, 1971. 13–35.

———. *Poetry and Repression: Revisionism from Blake to Stevens*. New York: Yale University Press, 1976.

———. *Agon: Towards a Theory of Revisionism*. New York: Oxford University Press, 1982.

———. *The Western Canon: The Books and School of the Ages*. New York: Harcourt Brace, 1994.

Bollas, Christopher. *The Shadow of the Object: Psychoanalysis and the Unthought Known*. New York: Columbia University Press, 1987.

Borch-Jacobsen, Mikkel. *The Freudian Subject*. Translated by Catherine Porter. Stanford, Calif.: Stanford University Press, 1988.

———. *Lacan: The Absolute Master*. Translated by Douglas Brick. Stanford, Calif.: Stanford University Press, 1990.

———. "The alibis of the subject: Lacan and philosophy." In *Speculations after Freud: Psychoanalysis, philosophy and culture*. Edited by Sonu Shamdasani and Michael Münchow. London: Routledge, 1994. 77–96.

Bostetter, Edward E. *The Romantic Ventriloquists: Wordsworth, Coleridge, Shelley, Keats, Byron*. Seattle: University of Washington Press, 1975.

Bracher, Mark. "Ideology and Audience Response to Death in Keats's 'To Autumn'." *Studies in Romanticism* 29 (1990): 633–55.

Brooks, Peter. "Fictions of the Wolf-Man: Freud and Narrative Understanding." *Diacritics* (Spring 1979): 72–81.

———. *Reading for the Plot: Design and Intention in Narrative*. New York: A. Knopf, 1984.

———. "The Idea of a Psychoanalytic Literary Criticism." In *Discourse in Psychoanalysis and Literature*. Edited by Shlomith Rimmon-Kenan. London: Methuen, 1987. 1–18.

———. *Psychoanalysis and Storytelling*. Oxford: Blackwell, 1994.

———. *Troubling Confessions: Speaking Guilt in Law and Literature*. Chicago: University of Chicago Press, 2000.

Brown, Marshall. "From the Transcendental to the Supernatural: Kant and the Doctors." In *Self-Conscious Art: A Tribute to John W. Kronik*. Edited by Susan L. Fischer. Lewisburg, Pa.: Bucknell University Press, 1995. 151–69.

Browning, Robert. *The Poems, Volume I*. Edited by John Pettigrew. Supp. and Comp. by Thomas J. Collins. New York: Penguin, 1981.

Bruhm, Steven. *Gothic Bodies: The Politics of Pain in Romantic Fiction*. Philadelphia: University of Pennsylvania Press, 1994.

Bruss, Elizabeth. *Autobiographical Acts: The Changing Situation of a Literary Genre*. Baltimore, Md.: Johns Hopkins University Press, 1976.

Buell, Lawrence. "The Question of Form in Coleridge's *Biographia Literaria*." *English Literary History* 46 (1979): 399–417.

Butler, James, ed. The Ruined Cottage *and* The Pedlar. By William Wordsworth. Ithaca, N.Y.: Cornell University Press, 1979.

Butler, Judith. *Gender Trouble: Feminism and the Subversion of Identity*. New York: Routledge, 1990.

———. *The Psychic Life of Power: Theories in Subjectivity*. Stanford, Calif.: Stanford University Press, 1997.

Cafarelli, Annette Wheeler. "De Quincey and Wordsworthian Narrative." *Studies in Romanticism* 28 (1989): 121–47.

Carlson, Julie. "Fancy's History." *European Romantic Review* 14 (June 2003): 163–76.

Caruth, Cathy. *Empirical Truths and Critical Fictions: Locke, Wordsworth, Kant, Freud*. Baltimore, Md.: Johns Hopkins University Press, 1991.

———. "Introduction." *Trauma: Explorations in Memory*. Edited by Cathy Caruth. Baltimore, Md.: Johns Hopkins University Press, 1996. 3–12.

———. *Unclaimed Experience: Trauma, Narrative, and History*. Baltimore, Md.: Johns Hopkins University Press, 1996.

Castle, Terry. *The Female Thermometer: Eighteenth-Century Culture and the Invention of the Uncanny*. New York: Oxford University Press, 1995.

Cavell, Stanley. "Freud and Philosophy: A Fragment." *Critical Inquiry* 13 (1987): 386–93.

Chapelle, Daniel. *Nietzsche and Psychoanalysis*. Albany: State University of New York Press, 1993.

Chase, Cynthia. *Decomposing Figures: Rhetorical Readings in the Romantic Tradition*. Baltimore, Md.: Johns Hopkins University Press, 1986.

Christensen, Jerome. *Coleridge's Blessed Machine of Language*. Ithaca, N.Y.: Cornell University Press, 1981.

———. "Philosophy/Literature: The Associationist Precedent for Coleridge's Later Poems." In *Philosophical Approaches to Literature: New Essays on Nine-*

teenth- and Twentieth-Century Texts. Edited by William E. Cain. Lewisburg, Pa.: Bucknell University Press, 1984. 27–50.

Clarke, J. J. *In Search of Jung: Historical and Philosophical Enquiries*. New York: Routledge, 1992.

Clej, Alina. *A Genealogy of the Modern Self: Thomas De Quincey and the Intoxication of Writing*. Stanford, Calif.: Stanford University Press, 1995.

Coburn, Kathleen. *Experience into Thought*. Toronto: University of Toronto Press, 1979.

———, ed. *Inquiring Spirit: A New Presentation of Coleridge from His Published and Unpublished Prose Writings*. 1951. Toronto: University of Toronto Press, 1979.

Coleridge, Samuel Taylor. *Collected Letters of Samuel Taylor Coleridge*. Edited by Earle Leslie Griggs. 6 vols. Oxford: Clarendon Press, 1956–1971.

———. *The Collected Notebooks of Samuel Taylor Coleridge*. Edited by Kathleen Coburn and Merton Christensen. 4 vols. New York: Bollingen Series: Pantheon Books, 1957–1990.

———. *The Friend*. Edited by Barbara E. Rooke. In *The Collected Works of Samuel Taylor Coleridge*. Vol. 4.1–2. Princeton, N.J.: Princeton University Press, 1969.

———. *Marginalia*. Edited by H. J. Jackson and George Whalley. In *The Collected Works of Samuel Taylor Coleridge*. Vol. 12.1–6. General editor Kathleen Coburn. Princeton, N.J.: Princeton University Press, 1980–2001.

———. *Poetical Works*. Edited by Ernest Hartley Coleridge. 1912. Oxford: Oxford University Press, 1980.

———. *Biographia Literaria; or Biographical Sketches of My Literary Life and Opinions*. Edited by James Engell and W. Jackson Bate. Princeton, N.J.: Princeton University Press, 1983.

———. *Lectures 1808–1819 on Literature I*. Edited by R. A. Foakes. In *The Collected Works of Samuel Taylor Coleridge*. Vol. 5.1. General editor Kathleen Coburn. Princeton, N.J.: Princeton University Press, 1987.

———. *Table Talk*. Edited by Carl Woodring. In *The Collected Works of Samuel Taylor Coleridge*. Vol. 14.1–2. Princeton, N.J.: Princeton University Press, 1990.

———. *Coleridge's* Ancient Mariner: *An Experimental Edition of Texts and Revisions 1798–1828*. Edited by Martin Wallen. Foreword by Donald Ault. Barrytown, N.Y.: Station Hill, 1993.

Cooper, Anthony Ashley. "On Enthusiasm." In *The Portable Enlightenment Reader*. Edited by Isaac Kramnick. New York: Penguin, 1995. 90–95.

Copleston, Frederick. "Schopenhauer and Nietzsche." In *Schopenhauer: His Philosophical Achievement*. Edited by Michael Fox. Sussex, U.K.: The Harvester Press, 1980. 215–25.

Corngold, Stanley. "On Death and the Contingency of Criticism: Schopenhauer and de Man." In *Intersections: Nineteenth-Century Philosophy and Contemporary Theory*. Edited by Tilottama Rajan and David L. Clark. Albany: State University of New York Press.

Corrigan, Timothy. "Interpreting the Uncitable Text: The Literary Criticism of Thomas De Quincey." In *Ineffability: Naming the Unnamable from Dante to Beckett*. Edited by Peter S. Hawkins and Anne Howland Schotter. New York: AMS Press, 1984. 131–46.

Crabtree, Adam. *From Mesmer to Freud: Magnetic Sleep and the Roots of Psychological Healing*. New Haven, Conn.: Yale University Press, 1993.

Culler, Jonathan. "Textual Self-Consciousness and The Textual Unconscious." *Style* 18 (1984): 369–76.

Cunningham, Andrew, and Nicholas Jardine. "Introduction: The Age of Reflexion." *Romanticism and the Sciences*. Edited by Andrew Cunningham and Nicholas Jardine. Cambridge: Cambridge University Press, 1990. 1–9.

Curtis, Jared, ed. *The Fenwick Notes of William Wordsworth*. London: Bristol Classical Press, 1993.

Darlington, Beth. "Two Early Texts: *A Night-Piece* and *The Discharged Soldier*." In *Bicentenary Wordsworth Studies*. Edited by Jonathan Wordsworth. Ithaca, N.Y.: Cornell University Press, 1970. 425–48.

———, ed. Home at Grasmere*: Part First, Book First of* The Recluse. By William Wordsworth. Ithaca, N.Y.: Cornell University Press, 1977.

Darnton, Robert. *Mesmerism and the End of the Enlightenment in France*. Cambridge, Mass.: Harvard University Press, 1968.

Deleuze, Gilles. *Kant's Critical Philosophy*. Translated by Hugh Tomlinson and Barbara Habberjam. Minneapolis: University of Minnesota Press, 1984.

De Luca, V. A. *Thomas De Quincey: The Prose of Vision*. Toronto: University of Toronto Press, 1980.

de Man, Paul. *Allegories of Reading*. New Haven, Conn.: Yale University Press, 1979.

———. "The Rhetoric of Temporality." In *Blindness and Insight*. 1971. Minneapolis: University of Minnesota Press, 1983. 187–228.

———. "Anthropomorphism and Trope in the Lyric." In *The Rhetoric of Romanticism*. 239–62.

———. "Autobiography as De-Facement." In *The Rhetoric of Romanticism*. 67–82.

———. "The Intentional Structure of the Romantic Image." In *The Rhetoric of Romanticism*. New York: Columbia University Press, 1984. 1–17.

———. "Keats: The Negative Road." In *English Romantic Poets*. Edited by Harold Bloom. New York: Chelsea, 1986. 343–61.

De Quincey, Thomas. *The Posthumous Works of Thomas De Quincey*. Edited by Alexander H. Japp. London: William Heinemann, 1891.

———. *Works of Thomas De Quincey*. Edited by Grevel Lindop et al. London: Pickering and Chatto, 2000–2003.

Derrida, Jacques. *Resistances of Psychoanalysis*. Translated by Peggy Kamuf, Pascale-Anne Brault, and Micheal Naas. Stanford, Calif.: Stanford University Press, 1998.

Descartes, René. *Meditations on the First Philosophy. A Discourse on Method, Meditations on the First Philosophy, Principles of Philosophy*. Translated by John Veitch. London: J. M. Dent, 1994. 59–131.

Donn, Linda. *Freud and Jung: Years of Friendship, Years of Loss*. New York: Scribner, 1988.

Dufresne, Todd. *Tales from the Freudian Crypt: The Death Drive in Text and Context*. Stanford, Calif.: Stanford University Press, 2000.

Durham, Margery. "The Mother Tongue: *Christabel* and the Language of Love." In *The (M)other Tongue: Essays in Feminist Psychoanalytical Interpretation*. Edited by Shirley Nelson Garner, Claire Kahane, and Madelon Sprengnether. Ithaca, N.Y.: Cornell University Press, 1985. 161–93.

Eagleton, Terry. "Schopenhauer and the Aesthetic." *Signature* 1 (Summer 1989): 1–22.

Eaton, Horace Ainsworth. *Thomas De Quincey: A Biography*. New York: Oxford University Press, 1936.

Edmundson, Mark. *Towards Reading Freud: Self-Creation in Milton, Wordsworth, Emerson, and Sigmund Freud*. Princeton. N.J.: Princeton University Press, 1990.

Ellenberger, Henri F. *The Discovery of the Unconscious: The History and Evolution of Dynamic Psychiatry*. New York: Basic Books, 1970.

Ellis, David. *Wordsworth, Freud, and the Spots of Time: Interpretation in* The Prelude. New York: Cambridge University Press, 1985.

Ellman, Maude. "Introduction." *Psychoanalytic Literary Criticism*. Edited by Maud Ellman. New York: Longman, 1994. 1–35.

Engell, James. *The Creative Imagination: Enlightenment to Romanticism*. Cambridge, Mass.: Harvard University Press, 1981.

Faas, Ekbert. *Retreat Into the Mind: Victorian Poetry and the Rise of Psychiatry*. Princeton, N.J.: Princeton University Press, 1988.

Faflak, Joel. "'the clearest light of reason': Making Sense of Hogg's Body of Evidence." *Gothic Studies* 5.1 (April 2003): 94–110.

———. "De Quincey Collects Himself." In *Nervous Reactions: Victorian Recollections of Romanticism*. Edited by Joel Faflak and Julia Wright. Albany: State University of New York Press, 2004. 23–46.

———. "Schopenhauer's Telling Body of Philosophy." In *Idealism without Absolutes: Philosophy and Romantic Culture*. Edited by Tilottama Rajan and Arkady Plotnitsky. Albany: State University of New York Press, 2004. 161–80.

Felman, Shoshana. "To Open the Question." *Yale French Studies* 55/56 (1977): 5–10.

———. "Turning the Screw of Interpretation." *Yale French Studies*. 55/56 (1977): 94–207.

Finch, John Alban. "*The Ruined Cottage* Restored: Three Stages of Composition." In *Bicentenary Wordsworth Studies*. 29–49.

Forrest, Derek. *Hypnotism: A History*. London: Penguin, 1999.

Foucault, Michel. *The Order of Things: An Archaeology of the Human Sciences*. Translated by Alan Sheridan. New York: Random House, 1973.

———. "Nietzsche, Genealogy, History." In *The Foucault Reader*. Edited by Paul Rabinow. New York: Pantheon, 1984. 76–100.

———. *The History of Sexuality. Volume One*. 1978. Translated by Robert Hurley. New York: Vintage Books, 1990.

Freud, Sigmund. "Preface to the Translation of Bernheim's *Suggestion*." 1888. Vol. 1. In *The Standard Edition of the Complete Psychological Works of Sigmund Freud*. Translated by James Strachey. 23 vols. London: Hogarth Press, 1953–1974; London: Vintage, 2001. 71–85.

———. "L'Herédité et l'étiologie des névroses." *Revue Neurologique*. 4 (1896): 161–68.

———. "Weitere Bemerkungen über die Abwehr-Neuropsychosen." *Neurologisches Centralblatt*. 15 (1896): 434–448.

———. *The Interpretation of Dreams*. 1900. In *The Standard Edition*. Vols. 4–5.

———. "The Dynamics of Transference." 1912. In *The Standard Edition*. Vol. 12. 97–108.

———. "On Beginning the Treatment (Further Recommendations on the Technique of Psycho-Analysis, I)." 1913. In *The Standard Edition*. Vol. 13. 121–44.

———. "On the History of the Psycho-Analytic Movement." 1914. In *The Standard Edition*. Vol. 14. 1–66.

———. "Remembering, Repeating and Working-Through (Further Recommendations on the Technique of Psycho-Analysis, II)." 1914. In *The Standard Edition*. Vol. 12. 145–56.

———. "Mourning and Melancholia." 1917. In *The Standard Edition*. Vol. 14. 237–58.

———. "From the History of an Infantile Neurosis." 1918. In *The Standard Edition*. Vol. 17. 3–122.

———. *Beyond the Pleasure Principle*. 1920. In *The Standard Edition*. Vol. 18. 1–64.

———. *Group Psychology and the Analysis of the Ego*. 1921. In *The Standard Edition*. Vol. 18. 65–144.

———. "A Short Account of Psycho-Analysis." 1923. In *The Standard Edition*. Vol. 19. 191–212.

———. *The Ego and the Id*. 1923. In *The Standard Edition*. Vol. 19. 1–66.

———. *An Autobiographical Study*. 1925. In *The Standard Edition*. Vol. 20. 1–74.

———. "Analysis Terminable and Interminable." 1937. In *The Standard Edition*. Vol. 23. 209–54.

———. "Constructions in Analysis." 1937. In *The Standard Edition*. Vol. 23. 255–70.

———. *An Outline of Psycho-Analysis*. 1940. In *The Standard Edition*. Vol. 23. 139–208.

Freud, Sigmund, and Ruth Mack Brunswick. *The Wolf-Man by the Wolf-Man*. Edited by Muriel Gardner. Foreword by Anna Freud. New York: Noonday Press, 1991.

Fruman, Norman. *Coleridge: The Damaged Archangel*. New York: G. Braziller, 1971.

Frye, Northrop. "The Drunken Boat: The Revolutionary Element in Romanticism." In *Romanticism Reconsidered: Selected Papers from the English Institute*.

Edited by Northrop Frye. New York: Columbia University Press, 1963. 1–25.

———. *A Study of English Romanticism*. Chicago: University of Chicago Press, 1968.

———. *Anatomy of Criticism: Four Essays*. 1957. Princeton, N.J.: Princeton University Press, 1973.

Fulford, Tim. "Conducting the Vital Fluid: The Politics and Poetics of Mesmerism in the 1790s." *Studies in Romanticism* 43 (Spring 2004): 57–78.

Gallant, Christine. *Tabooed Jung: Marginality as Power*. New York: New York University Press, 1996.

Galperin, William. "'Desynonymizing' the Self in Wordsworth and Coleridge." *Studies in Romanticism* 26 (1987): 513–26.

Gardner, Patrick. *Schopenhauer*. Bristol, U.K.: Thoemmes Press, 1963.

Gelley, Alexander. *Narrative Crossings: Theory and Pragmatics of Prose Fiction*. Baltimore, Md.: Johns Hopkins University Press, 1987.

Gill, Stephen. *William Wordsworth:* The Prelude. Cambridge: Cambridge University Press, 1991.

Goslee, Nancy Moore. *Uriel's Eye: Miltonic Stationing and Statuary in Blake, Keats, and Shelley*. University, Ala.: University of Alabama Press, 1985.

Gupta, R. K. "Freud and Schopenhauer." In *Schopenhauer: His Philosophical Achievement*. 226–235.

Hartman, Geoffrey H. "Romanticism and Anti-Self-Consciousness." In *Beyond Formalism: Literary Essays 1958–1970*. New Haven, Conn.: Yale University Press, 1970. 298–310.

———. "A Touching Compulsion: Wordsworth and the Problem of Literary Representation." *The Georgia Review* 31 (1977): 345–61.

———. *Wordsworth's Poetry, 1787–1814*. 1964. New Haven, Conn.: Yale University Press, 1977.

Henderson, Andrea. *Romantic Identities: Varieties of Subjectivity, 1774–1830*. Cambridge: Cambridge University Press, 1996.

Hertz, Neil. *The End of the Line: Essays on Psychoanalysis and the Sublime*. New York: Columbia University Press, 1985.

———. "The Notion of Blockage in the Literature of the Sublime." In *The End of the Line*. 40–60.

Hillman, James. *Re-Visioning Psychology*. New York: Harper Perennial, 1992.

Hobbes, Thomas. *Leviathan*. Edited by Edwin Curley. Indianapolis: Hackett, 1994.

Hogg, James. *The Private Memoirs and Confessions of a Justified Sinner*. Edited by John Carey. London: Oxford University Press, 1970.

Hogle, Jerrold E. *The "Undergrounds" of* The Phantom of the Opera: *Sublimation and the Gothic in Leroux's Novel and Its Progeny*. New York/London: Macmillan/St. Martin's, 2002.

House, Humphry. *Coleridge: The Clark Lectures 1951–52*. London: Rupert Hart-Davis, 1962.

Hume, David. *A Treatise of Human Nature*. Edited by L. A. Selby-Bigge. 2nd edition. Oxford: Clarendon Press, 1978.

———. *An Enquiry Concerning Human Understanding*. Edited by Eric Steinberg. 2nd edition. Indianapolis: Hackett, 1993.

Jack, Ian. "De Quincey Revises His *Confessions.*" *Publications of the Modern Language Association* 72 (1957): 122–46.

Jacobus, Mary. "The Art of Managing Books: Romantic Prose and the Writing of the Past." In *Romanticism and Language*. Edited by Arden Reed. London: Methuen & Co., 1984. 215–46.

———. *Romanticism, Writing, and Sexual Difference: Essays on* The Prelude. Oxford: Oxford University Press, 1989.

———. *First Things: The Maternal Imaginary in Literature, Art, and Psychoanalysis.* New York: Routledge, 1995.

———. *Psychoanalysis and the Scene of Reading.* Oxford: Oxford University Press, 1999.

Jameson, Frederic. "Imaginary and Symbolic in Lacan: Marxism, Psychoanalytic Criticism, and the Problem of the Subject." *Yale French Studies* 55/56 (1977): 338–95.

Japp, Alexander H., ed. *The Posthumous Works of Thomas de Quincey.* 2 vols. London: William Heinemann, 1891.

Johnston, Kenneth R. *Wordsworth and* The Recluse. New Haven, Conn.: Yale University Press, 1984.

Jones, Ernest. *The Life and Work of Sigmund Freud.* 1953. Edited by Lionel Trilling and Steven Marcus. New York: Basic Books, 1961.

Jung, Carl Gustav. *The Relations between the Ego and the Unconscious.* 1916. Vol. 7. *The Collected Works of C. G. Jung.* Edited by Sir Herbert Read, Michael Fordham, Gerhard Adler and translated by R. F. C. Hull. 21 vols. New York and Princeton, N.J.: Princeton University Press, 1953–83. 121–241.

———. "The Psychology of the Transference." 1946. Vol. 16. In *The Collected Works of C. G. Jung.* 163–201.

———. "Psychology and Literature." 1950. In *The Collected Works of C. G. Jung.* Vol. 15. 84–105.

———. *Memories, Dreams, Reflections.* Edited by Aniela Jaffé. Translated by Richard and Clara Winston. New York: Vintage Books, 1965.

Kant, Immanuel. *Dreams of a Spirit-Seer and Other Related Writings.* Translated by John Manolesco. New York: Vantage Press, 1969.

———. *The Critique of Judgement.* Translated by James Creed Meredith. Oxford: Clarendon Press, 1992.

———. *Critique of Pure Reason.* Translated by Norman Kemp Smith. 1929. London: Macmillan, 1993.

———. *Anthropology from a Pragmatic Point of View.* Translated by Victor Lyle Dowdell. Carbondale: Southern Illinois University Press, 1996.

Kaplan, Fred. *Dickens and Mesmerism: The Hidden Springs of Fiction.* Princeton, N.J.: Princeton University Press, 1975.

Keats, John. *Letters of John Keats.* Edited by Robert Gittings. 1970. Oxford: Oxford University Press, 1977.

———. *Complete Poems.* Edited by Jack Stillinger. Cambridge, Mass.: The Belknap Press of Harvard University Press, 1982.

Kelley, Theresa. *Wordsworth's Revisionary Aesthetics*. Cambridge: Cambridge University Press, 1988.

Klancher, Jon. "English Romanticism and Cultural Production." In *The New Historicism*. Edited by H. Aram Veeser. London: Routledge, 1989. 77–88.

Kneale, J. Douglas. *Monumental Writing: Aspects of Rhetoric in Wordsworth's Poetry*. Lincoln: University of Nebraska Press, 1988.

———. "Symptom and Scene in Freud and Wordsworth." In *New Romanticisms: Theory and Critical Practice*. Edited by David L. Clark and Donald C. Goellnicht. Toronto: University of Toronto Press, 1994. 135–63.

Knight, David. "Romanticism and the Sciences." In *Romanticism and the Sciences*. Edited by Andrew Cunningham and Nicholas Jardine. Cambridge: Cambridge University Press, 1990. 13–24.

Krell, David Farrell. *Contagion: Sexuality, Disease, and Death in German Idealism and Romanticism*. Bloomington: Indiana University Press, 1998.

Kristeva, Julia. *Powers of Horror: An Essay on Abjection*. Translated by Leon S. Roudiez. New York: Columbia University Press, 1982.

———. *Revolution in Poetic Language*. Translated by Margaret Waller. New York: Columbia University Press, 1984.

———. *In the Beginning was Love: Psychoanalysis and Faith*. New York: Columbia University Press, 1987.

———. *Tales of Love*. Translated by Leon S. Roudiez. New York: Columbia University Press, 1987.

———. *Black Sun: Depression and Melancholia*. Translated by Leon S. Roudiez. New York: Columbia University Press, 1989.

———. "The Adolescent Imaginary." In *Abjection, Melancholia, and Love: The Works of Julia Kristeva*. Edited by John Fletcher and Andrew Benjamin. London and New York: Routledge, 1990. 8–23.

———. "Psychoanalysis in Times of Distress." In *Speculations After Freud: Psychoanalysis, Philosophy, and Culture*, edited by Sonu Shamdasani and Michael Münchow. New York: Routledge, 1994. 13–26.

Kubiak, Anthony. *Stages of Terror: Terrorism, Ideology, and Coercion as Theater History*. Bloomington: Indiana University Press, 1991.

Lacan, Jacques. *Ecrits: A Selection*. Translated by Alan Sheridan. New York: Norton, 1977.

———. *The Four Fundamental Concepts of Psycho-Analysis*. Edited by Jacques-Alain Miller. Translated by Alan Sheridan. New York: Norton, 1981.

La Capra, Dominick. *Soundings in Critical Theory*. Ithaca, N.Y.: Cornell University Press, 1989.

Lacoue-Labarthe and Jean-Luc Nancy. *The Literary Absolute: The Theory of Literature in German Romanticism*. Translated by Philip Barnard and Cheryl Lester. Albany: State University of New York Press, 1988.

Laplanche, J., and J. B. Pontalis. *The Language of Psycho-analysis*. Introduction by Daniel Lagache. Translated by Donald Nicholson-Smith. London: Karnac Books and the Institute of Psycho-analysis, 1988.

Leask, Nigel. *British Romantic Writers and the East: Anxieties of Empire*. Cambridge: Cambridge University Press, 1992.

———. "Shelley's 'Magnetic Ladies': Romantic Mesmerism and the Politics of the Body." In *Beyond Romanticism: New Approaches to Texts and Contexts, 1780–1832*. Edited by John Whale and Stephen Copley. New York: Routledge, 1992. 53–78

Leder, Drew. *The Absent Body*. Chicago: University of Chicago Press, 1990.

Levinson, Marjorie. *The Romantic Fragment Poem: A Critique of a Form*. Chapel Hill: University of North Carolina Press, 1986.

———. *Keats's Life of Allegory: The Origins of a Style*. New York: Basil Blackwell, 1988.

———. "Introduction." *Rethinking Historicism: Critical Readings in Romantic History*. New York: Oxford University Press, 1989.

Lindop, Grevel. *The Opium-Eater: A Life of Thomas De Quincey*. London: J. M. Dent & Sons, 1981.

Little, Judith. *Keats as a Narrative Poet: A Test of Invention*. Lincoln: University of Nebraska Press, 1975.

Litvak, Joseph. "Back to the Future: A Review-Article on the New Historicism, Deconstruction, and Nineteenth-Century Fiction." *Texas Studies in Language and Literature* 30 (1988): 120–49.

Liu, Alan. *Wordsworth: The Sense of History*. Stanford, Calif.: Stanford University Press, 1989.

Locke, John. *An Essay Concerning Human Understanding*. Edited by Peter H. Nidditch. Oxford: Clarendon Press, 1975.

Logan, Peter Melville. *Nerves and Narratives: A Cultural History of Hysteria in Nineteenth-Century British Prose*. Berkeley: University of California Press, 1992.

Lukacher, Ned. *Primal Scenes: Literature, Philosophy, Psychoanalysis*. Ithaca, N.Y.: Cornell University Press, 1986.

Magnuson, Paul. *Wordsworth and Coleridge: A Lyrical Dialogue*. Princeton, N.J.: Princeton University Press, 1988.

Mallgrave, Harry Francis, and Eleftherios Ikonomou. "Introduction." *Empathy, Form and Space: Problems in German Aesthetics, 1873–1893*. By Robert Vischer et al. Translated by Harry Francis Mallgrave and Eleftherios Ikonomou. Santa Monica, Calif.: Getty Center for the History of Art and the Humanities, 1994. 1–88.

Maniquis, Robert M. "The Dark Interpreter and the Palimpsest of Violence: De Quincey and the Unconscious." In *Thomas De Quincey: Bicentenary Studies*. 109–39.

Marcus, Steven. *Freud and the Culture of Psycho-Analysis*. New York: W. W. Norton, 1984.

Massé, Michelle A. *In the Name of Love: Women, Masochism, and the Gothic*. Ithaca, N.Y.: Cornell University Press, 1992.

Masson, David, ed. *The Collected Writings of Thomas De Quincey*. 14 vols. Edinburgh: Adam and Charles Black, 1890.

Masson, Jeffrey Moussaieff. *The Assault on Truth: Freud's Suppression of the Seduction Theory*. New York: Harper Perennial, 1992.

McConnell, Frank D. *The Confessional Imagination: A Reading of Wordsworth's* Prelude. Baltimore, Md.: Johns Hopkins University Press, 1974.

McDonagh, Josephine. "Writings on the Mind: Thomas De Quincey and the Importance of the Palimpsest in Nineteenth-Century Thought." *Prose Studies* 10 (1987): 207–24.

McFarland, Thomas. *Coleridge and the Pantheist Tradition*. Oxford: Oxford University Press, 1969.

McGann, Jerome. "The Meaning of the Ancient Mariner." *Critical Inquiry* 8 (1981): 35–67.

———. *The Romantic Ideology: A Critical Investigation*. Chicago: University of Chicago Press, 1983.

———. *The Beauty of Inflections: Literary Investigations in Historical Method and Theory*. Oxford: Clarendon Press, 1985.

———. *The Poetics of Sensibility: A Revolution in Literary Style*. Oxford: Clarendon Press, 1996.

McKusick, James. "'Living Words': Samuel Taylor Coleridge and the Genesis of the *OED*." *Modern Philology* 90 (1992): 1–45.

Mehlman, Jeffrey. "French Freud." *Yale French Studies* 48 (1972): 5–9.

Mellor, Anne K. *Gender and Romanticism*. London: Routledge, 1993.

Meltzer, Françoise. "Unconscious." In *Critical Terms for Literary Study*. Edited by Frank Lentricchia and Thomas McLaughlin. Chicago: University of Chicago Press, 1990. 147–62.

Mesmer, Franz Anton. *Mesmerism: A Translation of the Original Scientific and Medical Writings of F. A. Mesmer*. Translated by George Bloch. Los Altos, Calif.: William Kaufmann, 1980.

Miall, David. "Coleridge on Feeling: Experience into Theory." *The Wordsworth Circle* 22 (1991): 35–39.

———. "Wordsworth and *The Prelude*: The Problematics of Feeling." *Studies in Romanticism* 31 (1992): 233–53.

———. "'I see it feelingly': Coleridge's Debt to Hartley." In *Coleridge's Visionary Languages: Essays in Honour of J. B. Beer*. Edited by Tim Fulford and Morton D. Paley. Cambridge: D. S. Brewer, 1993. 151–63.

Miller, J. Hillis. "The Stone and the Shell: The Problem of Poetic Form in Wordsworth's Dream of the Arab." In *Mouvements Premiers: Études critiques offertes à Georges Poulet*. Paris: Librairie José Corti, 1972. 125–47.

Milton, John. *Complete Poems and Major Prose*. Edited by Merritt Y. Hughes. New York: Macmillan, 1957.

Moi, Toril. *Sexual/Textual Politics: Feminist Literary Theory*. London: Methuen, 1985.

Muir, Kenneth. "The Meaning of 'Hyperion.'" In *John Keats: A Reassessment*. 2nd edition. Edited by Kenneth Muir. Liverpool, U.K.: Liverpool University Press, 1969. 103–23.

Nietzsche, Friedrich. *The Birth of Tragedy and The Case of Wagner*. Translated by Walter Kaufmann. New York: Vintage Books, 1967.

———. *The Gay Science*. Translated by Walter Kaufmann. New York: Vintage Books, 1974.

Onorato, Richard. *The Character of the Poet: Wordsworth in* The Prelude. Princeton, N.J.: Princeton University Press, 1971.

O'Quinn, Daniel. "Murder, Hospitality, Philosophy: De Quincey and the Complicitous Grounds of National Idenity." *Studies in Romanticism* 38 (1999): 135–70.

Paglia, Camille. "Christabel." In *Modern Critical Views: Samuel Taylor Coleridge*. Edited by Harold Bloom. New York: Chelsea House, 1986. 217–29.

Parker, Patricia. "Keats." In *Critical Essays on John Keats*. Selected by Hermione de Almeida. Boston: G. K. Hall, 1990. 103–28.

Perkins, David, ed. *English Romantic Writers*. 2nd edition. New York: Harcourt Brace, 1995.

Porter, Roy. *Mind-Forged Manacles: A History of Madness in England from the Restoration to the Regency*. London: Athlone Press, 1987.

———. *Madmen: A Social History of Madhouses, Mad Doctors, and Lunatics*. Stroud, U.K.: Tempus, 2004.

Pottle, Frederick. "Wordsworth in the Present Day." In *Romanticism: Vistas, Instances, Continuities*. Edited by David Thorburn and Geoffrey Hartman. Ithaca, N.Y.: Cornell University Press, 1973. 115–33.

Proudfit, Charles L. "Thomas De Quincey and Sigmund Freud: Sons, Fathers, Dreamers—Precursors of Psychoanalytic Developmental Psychology." In *Thomas De Quincey: Bicentenary Studies*. 88–107.

Punter, David. *The Romantic Unconscious: A Study in Narcissism and Patriarchy*. New York: New York University Press, 1989.

———. *Gothic Pathologies: The Text, the Body, and the Law*. New York: St. Martin's Press, 1998.

Quinney, Laura. "Wordsworth's Ghosts and the Model of the Mind." *European Romantic Review* 9 (1998): 293–300.

Rajan, Tilottama. *Dark Interpreter: The Discourse of Romanticism*. Ithaca, N.Y.: Cornell University Press, 1980.

———. "Romanticism and the Death of Lyric Consciousness." In *Lyric Poetry: Beyond New Criticism*. Edited by Chaviva Hošek and Patricia Parker. Ithaca, N.Y.: Cornell University Press, 1985. 194–207.

———. *The Supplement of Reading: Figures of Understanding in Romantic Theory and Practice*. Ithaca, N.Y.: Cornell University Press, 1990.

———. "Coleridge, Wordsworth, and the Textual Abject." *The Wordsworth Circle* 24, no. 2 (Spring 1993): 61–68.

———. "'The Web of Human Things': Narrative and Identity in *Alastor*." In *New Romanticisms: Theory and Critical Practice*. Edited by David L. Clark and Donald C. Goellnicht. Toronto: University of Toronto Press, 1994. 27–51.

———. "Language, Music, and the Body: Nietzsche and Deconstruction." In *Intersections: Nineteenth-Century Philosophy and Contemporary Theory*. Edited by Tilottama Rajan and David L. Clark. Albany: State University of New York Press, 1995. 147–72.

———. Review of *Keats, Narrative and Audience: The Posthumous Life of Writing*, by Andrew Bennett. *European Romantic Review* 6 (1995): 137–41.

———. "Keats, Poetry, and the Absence of the Work." *Modern Philology* 95 (1998): 334–51.

Rajan, Tilottama, and David Clark. "Speculations: Idealism and its Rem(a)inders." In *Intersections: Nineteenth-Century Philosophy and Contemporary Theory*. Edited by Tilottama Rajan and David L. Clark. Albany: State University of New York Press, 1995. 1–38.

Reik, Theodor. *Listening with the Third Ear: The Inner Experience of a Psychoanalyst*. New York: Grove Press, 1948.

Richardson, Alan. "Wordsworth at the Crossroads: 'Spots of Time' in the 'Two-Part Prelude'." *The Wordsworth Circle* 19 (1988): 15–20.

———. *British Romanticism and the Science of the Mind*. Cambridge: Cambridge University Press, 2001.

Richer, Charles. *L'Homme et l'intelligence. Fragments de Philosophie*. Paris: Alcan, 1884.

Rieff, Phillip. *Freud: The Mind of the Moralist*. 3rd edition. Chicago: University of Chicago Press, 1979.

Rimmon-Kenan, Shlomith, ed. *Discourse in Psychoanalysis and Literature*. London: Methuen, 1987.

Roe, Nicholas, ed. *Keats and History*. Cambridge: Cambridge University Press, 1995.

Ross, Marlon B. *The Contours of Masculine Desire: Romanticism and the Rise of Women's Poetry*. New York: Oxford University Press, 1989.

Russett, Margaret. *De Quincey's Romanticism: Canonical Minority and the Forms of Transmission*. Cambridge: Cambridge University Press, 1997.

Rzepka, Charles. "Christabel's 'Wandering Mother' and the Discourse of the Self: A Lacanian Reading of Repressed Narration." *Romanticism Past and Present* 10 (1986): 17–43.

———. *Sacramental Commodities: Gift, Text, and the Sublime in De Quincey*. Amherst: University of Massachusetts Press, 1995.

Schapiro, Barbara. *The Romantic Mother: Narcissistic Patterns in Romantic Poetry*. Baltimore, Md.: Johns Hopkins University Press, 1983.

Schapiro, Fred. "Neologisms in Coleridge's *Notebooks*." *Notes and Queries* 32 (1985): 346–47.

Schelling, F. W. J. *The Ages of the World*. 1815. Translated by Jason M. Wirth. Albany: State University of New York Press, 2000.

Schopenhauer, Arthur. *The World as Will and Representation*. 2 vols. Translated by E. F. J. Payne. New York: Dover, 1958.

———. *On the Fourfold Principle of Sufficient Reason*. Translated by E. F. J. Payne. La Salle, Ill.: Open Court, 1974.

Scott, Grant F. "Introduction." *European Romantic Review* 6.1 (1995): i-ix.

Shamdasani, Sonu. *Jung and the Making of Modern Psychology: The Dream of a Science*. Cambridge: Cambridge University Press, 2003.

Shamdasani, Sonu, and Michael Münchow, eds. "Introduction: the censure of the speculative." *Speculations After Freud: Psychoanalysis, Philosophy, and Culture*. Edited by Sonu Shamdasani and Michael Münchow. New York: Routledge, 1994.

Shelley, Percy Bysshe. *Shelley's Poetry and Prose*. 2nd edition. Edited by Donald H. Reiman and Neil Fraistat. New York: Norton, 2002.

Shorter, Edward. *From Paralysis to Fatigue: A History of Psychosomatic Illness in the Modern Era*. New York: The Free Press, 1993.

———. *A History of Psychiatry: From the Era of the Asylum to the Age of Prozac*. New York: John Wiley and Sons Inc., 1997.

Shuttleworth, Sally. "'The malady of thought': Embodied memory in Victorian psychology and the novel." In *Memory and Memorials, 1789–1914: Literary and Cultural Perspectives*. Edited by Matthew Campell, Jacqueline M. Labbe, and Sally Shuttleworth. New York: Routledge, 2000. 46–59.

Siskin, Clifford. *The Historicity of Romantic Discourse*. New York: Oxford University Press, 1988.Smith, Adam. *An Inquiry into the Nature and Causes of the Wealth of Nations: A Selected Edition*. Edited by Kathryn Sutherland. Oxford: Oxford University Press, 1998.

Smith, Andrew. *Gothic Radicalism: Literature, Philosophy, and Psychoanalysis in the Nineteenth Century*.

Smith, Robert. *Derrida and Autobiography*. New York: Cambridge University Press, 1995.

Smyser, Jane Worthington. "Wordsworth's Dream of Poetry and Science: *The Prelude, V*," *Publications of the Modern Language Association* 71 (1956): 269–75.

Snyder, Robert Lance. "'The Loom of *Palingenesis*': De Quincey's Cosmology in 'System of Heavens.'" In *Thomas De Quincey: Bicentenary Studies*. 338–60.

Sperry, Stuart. *Keats the Poet*. Princeton, N.J.: Princeton University Press, 1973.

Steele, Robert S., and Susan V. Swinney. *Freud and Jung: Conflicts of Interpretation*. London: Routledge & Kegan Paul, 1982.

Swann, Karen. "'Christabel': The Wandering Mother and the Enigma of Form." *Studies in Romanticism* 23 (1984): 533–53.

———. "Suffering and Sensation in *The Ruined Cottage*." *Publications of the Modern Language Association*. 106.1 (Winter 1991): 83–95.

———. "Literary Gentlemen and Lovely Ladies: The Debate on the Character of *Christabel*." In *Romantic Poetry: Recent Revisionary Criticism*. Edited by Karl Kroeber and Gene W. Ruoff. New Brunswick, N.J.: Rutgers University Press, 1993. 204–20.

Tatar, Maria M. *Spellbound: Studies on Mesmerism and Literature*. Princeton, N.J.: Princeton University Press, 1978.

Thomas, Ronald R. *Dreams of Authority: Freud and the Fictions of the Unconscious*. Ithaca, N.Y.: Cornell University Press, 1990.

Tillotson, Geoffrey, ed. *Eighteenth-Century Literature*. New York: Harcourt, Brace, 1969.

Todd, Janet M. *Sensibility: An Introduction*. London: Methuen, 1986.

Trilling, Lionel. "Freud and Literature." In *The Liberal Imagination: Essays on Literature and Society*. New York: Viking, 1950. 34–57.

———. "Freud: Within and Beyond Culture." In *Beyond Culture: Essays on Literature and Learning*. New York: Viking, 1965. 89–118.

Tuveson, Ernest. "Locke and the 'Dissolution of the Ego'." *Modern Philology* 52 (1955): 159–74.

Vallins, David. "The Feeling of Knowledge: Insight and Delusion in Coleridge." *English Literary History* 64 (1997): 157–87.

Von Hartmann, Eduard. *The Philosophy of the Unconscious: Speculative Results According to the Inductive Method of Physical Science.* Translated by William Chatterton Coupland. Westport, Conn.: Greenwood Press, 1972.

Wallen, Martin. "Body Linguistics in Schreber's *Memoirs* and De Quincey's *Confessions.*" *Mosaic* 24 (1991): 93–108.

———, ed. *Coleridge's* Ancient Mariner*: An Experimental Edition of Texts and Revisions, 1798–1828.* Foreword by Donald Ault. Barrytown: Station Hill, 1993.

Wasserman, Earl. *The Subtler Language: Critical Readings of Neoclassic and Romantic Poems.* Baltimore, Md.: Johns Hopkins University Press, 1959.

Weisman, Karen. "Romanticism, Kant, and the Prehistory of Psychoanalysis." Modern Language Association Convention. Washington, D.C. December 1996.

———. "Strange Silence: The Aesthetics of Sound in the Early History of Psychoanalysis." The Histories of Theory: A Conference of the Centre for the Study of Theory and Criticism. London, Ontario. April 1998.

Welch, Dennis M. "Coleridge's *Christabel*: A/version of a Family Romance." *Women's Studies* 21 (1992): 163–84.

Whale, John. "De Quincey's Anarchic Moments." *Essays in Criticism*. 33 (1983): 273–93.

Wieskel, Thomas. *The Romantic Sublime: Studies in the Structure and Psychology of Transcendence.* Baltimore, Md.: Johns Hopkins University Press, 1976.

Williams, Anne. *Art of Darkness: A Poetics of Gothic.* Chicago: University of Chicago Press, 1995.

Williams, Meg Harris, and Margot Waddell. *The Chamber of Maiden Thought: Literary Origins of the Psychoanalytic Model of the Mind.* London: Routledge, 1991.

Wilson, Douglas B. *The Romantic Dream: Wordsworth and the Poetics of the Unconscious.* Lincoln: University of Nebraska Press, 1993.

Winter, Alison. *Mesmerized: Powers of Mind in Victorian Britain.* Chicago: University of Chicago Press, 1998.

Wolfson, Susan. "Keats and the Manhood of the Poet." *European Romantic Review* 6 (Summer 1995): 1–37.

Woodman, Ross. "Freud and Jung: The Parting of the Ways." *Queen's Quarterly* 85 (1978): 93–108.

———. "Romanticism and Reading: The Case of 'The Fall of Hyperion'." "Romanticism and Reading" Special Session. MLA Convention. New York. December 1986.

———. "Nietzsche, Blake, Keats and Shelley: The Making of a Metaphorical Body." *Studies in Romanticism* 29 (1990): 115–49.

———. "Shelley's Dizzy Ravine: Poetry and Madness." *Studies in Romanticism* 36 (1997): 307–26.

———. "Wordsworth's Crazed Bedouin: *The Prelude* and the Fate of Madness." In *Sanity, Madness, Transformation: The Psyche in Romanticism.* Edited by Joel Faflak. Toronto: University of Toronto Press, 2005. 110–47.

Wordsworth, Jonathan. *The Music of Humanity: A Critical Study of Worsdworth's* Ruined Cottage. New York: Harper, 1969.

———. "The Five-Book *Prelude* of Early Spring 1804." *The Journal of English and Germanic Philology* 76 (1977): 1–25.

Wordsworth, William. *The Poetical Works of William Wordsworth*. Vol. 5. Edited by Ernest de Selincourt and Helen Darbishire. Oxford: Clarendon Press, 1959.

———. *The Letters of William and Dorothy Wordsworth*. Edited by Ernest de Selincourt. 2nd edition. Vol 1. *The Early Years, 1787–1805*. Rev. Chester L. Shaver. Oxford: Clarendon Press, 1967. Vol 2: *The Middle Years, Part 1, 1806–1811*. Rev. Mary Moorman. Oxford: Clarendon Press, 1969.

———. Home at Grasmere*: Part First, Book First of* The Recluse. Edited by Beth Darlington. Ithaca, N.Y.: Cornell University Press, 1977.

———. *The Prelude: 1799, 1805, 1850*. Edited by Jonathan Wordsworth, M. H. Abrams, and Stephen Gill. New York: Norton, 1979.

———. The Ruined Cottage *and* The Pedlar. Edited by James Butler. Ithaca, N.Y.: Cornell University Press, 1979.

———. *Poetical Works*. Edited by Thomas Hutchinson. Revised edition. Ernest de Selincourt. 1936. Oxford: Oxford University Press, 1988.

Wright, David. *Recollections of the Lakes and the Lake Poets*. By Thomas De Quincey. Edited by David Wright. 1970. Toronto: Penguin, 1986.

Wright, Julia M. *Blake, Nationalism, and the Politics of Alienation*. Athens: Ohio University Press, 2004.

———. "Growing Pains": Representing the Romantic in Gaskell's *Wives and Daughters*." In *Nervous Reactions: Victorian Recollections of Romanticism*. Edited by Joel Faflak and Julia M. Wright. Albany: State University of New York Press, 2004. 163–88.

Wu, Duncan, ed. *Romanticism: An Anthology*. Oxford: Blackwell, 1994.

Young, Michael Cochise. "'The True Hero of the Tale': De Quincey's *Confessions* and Affective Autobiographical Theory." In *Thomas De Quincey: Bicentenary Studies*. 54–71.

Young, Robert. "The Eye and Progress of His Song: A Lacanian Reading of *The Prelude*." *The Oxford Literary Review* 3 (1979): 78–98.

Youngquist, Paul. "De Quincey's Crazy Body." *Publications of the Modern Language Association of America* 114 (May 1999): 346–58.

Žižek, Slavoj. "Cartesian Subject versus Cartesian Theater." In *Cogito and the Unconscious*. Edited by Slavoj Žižek. Durham, N.C.: Duke University Press, 1998. 247–74.

Index